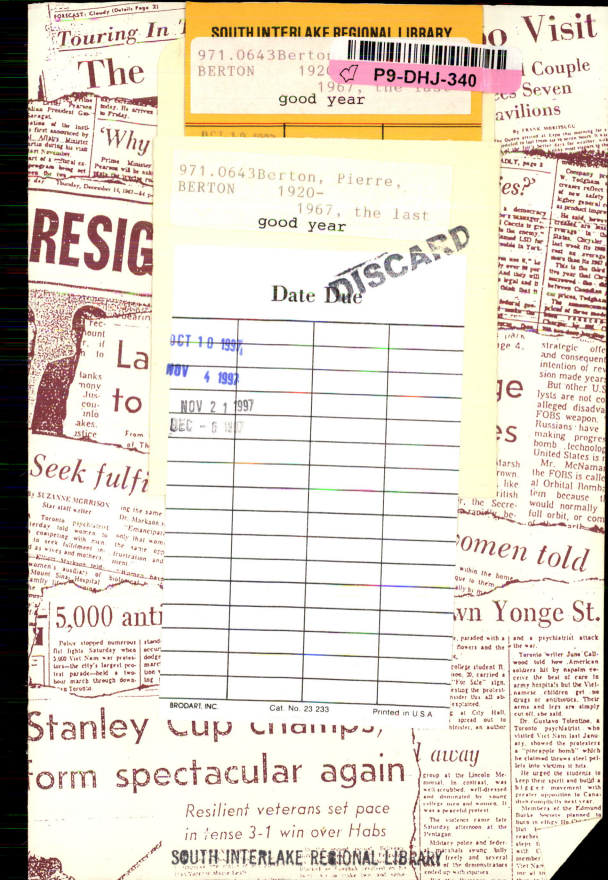

1967
THE LAST
GOOD YEAR

The Last
19

Not to hope for things to last forever,
is what the year teaches. . .
— *Horace*

Good Year

67

By Pierre Berton

Doubleday Canada Limited

Canadian Cataloguing in Publication Data

Berton, Pierre, 1920–
    1967, the last good year

ISBN 0-385-25662-0
1. Nineteen sixty-seven, A.D. 2. Canada – History – 1963– .*
I. Title. II Title: Nineteen sixty-seven, the last good year.

FC620.B47 1997 971.064'3 C97-930678-7
F1034.2.B47 1997

Jacket and text design by Andrew Smith Graphics, Inc.
Printed and bound in the USA

Published in Canada by
Doubleday Canada Limited
105 Bond Street
Toronto, Ontario
M5B 1Y3

To Charles Templeton

Books by Pierre Berton

The Royal Family
The Mysterious North
Klondike
Just Add Water and Stir
Adventures of a Columnist
Fast, Fast, Fast Relief
The Big Sell
The Comfortable Pew
The Cool, Crazy, Committed World
of the Sixties
The Smug Minority
The National Dream
The Last Spike
Drifting Home
Hollywood's Canada
My Country
The Dionne Years
The Wild Frontier
The Invasion of Canada
Flames Across the Border
Why We Act Like Canadians
The Promised Land
Vimy
Starting Out
The Arctic Grail
The Great Depression
Niagara, A History of the Falls
My Times: Living With History
1967, The Last Good Year

PICTURE BOOKS
The New City (with Henri Rossier)
Remember Yesterday
The Great Railway
The Klondike Quest
Pierre Berton's Picture Book
of Niagara Falls
Winter
The Great Lakes

ANTHOLOGIES
Great Canadians
Pierre and Janet Berton's
Canadian Food Guide
Historic Headlines
Farewell to the Twentieth Century

FICTION
Masquerade
(pseudonym Lisa Kroniuk)

BOOKS FOR YOUNG READERS
The Golden Trail
The Secret World of Og
Adventures in Canadian History
(22 volumes)

Contents

ONE: THE BEST OF TIMES

1

The centennial year began in a blaze of glory three hours early so the children could stay up to watch it. I don't mean the sacred flame, flickering at the behest of the Prime Minister on the slopes of Parliament Hill. I mean the full-scale bonfire that lit the winter sky and warmed the hearts of five hundred citizens of Bowsman, Manitoba, a frontier community 250 miles northwest of Winnipeg.

Bowsman's bonfire, fuelled by scores of outhouses, captured the imagination of the country. Here was a genuine centennial project (one of thousands) created at the last minute by a citizenry who hadn't put their minds to the country's hundredth birthday until the previous fall. When a member of the Manitoba Centennial Commission pulled into Bowsman and asked a group of council members and concerned citizens what they intended to do about the Centennial, there was a dearth of ideas.

All across the nation that year public officials and plain citizens, goaded into tardy action after a slow, four-year buildup, were grappling with the same problem. God knows, there were enough centennial arenas, community centres, parks, libraries, museums, and theatres going up—2,860 to be exact—thanks to dollar-for-dollar federal generosity. What was wanted in the villages and small towns of the nation was something quite different, something that sprang from the roots of the community—something not funded by a government department but by the people themselves. Something slightly kooky, perhaps, but eye-catching. Something that would help put their community on the map and at the same time demonstrate their faith in the nation.

In Bowsman it all began with a quip. Like so many Canadians, Bowsman's citizens hadn't given much thought to the Centennial. When the question, what did they intend to do was raised in council, it was met by puzzled frowns and knit brows. There was some laughter when one of the town councillors, Mrs. Pat Secombe, remarked in jest that since the community had finally got a new sewage treatment plant, maybe they should burn up all the now useless privies. The joke was quickly forgotten—or so everybody thought.

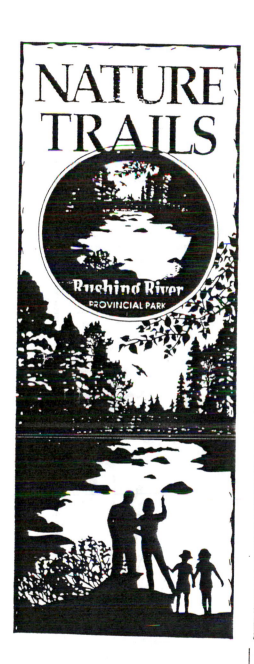

The story was leaked
illage clerk to ask for
ugh at that, too. Still,

Church minister, was
nstable, Cliff Nolan
nan, and garbage col-

pening. We just got a
here on the night of
My God, what're we

le. "There's only one
go out and get some

force in the commu-
ame afternoon when
ckup truck rumbling
nd loader came along
dvice seriously. Peo-
ses. Sometimes they
eached over a fence,
our-leave.

. "Dynie" (for Dyna-
n the campaign to get
blacc would be beside
a real hell raiser as a
hteen years on coun-
, and, as events tran-

d caught on. After a
e backhouse, symbol
washboard and the
d to organize a biffy

parade down the main street, complete with helium balloons, streamers of toilet paper, floats, marching bands, and placards on the outhouses themselves. "Beware of slivers, frostbite and wasps," one read, nostalgically. "Beware of down draughts," warned another.

It was a frosty night. The thermometer dropped well below zero, but the flames, rising forty feet into the sky, toasted the crowd of four hundred as they sang "Auld Lang Syne." Mrs. Secombe and Reeve Sutherland were presented with scrolls designating them as members of the Bowsman Privy Council. The reeve had thoughtfully purchased a quantity of spirits for the CBC crew, who virtuously refused to drink on the job. Rather than waste the taxpayers' money, the reeve drank most of it himself.

Just before the bonfire was set, Jim Liles offered a funeral oration. "The time has come," he intoned, straight-faced, "to destroy friends who have held up their ends through the years. They have fulfilled their duties under fair and foul conditions. They have always stood ready to meet the needs of anyone and give them support as well as providing a good place to read the most recent catalogues. As the blaze is kindled and these outmoded buildings go to their final rest, shed not tears, for they have served us well and the light they provide as a final service is fitting as we enter our centennial year."

A reporter asked if he could be quoted. "Yes," Liles said, "but for Heaven's sake don't say I'm a United Church minister." When the published reports were flashed around the continent, he was invariably cited with "Rev." before his name.

All across Canada, as Bowsman's flames crackled in the cold northern night, the country was caught up in a wave of uncharacteristic whoop-de-do, of torchlight parades, hundred-gun salutes, pealing of church bells, air-raid siren and industrial whistle serenades, centennial flames, balloons, and exploding fireworks. In civic centres and in public squares, thousands sang the national anthem, standing on guard for their country no fewer than five times in the space of less than one minute, a bit of poetic overkill that Lester Pearson, the prime minister, was determined to tone down. They were all driven by what Peter Aykroyd of the

Centennial Commission has called "the anniversary compulsion"—the emotion that drives people to mark certain milestone dates, from birthdays to millennia, with ritual pomp and celebration.

This would be Lester Pearson's last year in office, but he had no intention of retiring until the big birthday party was over. Here he was on Parliament Hill, seen by millions on television, swaddled in his black cashmere overcoat, red wool scarf, and fur-lined gloves, his frozen breath easily observable on black-and-white TV (colour had only just arrived), setting alight the flame that would burn for the next twelve months.

The ceremony brought tears to the eyes of those who watched it, including a group of supposedly hardbitten newsmen who had gathered in the Toronto apartment of broadcaster Gordon Donaldson to see the new year in. "Tonight," the Prime Minister was saying, "we let the world know that this is Canada's year in history. We have laid a strong foundation on which to build our second century. If we have the will and the goodwill there is no limit to our progress."

The spectacle of the thousands gathered on Parliament Hill, with the new maple-leaf flag fluttering in the klieg lights and the sounds of "O Canada" echoing off the familiar Gothic pile in the background, was too much for Norman DePoe, the CBC's gravel-voiced newscaster. Misty-eyed, he sprang from his seat and insisted that everyone in the room sing the national anthem. Everybody stood up except one man, a newly arrived Englishman, Alan Edmonds, who would soon make his mark in Canada as a journalist and broadcaster. Edmonds was baffled. Why was this group of supposedly jaded journalists warbling "O Canada" into a television set? He kept his seat.

At this cavalier treatment of a sacred Canadian moment, DePoe went berserk. He lunged at Edmonds so ferociously that he had to be pulled away before doing him serious injury. Abashed, the newcomer stood with the others and helped salute his adopted nation's centenary. "It was really a special moment," one who was present recalled, "because we all had such pride in being Canadian and such anger at this Brit making fun of us."

The country was in love with itself. To read the daily and periodical press for that time is akin to being transported to a strange and distant planet. Traditional Canadian modesty was jettisoned. Knowlton Nash, the CBC's Washington correspondent who had lived in the U.S. capital for fifteen years, was struck by "the real sense of verve" that hit him like a warm shower as soon as he crossed the border. "It was almost an innocent kind of effervescence," he recalled. "You really felt joy in coming here. That was the best of times. There was real pride in being a Canadian."

As the year opened, the newspaper editorials matched Pearson's sunny prediction that "the future promises a destiny beyond the dreams of those who made our Confederation." Superlatives abounded. The *Edmonton Journal* announced that the country had launched "the most spectacular birthday party the world has ever seen." To the *Vancouver Sun*, the country was "the most fortunate in the world." The *Winnipeg Free Press* declared that "no people on earth have been more fortunate; none can look forward to fairer prospects."

But in spite of all this editorial tub-thumping, some editors expressed subtle reservations. The St. John's *Evening Telegram* wrote of adapting the Canadian family structure to the next century and added, wistfully, "there is no reason why, with toleration, understanding and insight, this adaptation cannot be accomplished without bitterness and strife." The Regina *Leader Post* remarked that although "there is a place for all the Centennial whoopla, it would fail to achieve a useful purpose unless as a nation we re-emerge from our Centennial re-dedicated to this basic principle which motivated the Founding Fathers—one nation with dominion from the Atlantic to the Pacific." Every Canadian understood those code words and why, in the phrase of the Halifax *Chronicle-Herald*, a "time of resolution was needed." Exactly thirty-eight minutes after the centennial flame was lit, an explosion of a different kind ripped into a mailbox in Montreal's financial district. It was not the first time a bomb had destroyed the royal coat of arms on a piece of federal property, nor would it be the last. Every Canadian knew that the young terrorists of the Front de Libération du Québec—

the FLQ—had made their presence known and their message explicit.

Yet it was impossible in that glorious year to dampen our spirits. In Winnipeg that July, when the city proudly played host to the Pan-American Games, nineteen thousand braved pelting rain on opening day and refused to budge, cheering the athletes of twenty-eight competing countries as they marched onto the field at the Winnipeg Stadium. In spite of the deluge they stood and cheered, waiting for the Canadian contingent to leave the building. "Smile!" they shouted as the athletes from the hemisphere plodded through the downpour. As hosts, 368 Canadians were the last to appear, and just as they emerged the rain stopped. That symbolism was not lost on the exuberant crowd.

It was a special year—a vintage year—and it is probable that we will not see its like again. It was a turning-point year. An aging political establishment was about to fade away to be succeeded by a younger, more vibrant one. A past royal commission—into bilingualism and biculturalism—delivered its report; a future commission, dealing with the status of women, was launched. Canadians talked about economic nationalism, women's place in society, the outmoded divorce laws, national unity, the drug culture, and whether or not the state had any business in the bedrooms of the nation. All these diverse subjects reached a kind of realization in 1967.

Babies born in the glory years of the late forties when the boys had come home from the war had now reached voting age. They saw the world differently from their parents. And so 1967 was a psychedelic year, a McLuhanesque year, a crazy, mixed-up year, to use the buzz phrases of the day—a year of arguments over hair lengths and skirt lengths, of hippies, draft dodgers, love-ins, and ban-the-bomb marches. But above all it was a year in which most Canadians felt good about themselves and their country.

And why not? The Organization for Economic Cooperation and Development had just named Canada the second most affluent country in the world (after the United States). Money and credit had become cheaper and easier to get. Government dollars flowed freely. Peter Aykroyd, director of public relations for the Centennial Commission, recalled that when he went to his minister to ask for more money, the response was: "Are you sure you're asking for enough?" As Aykroyd put it, "Those were the good old days."

The stock market was rising. Dividends were at a record high. On the prairies it was the year of the miracle crop—329 million bushels harvested, almost 50 million more than forecast. The mining industry was expanding at a rate double that of the western world. The Gross National Product had doubled in a decade. As the year ended, John Holmes, director-general of the Canadian Institute of International Affairs, wrote that "twenty million people, more abundantly endowed than any comparable group on earth, are wondering if for them extravagance may not be a more appropriate virtue than thrift."

The word "deficit" was not yet implanted in the national lexicon. Every province save Newfoundland reported a surplus in 1967. At the federal level the story was different. In May, the finance minister, Mitchell Sharp, budgeted for the second-largest federal deficit in Canada's peacetime history—the largest in an uninterrupted string of deficits since the last surplus was recorded in 1957. Was Sharp concerned? Not a bit. In his "stand-pat budget," as it was called, he took into account "the enthusiasm and persistence of my colleagues and other honourable members in support of worthy but expensive ideas." Sharp's budget speech was laced with the optimism of the day. "With care and restraint," he said, the country could lick the cost spiral, "pace our prosperity," and look forward to an economically buoyant 1968. How he proposed to accomplish this was unclear, for he neither raised nor lowered taxes. The national debt had reached a new high, almost doubling since 1950, accruing interest rates that put every man, woman, and child in hock for an annual $785.14 a year. Nobody worried.

From British Columbia to Labrador the boom rolled on. A few weeks before the Big Year, *Time* magazine gave the country its seal of approval with a cover story about the country's yeasty economy featuring B.C.'s ebullient premier, W.A.C. "Wacky" Bennett. A delighted Bennett said it would be another boost for business. The following July at the other end of the nation, in the presence of 450 high-powered guests, including Sir Winston Churchill's grandson and Baron de Rothschild, Joey Smallwood, the premier of Newfoundland, sank a silver shovel into a square of Labrador moss to symbolize the start of the $1.1-billion Churchill Falls power project.

The world was in turmoil that year. American bombs thudded down on North Vietnam, and American youth marched in protest. The Six-Day War between Egypt and Israel forced the closing of the Suez Canal. China was close to civil conflict as the Red Guard roamed the countryside. Greece abandoned democracy in favour of a military junta. The breakaway republic of Biafra threatened new bloodshed in Nigeria. No fewer than 127 cities in the United States endured savage race riots. But in Canada, peace and prosperity reigned.

An unemployment rate of 3.7 percent meant that virtually anybody who wanted a job had one and any young man or woman who didn't like the job could quit and travel the country with backpack and guitar in the certainty of finding work again when the money ran out.

Now, with affection and nostalgia, we remember those times when anything seemed possible and the future looked rosy. How sunny it all seems, viewed through the golden mist of memory. On the eve of the big birthday party more than one public leader, including the labour minister, echoed the words of Sir Wilfrid Laurier at the dawn of the twentieth century, which he had called "Canada's Century." "It is even more valid now," said John Nicholson, "to regard Canada as a land of opportunity."

But it was left for Irving Layton, the raunchiest of Canadian poets, to create in blank verse a metaphor that any Alberta rancher could understand:

Like an old, nervous and eager cow
my country
is being led up to the bull of history.

2

John and Judy She was christened Julia, but no one ever called her that; it was a name she hated. She was one of the few public figures—and certainly one of the very few women in public life—who was recognizable by her first name alone. She was Judy in the headlines, and every Canadian knew the reference wasn't to Judy Garland. And as secretary of state with responsibility for both the Centennial and the CBC, she was in the headlines, front and centre, for all of 1967.

She was her father's daughter. He was a man "of mercurial temperament, strong likes and dislikes," in her words. "No one," she wrote, "was ever long in doubt as to where he stood on any issue." Like his father before him, he was a Grit, "and no mistake." So was she.

She was a hard worker—fiercely so. As a member of the Canadian Women's Army Corps during the Second World War, she had learned Japanese in one year—"the hardest work of my life" she called that course. She "slaved like a demon to excell [*sic*] in it." Now she was a member of the Liberal cabinet, a solitary female on the periphery of a male preserve, but giving no quarter for all that. In one meeting, it was said, she had thrown all her documents at the head of a colleague who had expressed a doubt about her ability as a woman to run a large department.

As minister of national health and welfare, she had proved herself. The Canada Pension Plan and the Canada Assistance Plan had been her babies, and she had paved the way for medicare. The opposition, especially from the insurance lobby, was formidable. Between 1963 and 1965 she felt herself "bruised and buffeted." She had been attacked as violently partisan when she spoke in the House at the time of the introduction of the White Paper on Pensions. The battle that followed stamped her in the minds of many as a "quarrelsome, stubborn, heavy-handed fighter." But she got the plan on the books. She could be unforgiving. When Arthur Laing, the Indian affairs minister, didn't carry out what she considered was a promise to put a federal park in her Niagara Falls riding, she refused to sit next to him in Parliament.

18

In the cabinet shuffle that followed the 1965 election (another minority government for the Liberals), any man with Judy LaMarsh's qualifications might have expected a powerful position on the Government's front bench. What she got was a consolation prize—the choice of one of three minor (and non-controversial) portfolios: postmaster general, solicitor general, or secretary of state. The latter was the only one, she thought, where some energy was required, and so she took it.

It needed someone with energy, for the Centennial was not uppermost in the mind of the Canadian government let alone those of most Canadians. As Peter Aykroyd remembered, it was a peculiarly difficult time in which to create any awareness of the coming celebration. "We were slaving in the dark four years before the event, three years before the event, even two years before the event—with no recognition. No one seemed to know what we were doing. And it was just drip, drip, drip, waiting for the rock of unknowingness to break." When LaMarsh took over she found that she was unable to interest the Prime Minister, or his cabinet, in the subject. Although she made frequent appointments with Pearson to discuss centennial matters, he never kept them. There was probably more to this than mere inattention. LaMarsh was not his favourite minister.

Her reputation had preceded her. In the spring of 1967, Gérard Pelletier, one of the "three wise men" recruited from Quebec to join the Government, was offered a post that every new member craves: that of parliamentary assistant. He got a call from another wise man, Jean Marchand (the third was Pierre Trudeau), who left a cabinet meeting to give his old friend the good news: he would become parliamentary assistant to the secretary of state. Pelletier told Marchand bluntly that he couldn't accept the job, and if it was announced he would stand in the House to say he hadn't been consulted, wasn't interested in the job, and refused it outright.

Marchand was astonished. It was unheard of for any member to turn down such a promotion. But Pelletier had a reason for his refusal, and "the reason was called Judy LaMarsh." He liked her, or so he claimed in his memoirs. He found her intellectually lively, nimble, and inventive, but she "was as impulsive and petulant in the management of her department as she was in her friendships." As a former chairman of the Commons Committee on Broadcasting, one who had spent his career in the media, Pelletier felt he knew more about communications than she did. He did not feel that he could defend all her decisions or support her initiatives in public; he knew that influencing her choices or deflecting her train of thought would be impossible.

We tend to forget that the year-long birthday party, which to this day inspires so much nostalgia, was not a government initiative. Without the extensive lobbying, as early as 1959, by a wide range of non-governmental groups—ranging from the YMCA and the Canadian Citizenship Council to the Canadian Conference of Christians and Jews and the Royal Architectural Institute of Canada (which undoubtedly foresaw a harvest of architecturally designed centennial buildings)—it is doubtful that Ottawa would have acted. This mini-movement of more than twenty organizations formed the Canadian Centenary Council, chaired by Dr. Norman MacKenzie, president of the University of British Columbia. It lobbied hard for a celebration in 1967. In autumn 1961, the National Centennial Conference (soon to be renamed the Centennial Commission) was belatedly formed. Even then the prime minister, John Diefenbaker, could never make up his mind to put someone in charge. A year passed; nothing happened. Eventually Diefenbaker appointed a man who seemed to most Canadians the obvious choice for the job of chairman—Mr. Canada himself, John Wiggens Fisher, whose love affair with the country was known and hailed from coast to coast.

Fisher had been executive assistant to Diefenbaker since 1961, a frustrating job since the Prime Minister never even bothered to look at the speeches Fisher wrote for him, much less use them. Diefenbaker promised him a Senate seat—lifetime security for a man who invariably worried about the future. That pledge went unfulfilled because the Conservatives lost the 1963 election before the dallying prime minister ever got around to ensuring the appointment. As a result, Fisher remained embittered for the rest of his life.

Yet more than anyone else Fisher deserves credit for waking up the country and igniting the imaginations of ordinary people to do something special for the Centennial. He had been a CBC talks producer who produced only his own fifteen-minute radio talks, but these were so phenomenally successful that the CBC let him run with them. His first broadcasts in the early fifties had produced a flood of 27,000 enthusiastic letters. He set out to tell Canadians, in language of unabashed praise, about their country—its geography, its history, its culture—something that others had failed to exploit in the postwar years. A stocky, balding man with full, sensuous lips and an impressive gift of the gab, he laid on patriotism as thick as maple syrup in a barrage of nationalistic overkill that made him the most popular and eloquent after-dinner speaker in the country. "If Canada did not have a John Fisher," *Maclean's* magazine wrote at the time of his appointment, "we would have to invent one. . . . He is probably the only Canadian able to say, with a straight face: 'Each corner of Canada stabs my soul, for I am in love with the whole.'"

Fisher had been calling for a centennial celebration since the mid-fifties. (One of the ideas he pushed was a Canadian "freedom train" to travel the country filled with treasures, such as the Confederation table.) His purpose, he once said, was to jolt Canadians "out of their apathetic rut. I am a Canadian," he declared, "trying to develop a strong Canadian spirit so we can show the world a beautiful new way of life, the Canadian way, and my job is to hit at this strange Canadian disease of apology and non-support for things Canadian."

In 1963, when he took over as chairman of the new commission, Fisher had just four years to wake up the country. Fortunately he had star quality. Every community wanted him. He received two thousand speech requests a year and accepted at least three hundred. He spoke in factories, hotel dining rooms, schools, theatres, skating rinks, drill halls, on bandstands, and, on one occasion, at the Winnipeg Grain Exchange. He travelled alone. Some years earlier his wife had been raped in a motel; she suffered a nervous breakdown and became a recluse. As Peter Aykroyd put it delicately, "he accepted comfort from wherever it might come," for he had a vast and devoted female following from coast to coast.

By 1965, the growing separatist movement in Quebec had lent a certain urgency to the centennial plans. The political buzz phrase was "national unity," and the big birthday party was now seen as a heaven-sent opportunity to get Canadians feeling good about themselves and about their country. This attitude—that by spending large sums of money on feel-good events the country could deflect the threat from French Canada—would still dominate Liberal Party thinking in 1996, when the government set aside $25 million to buy flags to boost Canadian unity. That the Centennial was seen as something more fundamental than a simple celebration of the past was made clear by Fisher himself as early as 1963, when he stated: "I am not naïve. I know something is wrong somewhere. One of our prime jobs during the Centennial will be to promote Canadian unity. If we were not having a Centennial, we would have to invent one." Given Ottawa's apathy, would there have been a Centennial at all, had not the move towards Quebec independence made it necessary? Certainly the Government would not have lavished such largesse upon it. The irony is, of course, that Quebec was the one province that officially refused to have anything to do with the birthday party.

When Judy LaMarsh took over, the staff of the Centennial Commission was labouring under the dead weight of a number of patronage posts—defeated candidates, wives of dead Tory MPs—who had no real jobs. It had already hired and fired one associate commissioner, Robert Choquette, known as "the Prince of Poets," a major literary figure in Quebec but, like Fisher, a bad administrator. He was chosen for one reason only—that he was a French Canadian. Choquette was replaced by a better manager, Georges Gauthier, whom LaMarsh admired but found "wary, watchful, over-sensitive and suspicious." Gauthier disapproved of Fisher, who was not only a terrible administrator but who deeply distrusted French Canadians. Fisher was touted as bilingual because he could pepper his speeches with a few polite phrases learned in a summer course he had taken in

St. Pierre, but he could never address a Québécois meeting in French.

He was a lone wolf, out of the office most of the time because his chief job was crossing the country to make speeches boosting the centennial idea. On his return he tried to run the office as if he'd never been away, insisting on involving himself in a jungle of details he hadn't time to handle. His mother once remarked that he was a little boy who had never grown up. LaMarsh described him as "an untidy-looking man. . . warm, friendly, and outgoing." He suffered, she said, "from a lifetime of over-patted ego and a fear of the future." Fisher worried that, as a Tory appointee, he might lose his job under a minister as partisan as LaMarsh.

As soon as she took office Judy called him in to reassure him. Stay sober, she told him; be loyal and honest and stick to your job. Get out and beat the drum; that's what you're best at. But if Fisher started any trouble, she warned, she'd throw him out, even if it meant her own neck. The problem was that Fisher and Gauthier couldn't work as a team. LaMarsh likened them to "two strange cats, circling one another, looking for a claw hold." It was all very disheartening. The English–French split on the commission was deepening. The whole purpose of the Centennial was to develop a sense of unity among Canadians, and that couldn't be accomplished even on the centennial staff. Gauthier quit early in 1967, and LaMarsh persuaded a top administrator, Gilles Bergeron from Quebec City, to take the job. He did it so well that the commission returned more than a million dollars, unspent, to the Treasury Board.

Judy LaMarsh seemed to be everywhere that year. She was in Victoria to launch the Confederation Train, at Rocky Mountain House to meet the voyageur pageant, and in Fort William to attend a performance of Les Feux Follets, the first of Festival Canada's impressive array of travelling cultural events.

Once she found herself in the Yukon standing on top of an unnamed mountain peak in the heart of the St. Elias Range, waist-deep in crusted snow that had never before been trod by any human, surrounded by the ghostly shadows of a neighbouring frieze of mountains. This was to celebrate the Alpine Club's centennial project (carried out in co-operation with the Yukon government and the Arctic Institute of North America) to climb twelve hitherto unscaled mountains. Eleven were named for a Canadian province or territory, the twelfth for the nation. There she stood in her heavy boots, thickly padded pants and parka, on a space no more than fifty feet square. Before the helicopter lifted off, the Secretary of State gave vent to a series of yodels that echoed and re-echoed through the mountain wilderness, giving her a sense of peace and freedom she had never known before.

Sandwiched in between these junkets was the business of her department. This included the difficult and laborious preparations for a new broadcasting act—the one that would replace the patronage-controlled Board of Broadcast Governors with the Canadian Radio-television Commission—as well as formally greeting most of the state visitors who came to Canada in 1967. More VIPs would descend on the Dominion in that one year than in all the previous hundred.

It irked her to have to bend the knee to a man—none of the male members of the entourage were required to do so—and she was relieved when, probably at the instigation of his independent wife, Maryon, the Prime Minister decreed that curtsies would no longer be required for the governor general and his consort. But LaMarsh still had to curtsy to all visitors if their head of state seemed to expect it. During that hot centennial summer, she had to pull on stockings and gloves some forty times and revise her crowded schedule to greet various VIPs on the lawn of Parliament Hill. As thousands of visitors watched and goggled she tried her best to put forward the proper foot for the inevitable curtsy—and usually muffed it.

Judy LaMarsh's position as the only female cabinet minister led to more than one embarrassment. Her tale of Norah Michener's bouquet reads like a Feydeau farce. Governor General Georges Vanier was dead; Roland Michener was about to be inaugurated. But who would present the governor-general-designate's wife with the customary bouquet? Maryon Pearson resisted that traditional duty, possibly because the Micheners were staunch Tories. But Judy refused to be turned into a flower girl. Would a man in her job have been expected to perform such a function?

In the end, nobody was chosen; the flowers went to Mrs. Michener by courier and without ceremony—a real snub. Judy was "mad clear through that a morning which should have been so special in the life of this woman was to be spoiled by Mrs. Pearson's pettiness." In the end, she took on the task herself, retrieving the flowers, racing down the Senate steps, and breathlessly thrusting the bouquet into the hands of a startled Norah Michener, who had already received the official greeting and was on her way back up the stairs with the vice-regal party. "Welcome back to Parliament!" Judy blurted and then raced up ahead of the party to the Senate anteroom, where her colleagues were already assembled. "Trust a woman to be late," one of them remarked acidly to another. It is small wonder that the strongest cabinet supporter of the burgeoning women's movement was the Secretary of State.

LaMarsh had another problem that didn't trouble any of her male colleagues. As secretary of state, she had to greet officially all VIPs who came to Ottawa for the Centennial. She met with royalty and near-royalty. She turned up in photographs smiling and shaking hands with world leaders. At these functions a man could wear a dark suit and a white shirt, merely changing his tie from time to time in the course of the Centennial. But she could not wear the same dress day after day. Her duties called for a considerable wardrobe—a dress for almost every occasion, but never an ordinary dress. It must have style and it must be in fashion. Her size made it impossible for her to buy clothes off the rack. Everything she wore needed a good deal of material; it had to be handmade, and it had to match her purse, shoes, and stockings. By the time the centennial year was over the Secretary of State had run up a bill of $100,000 just for clothes.

She couldn't afford it. She lived on her salary and her salary wasn't enough. Max Ferguson, the CBC's longtime satirist, remembers sitting next to her at a Young Achievers' banquet. Judy sat down beside him and asked if that was the first vice-regal affair he'd ever attended.

25

It was. She then told him that before she attended her first, Pearson had asked her to "dress properly." As she put it, in a very loud voice, she "didn't have a pot to piss in" at the time, and when she'd bought a bra for the event found she couldn't get it on and abandoned trying. She added that she didn't care "if they fell out into the soup." Pearson, who'd heard her, interrupted. "Now, Judy. . ." he kept saying, but she was irrepressible.

During the centennial year she appeared on public platforms at least 150 times. Surely, she argued, the Government should pay for her various public costumes. But the Government balked. She talked to John Turner, a close friend, who took the problem to the Prime Minister. It was a legitimate expense, Turner argued: you and I don't need a bunch of outfits; Judy does. After all, she's representing the people of Canada.

Pearson thought it over and turned it down. Judy, he ruled, would have to pay for her public attire. That was the end of any vestige of warmth the two had enjoyed. In her memoirs she made no bones about it. "Like everyone else I found to know Mike Pearson a little was to love him—a little. To know him better was to be disappointed and disillusioned. . . ." She described him as "sometimes petulant and irritable, forgetful, child-like, and not to be depended upon." She could never forgive him for hanging Guy Favreau, her greatest political friend, out to dry after a minor scandal and for cooling his friendship with his closest political crony, Walter Gordon—another LaMarsh booster. "I wonder if," she wrote, "in his retirement, he has left as friends any of the people in politics who helped him on his way and kept him in office. I imagine he will spend his retirement cosied up with the mandarins of the civil service. . . (he always deferred to their views over a member's), shrugging wryly over the shortcomings of mere politicians."

That tells as much about Judy LaMarsh as it does about Lester Pearson. Their temperaments did not mesh. As she herself noted, Pearson's favourite word was "flexible." It was not one that fitted the personality of the Secretary of State, as Gérard Pelletier suspected when he turned down the post of parliamentary assistant.

One cannot imagine two less compatible people than these two who that year greeted dignitaries from abroad on behalf of the people of Canada. Pearson, the trained diplomat, was master of the art of the subtle. LaMarsh, the hard-nosed politician, saw the world in black and white. Pearson himself wrote that "there were no varying shades in between. She liked to have decisive statements and decisive postures." As C.D. Howe once remarked to Donald Gordon, she was like a bull in a china shop, but she brought her own china. "I am sure she did not like my way of doing business by trying to find agreement rather than standing up in confrontation," Pearson remembered. He must have cringed when he read a copy of a letter she had sent to a cabinet colleague referring to his "limited intelligence" and suggesting that he had enough difficulties with his own department and should keep his nose out of hers.

This would be the Prime Minister's last year in office. He turned seventy in April, determined to see the centennial year through and then retire. Even without the birthday celebrations the burden would have been heavy, for his was a minority government. In question period each afternoon, he was forced to face the biting sarcasm of John Diefenbaker, breathing fire from the opposite bench. Now, having invited every head of state in the world to come to Canada to celebrate the birthday and visit Expo, he found his political and social calendar overcrowded.

Fifty-nine VIPs, ranging from a Japanese prince to a Dutch queen to a Monaco princess to the Lion of Judah, accepted Pearson's invitation. Each had to be treated equally with red-carpet hospitality. For each, Pearson had to prepare a welcoming address. Each was given a dinner by the governor general and a luncheon by the prime minister, or vice versa. Each arrived with a retinue that had to be housed and fed. When Haile Selassie of Ethiopia arrived, his vast entourage included a tiny brown dog, Lulu, that never left the emperor's side. Even at the state dinner, as the diminutive monarch marched in, his dog followed, to disappear under the table where the King of Kings fed her tidbits. At one point LaMarsh was alarmed to feel a rough tongue on her ankles as Lulu tugged at her evening slippers.

Each visitor was to receive a gift from the government worth no more than four hundred dollars. LaMarsh, with the help of Maryon Pearson and Mme Pauline Vanier, had looked over a suggested list while the former governor general was still alive. A treasure trove of Inuit sculpture, native masks and baskets, hand-woven blankets, buffalo carvings, Canadian tapestries, paintings, hand-crafted jewellery and enamel work was chosen and kept in a storehouse until needed.

To Harold Holt, the Australian prime minister, Pearson handed a spectacular wood carving of a musk ox. Holt, in his turn, gave Pearson a set of exquisite gold goblets, one for each Australian state. Pearson interrupted Mrs. Holt in mid-conversation to show her the Australian gift and thank her for it. "Oh," exclaimed the delighted lady. "It's just what I wanted. You couldn't have given us anything that would make us happier."

Her husband stared at her despairingly. "You're not getting it," he said, "you're *giving* it!"

The most difficult of all the bigwigs was almost certainly the American president, Lyndon Johnson, who had been unable to make up his mind about coming to Canada and had changed it twice overnight. He turned up at the last minute, giving Pearson's staff no time to prepare any kind of welcome. The Prime Minister wanted to entertain him at lunch at the official residence on Sussex Drive, but Johnson's security people wouldn't allow him to come into the city. Pearson suggested the summer residence at Harrington Lake, and that they agreed on. Off they went, scouring the shore in rowboats and clambering through the bushes with walkie-talkies. Pearson said later that a couple of Mounties could have done the job as easily. Lyndon Baines Johnson was not his favourite American. When the Prime Minister entered the house and went up the stairs, a hard-faced security man stopped him at the top.

"Who are you?" he asked.

"I live here and I'm going to the bathroom," Pearson told him. The incident irritated him. Johnson arrived by helicopter (which sheared off the top of a maple tree), attended a swift state luncheon, and was back in Washington by five that afternoon. Pearson, the diplomat, did not take kindly to this curt treatment. Here was the president of Canada's closest neighbour and trading partner, arriving unexpectedly and leaving abruptly, virtually without ceremony. "It was not good enough," Lester Pearson commented quietly in his memoirs.

Judy LaMarsh, one suspects, would have had a lustier reaction and one that would not have eased relations between the two countries. All that year, as VIPs came and went and the pressures of her job continued, she threw herself, heart and soul, into the Centennial. It was her moment. The job may have been handed to her as a consolation prize, but it is difficult to imagine any other politician doing it better. Work was her solace, and fortunately 1967 was, for her, a year of hard work. She was a lonely woman, and that loneliness was not alleviated by a romance that went sour. She had gone so far as to announce her upcoming marriage to a young Englishman at a small engagement party. Ten days later it was over, and she was shattered.

John Turner and his wife encountered her about this time at the Grenada Beach Hotel in Grenada. As they left the bar for the dining room, the Turners spotted Judy, all alone. The woman who had officially greeted some of the most famous people in the world didn't even have an escort.

"What can we do?" Geills Turner asked her husband.

"We can't have Judy sitting alone at a bar," he said.

Geills Turner was not a fan. "It could be an unpredictable evening," she said.

"It *will* be an unpredictable evening," he replied, and it certainly was. As Turner later put it, "Judy just had too much to drink and she went ape. But there she was, all alone. What could we do?"

3

For those of us who remember the centennial year with affection and
nostalgia, a singular image remains imprinted on our memories: a group
of small children traipsing along behind a tall piper with a jewelled
horn, singing a song about Ca-na-da.

Who could resist it? The infectious enthusiasm of the eight-year-
olds, the catchy, bilingual lyrics, the bouncy tune, and the zesty rah-
rah patriotism of the man with the horn did more to make the centennial
celebrations a success than any other project save Expo. Canadians are
a prickly lot when it comes to unabashed tub-thumping. A male chorus singing a bilingual song in Vancouver? Forget it! But, as Al Scott,
the executive vice-president of Vickers and Benson, the government
(i.e., Liberal) advertising agency, put it, "Even the wise guys in the
communications dodge can't knock kids."

Hired to promote the Centennial, the agency was, in the words of
one staff member, "going out of its mind" in the spring of 1966 seeking some sort of gimmick to kick off the big birthday bash. Ottawa was
making plans to launch a centennial hymn or anthem—or both. A *hymn*,
for God's sake! For a birthday party? The proposal sent a chill through
the hearts of the Toronto flacks. Expo had run a six-thousand-dollar
contest to find a suitable song. It came up with "Hey Friend, Say
Friend." But who remembers it?

And then, on an April morning, like a seraph descending from above,
Bobby Gimby walked into Vickers and Benson's Toronto office, blue
eyes shining, and began to sing "CA-NA-DA, we love thee!" It was almost
too good to be true. For weeks the collective minds of the flacks had been
wrestling with the old Canadian problem—how to produce the kind of
song that could be warbled in both official languages without sounding
awkward or patronizing. And here was this tall, skinny, incredibly youth-
ful-looking forty-six-year-old band leader, tapping the rhythms on a desk
with a pencil and belting out rhymes that, he assured them, could easily
alternate between French and English. *Bilingual togetherness* out of the
mouths of babes! Al Scott knew immediately that he had a grabber.

Gimby was a seasoned and successful musician with an enviable background—a veteran of thirteen years with CBC Radio's incredibly popular (and incredibly corny) "Happy Gang" show and a graduate of the Saturday night TV show, *Meet Juliette*, with which every hockey fan was familiar. He was a small-town boy from Cabri, Saskatchewan, so insignificant that "the train doesn't actually stop there; it just hesitates."

There was nothing hip about Bobby Gimby. Schooled in the meat-and-potatoes music of the West Coast's Mart Kenny orchestra, "a naïve country boy at heart" by his own admission, a sincere but non-controversial patriot without a trace of smart-aleckism, he was so mainstream Canadian that he seemed almost too good to be true— the invention, perhaps, of a parliamentary committee.

But he was real and he was commercial. He ran three society dance bands. He had written some thirty advertising jingles ("Stay away from snacks. . . chew Chiclets and relax"), a slew of novelty pop tunes, and, astonishingly, two patriotic ballads designed to be sung by Malaysian children that had become hits in their country, just as "Ca-na-da" was to become *the* hit of Canada's Centennial.

North, south, east, west,
There'll be happy times
Church bells will ring, ring, ring
It's the hundredth anniversary of
Con-fed-er-a-tion
Ev'-ry-bo-dy sing (together!).

The song had its genesis in the summer of 1965 when Gimby's band was playing at the upper-crust Manoir Richelieu on the St. Lawrence River. Visiting the town of La Malbaie on the feast day of Jean-Baptiste, patron saint of Quebec, Gimby spotted a group of fifty or so small children holding a celebration of their own. The crocodile of moppets paraded through the streets—the boys in a quaint sacking material, the girls with flowers in their hair—all singing French folk songs at the top of their lungs. The image stayed with him, and by the following April when he walked into the Vickers and Benson offices, he had the song roughed out.

31

The original plans for the song were modest enough. It would be put on tape and used as background music for a film promoting the Centennial among businessmen. It was not yet considered an attention-getter for the general public. Two groups of eight children from Toronto and from Montreal were recorded separately, and the results fitted together. Then thirty boys and girls from the Grade 7 class of Princess Margaret Public School in Toronto were given a day off to march around the Boyd Conservation Area north of the city, waving banners and giving their school cheer. The resultant mixture of professional voices and fresh-faced children gambolling about was used as the opening shot in the film. Everybody who saw it was bowled over. The agency was ordered to make a commercial of the song as quickly as possible. That wasn't difficult. They simply clipped the first sixty seconds of the documentary, to be shown on every Canadian TV station for twenty-six weeks. The overwhelming reaction startled sceptical officials. Thousands phoned in asking for the words and music. The firm of Gordon V. Thompson published ten thousand copies of the sheet music at seventy-five cents a copy. The entire edition sold out in five days.

In his twenty years in the business, Thompson's president, John Bird, had never seen anything like it. "Three-year-old kids are dancing to it," he told the *Canadian* magazine. "High school swimming classes want to swim to it. Bike riders want to cycle to it, and drum corps want arrangements so they can beat a tattoo to it. . . . By the end of 1967 I predict that every school choir, every school band, every family with a piano in the parlour will be playing it." He wasn't far out.

For a Canadian song it was an all-time smash record-breaker. On some radio charts it was running ahead of The Monkees, whose own records, sparked by their TV show, were popular hits. By the end of the year Gimby's song had sold 85,000 copies of sheet music and 200,000 45-rpm recordings.

The Centennial Commission not only bought the song ("the only centennial project that will make money for the government," was Judy LaMarsh's boast) but they bought Gimby, too, for a year and a half, for thirty-five thousand dollars.

CA-NA-DA
Notre pays
CA-NA-DA
Lon-gue vie

That year Bobby Gimby crossed the country eleven times, leading groups of enthusiastic children down the streets and byways of the nation. Everybody wanted him—to adjudicate a band festival in Moose Jaw, to autograph records at a youth festival in Winnipeg, to ride a balloon at St. Paul, Alberta, to lead two thousand children past the Queen on July 1.

In my village of Kleinburg, Ontario, we certainly remember him. There he was, rehearsing the local school children for a couple of hours, then leading them down the main street at the head of a Binder Twine Festival parade, itself a centennial project. No wonder that when he finally reached his home town of Cabri, the entire population of six hundred spread out a red carpet in the mud for him and gave him the keys to the town.

When Tom Spaulding, the design director of the Confederation Train, first heard Gimby's song, he said, "This music is exactly the finishing touch we need for the last coach of the train." As a result, the train and Gimby became inseparable. Every time the train crossed a provincial border, the piper and his singing tots were on hand to welcome it.

Like Gimby, the train, originally inspired by John Fisher, made musical history. It was dedicated on New Year's Day in Ottawa's new railway station. Swathed in fur, Madame Vanier, wife of the ailing governor general, was invited to press a small green button that would set the inaugural mood. She did so, and to her manifest delight and that of the audience, the organ-like sounds of a diesel whistle intoned the first four notes of "O Canada." Madame Vanier clapped her hands like a small child presented with a new toy, a gesture of spontaneous enthusiasm that captivated the crowd. "For the first time," Judy LaMarsh recalled, "I began to feel that perhaps the Centennial spirit would really catch fire."

If Bobby Gimby was to become a symbol of the Centennial, so was the purple train. They complemented one another as each travelled from coast to coast, one blaring out the deep-throated notes of "O Canada," the other warbling the new national anthem. They made an ideal combination—the train with its historical exhibits gazing nostalgically back into the past, the Gimby choruses looking optimistically towards the future.

The railway was embedded deeply in the Canadian psyche. The feat of its construction was the nation's defining moment, a bloodless kind of conquest no other could claim. (In 1967, emboldened by the country's new enthusiasm for its past, I was beginning the research that would result, three years later, in *The National Dream*.) The railway celebrated Canada's unique geography and heritage. Our schoolbook heroes were railway builders, not conquering generals. Canada's West was peopled not via covered wagons but by colonist cars. How appropriate then that this purple train—a kind of circus train, really—should be launched from the one Canadian province that had joined Confederation because it was promised a railway to connect it to the rest of Canada.

Nine days after its Ottawa dedication the train arrived in Victoria, having been ferried across the Strait of Georgia from the mainland. Now everybody in the official party wanted to press the little green button. Judy LaMarsh, who had flown out for the ceremony, pressed it first, and the whistle responded. Mrs. Bennett, the premier's wife, pressed it, and it responded again. The lieutenant-governor's wife followed, and after that the lieutenant-governor himself, George Pearkes, asked if he could try. Once again the opening notes of the national anthem were heard. Pearkes laughed with pleasure and the crowd laughed with him as a trio of RCAF Voodoo jets roared past. In the harbour, a scant hundred yards distant, every ship tooted its whistle. At the same time a thousand balloons, each bearing the Centennial Symbol, floated up into the sky.

Bobby Gimby turned up wearing a pied piper's cape—a two-toned red robe with gold lining and embellished with gold buttons. In his hands he carried a four-foot trumpet festooned with beads, bangles, and century-old pennies. Behind him trooped a forty-voice boys' choir, each

34

member decked out in a green-and-blue centennial tartan vest. They had marched through a typical Victoria drizzle from the Empress Hotel singing "Ca-na-da." Gimby admitted later that he was "terribly worried" at the time. What was the Canadian government doing in show business? Would the gamble pay off? But then an elderly woman came up to him, wiping the tears from her eyes, to say, "I'm *proud* to be a Canadian."

"Holy cow," Gimby thought, "we've scored a bull's eye."

As soon as the six windowless cars that contained the confederation exhibits were opened, the crowds began to line up. Mary Isobel Winstone, a forty-five-year-old Victoria widow who decided to visit the train with her ten-year-old daughter, Jenny, learned that the best time to go was between five-thirty and six in the afternoon. And so, at half-past five on January 11, she and Jenny took their places. If this was supposed to be a lull, she wondered, what was it like during peak hours? The rain drizzled down as they arrived, but each had brought an umbrella and the queue seemed to be moving ahead in fairly frequent spurts. A policeman told them that it would take three hours to reach the entrance, but they didn't believe him.

After half an hour the rain stopped. In another half hour they reached the railway yard office that was doing duty as an emergency first-aid post and unofficial comfort station. A stiff breeze chilled them, and the line seemed to move more and more slowly; but they kept on. At last they reached the end of the train proper. Visitors who had already gone through cheered them as they passed by. "It was worth that long wait," Mrs. Winstone heard one remark. She felt relieved.

At the two-hour mark, a small child, tired but still game, sighed, "Isn't it lucky the Centennial comes only once in a lifetime?" Mrs. Winstone longed for something hot to drink; a sign announced "free coffee after the train," but the need was now. Mrs. Winstone took heart from the fact that they were inching closer. "We felt we were paying a tribute to Canada by being there," she recalled later, "and that we would somehow be letting her down if we left, so we continued to wait."

At last, after three hours in the queue, they reached the intricately designed entrance to the travelling museum. A ripple of excitement ran down the line. "Is the train going to leave now?" a tiny three-year-old wanted to know.

At 9:09 p.m. they made it inside. The train was an experience on wheels, complete with the sights, sounds, and smells of a country one hundred years in the making. Mary and Jenny Winstone entered Car No. 1, walking the floor of a primeval forest, listening to sounds the archaeologists told them were heard long before the ice age. They walked past a huge photograph of a family of eight huddled on an English dock in the 1920s, preparing to leave hearth and home for Canada, then entered a replica of a steerage cabin on an immigrant ship, complete with bunks housing plastic figures of sickly, emaciated passengers in rags. A lantern swayed above them as they heard the cries of children, the coughs of men, and the groan of timbers as the musty smells of crowded humanity assailed their nostrils. They stood on a plank floor and looked out at a Great War no-man's-land from inside a trench, with machine-gun fire bursting all about and the occasional star shell lighting up the sky. When they walked through a beaded curtain, there was a 1920s dress, shimmying to the Charleston, while a Mack Sennett film flickered above an ancient player piano and a nearby stock ticker recapitulated the Crash of '29.

They found buttons to press. One caused an ice cap to descend over a map of Canada; another showed a jigsaw puzzle of the country's provinces and territories coming together between 1849 and 1949. They walked on the steel deck of a World War Two fighting ship, put their hands on the huge wheel of a Red River cart, sat in an eighteenth-century French-Canadian chair, played with Joseph Howe's flat-bed press, stroked a 1920s coonskin coat, picked up a few grains of Marquis wheat, goggled at Louis Riel's pistol and Sitting Bull's tobacco pouch. And once every hour, some small fortunate child was allowed to press the button that sounded the train's familiar whistle.

After spending an hour among the displays, Mrs. Winstone and her daughter were exhilarated by a sense of Canadian history. To plan and build the train had taken two years and $1.5 million. Mary Winstone considered it time and money well spent.

The purple train caught the imagination of the country. In Calgary, thousands waited four hours in a blizzard to climb aboard. Although the train was designed to handle no more than four thousand visitors a day, the attendance was never less than five thousand. In a single day in Vancouver twice that many lined up, uncomplaining. The long wait was an act of affirmation in the country. Like Mrs. Winstone, visitors saw themselves as bearing witness to something profound and mystical. The nation had survived for one hundred years; who were they to complain about a three-hour wait?

Every community desperately wanted the train to stop there and was aggrieved when the tight schedule made additional or undesignated stops impossible. The people of Terrace, a B.C. logging town, actually plotted to halt the train by stalling a logging truck on the tracks, after which they proposed to entertain the crew with a barbecue and square dancing. The Mounties got wind of the scheme, and the train roared through town, unimpeded, two hours ahead of schedule.

There were a few complaints—neither the Bible nor the Queen's picture was on display—but there was only one unruly incident when a separatist group in Montreal tried to daub the train with paint. It visited sixty-three cities and every province except Newfoundland, where the gauge of the tracks, though suitable for the famous Newfie Bullet, was too narrow. Instead, the Centennial Commission dispatched to the island one of its eight motorized caravans. The largest ever constructed, they had been designed to get to communities not served by rail. This was a mammoth operation. Each caravan was made up of eight tractor-trailer assemblies more than seventy feet long and ten feet wide, containing the same exhibits as the train. Because nothing like this had ever been attempted before, the commission had difficulty finding enough skilled and disciplined drivers to handle them. The caravans travelled by night in order not to disrupt traffic and, being too wide for provincial highway regulations, needed permission to travel in each province. They rumbled down forty thousand miles of road and highway, visited more than 655 communities, and suffered only one minor accident when one rolled over in a high wind in Cape Breton. Save for a single episode (quickly hushed up) when shots were fired at Caravan No. 2 as it crossed from Ontario into Quebec, there were no major problems.

The trackless North presented a different kind of problem. The caravans weren't heated, nor were they designed for the tough, twisting northern roads. Labrador hadn't even been on the schedule until Judy LaMarsh arranged to have a caravan piggy-backed by train from the North Shore area of Quebec to Labrador City. On the Mackenzie River two centennial barges, each 115 feet long, set out on a twenty-five-hundred-mile journey to Tuktoyaktuk north of the Arctic Circle. On board were a model of downtown Edmonton, a miniature Toronto subway, and a mixed group of Inuit, Indian, and white rock and rollers, called the Centennaires.

But the highlight of this unexpected museum-cum-floating-carnival, which brought native families from hundreds of miles distant, was the inspired installation of a real, working Ferris wheel, something the delighted children of the North had never seen before. And just to make the experience authentic and satisfying, the centennial planners had added one more artifact.

Alongside the Ferris wheel, they provided a popcorn machine.

4

The response of ordinary people John Fisher was astonished at the result of his four-year cross-country campaign to wake Canadians up to the Centennial. No country in the world had ever before planned a year-long birthday party, and there had been doubts as to whether the traditionally phlegmatic Canadians would warm to the idea. Fisher travelled constantly, making close to one speech a day in every hamlet, village, and small town, clocking upwards of a quarter of a million miles, to spread the message: "The Centennial belongs to you! It doesn't belong to governments. Do something. It doesn't matter how small your effort is!"

To Fisher's delight, the country responded, surprising him "at the dropping of inhibitions and the sheer delight that Canadians showed in celebrations." It had changed the country, he declared. "There's a new emphasis on Canadianism now and it was the response of the little people that brought it about."

Ordinary Canadians responded in a fashion so boisterous that it startled official observers. John Holmes of the C.I.I.A. echoed Fisher's remarks. The country, he noted, had been in a "tiresomely depressing state but now the almost embarrassing naïve enthusiasm of people I know, makes me think that may be a thing of the past."

It almost seemed that every man and woman in the country was determined to mark the anniversary with a personal effort, even if to somebody it meant throwing a hammer through the window of the U.S. Consulate in Toronto. A note from the anonymous vandal attached to the hammer announced that this was *his* centennial project.

Some celebrants went underwater for the Centennial; twenty members of an Edmonton diving club managed to construct a bathroom, of all things, below the surface of Hubble Lake. One went to the end of the earth: Jim Cameron, a bush pilot, landed his Twin Otter on an Arctic ice floe with the express purpose of planting the centennial flag on the site of the North Pole. Only centennial fever could have caused the members of the Bethel Pentecostal Church of Edmonton to write out the entire Bible by hand (the result weighed forty-eight pounds), or a Newfoundlander named Harold Macey to spend six months constructing a model of a destroyer out of 5,700 match sticks.

All year long, Canadians treated themselves to a continuing history lesson. Why not recreate the Battle of the Thames, Tecumseh's last stand near London, Ontario, in 1813? A bunch of history buffs did just that, even though it was one of the few battles of that war the Canadians lost. And why not revive the spirit of William Lyon Mackenzie in Toronto? The residents of Rathnelly Avenue went the limit—by seceding from the city. They set up barricades around the "Republic of Rathnelly," organized a group of barefoot boys to hold off all comers with rifles, and demanded that the mayor produce a passport before they allowed him in.

This was the year in which Canadians began to realize that they had a past—not the drab, date-oriented past of the school texts but a vibrant and exciting history. Few people spoke of "heritage" in those days, but there's little doubt that the Centennial helped put that word into the lexicon before turning it into a cliché. The idea of heritage has become so popular that the government has even invented its own department of heritage, which the press calls Heritage Canada, confusing it with a private foundation of the same name created twenty-five years ago, also with public money, as a sort of footnote to the Centennial. The 1997 Toronto phone book reveals that thirty-six businesses and institutions have appropriated the term, even though they have little connection with a rich and varied past. There are Heritage restaurants that don't serve heritage food and there's a Heritage Fine Clothing emporium that certainly doesn't specialize in bustles or wing collars. There's a Heritage Paving Company, of all things, and even a Heritage Duct Maintenance firm. Does Heritage Ford Sales peddle Tin Lizzies? Does Heritage Landscape Management specialize in nineteenth-century gardens? What's a Heritage Tile? What on earth are Heritage Soups? Does the Heritage Pharmacy feature Lydia Pinkham's Vegetable Compound? Hardly.

In 1967, the idea of preserving something of the past by restoring old buildings and preserving historic landscapes was a novel one at a time when local governments were still applauded for bulldozing entire neighbourhoods in the name of "urban renewal." The Centennial marked the beginning of the end of that philosophy. "Heritage" had come into its own when Victorian mansions that had once seemed grotesquely ugly began to be viewed as monuments to a gilded age. Old railway stations, banks, even 1930s gas stations would be seen as living history lessons. That, even more than the new sports arenas, was the true legacy of the centennial year.

The Centennial Symbol was everywhere to remind us that Canada was no longer a young country. Along with the new flag the Pearson government had introduced in 1964 it was there in the millions—a five-pointed maple leaf built of eleven triangles like a set of children's blocks, one for each province, another for the territories. It appeared on postage stamps, coins, paper money, flags, banners, lapel pins, federal government cheques, billboards, pamphlets, stationery, and every piece of literature dealing with every centennial project. One  school fashioned a huge centennial flag out of macaroni and another sewed sixty bed sheets together to make a flag two thousand feet long. No visitor could arrive in Canada and remain unaware of the country's birthday. There were centennial pageants, centennial roses, centennial quilts, centennial beards, centennial scrapbooks, and even a new centennial typeface.

Between July 1, 1966, and March 31, 1967, the Centennial Commission contributed to various community organizations some $300,000 in grants, ranging from $250 for a Kentville, Nova Scotia, writer to prepare a historical play to a $5,000 grant to hold a soapbox derby in the Gatineau. These amounts seem small to us, but we must remember, in these post-inflationary days, what a dollar would buy in 1967. A five-bedroom house in Toronto could be had for $15,000. A three-bedroom house at 49th and Fraser in Vancouver sold for $13,500. A loaf of bread cost twenty-seven cents, a dozen Grade A Large eggs, thirty-nine cents. The average secretary was paid about one hundred dollars a week.

From ocean to ocean the country went centennial crazy as each community tried to compete with its neighbours in the scope and ingenuity of the birthday binge. The nation indulged in an orgy of sports events, folk dancing, historical pageants, parades, and youth exchanges. But no place could match St. Paul, Alberta, a small bilingual community northeast of Edmonton.

Judy LaMarsh called it "the greatest centennial town in Canada." To John Fisher it was *the* "Centennial Star of Canada." In this case the hyperbole was justified. St. Paul boasted no fewer than one hundred individual centennial projects, ranging from a bubble-gum-chewing contest to a trailer built by a local photographer in the shape of the Centennial Symbol.

It was not possible to avoid that symbol in St. Paul. It was on everything—on the beadwork crests and ties made by young Indian girls from Saddle Lake, on the petit point collection of a local housewife, on the suntanning cutouts distributed with the help of a local judge, on the automobile decal transfers given away by a local dentist, on the special neckerchiefs designed for the St. Paul Scout troops, on the lapel buttons handed out by Mr. and Mrs. Alphonse Gagne, on the centennial school report cards distributed by the superintendent, Nick Chamchuk, on the play money mailed out to raise funds for retarded children, on the ear tags for newborn calves given away by a local druggist, and on the centennial tuques sewn by St. Paul women to raise funds to send peewee hockey players to Montreal.

Every family in St. Paul got a Canadian flag from the Knights of Columbus. Every church got a picture album put together by a local priest. Every trailer in town carried a sign boosting the Centennial, all put together by a local resident. Thanks to a St. Paul building-supply operator, fourteen streets were renamed in honour of the first fourteen Canadian prime ministers. The ladies' auxiliary at the hospital raised enough money to buy a heart-lung machine as their part in the anniversary. Wilbert Kelley, who ran a typing class, used his machine to create a black-and-white drawing of every provincial legislature building in Canada as well as the Parliament Buildings in Ottawa.

"Centennial Fever is the desire to do something good for Canada," the *St. Paul Centennial Progress Report* declared in November 1966. "It is a state of mind, a way of life, it can change the very fabric of our society. Are there specific needs in your community which are crying out for correction? How many of your local Canadians are prepared to do something about it? If we have ever needed an excuse to go out crusading for Canada, we have it now. . . . It must transcend petty politics; it must go beyond regional and local ethnic, social, and religious differences. It must unify individuals, clubs, groups, and organizations in each locality into one dynamic, unstoppable force of energy and goodwill which will leave its Centennial mark on all of us and carry us far beyond 1967. . . ."

When the big year arrived, St. Paul was ready. Years of planning had been led by the secretary of the St. Paul Centennial Committee, a tireless promoter and local lawyer, John Lagasse. The celebrations got under way at midnight, December 31, 1966, thanks to Paul Droley, who asked communities across the country to ring bells at midnight. Seventy-five responded, and ships' bells, train bells, church bells, and hand bells were rung that night in response to Droley's requests. St. Paul had its own centennial symbol—a small reproduction of a bell. And three local residents set off for Ottawa where they distributed 265 bells and 265 centennial toques, one for each Member of Parliament.

All this earnest activity paled before St. Paul's goofiest and most celebrated centennial effort—construction of a landing pad for flying saucers at the Centennial Community Centre. The local chamber of commerce offered $500 for the design, and a local construction company agreed to build the plan for free. The design contest was won by Alex Mair, a professional engineer from Edmonton. On a forty-foot-long concrete wall he fashioned a vast map of Canada to orient visitors from outer space when they landed in the community. Each province was marked out in stones dug from its own soil. The map showed those communities that had been active participants in the Centennial. The oval landing platform, twenty by forty feet, would be used as the official entrance to St. Paul's new recreation grounds as well as a speaker's podium and a dance floor for teenagers. As Lagasse declared: "The shareholders of Car-Ouel Construction are convinced that the only reason why UFOs have never landed in Canada is that no one has, until now, made them officially welcome." A large sign welcoming outer-space visitors was displayed beside the pad.

With radio and television crews arriving from as far away as Great Britain, the people of St. Paul flung themselves enthusiastically into the flying saucer project. It was generally assumed that the spacemen would be Martians. The Lavoie Hotel produced special wooden Martian currency, each coin worth fifty cents as a room discount. Other souvenirs included Martian medallions, paper matches, postcards, and new landing-pad coins sold to boost the Retarded Children's Fund. The St. Paul Centennial Committee sponsored a flying saucer kit for kids. The local soda-pop plant offered free Coca-Cola for all outer-space visitors for the duration of their stay. The IGA store came up with an outer-space menu guaranteed to satisfy any Martian. The manager of the local Toronto-Dominion Bank, Bernard Girard, wrote to each province asking to be sent a pint of local water; the plan was to mix all the water together as a symbol of unity and give it to the bishop to bless the landing pad.

The Flying Saucer Pad, of course, is still in St. Paul and still in use. A great many other centennial projects had a life beyond 1967. In Nanaimo, the local centennial committee launched a thirty-mile National Bathtub Race across the choppy waters of the Strait of Georgia to Vancouver. The purpose of the race, Chairman Frank Ney announced, poker-faced, was "to show the world that Canada leads in bathtub technology." Two hundred and fourteen vessels, each one resembling a bathtub and powered by a 6-hp outboard motor, set off on the crazy odyssey. Forty-seven actually made it, led by a telephone lineman, Rusty Harrison, who was awarded the Centennial Order of the Bath and one hundred dollars in cash. He clocked in at thirty hours, twenty-seven minutes, twenty-nine seconds. The last to arrive, thirty hours later, was an actual bathtub, forty years old and powered by sail. Like many other centennial projects, the bathtub race has become a West Coast fixture.

All the activities pale before the personal centennial project of Blake Brown, a twenty-three-year-old house painter from Edmonton, whose mad plan was to drive a centennial dog team out of Tuktoyaktuk in the Mackenzie River delta to Edmonton's Mukluk Mardi Gras in the coldest, most brutal months of the winter. One Edmonton newspaper columnist called it "one of the toughest, craziest, most dangerous, and least publicized projects of this whole weird year." And so it turned out to be.

Brown had never driven a dog team in his life. But he had a philosophy that "everyone when he gets older should be able to pick up a scrapbook with an old newspaper clipping and say: 'That was me.' Just one big spectacular thing. . . the longest, or the highest, or the fastest. After that you can relax."

As it did for many ordinary Canadians, and some not so ordinary, the Centennial gave Brown the excuse he needed for his wild adventure. It was rather like a war or a gold stampede, when men seize on a plausible goal to test themselves—patriotism in one case, the prospect of sudden wealth in the other. "I just had to do something for the Centennial," Brown remembers. "The part that really got me in 1965 was that they had changed the Union Jack to the Canadian flag. It was the greatest thing I'd ever seen—that damn flag going up. I thought it was beautiful. It was then this idea came to me. I thought about Canada and the Centennial coming up in 1967 and all that, and I said: 'I've got to do something!'"

Brown had been a city dweller all his life, but there was an adventurous demon in him waiting to get out. It had manifested itself when at the age of four he set off to cross Edmonton, riding a tricycle and pulling an even younger child in a red wagon hitched on behind. His objective was his grandmother's house and the jar of chocolate cookies for which she was renowned. Astonishingly, he made it.

Now, in 1965, he was still a city boy. He had never lived in the wilderness, had very little money, and knew nothing about mushing behind a dog team. That didn't stop him. He moved to Inuvik near the Mackenzie's mouth, got a job as a house painter, rented a shack at the native end of town, and bought himself a good sled dog. By December she had presented him with a litter of seven pups.

He had less than a year to train himself for the journey. He had his pups in harness as soon as they could walk, so that by March they were trained to the point where they were able to pull a toboggan at a local festival. At the same time he conditioned himself by touring traplines with his Loucheux Indian friends. They christened him *Injut Nachi*— the Crazy White Man. When the dogs grew to adulthood and began devouring enormous quantities of food, Brown got himself a small boat and went fishing for his own dog food.

To reach Edmonton in time for the Mardi Gras in February, Brown knew he would have to leave no later than the last week in November 1966. But now he faced a series of setbacks. First, the partner he had chosen to make the trip with him "chickened out at the last minute." He figured his brand-new wife Karen could take his place, but after a day's outing on the Arctic ice, she told him no way and said she'd rather wait for him in Edmonton. Undaunted, Brown decided to go off on his own—a hazardous decision in the North. In Inuvik, bets were placed that he would not survive.

The first lap of the journey was easy enough; he started out from Tuktoyaktuk and reached Inuvik in a day. The rest was pure hell. He'd intended to follow the new land line that had been slashed out of the forest to provide Inuvik with its only contact with the outside world. But he hadn't realized how the snows would drift so wickedly into this broad gap in the woods. The route along the twisting Mackenzie would have been easier, even though longer.

Now he realized he would have to break trail on snowshoes every step of the way before the dogs and sleds could get through. He had hoped to make twenty miles a day, but this exhausting work slowed him down. Then the temperature began to drop alarmingly until it reached -70°F. The very air seemed to freeze. He couldn't breathe. He could scarcely move. He and his dogs would certainly have frozen to death if he hadn't come upon one of the small relay stations established along the line. It was no bigger than a bathroom, but it had a stove and a handy pile of firewood, with just enough room to lie down. He was imprisoned there for three days. Each night he was forced to tramp out a bed for his dogs, which could not work in the intense cold. He covered them with branches and more snow to prevent them from freezing to death until he was able to move again.

He left the land line and followed a small creek to the valley of the Mackenzie. In the distance he noticed a column of smoke, and his heart leapt at this evidence of other human beings. It turned out to be a native hunting party. They welcomed him with a feast, complete with home brew, for they knew who he was; the radio had told them. The festivities outlasted Blake Brown, who unrolled his sleeping bag under a table and climbed into it so nobody would step on him.

He set off again next day, heading for Fort Good Hope. This was lonely country, dark, silent, and more than a little spooky. At dusk one night he spotted a light in the distance. Again his spirits rose at this sign of civilization. He decided to make camp, freshen up, and change into his Sunday mukluks, all beaded and decorated, before heading into town. But there was no town, only a solitary marker light, flickering wanly on the cold and empty expanse of the great river.

He was sick with disappointment. The cold, the desolation, and the loneliness were telling on him. He attempted to dry his mitts over a fire and lost them to the flames. The dogs, which had strong homing instincts, kept trying to turn about. When he struck them on the nose, they tried to attack him. At night he was haunted by wolves howling just beyond his tent—the eeriest sound in the North.

When, at last, he reached Fort Good Hope he radioed Inuvik for messages; there weren't any—not a whisper from his friends, not a word of encouragement. It was as if they already considered him lost. He set off doggedly for Norman Wells, but his heart was no longer in it. He spent another day on the trail before he decided, reluctantly, to pack it in. "This is stupid," he told himself. "Christmas is coming. I've almost killed myself three or four times. And I've got a young bride waiting for me in Edmonton." He sledded back to Fort Good Hope, sold his dogs, sleds, and equipment, packed his sleeping bag and gun, and caught the next plane south.

Karen was waiting for him at the airport. "Thank God you're alive," she said. He had made his obeisance to the anniversary compulsion, and even though he hadn't gone the limit he had tried his damnedest. Trying manfully but failing—that, too, was part of the spirit of the Centennial.

5

During 1967, half the country seemed to be on the move. One man actually managed to drive a Model A Ford all the way from Inuvik to Vancouver as a centennial gesture. An entire brigade of vintage cars somehow rattled its way from Victoria to Expo 67 without too many breaking down—a Herculean feat for cherished antiques more accustomed to parades than endurance tests. Canadians by the tens of thousands were exploring their own land, sometimes as a new venture, partly because of the lure of Expo and partly out of sheer enthusiasm. They crossed the country not only by conventional methods but also on roller skates and horseback, in covered wagons and hot-air balloons, and even in wheelchairs.

It was a year in which thousands went walking for a purpose—to understand and recreate their own history. For this was the year when Canadians gained a sense of their own past, often for the first time, and an understanding of how the Canadian experience differed from the American, as exploited by Hollywood. The outpouring of books that accompanied the Centennial turned many Canadians into history buffs— an enthusiasm that carried over into the next decade, a phenomenon to which I and many other writers can attest.

Retracing forgotten historical routes became a popular centennial exercise. A Niagara group staged Laura Secord's famous trek from Queenston to Beaver Dams, while the citizens of Galt organized a hike to Guelph to celebrate John Galt's birthday and his founding of that town. One hundred men trudged south from Lloydtown to Toronto to re-enact the Lloydtown March of William Lyon Mackenzie's rebels. Les Fusiliers de St. Laurent followed the route of the king's soldiers in the Loyalist trek from Edmundston, New Brunswick, to Notre-Dame-du-Portage on the St. Lawrence. Some didn't walk; they paddled— like the fourteen Nova Scotia Micmacs who made a one-thousand-mile, forty-five-day canoe trip from Cape Breton to Montreal to relive an 1894 treaty signing between their people and the Quebec Iroquois.

Yet none of these exhausting passages could compete with the mobile history lesson experienced by one hundred canoeists who followed the historic voyageur route from the headwaters of the North Saskatchewan to Montreal, a 3,283-mile trek by paddle and portage unprecedented in modern times.

The adventure began on a Sunday afternoon in May with Judy LaMarsh riding shotgun aboard a stagecoach at Rocky Mountain House in the shadow of the continental divide. The symbolism may have been a little skewed: the stage and its shotgun defender belong more to the American West, with its whooping Indian braves, than to the relatively peaceful foothills of Alberta; but that historical anomaly was set right the following drizzly afternoon, Victoria Day, when the great voyageur pageant got under way. Here the specially picked paddlers from eight provinces and two territories were about to embark on what LaMarsh called "the most difficult and personally hazardous of all the national celebrations." The men would set off from a post of the North West Company on the North Saskatchewan and spend 104 days following the main fur trade route all the way to Montreal.

Each canoe would be following in the tracks of schoolbook heroes— McGillivray, Henry, La Vérendrye—along water routes that had helped give Canada its horizontal shape. In a continent where the mountains, prairies, and sea coasts run from north to south, the lake and water system challenges the vertical geography. From a population point of view, Canada is a long, narrow country. Eighty percent of its people live within three hundred miles of the international border. This skinny, four-thousand-mile stretch of populated land helps explain why transportation and communication have always been at the heart of public policy, so that canals, railways, airlines, and broadcasting networks have enjoyed public support. The country is an archipelago of population islands, separated by impossible natural barriers—ocean, Shield, cordilleran spine. And yet it is possible to travel by river, lake, and portage all the way from the St. Lawrence's yawning mouth to the fjords of the Pacific. Like the railway train, the canoe is an authentic Canadian symbol, part of a romantic past that every Canadian—anglophone or francophone—shares. The Sieur de La Salle, paddling his canoe across those boisterous inland seas, searching for his lost ship *Griffon*, belongs to Ontario as much as David Thompson, besting the wild Columbia on its big bend around the Selkirks, belongs to Quebec. One can scarcely imagine a centennial pageant more rooted in the country's past than this one.

The ten brightly painted canoes, each bearing the name of a Canadian explorer, would bring the Centennial to some ninety communities along the route. It was a race as well as a pageant. Although all the canoes in the brigade left the camping spot at the same hour and arrived at the next more or less simultaneously, there were sprint races at most communities, with prize money put up by the towns and villages, and lap races, as long as ninety miles each, all along the route.

The hundred voyageurs came from all across the land. All were seasoned paddlers. They included lawyers, miners, farmers, trappers, students, rail workers, high-school principals, labourers, and professional skiers. The youngest was seventeen, the oldest fifty-one. They were a hard-muscled bunch, having taken part in two gruelling trials in 1965 and 1966. For many the pageant meant a considerable sacrifice. All had taken a three-month leave of absence from their jobs.

Don Starkell, a thirty-four-year-old salesman from the CPR's freight service, was a member of the Manitoba team, whose canoe bore the name of one of his heroes, Pierre-Esprit Radisson. Three years before, when the Centennial Commission had planned the affair as a simple two-man race, Starkell, a seasoned paddler, had written to John Fisher suggesting something more exciting and more in keeping with the hundredth anniversary. He was married, the father of three children, and had held his job with the railway for seventeen years, but he had no intention of letting any of that stand in his way. He would later produce two books, *Paddling to the Amazon* and *Paddling to the Arctic*, which gave more than a hint that canoeing was close to being an obsession with him.

Starkell worked out two hours every day in the weeks before the pageant. The week before the race he was running fifteen miles nonstop with twenty pounds of lead strapped to his waist. Now, in his caribou shirt, headband, and moccasins, he joined his fellow Manitobans as they struggled in the snowbound river to launch their heavy fibreglass canoes. For miles along the route crowds on the banks cheered them on.

It would not be an easy trip for Starkell. He was the only member of the ten-man team who had not been born and raised in Flin Flon, which considered itself the canoeing capital of the country. But the provincial centennial commission wanted at least one paddler from Winnipeg, and Starkell was the obvious choice. He felt a bit of a stranger and was certain the chief Manitoba voyageur, Norm Crerar, wanted him off the team. But he decided to stick it out, and stick it out he did.

For the first four days it poured. The banks of the river were reduced to a muddy glue, but that didn't keep the crowds away. At each community, thousands turned out to watch the brigade of canoes slicing through the choppy waters—three thousand at Duvernay, twelve thousand near Elk Point, eight thousand at Lloydminster, where a clothing company presented each paddler with a complete cowboy outfit. It was as exhilarating as it was exhausting. They paddled all day and made whoopee all night. At every stop there was a banquet and dance in their honour and usually a parade through town. And the food! A fish fry at Prince Albert, a moose and sturgeon banquet at Cumberland House, fresh lobsters flown in from New Brunswick at Winnipeg. Starkell reckoned that by August he and his fellow paddlers had been guests at more than sixty of these mammoth repasts.

In the unpopulated sections of the route they carried and cooked their own food. During the 104 days they consumed 30,000 eggs, two and a half tons of bacon, 60,000 pancakes, half a ton of honey, 10,000 quarts of milk, six tons of steaks, two and a half tons of potatoes, 5,000 loaves of bread, and a ton and a half of butter. But they were never able to dip a mug into the shining waters beneath them. Since the days of the original voyageurs, these waters had become unfit to drink. They drank on the move from bottles with angled straws and ate by snatching a bite here and a bite there without missing a stroke.

They paddled all day from early morning until five in the afternoon.

At each community they rested for an hour or so, then leapt back into the canoes to stage a timed sprint for the town, which had raised the prize money. At night, after the inevitable banquet, they danced. The Yukon team, whose canoe was named for the legendary Robert Campbell (who had once travelled, mainly on snowshoes, from Fort Selkirk to Crow Wing, Minnesota), was the raunchiest and most colourful of all. One or two members spent a night in jail as a result of a spree that did not improve their paddling. The Yukoners generally placed last during the sprints and lap races, having imbibed too heavily the night before. At Kenora they agreed to stop tippling and switch to milk. The following day they managed to finish fourth. That was the best time they ever made, but they agreed it wasn't worth it. Having made a point of sorts, they went back to partying.

During the thirty-four lap races, the voyageurs paddled at a rate of at least sixty strokes a minute; in the short sprints, the rate went up to more than seventy. Only six of the ten-man teams paddled at any one time. The other four travelled by truck or in the accompanying naval boats, performed odd jobs, and alternated with their fellow paddlers. Each paddler had his own seat, which meant he had to shift himself across the four-foot thwart every time he switched sides to dip his paddle in the water without missing a stroke.

For Don Starkell it was a memorable three months. He would never forget the spectacle of the Saskatchewan team struggling to push their craft through a set of rapids, up to their waists in the freezing water, and, out of sheer frustration, breaking out into a knock-down, drag 'em-out fistfight. Once while paddling furiously during a lap race, his own team spotted a moose in the water. Nothing would do but that they try to catch up with the animal. They got close enough to enable one man to make a grab for the moose's rear. It took off, leaving a handful of hair behind. The paddlers put the hair in a plastic bag and mailed it to the Secretary of State. "Dear Judy: A handful of hair from the ass of a Manitoba moose, captured on our waters in northern Manitoba."

A steady downpour across Lake Winnipegosis forced the cancellation of a sprint at Duck Bay. Here the townspeople opened their homes to the dripping canoeists, all of whom enjoyed a hot bath while their clothes dried.

For most of the pageant the Manitoba team stayed in the lead. Indeed, it was well ahead of its closest rival, British Columbia, until it lost its way in the maze of islands in Lake Winnipegosis. That diversion cost it its lead of one hour, forty minutes. It made up the time a week later in Lake Manitoba when the other crews, fearing that the Manitoba team would again get lost and lead them off course, made a wrong turn themselves and came into Delta Beach one hour late.

There were other diversions. On the longest portage in Canada—twelve miles from Delta Beach to the Assiniboine River—the paddlers were allowed to transport their canoes by any means available to the voyageurs of old. Alberta and Quebec were the only teams to portage the canoes by hand. Several used horse-drawn wagons. But the New Brunswick team, recalling that the Indian women did most of the work around the campfires, found six local girls, whom they dressed in burlap clothing, to help carry the craft.

On Lake of the Woods the voyageurs suffered their first delay since leaving Rocky Mountain House. Twelve-foot waves forced them to beach their craft for five hours, and that threatened to disrupt an already tight schedule.

The voyageurs were often out of touch with the world for days at a time, with radio their only link. After thirty-six hours in the wilderness of Northern Ontario, they finally encountered civilization in the person of the indefatigable Judy LaMarsh, who turned up in Kenora to address a crowd of three thousand.

When the canoes reached Sandy Point, a remote reserve on Lake of the Woods, one man collapsed from exhaustion. He was Joseph Deorchie, not only the best paddler on the Ontario crew but also the Canadian and North American single-blade champion. It was a sobering moment. If this crack canoeist couldn't take the pace, what hope was there for the others? But fortunately Deorchie recovered after a two-day rest.

By the time the voyageurs entered the wilderness of Quetico

Provincial Park, Don Starkell was experiencing an overpowering impact of history. Here, no roads or wagon trails existed; moose, bear, and deer prowled through the virgin forests in full view; and aboriginal cliff paintings still remained undisturbed. The land was exactly as it had been since the days when the light *canots du nord* had followed these waters for their rendezvous with the big *canots de maître* from Montreal, loaded with trade goods to exchange for a fortune in beaver pelts brought down from the North.

In the days that followed the crews developed the camaraderie that comes to those who share moments of triumph and travail. The leading teams were taking extra time to help the last-placed teams over the difficult portages. The strength and skills of even the most experienced paddlers were taxed by some of these arduous overland treks. The worst was the notorious Staircase Portage, one of five between Gunflint and Mountain lakes in Quetico Park. "Only those who have travelled this can understand the agony," read a radiogram from the chief voyageur, W.H.A. Mathews, a retired colonel of the Canadian army.

The portage consisted of a wide wooden ladder, three or four canoe lengths high, which rose straight up a rocky cliff. To Don Starkell it didn't look challenging until he realized that the six-man crew had to up-end their five-hundred-pound craft and hoist it up the ladder. The trouble was that the weight of the canoe did not fall evenly on all. The two men at the base got most of it.

It was at Grand Portage that the sense of history struck Don Starkell most strongly. He had felt it back at Lac du Bonnet in Manitoba where, it was said, La Vérendrye had once camped and tossed his hat in the air when the Indians met him. The hat landed on a tree and hence the name. To paddle in La Vérendrye's wake! The scene with the hat had been re-enacted by Eddie Marchand of Shawinigan before an enthusiastic crowd. But there were no spectators to witness the gruelling portage—*Le Grand Portage*—to Lake Superior through the muskegs and tangled deadfalls on the notorious nine-mile trail. Here, in the early nineteenth century, the men from the northern outposts had dragged their load of furs down to Superior's shore.

There were no wagons to aid them here; no young girls in sacking to help carry the twenty-six-foot canoes. They would have to be man-handled all the way. The voyageurs did the entire nine miles non-stop, even though some tumbled into the muskegs and others stumbled on the rocky Precambrian ground. Here on Superior's shore—U.S. terri-tory at this point—stood a reproduction of the old fort where the men from Montreal had once whooped it up after their exhausting race across the wild inland sea. Starkell did not stop. Played out by the journey and burning with thirst, he helped drop the canoe, then walked—limped rather—to the water's edge, not stopping until he had waded out into the freezing water to put his head under the surface and drink his fill.

From this point the voyageurs followed the route of the "pork eaters," as the original Great Lakes voyageurs were dubbed. This was no mean feat because the canoes built for the pageant were shorter than the big Montreal canoes and were thus unable to breast the great breakers that roll across Superior and Huron. Here, too, there was fog so thick that the naval craft accompanying the pageant for safety reasons asked the voyageurs to cover a rear paddle with aluminum foil so they could get a radar fix on the flotilla. Yet the canoeists managed to cover eighty-three miles in a single day even though several, including some naval men, got seasick.

As they entered the locks at Sault Ste Marie, John Fisher was on hand to meet them along with a cheering crowd of ten thousand. Six-teen days later he welcomed them again at Ottawa after they had successfully paddled the old voyageur route up the French River to Lake Nipissing and down the Ottawa. By this time the voyageurs and all who followed their exploits in the press had been treated to a lesson in the history and geography of the fur-trading days when beaver was king and only a canoe could traverse the trackless expanse of the hinterland.

For Starkell, the highlight of the journey was the Ottawa reception with its welcoming ceremonies at Rideau Hall and Parliament Hill and more speeches by the Prime Minister and Judy LaMarsh. Five days later, still following the voyageur route along the Ottawa, they reached the Expo site on schedule, to be greeted by an enthusiastic crowd, twenty thousand strong. One hundred paddlers had started out at Rocky Mountain House; one hundred had made it safely to Expo. It had long been clear that the *Radisson* canoe could not be beaten. Manitoba's time for sprints and laps was 531 hours and 6 minutes—eighty minutes shorter than that of the runner-up, British Columbia. As Starkell put it, "after thirty-two hundred miles, that's not an awful lot."

The exposition gave the voyageurs a grand ball and flew in their wives and girlfriends from across the nation. As a member of the winning team, Starkell received $2,500 (runners-up received sums varying from $2,000 to $1,000 each). Like most of his fellow paddlers, he spent most of it enjoying the glitter and wonder of the big show.

Some years later it occurred to him that the voyageur pageant should be immortalized in the *Guinness Book of World Records*. It was unquestionably the longest canoe race in modern times, almost three thousand miles longer than a race in Texas that Guinness had previously recorded. Starkell didn't get around to entering it until 1982, but the record still stands.

TWO: UNCLE SAM'S LONG SHADOW

1
The attempted resurrection of Walter Gordon
2
Hockey's last hurrah
3
The CBC's loss of nerve
4
The Tories change their image

1

As the centennial year opened, Walter Gordon returned to the Liberal cabinet carrying with him the grudging assurance of his friend the Prime Minister that he would be given latitude to do battle for the economic independence of the nation.

It was a propitious time for the former finance minister to recharge his campaign to reclaim the country from the Americans. The growing euphoria over the Centennial was sparking a new nationalist movement that would prevail well into the seventies. On the day that Gordon's return was announced—January 3—the *Toronto Daily Star*, which sounded more and more like his personal organ, published a poll showing that six out of ten Canadians believed foreign control of a large portion of Canadian industry endangered the country's political independence. The same proportion thought the Canadian government didn't show enough independence of U.S. foreign policy. That month a Gallup poll revealed that the strongest feeling its respondents had about Canada was one of pride. It was the first emotion they felt when given the phrase "I am a Canadian." Significantly, "happiness" and "freedom" came second and third.

As the centennial festivities started to catch the imagination of the nation, more Canadians began to fear that they were no longer masters in their own house. (There was irony here. That same year French Canadians were responding to a similar rallying cry, *"Maîtres chez nous,"* directed less at Americans and more at Ottawa.) By March another poll showed that among Canadians, respect for the United States was at its lowest ebb in several years. Four months later, when Gallup polled those Canadians who felt dissatisfied with their country's development, half gave American dominance and the reliance on outside capital as their reasons.

This unease, some of it fostered by Gordon himself in his public speeches and in his book *A Choice for Canada*, had a statistical basis. Foreigners, mainly Americans, controlled 46 percent of Canadian manufacturing, 62 percent of the oil and natural gas industry, and

35 percent of the pulp and paper business. No other Western nation had given up so much of its economic control.

The growing nationalist movement, seeded by such influential left-wing publications as *Canadian Dimension* and the *Canadian Forum*, was on a roll that year. In April, the *Toronto Daily Star* opened its columns to three *Dimension* editors who issued an open letter—a manifesto, really—proposing the formation of a "non-partisan, non-sectarian, non-regional, non-racial alliance for independence." This helped pave the way for the formation, in 1971, of the Committee for an Independent Canada, one of whose founders, Abraham Rotstein, signed the open letter.

"We are Canadian nationalists," it read, "because we are not satisfied with being a comfortable satellite of the United States. A miniature replica of the Great Society is not our vision of the future of Canada. We are anxious to diminish the economic and cultural influence of the United States in order to preserve the possibilities of building in this country a society better than the Great Society."

This fervent nationalism did not sit well with the right wing of Gordon's party, and his return to cabinet was not greeted with unanimous huzzahs. Some saw him as a loose cannon, best kept on the outside; others saw him as a loose cannon better controlled by being *inside*. To Judy LaMarsh and her cabinet cronies, he was the conscience of the Liberal Party. "In wanting to retain our independence," he had written in *A Choice for Canada*, "we are no different than. . . the people of other countries. . . . Some may call this nationalism, and so it is. It is a proper respect, loyalty, and enthusiasm for one's country and legitimate optimism and confidence about the future." He openly challenged his own party to stand up to American interests and not buckle under big-stick diplomacy. "Canadians," he wrote, "are much more likely to be respected in the United States if they fight for their interests and their independence, than if they give in silently and without protest every time Uncle Sam looks cross."

Gordon was no longer the Liberals' golden boy, the man who, with Pearson, had reorganized the party and helped restore its commitment to social reform. He now bore the stigmas of both his disastrous and short-lived 1963 budget as minister of finance and the equally disastrous 1965 election, which he had urged Pearson to call. He took full responsibility for that débâcle, in which the party made no substantial gains, and resigned immediately for giving his leader bad advice. That was an honourable decision; many other ministers of the Crown would not, in similar circumstances, have displayed such political integrity.

But then, Walter Gordon did not fit the stereotype of the political animal. Somebody once remarked that he seemed to be carrying his resignation about in his pocket. On the hustings it is commonplace for every office seeker to announce that he is entering politics, not for reasons of selfish ambition, but "to get things done." In Walter Gordon's case that was true. If he was ambitious it was only to see his ideas prevail. His background and upbringing had made him impervious to the usual siren calls of power and prestige. A businessman's businessman (accounting; management consulting), he had been raised with a patrician disdain for politics. He did not hunger for office; he did not, in fact, appear to hunger for anything, apart from his desire to save the country from the Americans.

He did not wear his heart on his sleeve. There was no passion in his speeches, no arm waving, no clarion call for reform or for anything else. To him, stridency was unbecoming (and, possibly, too American?). At an Ontario caucus dinner held in his honour the previous November—a dinner at which there was a good deal of tearfulness and affection—Gordon stood up and remarked blandly, "I'm very moved by this demonstration." At which somebody shouted, "Well, then, for Chrissake, show it!"

In private he could be a charmer, if a little patrician. He was the son of a well-to-do father, described by one Anglican layman as "an old Toronto WASP. . . born with a silver adding machine in his hands," who, in effect, bequeathed him his profitable accounting business.

The son had "Rosedale" written all over him, from the cut of his clothes and his hand-tailored shirts to the guise of mild boredom and superior amusement that were the outward manifestations of an inner shyness. Because of his commitment to the traditional Liberal social philosophy, he was, to the Eastern business community, a traitor to his class. To the Western Liberals, he was a "tab-collar Castro." Ross Thatcher, the Saskatchewan premier, himself a former socialist, called him "the most dangerous socialist in Canada."

When the party, especially its Western wing, rejected his stand on economic nationalism and supported free trade at its 1966 policy conference, Gordon threatened to get out. That horrified the so-called progressive wing of the party, which included Judy LaMarsh, Jean Marchand, Edgar Benson, and Donald Macdonald. The New Democratic Party was climbing in the polls. If Gordon left, they told Pearson, much of the party's left-of-centre support might opt for that alternative.

Pearson's long friendship with Gordon went back to the mid-1930s when the two had served on Harry Stevens's Price Spreads commission—Pearson as secretary, Gordon as a research resource. Now that friendship was beginning to fray. Pearson was weary, and his fatigue was reflected in the party itself, which Gordon hoped to reanimate. Pearson had been a politician—a role that did not suit him—for almost twenty years. The last ten had been especially hard, since in the House he was plagued by the formidable figure of John Diefenbaker, a master of the kind of political cut and thrust that Lester Pearson abhorred.

For Pearson, the Nobel-prize-winning diplomat, compromise was the name of the game. The last thing he needed, as the centennial year opened, was a knock-down battle between two extremes on the subject of economic nationalism. On that topic there was little agreement between Walter Gordon and his successor as the minister of finance, the flinty Mitchell Sharp.

Pearson was not a committed nationalist of the Walter Gordon school. Indeed, he didn't appear to be fiercely committed to anything except such motherhood concepts as "democracy" and "international understanding." When Canadians pay homage to "peace, order, and good government," they really mean *strong* government; among his critics, especially in his final year, Pearson wasn't seen as a strong leader. As a career diplomat he could not view the complicated political scene in the simplistic, black-and-white terms that made John Diefenbaker such an effective leader of the opposition.

That was hard enough, but with Gordon's return to the cabinet, Pearson found himself presiding over two warring camps in his party, neither of them prepared to compromise. To Sharp's followers, Gordon was the Bad Guy, depriving his fellow citizens of the benefits of American largesse. But to the left wing of the Liberal Party, Gordon was the man in the white hat, fighting to save his people from the incursions of the wicked Yankees. This longtime Canadian dilemma goes back beyond the Reciprocity election of 1911 to the Canada First movement that followed Confederation. Now, after lying relatively dormant for half a century, it was revived in the centennial year.

Months of enthusiastic flag waving had helped turn the eyes of the nation inward. After a long dry period of war, depression, and reconstruction, the new nationalism was making itself felt, and the old queries were being asked again: How cosy should we get with the Americans? Are we selling our souls for a mess of pottage? How much of the country's resources can we afford to peddle to foreigners? How can we accept Yankee dollars and Yankee institutions and still retain a measure of independence? These composed the great Canadian quandary that the politicians talked about, the journalists wrote about, and the people argued about in 1967. Thirty years later, they still do.

We look back now on the Pearson era as one of achievement. It was in this, Pearson's final year in office, that the Canadian welfare state reached its high point. A Canada Pension Plan, a universal medicare system, loosening of traditional attitudes to divorce and homosexuality, a new flag, a revised national anthem, unified armed forces, and a revised transport act—all these were part of Mike Pearson's legacy.

Yet, such was the distemper of those times (Peter Newman's phrase) that Pearson, unable to match Diefenbaker's fiery and sardonic appeal at the hustings, was never able to enjoy the luxury of a majority government. His colleagues, including Gordon, began to think of him as a weak and indecisive leader. In the House, as Gérard Pelletier noted,

62

the Prime Minister "tripped more often than he triumphed." Had he enjoyed a strong majority it wouldn't have mattered, but now his gaffes made everybody nervous. As Pelletier pointed out, "all minority governments are fragile, and every slip made by the prime minister threatens the very existence of his mandate." Nor was the Liberal Party in any sense united: it was well known that this was the Prime Minister's last year, and several members of the cabinet were already scrambling to succeed him. It seemed impossible to keep anything secret, even for a few days. Reports of cabinet decisions leaked out like liquid from a colander. As the Japanese ambassador murmured to his neighbour at a diplomatic reception: "The Canadian Ship of State is the only ship I know that leaks from the top."

Pearson had tried his best to solve the dilemma of Gordon in the cabinet by kicking him upstairs—to the Senate, or the high commissionership in London, or the presidency of the CBC. Gordon would have none of it. Now, with the extra burdens of the centennial year facing him, the Prime Minister was forced to mediate between Gordon and his successor. Gordon had made it clear—and Pearson had agreed—that he would find it difficult to be part of any cabinet that included Mitchell Sharp, whose "back stabbing tactics" he complained of to Pearson. Sharp was dead set against the kind of economic nationalism that Gordon espoused and to which the Prime Minister had paid some lukewarm lip service. He had to support his finance minister and he had to be seen to support him. Yet, with the Ontario caucus solidly on Gordon's side, Pearson had to throw him a bone meaty enough to keep him in line.

Gordon was in a strong position. He wanted the Government to commit itself to a program of full control of the Canadian economy—a commitment Sharp would be unable to block. He wanted the Government to issue a white paper dealing with the entire question of foreign control. And he wanted a senior cabinet post that would make him, in everything but name, deputy prime minister—a phrase, according to Keith Davey, that Pearson himself had used. On the eve of his appointment, he, Sharp, and Pearson met and papered over their differences, including the question of the powerful First National City Bank of New York (Citibank), which had been trying to get a foot in the door by buying a small Canadian bank, the Mercantile, from Dutch owners. Gordon was absolutely opposed to any concessions to Citibank. Though Pearson and Sharp agreed, when Gordon returned to the cabinet on January 9 he was convinced that "Mike will renege if he can."

His reception was, in the words of a fellow cabinet minister, Paul Hellyer, "good, but not terrific." Hellyer noted in his diary that day that "he will have a tough row to hoe." The business world was not happy. Robert Winters reported to Pearson that his contacts for raising money had dried up and that a committee to work on trade promotion had called the whole thing off. Yet the *Vancouver Sun*, in an editorial that bore all the earmarks of its veteran editor, Bruce Hutchison, wrote that "Mr. Gordon is almost, but not quite, co-prime minister. [His] resurrection and restoration is Mr. Sharp's demotion. Mr. Sharp will now fight for his policies in a split cabinet and his chances of success are small."

Gordon was more sceptical. At their January 3 meeting with Sharp the Prime Minister had been suspiciously vague. Persistently questioned by reporters at a press conference the following day, Pearson, using the double negative often preferred by politicians, declared that "we have never, as a government, felt that policies for the maximum Canadian control of Canadian economic development and Canadian resources should not be a primary objective of Canadian government policy." He also added, no doubt for Sharp's benefit, that "this kind of thing has to be reconciled with the need for Canadian capital and indeed foreign capital for Canadian development." After a good deal of study, he promised, the Government would be announcing "new measures" dealing with this "vital issue" but not in the immediate future. Buttonholed by a reporter after the meeting, Sharp took advantage of the Prime Minister's vagueness by insisting that no measures concerning foreign investment were contemplated. By the end of January, Gordon later wrote, he "was thoroughly sorry [he] had agreed to return to the cabinet." Pearson had not lived up to the various understandings he had given him and now he found himself involved in a serious disagreement with Sharp.

Gordon's main concern was the incursion of U.S. banking interests into Canada, specifically Citibank (the third largest in the United States), which was planning to expand its newly acquired Mercantile Bank into a full-blown enterprise. Gordon's draft revision of the Bank Act proposing to restrict foreign ownership of shares in Canadian banks had died on the order paper in 1965. Since that time the Americans had exercised enormous pressure on the government to allow foreign-owned banks and bank agencies to operate in Canada without discrimination. Intense lobbying from James Rockefeller of Citibank, a "very rough" note from the U.S. undersecretary of state threatening retaliation, and some arm twisting by the U.S. ambassador to Canada, Walton Butterworth (including several uncomplimentary off-the-record remarks about Gordon) didn't shake the Canadian government. Sharp and Pearson promised to stand up to the Americans and make no changes in Gordon's earlier draft for a revised Bank Act.

Sharp, however, wanted to give special consideration to Citibank. He proposed that the American firm be given a three-year period of grace before being forced to sell three-quarters of its stock to Canadians—a privilege denied all others. During that period it could, of course, expand without limit, carve itself a hefty chunk of the Canadian banking business, and, as the largest single shareholder, control the Mercantile subsidiary from New York. To Gordon this meant that Sharp wanted to open the door to American banks in Canada.

The press saw the whole argument as a battle for power between Sharp and Gordon. To the *Star*, the new deal for the Mercantile "represents an almost complete backstage victory for Sharp." The situation was exacerbated by the fact that Sharp was an undeclared but active candidate in the coming battle for the Liberal leadership. His supporters were urging him to stand fast: if he lost this duel with Gordon he would have little chance of succeeding Pearson. Sharp stood firm. The parliamentary committee amended the draft bill in his favour in what the *Globe and Mail* reported "appeared to be a well-planned maneuver for Mr. Sharp."

If Sharp got his way, Gordon was prepared to resign. He cut short his Jamaica vacation to return to Ottawa for a "flaming row" in cabinet on March 7. There he stated what he believed to be the substance of the issue: "Very simply, the problem was foreign control. . . . The Mercantile question was symbolic for three reasons: Were we to give way to intensive pressures including those from the U.S. State Department? Were we to clear the way for the full scale entry into Canada of U.S. banks? Were members of the cabinet to be able to trust each other's commitments?"

In the end Gordon prevailed. Citibank would either have to forgo its expansion plans or eventually reduce its share of the mandatory ownership to 10 percent. If Mercantile floated more stock, those additional shares would have to be sold to Canadians until Citibank's percentage of ownership dropped to 10 percent.

Gordon, however, was becoming more and more frustrated by politics in general and what he saw as the equivocations of his leader. He had believed, when he returned to the cabinet, that he would be made president of the privy council by the end of January. He was not sworn in until April 4 and even then had no clear idea of his duties. "It was obvious," he wrote in his memoirs, ". . . that the undertakings made to me when I rejoined the government were not going to be implemented, either because Pearson had changed his mind about them or because his own position was not strong enough to force them through." He was not, in short, going to be deputy prime minister; his new post as president of the privy council was merely titular.

The breach between the two old comrades was widening. Once they had been the closest of friends, but since Gordon's unfortunate advice to the Prime Minister to call an election in 1965, the atmosphere between them was cool and getting cooler. The time was coming when they would cease speaking to one another, and no amount of importuning by Keith Davey, a friend to both acting as a go-between, could reconcile them.

Gordon also felt strongly that the Government should take a strong stand against the war in Vietnam. The question was troubling much of the country in 1967, especially the young people. Gordon was, in his own words, "sick at heart" over the bombing of North Vietnam and fearful that it might lead to an all-out nuclear war. Since he knew he would get nowhere with the cabinet, he broke with tradition, defied convention, and spoke directly to the people. He had already told the National Press Club that Canada should probably get out of the North Atlantic Treaty Organization, something that no other member of the Government had even hinted at. Then, on May 13, in a speech to the Arts and Management Conference of Professional Women in Toronto, he stated baldly that the Vietnam War could not be justified on either moral or strategic grounds. He urged all Canadians, and especially the Canadian government, to press the United States to stop the bombing.

That was a direct counter to Lester Pearson's famous policy of "quiet diplomacy." Gordon hadn't even followed the standard practice of showing his speech in advance to the Prime Minister or the secretary of state for external affairs, Paul Martin, with whom he often disagreed. In Gordon's view, Canada was too anxious to cosy up to the policies and actions of its neighbour.

The Prime Minister called a cabinet meeting and read the riot act to Gordon. Cabinet solidarity, he made clear, could not be broken, and any criticism of this kind should be delivered to the PMO or External Affairs. At the same time, Pearson's statement contained a specific request that the United States end the bombings and enter peace negotiations. Gordon could accept that. When Pearson delivered an even tougher rebuke at the caucus, Gordon remained unchastened and unapologetic. The deluge of letters and phone calls supporting his stand suggests that on this issue, as on the issue of American control of Canadian resources, he was closer to the people than the Prime Minister was. Certainly the response served to soften the attacks on him.

He was ready to get out of politics. First, however, he would have to wait for the report of the task force on foreign investment in Canada that had been one of the lures offered for his return to cabinet. He had trouble getting Pearson to act on the matter, but an eight-man group under Professor Mel Watkins of the University of Toronto was eventually approved. Its mandate was to report to a small cabinet committee, which Gordon himself chaired and dominated. Gordon was convinced that if he quit, the task force's recommendations would never see the light of day. Watkins's report, whose recommendations, among other things, led to the creation of the Canada Development Corporation, was supposed to be tabled in September but was not complete until January 1968.

Gordon chose Watkins to chair his task force on the recommendation of Abraham Rotstein, editor of the *Canadian Forum*. Gordon was impressed because Watkins, a one-time critic of economic nationalism, had given *A Choice for Canada* a favourable review. The Vietnam War had completed a change of heart. Watkins had not been interested in politics in his undergraduate days, but a stay in the United States had disillusioned him and led to a conviction that Canada ought to set her own course. Like Gordon, Watkins now believed that Canada needed more autonomy in her foreign policy.

When Watkins first met Gordon in Gordon's big Rosedale home, he warned him, "I'm actually an NDP supporter." Gordon replied that "some of my best friends are, some of my strongest supporters are." Watkins later remarked that of all the people he had met in politics, no one else had Gordon's kind of principles. The career mandarins in External Affairs did not take kindly to the makeup of his task force, which also included Rotstein. When its members tried to get access to External Affairs files they were treated to a lengthy diatribe against the anti-war movement, especially the teach-ins at the University of Toronto. It was, Watkins remembered, "one of the most chilling things" he'd encountered at that time. As far as the war was concerned, the political establishment stood foursquare with the United States.

Gordon, who chaired the cabinet committee overseeing Watkins, turned it into a one-man band. He kept a tight rein on the proceedings, meeting weekly with Watkins. Watkins would occasionally ask whether something should be approved by the cabinet committee, and Gordon would tell him that the committee, which rarely met anyway, didn't need it.

68

In all this Walter Gordon had the unswerving support of Beland Honderich's *Toronto Daily Star*, which gave him a political platform whenever he needed it. With the help of the *Star*'s Ottawa correspondent, Val Sears, Watkins and his committee got regular access to the front pages and enthusiastic support from the editorial columns. It was a situation that once prompted Sears to shout across a crowd at a cocktail party, "Shut up, Watkins, you wouldn't exist if I hadn't invented you."

As soon as the Watkins Report was tabled in February 1968, Gordon submitted his resignation. He had been in constant pain for some time as the result of a herniated disc and had hung on only long enough to see his baby born. Keith Davey wanted to host a celebratory dinner for him to mark his exit from politics, but Gordon vetoed the idea. It was not possible, he told Davey, to hold such a dinner without Pearson's presence, and he wasn't willing to have Pearson invited. And so, with his friendship with the Prime Minister in tatters, he slipped quietly out of public view.

2

Hockey's last hurrah

Halfway through the centennial year, Canada lost control of its national game. In the spring of 1967, six teams made up the National Hockey League. The two dominant teams—the ones that had won more Stanley Cups than all the American teams put together—were the Toronto Maple Leafs and the Montreal Canadiens. But that fall the league doubled in size. Now there were twelve hockey teams, of which ten were based in American cities. Hockey would never be the same again.

The game was still played by Canadians. In 1967 every league player but one—a Duluth-born Boston forward, Tommy Williams—had been born and raised in Canada. Many had learned to handle the puck as spindly youths playing shinny on frozen ponds in small frontier towns. They'd been nurtured on the Saturday night hockey broadcast—the only program in the world that turned a radio announcer into a national icon.

As small boys with big dreams, they had been fed the lore with their morning porridge. They knew more about the Big Train, Cyclone Taylor, and the Silver Fox than they did about the prime ministers of their country or the kings and queens of England in the Grade 5 school texts.

Never mind the Stratford Festival, the Royal Winnipeg Ballet, or the Montreal Symphony! Hockey Night in Canada was Canadian culture writ large. If the CPR helped tie the nation together, Hockey Night helped to hold it together. Like the long, remorseless winter, it was something Canadians shared—a hot game for a cold country that reached its climax by the end of March when the frost was still in the ground.

And it *is* a hot game, whose icons are themselves hot-tempered. I've always been amused and puzzled by the fact that Canada's national game is an anomaly. The stereotypes just don't mesh. Some of the greatest and most admired players have been brutes, using hockey sticks as spears, untangling themselves from pile-ups of bodies that often begin with a fistfight or a low blow. These are typical Canadians, playing the typical Canadian sport? It requires an Orwellian form of double-think to match the image of these violently aggressive young men with that of the polite and deferential Canadian. We are not a nation of bruisers, yet fighting has always been a part of hockey. Sportswriters decry it, politicians demand that it be stopped, parent-teacher groups rail against it, the more decorous European teams sneer at it. But it continues because the fans like it and want it. In moments of high emotion our national game becomes a blood sport, and we are mesmerized by it even as we lament its violence. That, no doubt, helps give us a distinct identity.

In the long discourse about identity, the Saturday night hockey broadcast was often passed over, yet it could be argued that this single program did more to give us a wacky kind of unity than all the rest of the CBC combined. Television's unifying force was even more potent. No matter what language you understood—French, English, or Ukrainian—the spectacle of the game was there for all to see and argue about the following morning, in beautiful black and white—darting figures silhouetted against the alabaster expanse of the ice. Was it significant that the CBC switched to colour just before the league expanded?

It was something we had in common—all of us, West Coast loggers, Slavic farmers, *habitants*, Bluenoses. A tiresome cliché holds that Canada has no heroes. Nonsense! How about Howie Morenz, Charlie Conacher, Bobby Orr? How about the Rocket? Boom-Boom? The Big M? The Golden Jet? The Great One? The nicknames are instantly recognizable to any Canadian. Gump Worsley is remembered today; the chinless comic-strip figure for whom he was named is forgotten. These, not the politicians, are the national heroes we revere. But after the centennial year, everything began to change as hockey slowly became an American spectator sport. How does one create a national icon out of a team named the Mighty Ducks?

It was Canada's game in more ways than one. The National Hockey League was rigged in favour of the two Canadian teams; under its rules any team could protect a player living within a fifty-mile radius of home ice from being drafted by another team. That was a cinch for the Canadiens, the majority of whose players came from Quebec, or the Leafs, where so many hailed from Northern Ontario mining towns. It wasn't so easy for, say, New York. How many hockey players ever came out of Westchester County? No wonder the two Canadian-based teams won all but five Stanley Cups in the years that followed the Second World War. They also dominated the play-offs, meeting seven times over the previous nine years.

Saturday nights were home game nights, which meant that one or other of the Canadian teams, and often both, would be on the air. It was the rivalry between the Leafs and the Canadiens that made *Hockey Night in Canada* so compelling—even more compelling than *The Jackie Gleason Show*, *Mission Impossible*, *Lawrence Welk*, or *Hollywood Palace*, all of which were in the ten top-rated TV programs.

The players themselves had been raised on these Saturday night hockey broadcasts. As Terry Harper, a Montreal defenceman, told the author Stephen Cole, "The thing you have to appreciate is that all the players were Montreal and Toronto fans growing up. You listened to your team on the radio; they were your heroes. And if you were a

Montreal fan, you fought with the kids who liked Toronto. Then you got signed up to play for the Canadiens or the Leafs when you were a teenager, and you fought against each other's junior teams. Then, oh, geez, you made the NHL, well, no one had to prepare you for a game against Toronto. Any time we played the Leafs was a special game. Everybody got all pumped up. . . . You could never get hockey that good anymore as far as I'm concerned. Never."

Then suddenly, it was over. As Cole wrote in his definitive book, *The Last Hurrah*, "we all thought the Leaf-Canadien rivalry would last forever. It didn't. The 1966–67 season was the last hurrah for a rivalry that sustained Canada through more than forty winters. The last time that hockey seemed securely, yes, perhaps even smugly ours. Those who were there will never forget it. Those who weren't will never understand. There's not much the former can say to the latter, except to explain that for four decades there were two professional hockey teams in Canada. One of two hockey sweaters was passed out under the tree at Christmas. Somewhere along the way the dye from those scratchy wool sweaters must've seeped into our skins."

It was this that made 1967 a miracle spring for hockey fans. For this would be the last time the two teams would meet in the twin temples of sport—Forum and Gardens—in the Stanley Cup finals. The play-offs had always been staged in early April. A stranger might wonder why there were play-offs at all, since there were only six teams in the league. Two had been eliminated in the regular season. Why not four? Why not go directly to the Cup finals?

What, and lose all those extra admissions? The day was coming when the play-offs would seem to go on forever, with summer around the corner, the lilacs in bloom, and the iris already fading. But in 1967, the advent of the finals spelled, for most people, the end of winter. There were still blizzards in some parts of Canada. The Yukon River remained frozen until early May. The idea that a professional hockey game might one day be played on a hot June night would have met with wide-eyed disbelief, if not anger.

In 1967, the Maple Leafs were the underdogs. In the past dozen years the Canadiens had won seven Stanley Cups (five in a row between 1956 and 1960), the Leafs only three. There was no "typical" Leaf player—no stereotype. Eddie Shack, "The Entertainer," who inspired the song "Clear the Track, Here Comes Shack," was a grammar school dropout who could scarcely read or write when he joined the league. By contrast, Brian Conacher, the current scion of a famous hockey family, had gone to Upper Canada College and held a university degree. Bob Pulford, "the hockey player's hockey player" (as Pulford goes, so go the Leafs), managed to play the game professionally and at the same time earn a Bachelor's degree at McMaster University. Red Kelly represented York West as a Liberal Member of Parliament. Frank Mahovlich, the sensitive son of Croatian immigrants, liked to visit art galleries when the Leafs were on the road. Tim Horton ran a doughnut shop chain. Terry Sawchuk, one of the team's two superb goalies, was nicknamed "Ukie" because of his Ukrainian heritage. George Armstrong, the captain, had an Irish father and a native Algonquin mother; his teammates called him Chief.

The day of the millionaire defenceman had not yet arrived. These men played hockey for the love of it. Some of the best came out of northern mining camps—Noranda, Sudbury, Timmins, Cochrane. Most held summer jobs to help make ends meet. Many had grown up poor in the Depression, like Johnny Bower, whose childhood goalie pads were made from strips of an old mattress held together by pieces of inner tube.

The day would shortly come when hockey stars were bounced about from team to team so that a player might easily find himself facing an opponent who had been his roommate the season before. But in these pre-expansion days, the line-up was remarkably consistent. In Punch Imlach's first season as Leaf coach—1958–59—the guts of the club consisted of Armstrong, Horton, Pulford, and Allan Stanley (and later Red Kelly). In 1967 all were still on the team.

Imlach made a bold prediction that first season. He announced that within four years the Leafs, then one of the poorest teams in the league, would win the Stanley Cup. His prediction came true. By 1967, the Leafs had managed to win three Stanley Cups while the aging players who would help him win the fourth remained the backbone of the team.

What they lacked in youth they made up in experience. Half a dozen were over the age of thirty. Pulford was now thirty-one, Sawchuk, Horton, and Armstrong would all be thirty-seven by the next season. Red Kelly was crowding forty. Allan Stanley was forty-one. And Johnny Bower, who seemed to have been playing goal for the Leafs since the Great War, was forty-two.

Holding it all together was the highly controversial and highly successful coach George "Punch" Imlach, a man of many moods who could treat his rookies with infinite patience and chill out any veteran who didn't produce. He was not loved by his players, but he was certainly admired. "My job," he said, "is to win hockey games and the Stanley Cup. If I have to bruise a few guys to do it, that is just too bad. I do what I think is necessary to win."

He had his fans and he also had his detractors, on his own team, in the press, and among his opponents. "As a player," his mentor, Lex Cook, remembered, discussing his early days, "he only knew one way to play—all out." As one opposition player remarked, not without a touch of respect, "he gets everything out of those guys, even the whites of their eyes." His personal Bible was Norman Vincent Peale's *The Power of Positive Thinking*. In 1964 he had handed out paperback copies to every player on the team.

He was a bundle of superstitions. He thought two-dollar bills were unlucky and wouldn't accept them. When one of his teams was billeted on the thirteenth floor of a hotel, he had all the players re-assigned. When the Leafs were on a winning streak, he refused to change his suit. His favourite number was eleven. As a rookie, Ron Ellis wore that number, scoring twenty-six goals and sixteen assists. The following year Imlach assigned the number to a new rookie, hoping the magic was catching.

Imlach's moods matched the fortunes of his team. Between mid-January and mid-February in 1967, the Maple Leafs lost ten games in a row, dropping to fifth place in the league. Imlach's response was to work his players and himself harder—so hard that he ended up in hospital. At that juncture the Leafs started to win. King Clancy, his second-in-command, took over for him and was hailed as a wonder coach. The sports press began to call for Imlach's head, but two of his key players made a point of publicly supporting him. "Punch had us straightened out before his health gave out," Tim Horton explained. "He proved he was a real man during that ten-game losing streak. He could have blasted us in the news media, made a lot of line-up changes, and taken us apart verbally behind closed doors. He did none of those things. Instead of criticizing, he went out of his way to build up our confidence. . . it took patience and courage. . . ." Red Kelly agreed. "Instead of threats of demotion, I got sound advice and encouragement," he said.

Imlach returned after a three-week recuperation. By the end of the regular season his team had bounced back from fifth place to third. In the logical order of things, the Maple Leafs would have had no business being in the Stanley Cup finals that spring. By actual statistics, the Chicago Black Hawks were the best team in the NHL. They played seventy games in the regular season, won forty-one, lost seventeen, tied twelve. That put them at the top of the heap, seventeen points ahead of the Canadiens, who were themselves two points up on the Leafs who were three points ahead of the New York Rangers.

By the peculiar reasoning of the hockey moguls, first-place Chicago did not battle it out with second-place Montreal but with third-place Toronto, while Montreal took on New York. The Canadiens-Rangers series was no contest. Montreal took the semi-finals in four games straight: 6–4, 4–3, 3–2, and the last game, which was the toughest of all, 2–1 in overtime.

It was not so easy for the Leafs, who skated onto the Chicago ice wearing a new symbol on their white jerseys—a blue maple leaf, remodelled for the Centennial, with five points instead of eleven, like the one that graced Mike Pearson's new Canadian flag. They had been dismissed by sports experts as an "over the hill team," too old and too tired to prevail against the powerhouse Black Hawks. Imlach defiantly reminded his aging players that the team had been together for ten years. Next season's expansion would tear it apart. These would be the last moments that most of them would spend as members of the Toronto Maple Leafs. The result was a hard-fought contest.

New symbol or not, the Leafs were clobbered 5–1 by their opponents in the first game. For that, however, Chicago paid a price. The Leafs' aggressive defence was damaging. "I felt like an eighty-year-old man," said Bobby Hull at the end of the game.

Surprisingly, the Leafs did not stay in Chicago between games. Imlach insisted on taking the last flight out of O'Hare, which meant the team didn't reach Toronto until three the next morning. For that Imlach was criticized, but he knew what he was doing. The Ice Capades had booked the Chicago stadium for their exclusive use. If the Leafs had stayed, they'd have had to practise in a mall far out in the suburbs—not a major league facility. As a result the Toronto team got two practices on its home ice while most of the Black Hawks took two days off.

The ice show left the Chicago skating surface in bad shape. The *Chicago Tribune* reported that the "stadium ice looked like a frozen sewer. There was enough mud to satisfy the most finicky hippopotamus." That suited the Leafs' checking game, but not the Hawks' skating game. Greed had done Chicago in. The stadium and the hockey team had the same ownership, yet the stadium management booked the ice show even though they knew the Hawks would be needing the ice for the play-offs. "Didn't they think the Hawks would make the play-offs?" the *Tribune* asked. "Or didn't they care?"

The Leafs cared. When their plane touched down in Toronto in the early hours of the morning, Imlach told his players that the practice session, only a few hours away, would be optional. In spite of very little sleep, every Leaf was on hand for it. Chicago had an optional practice too, but only four regulars turned up.

Imlach had another reason for returning to Toronto. "If I let them loose in this town for two days I'd never find them," he explained to a Toronto reporter, who himself seemed the worse for wear after a tour of the Loop bars. "Christ, from the looks of you, I'd never let my team stay here."

The second game was no contest. Toronto beat Chicago, 3–1, and repeated that score on home ice a couple of days later. In the fourth game Chicago struck back, 4–3, tying the series. In the fifth game the score was tied 2–2 after the first period. At that point Imlach replaced Bower with Terry Sawchuk, the best goalie in hockey history. Now Sawchuk showed some of the spirit that inspired the Toronto team. In Stephen Cole's words, the two teams entered the second period "like charging rams." Allan Stanley of the Leafs slammed into Kenny Wharram, knocking him senseless and incurring a penalty. In the power play that followed, Bobby Hull fired a shot from thirty feet directly at the net. As Red Kelly put it, "that puck got off the ice so high, so fast, it was like a golfer using a sand wedge. You wouldn't have thought a hockey stick could make a shot like that." Sawchuk never saw the puck, which caught him high on the shoulder as he moved out of the net. "He went down," Kelly remembered, "like somebody shot him."

Sawchuk had been knocked out cold. When he came to, he lifted himself on one elbow and gave his head a shake.

"Where'd you get it?" Bobby Haggart, the Leafs' trainer, asked.

"My bad shoulder."

"Think you're all right?"

Sawchuk's riposte has gone down in hockey legend.

"I stopped the shot, didn't I?" he said.

What followed was the most remarkable demonstration of goaltending that veteran reporters had ever seen. Thirty-seven times Sawchuk's opponents fired the puck at him. Thirty-seven times he stopped it. By the end of the game his arms and shoulders were a mass of bruises. One shoulder was swollen. He could hardly move. But thanks to him, the Maple Leafs had bested the Black Hawks, 4–2.

It had taken courage to rush out time and time again as Hull fired shot after shot. Sawchuk's teammates knew it, and as Ron Ellis put it, "we were determined to go out that next game and give him the kind of support he deserved." They did just that. The Hawks had set twelve scoring records that season, but the Leafs beat them in the sixth and final game, 3–1. The Chicago team seemed to have run out gas, perhaps because their aggressive style of play had exhausted them, perhaps because of sheer frustration at their inability to get the puck past Sawchuk, or perhaps because the Leafs fitted together better as a team. Imlach's style was such that if one man went down, another was on hand to replace him. And so the team that had been given little chance in the early months of 1967 to make the play-offs was now in the Stanley Cup finals. But there was no champagne in the dressing room that night. The Maple Leafs would be facing Toe Blake and the Canadiens soon enough.

Once again the Leafs were the underdogs, facing the most formidable hockey team in history. The Canadiens had won the Stanley Cup nine times since the end of the war, including 1965 and again in 1966. The experts were still saying that Imlach's team was too old and too slow. To which Imlach responded, "Yeah, they may be bums, but they're my bums, so that's the end of that."

Only Imlach believed the Leafs had a chance. The consensus was that Montreal was again a cinch to make it three Stanley Cups in a row. Hector "Toe" Blake was a man who hated to lose, a man who knew how to fire up his players, a man who, as Red Fisher, the Montreal sportswriter, once said, could be intelligent, thoughtful, funny, and cruel—sometimes all in the same afternoon.

Blake had a ferocious temper. He was so infuriated by the team's loss to Chicago in the 1961 play-offs that he walked across the ice and smacked the referee, Dalt MacArthur, on the nose, thereby drawing a huge, two-thousand-dollar fine. He had a wicked tongue, which he used against players he thought weren't doing their best. He claimed defenceman Doug Harvey was so relaxed "he played the game in a rocking chair," and when another player offered him a cigar to celebrate the birth of a child, he responded, "Good; now maybe you'll get off your ass and play hockey."

His players feared him. After a rough loss he could reduce them to tears. But he never railed at a sensitive player in public, only against those veterans who knew how to take it. And he never criticized a player during a press or TV interview. Jean Béliveau called him "a player's coach. . . a very fair hockey man."

Blake had been a player himself for fifteen seasons, scoring so many goals and thereby causing the red light behind the net to light up so often that he earned the nickname the Old Lamplighter. By 1967 he had coached eleven Montreal clubs; seven won the Stanley Cup. It was generally conceded that of all the play-off coaches, he was the best ever.

His was an all-star team, dominated by French Canadians. Jean Béliveau, the captain, was one of the classiest players in the league, the third-highest scorer in hockey history, and in Punch Imlach's own estimation "the best that ever came down the pike." Imlach said, "He could play for me, anywhere, anytime, in this world or the next." Henri Richard, the Pocket Rocket, younger brother of the legendary Maurice, was one of the fastest skaters in the league and so obsessed by the game that he hated to come off the ice when the whistle blew; often he pretended he hadn't heard it. He was happy only when playing and, in the phrase of the sport, "puck lucky"—it seemed to be either at the end of his stick or behind his legs. The newer players, such as little Yvan Cournoyer, the "Roadrunner," were already making their names in French Canada. One of the most potent scorers on the team, a power-play specialist—small, fast, and deadly—Cournoyer had the potential to become the greatest player of all time, with an ability to get shot after shot away faster than any of his contemporaries.

These three players won the first game in the Montreal Forum. Among them they scored six goals to Toronto's three (Béliveau scored one, Cournoyer two, and Richard three). In the Montreal net was a rookie, Rogatien Vachon, a kid of twenty-one just called up from a Junior B club. He felt no pressure until Imlach, in a carefully orchestrated attempt to get Blake's goat, told a sportswriter, "There is no way that [they] can beat us with a Junior B goaltender." That rankled, as Imlach knew it would. Reporters covering the finals seized on the remark, which stuck to Vachon for the rest of his career.

The Leafs had two of the most experienced goaltenders—the moody Terry Sawchuk and the veteran Johnny Bower. Lester Patrick of the New York Rangers was on record as declaring that goaltending represented 70 percent of a team's effectiveness. Other players could make mistakes; a goaltender's mistakes could cost his team the game. Because the goalie was usually on the ice for the full sixty minutes, the pressure never ended. In that sixty minutes he would have to stop twenty, thirty, or more hard rubber pucks, fired at a speed of up to 120 miles an hour. The Canadiens' veteran, Gump Worsley, once said that the only job worse than tending goal was that of a javelin catcher at a track-and-field meet. Two earlier Leaf goalies had been forced to quit because of ulcers.

Terry Sawchuk, whom Imlach picked to mind the net in the first game with Montreal, had not yet recovered from the exhausting and bruising play-offs. High-strung and understandably nervous, he had shocked the hockey world in the middle of the 1956-57 season with the Boston Bruins by announcing that he was quitting the game forever. For that arrogance he was attacked in the press until it was discovered that he had been playing on his nerve for a month, the victim of a debilitating attack of mononucleosis. That he did return was a tribute to his fierce intensity to excel. By 1962, when he donned a face mask for the first time (a protection that neither Bower nor Worsley would accept), Sawchuk's Slavic features were crisscrossed with more than 250 scars.

His many bouts of surgery were legendary. At the age of two he had injured his elbow so badly he couldn't raise it to lift a glass of water. His right arm was two inches shorter than his left. In three operations doctors had removed sixty bone chips, twenty-two of which he kept as keepsakes in a jar. In 1947 a blow from a hockey stick almost blinded him, putting him out of action for three weeks. In 1953 an acute attack of appendicitis again put him under the knife. In 1954 his chest was crushed in an automobile accident. In 1966 a ruptured spinal disc brought more surgery.

Now he was facing the ferocious Canadiens, his weight down from 228 to a skinny 150 pounds, his ankle dented, his nose crinkled, his fatigue showing, and his mind in turmoil because of marital problems. Sawchuk was not up to that first game. In the middle of the third period, with the score at 5–2, Imlach pulled him out "to conserve energy," in effect conceding the game to Blake. The experts began to predict a Montreal sweep.

In the second game the Canadiens fired thirty-one shots at the forty-two-year-old Johnny Bower, who deflected them all. Three times the Canadiens' John Ferguson accidentally struck Bower on the shoulder. The third blow also opened up a gash on the goalie's unprotected nose. Up rushed the Leafs' trainer, Haggart, brandishing a towel. Did Bower need a bit of time on the bench to recuperate? Bower waved him away. "I'm hot!" he hissed. "Hot! Just leave me alone. Don't bother me." For Bower it was a 3–0 shutout, and the series was tied.

The third game, at the Gardens, was a goaltenders' battle. After three periods the teams were tied at two all. Montreal fired a phenomenal sixty-two shots at Bower; Toronto fired fifty-four at Vachon. After the first period of overtime the score was still tied. Part way through the second, Pulford scored the winning goal and left the Montreal players in a state of blue funk.

Imlach couldn't resist rubbing it in. "How's your team?" he asked a Montreal sportswriter the following morning. "Ask them if they want to be humiliated any more." King Clancy tried to get him to stop, but Imlach insisted on taking another crack at Vachon. "He's up to Junior A now. He's graduated from Junior B to Junior A. There's no way we can lose. . . ."

But in Game 4, Vachon came through. Sawchuk found himself in the Leafs' net because Bower had pulled a muscle in his left thigh. Sawchuk, who hadn't expected to play, had been out drinking the night before and wasn't up to form. Montreal won, 6–2, and once again the series was tied. Blake went out of his way to praise Vachon in his postgame press conference. Imlach was so depressed he fled the Gardens and let Clancy handle the reporters.

Before Game 5, Imlach assembled his players and told them it was now or never. They *must* win this one because if the series were to go to seven games the Canadiens would end up on their home ice, and there was little chance of Toronto prevailing before the screaming fans in the Forum. The Leafs needed this game to give them a three to two lead in the series.

To the delight of the Montreal team, Sawchuk again replaced the injured Bower. They thought he was a softer target and launched the first period with a whirlwind attack. It may have unnerved some of the Leafs, but not Terry Sawchuk. The Leafs stuck to Imlach's defensive strategy, their hard checking nullifying the speed and expert passing of their opponents. Montreal drew first blood, but after that it was no contest. Toronto won, 4–1.

Toronto, Tuesday, May 2: events were unfolding as a nervous Punch Imlach hoped they would. "We have to win this game tonight," he reminded his players. "If we go back to Montreal for a seventh game, all bets are off." He reminded his younger players that they were a mere sixty minutes away from a Stanley Cup win. Then, to the veterans: "Some of you have been with me for nine years. It's been said that I stuck with the old ones so long we couldn't possibly win the Stanley Cup. For some of you it's farewell. Go out there and ram that puck down their goddamn throats."

In this sixth game the Canadiens played with all the panache and aggressiveness that mirrored the French-Canadian flair of their home city and the dazzle of Expo 67. The Torontonians were stereotypically cautious, self-controlled, and co-ordinated. In the first period the Leafs let the Montrealers carry the game deep into their own territory, where Sawchuk stonewalled them. In the second period they scored twice and entered the third period with a 2–0 lead. Dick Duff of the Canadiens cut it to 2–1. Toe Blake desperately needed a tie to stay alive. His team played a furious game but could not get past Sawchuk. With one minute to go in regulation time, Blake had only one hope: yank Worsley, leave the net empty, and send six players down the ice in a last-minute gamble. If they succeeded it was still anybody's series.

Punch Imlach, defiantly thumbing his nose at critics who had charged his team was too old, too tired, and too shopworn, turned to his veterans: Horton, Stanley, Pulford, Kelly, and Armstrong. These aging stick-handlers, all resisting normal retirement, would support Sawchuk in the net. It seemed an unequal contest: five old men challenging six of Blake's youngest and most energetic players.

82

Forty-one-year-old Allan Stanley took the face-off. In his early years as a defenceman, before the rules changed, "Big Sam" had been the choice because the centremen were always smaller than he was. When the referee dropped the puck, he would surge right over his smaller opponent. But now that kind of face-off interference was no longer allowed, and Stanley hadn't taken a face-off in years. As he skated out to the circle, he saw big Jean Béliveau waiting for him and asked himself, "Jesus Christ, what am I gonna do?" There was only one thing *to* do, and that was to play it as he always had before the new rule came in.

He asked Red Kelly to line up a little behind him. "That's where I'm going to put the puck," he told him. He kept his eye on the referee, and when the puck was dropped, he later recalled, "I played Béliveau so he couldn't get his stick on it and I ran the sonofabitch right out of there with his stick between my legs."

The puck rolled back to Kelly, who threw it to Pulford, who passed it to Armstrong, who shot it one hundred feet directly into the centre of the empty Montreal net. Béliveau was running after the referee shouting "Face-off interference! Face-off interference!" but nobody paid much attention. A few seconds later the game ended and the Leafs had won the Stanley Cup.

In the visitors' clubhouse, Blake was shaking hands with his players. "Tonight," he said, "Sawchuk was too much." And so ended what was to become known as the Golden Age of Canadian Hockey. By 1972, the number of professional hockey teams would have risen from the original six to twenty-seven. The Leafs and the Canadiens in 1974 were assigned to separate divisions, which meant that they would never again meet in the playoffs unless they met in the finals.

The black-and-white game was gone with the black-and-white rivalry. TV profits helped boost players' salaries to astronomical heights. Colour television arrived on the eve of the centennial year. The Americans, who hadn't even bothered to telecast hockey's greatest season, soon made hockey their own game.

Two years after his big win, Punch Imlach was fired as coach of the

Leafs. A year later the man who had made that win possible (by common consent the greatest goalkeeper in hockey's history), Terry Sawchuk, now despondent, died of injuries suffered as a result of drunken horseplay with a fellow player. There were those who said that the great Canadian game—the game of Foster Hewitt, Charlie Conacher, Rocket Richard, and Conn Smythe—died with him.

3

The CBC's loss of nerve

In the final month of the centennial year, Roy Shields, the *Toronto Daily Star*'s influential television critic, put into words what many Canadians were thinking. Can Canada, he asked, survive the impact of American television?

The previous night—December 3—the National Broadcasting Company had aired a documentary, with commentary by John Steinbeck, entitled *America and the Americans*. As Shields pointed out, all the sights and sounds from a thousand pictures could just as well have been from Toronto, Hamilton, Winnipeg, or Vancouver. "The America and the Americans presented to us were ourselves. Indeed, most of Steinbeck's observations about his country could also have been made about ours. All save Quebec, and that's the rub."

It was curious how blind Canada's politicians and intellectuals had been to the merciless effect of Canada's Americanized television on Canadian life. The cruel truth was that American television had changed the way Canadians looked at themselves.

Not only did Canadians watch far more American than Canadian television but they also seemed completely hooked on the medium. The middle economic class—54.1 percent of the population—watched TV for six hours and twenty-six minutes every day. The higher income group watched almost as much—five hours and twenty-four minutes a day. No other country in the world was so willingly bombarded by the mass culture of a neighbour.

Under the rules of the soon-to-be-defunct Board of Broadcast

Governors, every channel was required to carry 55 percent Canadian programming. Little of this was carried in prime time; in 1967 only three of the ten most watched programs were Canadian. Though the CBC produced some shows of quality, many imitated American-style programming. Two of the three shows in the top ten, *Front Page Challenge* and *Flashback*, both undeniably popular, were adaptations of the American panel show format that had been made familiar by the producers of *What's My Line?* and *I've Got a Secret*. (The third was the quintessential Canadian musical program, *Don Messer's Jubilee*.)

One might have expected a publicly owned network to specialize in the kind of broadcasting that the private channels could not afford, not only because of their financial situation but also because they were not in the boat-rocking business. Two incidents in 1967 revealed that the CBC's hierarchy actually feared controversy and stifled the kind of bold, experimental programming that reflected the new psychedelic age.

The year before, Patrick Watson, a producer of *This Hour Has Seven Days*, assigned a documentary about Warrendale, a residential treatment centre for emotionally disturbed children on the outskirts of Toronto, to a respected filmmaker, Allan King. *Seven Days* itself was far too controversial for the CBC and was killed in 1966, but the Warrendale project survived.

At Warrendale the child patients lived in houses in groups of twelve with a trained staff providing, in Watson's description, "a warm and supportive atmosphere that not only tolerates but welcomes and encourages expressions of all feelings, even the most violent and destructive."

These children's lives had gone off the track. Their fears and rages had become so extreme that their parents, teachers, and friends could no longer reach them. The treatment devised by John Brown, in charge of Warrendale, did not attempt to control or curtail the violent and destructive outbreaks through the traditional use of drugs, "quiet rooms," and straitjackets. Instead it called for the firm and safe physical holding of children who blew up. Since they could not hurt themselves or others, they had the opportunity to express their inner, terrifying feelings. King spent two months at Warrendale, and the result was a film that won international prizes and critical praise—but was rejected by the CBC.

It broke new ground. That, more than anything else, made it unacceptable for television. At that time, as King recalled, "we weren't allowed to look at people who were shameful. Just to *show* them was shameful." The head of the Children's Aid Society even attempted to block screenings of the film and tried unsuccessfully to get an injunction to stop anybody from seeing it.

It had been the custom in films of this kind to block out the faces of the key people. The kids objected. Why did they need to be wiped out? they asked. Why were they being treated as a bunch of freaks? In the end, King used identifiable children who talked in a normal way and used a number of four-letter words, especially the dreaded F-word, which in those days didn't turn up in films anywhere.

After *Warrendale* was completed, King faced six months of negotiations with the CBC. It seemed at times that they were discussing two different films. King thought he had made a documentary about the treatment of disturbed children, but the CBC's official reason for refusing to release it was that the corporation felt the film itself was an *abuse* of children. They couldn't have chosen a more insulting way of dismissing his work.

King had known in advance that *Warrendale* would be controversial. He and Watson decided to forge ahead and argue later. After all, this was the sixties, when social values and mores were in flux and nobody really knew what the rules were because the rules were changing so swiftly.

The CBC executives began to advance other reasons for keeping the film under wraps. The most patronizing was that expressed by Eugene Hallman, the one-time weatherman who had risen to become the corporation's vice-president of programming. Hallman said that although sophisticated Toronto audiences might understand the documentary, "if you lived in Swift Current and had never heard of Warrendale, and one night you saw this film, what would be your reaction?" There were other complaints. The film seemingly had no structure—no beginning, middle, or end, no voice-over commentary, no musical background, no point of view. It was simply a slice of life at the institution, forty hours of celluloid edited down to an hour and forty-two minutes. It was, in short, *McLuhanesque*, a word in constant use in 1967. Like so many of the films shown at Expo 67, it did not conform to tradition and follow the accepted and acceptable documentary format. Its content was disturbing—scenes of screaming, hysterical children being held by staff workers. It was raw, impressionistic, and agonizing. And it was *formless*.

The real reason that *Warrendale* was shelved, however, was simple enough. It was riddled with obscenities—and out of the mouths of babes! All the obfuscation from the CBC's top brass was designed to paper over that problem. Thirteen-year-old children crying "Fuck!" over and over again! That, of course, was reality, but the CBC didn't want reality. Hallman tried to hide behind the legal department, which, in the craven fashion of lawyers everywhere, had assured him that under Canadian law the corporation would be found guilty of broadcasting obscenity. Nobody swallowed that one, especially after the Ontario Film Review (i.e., censor) Board passed it for public showing in Toronto. In May *Warrendale* won two awards at Cannes, and in June it opened at the New Yorker Theatre in Toronto to critical applause. It remains a landmark film, the *Citizen Kane* of documentaries, "the most appealing and affecting film I have even seen," the *New Statesman*'s critic called it.

That year the CBC muffed another chance to move with the changing times and to establish itself as a unique public television network unencumbered by the commercial and social restraints that were inhibiting American broadcasting. Having put the kibosh on the pioneering and often incendiary program *This Hour Has Seven Days*, the corporation settled for what it hoped would be a more traditional Sunday night flagship program. But *Sunday*, as it was called, turned out to be almost as controversial as *Seven Days* and was jettisoned after a single season.

Its producer was Daryl Duke, one of the bright young men who had cut his teeth on Ross McLean's *Close-Up*. An early press release announced that the program would be "an attempt at total journalism using a combination not only of politics and other significant current events, but also drama, music, and the arts." This too was a novel concept. Duke would not package his various segments as features, drama documentaries, and so on, but would arrange them to flow in a single framework. His manifesto must have given the CBC's bureaucrats cause for alarm:

"*Sunday* is a show which will run the gamut of human experience, mixing raw journalism with the emotional intensity of a medieval bear pit or bull fight arena. With *Sunday* I hope to give a mind-expanding view of life. . . a view which has all the intensity and chaotic clarity of an LSD trip. . . . Since the world is exploding and changing in new ways, the inevitable desk and neat studio look seem sterile to me and incapable of conveying to the viewer the true impact of the exciting but irrational world . . . . In short, I am trying to approach a format which, in its ultimate form, could provide the first experience in psychedelic television."

Duke, then, was very much a product of his times. But "psychedelic" was not a word that the CBC or its critics would appreciate. The country was on the brink of a sexual revolution, and, as is always the case when accepted values are about to crumble, conventional society fought back. *Sunday* was attacked for the usual reasons—undermining "Christian values," public morality, and the establishment. The former justice minister, Davie Fulton, called it "utter garbage." A Tory senator, noting with horror that an unmarried couple had been shown on the program living together, attacked it as "a diabolical scheme to tear down the sanctity of marriage." A Quebec senator (also a Tory) said it "carried the flavour of perversion." The CBC's president, Alphonse Ouimet, who had peremptorily cancelled *Seven Days*, made the front pages with an unprecedented apology because *Sunday* had included what he called "a sex film" produced by the British Broadcasting Corporation and shown on television to an apparently uncorrupted British public. Senator Grattan O'Leary galloped into the controversy crying that the CBC was plagued with "a number of young producers [who] apparently have just discovered sex. . . and appear to have discovered that it is wonderful."

Duke saw *Sunday* as a live program in which anything could happen and nothing could be edited. In his bear-pit setting the guest was challenged by an audience ringed around from above. That was where Duke wanted to put Adolf von Thadden, a German right-winger so contentious that he had even been ousted from the extremist National Democratic Party in his homeland. What he didn't want was a cosy little interview on von Thadden's own turf. But that was what he got. The CBC feared a public outcry if this would-be Nazi was brought to Canada under its auspices. As a result, the interview that was filmed in Germany in von Thadden's home was a far cry from the abrasive encounter that Duke hoped for. The chatty tête-à-tête with a neo-Nazi harmed the CBC far more than his presence in Canada would have done.

The CBC feared public opinion in the same way that the U.S. networks feared the pressure of commercial interests. In the year of Expo, new techniques, especially in films, were being tackled by bright young artists, yet the one transcontinental institution dedicated to holding the country together refused to build for itself a bold, imaginative persona that differed from the one flourishing south of the border.

The original Broadcasting Act had stated simply that the corporation was established for the purpose of offering a national broadcasting service. Now a new act that went before Parliament in 1967 declared that the CBC must contribute to the development of national unity and provide for a continuing expression of Canadian identity. "National unity" was the buzz phrase of the year. But the act, as Patrick Watson among others pointed out, was fraught with pitfalls. He feared that "national unity" could become an excuse for the hierarchy to keep a program off the air because it might be thought divisive.

Certainly there was no doubt that Canadian broadcasting should be less dependent on American programming. That was the thrust of the campaign launched by the Association of Canadian Television and Radio Artists (ACTRA) in the fall of 1967. Noting that the response to both the Centennial and Expo had been "immediate and overwhelming," the association declared "that there has developed as never before a pressing need by the Canadian people for information about their country." And the only way that demand could be satisfied was through broadcasting.

"The schism that has developed between Quebec and the rest of the nation must be closed. . . . The people of Quebec have always fought with all their might to preserve their own way of life. . . ." The problem, the ACTRA brief said, was that it was difficult for a Quebecker to distinguish an English-speaking Canadian from an American. The culprit was television. "The monster. . . has been disseminating an alien way of thinking, an alien culture in every hearth and home in English Canada, and at the same time it has been used in Quebec to nurture native indigenous ideas." Thus, TV had become a wedge to divide the two peoples of Canada, and it was time for broadcasting to concentrate on Canadian culture and ideas and "to insist that the Canadian broadcasting system be predominantly Canadian in character."

Judy LaMarsh, who bore cabinet responsibility for broadcasting, was in tune with the import of the ACTRA brief. Alphonse Ouimet, who reported to her, was a brilliant engineer but in no sense a programming expert. He was due to retire at the end of the year, and LaMarsh had already announced that she was looking for a young, "brilliant rising star" to run the corporation—a national figure, who, in her words, was "with it."

"For instance, one of the people who has worked with the CBC for quite a long time and recently came back, who is in his thirties, has been suggested as president." She was, of course, referring to thirty-six-year-old Patrick Watson, who was actively lobbying for the job. His chances of getting it were no more likely than the chances of striking oil in Toronto under the CBC's Jarvis Street headquarters. How could the government hand over the presidency of the corporation to the very broadcaster who had been one of the point men in the bitter public struggle over *Seven Days*? That would be seen as a slap in the face to the retiring president.

But Alphonse Ouimet was about to get his face slapped anyway, by the very minister to whom he reported. LaMarsh had already said that whoever his successor might be, the new president should concentrate on programming—an expertise Ouimet lacked. I have reason to remember what happened next, for it was on the nightly *Pierre Berton Show* that it occurred. I had asked LaMarsh why the CBC couldn't find enough money to fix up the shabby studio from which the top-rated *Front Page Challenge* program was produced.

"Well, quite frankly," she said, "I think there is some rotten management in many places in the CBC and with a little better management there will be money, at least for necessary things."

It tells something about the state of matters at the corporation that we all passed over that incendiary remark—did not even make it the lead paragraph in the press release and transcript we sent out to the media. Rotten management was old stuff, hardly news at all. Or so I thought.

Next day, quite properly, the story was all over the front pages. A cabinet minister had reached down and chastised a public servant in public! We had thought of bad management in terms of Eugene Hallman or Bud Walker, another ineffective executive banished to the Caribbean after the *Seven Days* débâcle. But the buck stopped at Ouimet's desk, and it was, as the *Globe and Mail* declared, "a kick in the teeth to every single CBC employee with management functions."

Ouimet was furious. He shot off an angry letter to LaMarsh demanding that she supply evidence of her charges, then took the highly unusual step of releasing the letter to the press. LaMarsh didn't buckle. In a blunt, four-paragraph reply she called Ouimet's request "arrogant." And in Parliament, during the debate on the new broadcasting bill, she magnified her televised remarks by suggesting the situation at the CBC management level was far worse than she'd implied. "It is really in the past two weeks that from some exceptionally knowledgeable people, I have been given some examples, which caused the use of language, which might otherwise be considered as too colourful."

What did she mean by this? Had she brought the matter to the attention of Ouimet? Who were the knowledgeable people? They included

Patrick Watson and several of the young Turks at the CBC, but LaMarsh evaded these questions.

David Lewis, leader of the NDP, bored in: "The low ebb in the affairs of the CBC is the refusal of the government to make appointments to the top positions in the last year." Ouimet's resignation had been in the Government's hands for a year. Two other senior officers had quit. The corporation was being led by caretaker officers with a resultant loss of morale. Why hadn't LaMarsh acted? It was her duty to make sure she knew about the failure of management.

LaMarsh admitted there was a problem: two recent studies, the Glassco Royal Commission Report and the Fowler Committee Report, both of which condemned the CBC management, had made that point. "But what I learned in the past few weeks was very much worse than that." Those tantalizing words caused another uproar. Lewis insisted that LaMarsh should make her charges stick or drop them—they had thrown a shadow over a good many CBC executives. Michael Starr, temporary leader of the opposition, demanded she provide the government with evidence of mismanagement. But LaMarsh refused to name her sources (to protect their privacy, she said) and claimed that the entire matter could not be addressed until the new regime at the corporation was in place.

While she stonewalled, the debate raged on. The whole subject of CBC programming was under fire. Erik Nielsen, an old Diefenbaker loyalist, had already accused the corporation of treating its viewers to "an unending parade of drug addicts, black power advocates, prostitutes, purveyors of filthy literature, Nazis and pseudo-Nazis. . . all the scrapings and leavings of society," a declaration that must have bemused those critics who felt the CBC's programming was far too bland. These charges threatened programs like *Sunday*. Nielsen's attack was abetted by Robert Thompson, leader of the national Social Credit Party, who pointed to "the small, mischievous or misguided minority who all too often gain control over peak broadcasting hours in order to air controversial and degrading programs." Thompson suggested that the CBC should concentrate on "human and family oriented" plays such as *Anne of Green Gables* and not something "degrading to human personality." Reading these remarks in the Hansard of 1967, one cannot help but sympathize with a nervous corporation for cancelling Daryl Duke's new and sometimes outrageous flagship program.

LaMarsh's broadcasting bill survived these attacks and became law. The BBG, a collection of tired party hacks whose main objective seemed to be to award licences to political friends, was scrapped. It was replaced by the Canadian Radio-television Commission, whose tough new rules on Canadian content, and especially on the playing of recorded music, helped to create international stars such as Anne Murray, Gordon Lightfoot, and Stompin' Tom Connors.

Alphonse Ouimet was leaving, his bruised feelings assuaged by a testimonial banquet hosted by the Prime Minister himself, who went out of his way to praise the retiring president for his term in office. Any hopes that a show business entrepreneur might take over the CBC were dashed when Ouimet was replaced by George Davidson, a good, grey mandarin from Treasury Board. He was no "rising star" who was "with it," but he was certainly safer than Watson. It could scarcely be said that George Davidson did much for the CBC—he was undoubtedly the worst president the corporation ever had—but the CBC did a good deal for George Davidson. In fact, it changed his life. In his new job, Davidson rubbed shoulders with a series of glamorous young people, one of whom he married. At the end of his term Davidson went to his reward at the United Nations and presumably lived happily ever after.

4

The Americanization of Canadian politics began in September 1967, when the Progressive Conservative Party staged the largest political convention in Canadian history within the cavernous confines of Toronto's Maple Leaf Gardens. It was also the liveliest. Because of television it was inevitable that American-style hoopla would spill across the border to transform otherwise staid Tory politicians into

The Tories change their image

93

something close to snake-oil salesmen. Without TV it is doubtful that John Diefenbaker, arriving at the Royal York Hotel on the eve of this convention, would have been greeted by a ten-piece marching band, a kilted piper, and a chorus line of elderly women so wound up by the ballyhoo that one tried to clobber Dief's chief supporter, Jim Johnston, in the belief that he was Dalton Camp, the architect of Diefenbaker's humiliation.

Since the days of the young John Kennedy, Canadians had been glued to their television sets whenever American politics dominated the screens. They were so *watchable*, so much fun compared to the solemn, heavy-handed styles of King, St. Laurent, and yes, Mike Pearson. Now in the centennial year, when Canadians of every stripe were shaking off their inhibitions and engaging in a national romp, it was obvious to the Tory inner circle that the party was going to have to change its image and use American techniques to grab the TV audience. That meant marching bands, raucous demonstrations, miniskirted girls in cardboard hats, and monster signs—huge cardboard images of Robert Stanfield or billboards heralding Wallace McCutcheon, Man of Distinction. Some veteran Tories such as Frank McGee, who had been the youngest cabinet minister in the Diefenbaker government (his father-in-law was the Tory eminence Grattan O'Leary), deplored this departure from the old style as "some sort of Rotarian romp." The lobby of the Royal York on convention eve, he declared, "deteriorated into some sort of psychedelic nightmare." It was his hope that the leadership convention "might well mark the end of the Americanization of Canadian politics." It was actually the beginning. In spite of his twenty years' experience—or perhaps because of it—McGee was well off base. It would be as hard to stop the Americanization of Canadian politics as it would have been to stop the Americanization of Canadian television.

Donald Fleming, the former Tory finance minister, whose shirt had long since been stuffed to overflowing, was equally repelled by the "sheer noise, brassiness, rough and tumble, manoeuvring and pandemonium" of the convention. Why couldn't party leaders be chosen "with dignity, fair play, and courtesy?. . . It irks me," he wrote in his memoirs, "to see leaders who are to bear supreme national responsibility and discharge sacred trusts chosen to the accompaniment of carnival heroics and organized circus shows." But Fleming, who was going nowhere, was a walking memorial to a dying era, as anachronistic as a pair of pinstripe trousers at a hoedown.

The Tory convention was a carefully orchestrated piece of mass entertainment. Eddie Goodman, the chairman, took no chances. He and a colleague flew to Washington to pick the brains of American party organizers about how to increase efficiency as well as excitement. The convention had everything a TV addict could desire. It had a contest that encompassed much of the excitement of the Academy Awards—nine prominent Tories vying for a political Oscar. It had mystery and suspense: would Diefenbaker run or not? When the convention opened no one had the slightest idea. It had a bitter and much publicized feud: Dief versus his one-time supporter, Dalton Camp. Here was something more than a battle for the soul of the Tory party: it was a conflict between the old and the new, the past and the future. Could Canada manage to exist as one nation with a set of ten provinces, each equal in every way to all the others? Or was it moving to a new kind of confederation, in which two distinct cultures—*deux nations*— co-existed under the new maple leaf flag? That, in effect, was why the convention had been forced on Diefenbaker by the party's national president. A stocky, balding, former advertising man, Camp realized that Canada had become a different society from the one that had nurtured his old chief. Politics had changed and so had the population, both in age and in ethnic composition. "We are talking now about politics that didn't exist ten years ago," Camp remarked that fall. "Foreign policy and defence are different. It is not the same technology and science. The vital considerations that have to be made in the country, increasingly, are going to involve external considerations. We're going to have to get away from the eternal contemplation of ourselves."

People no longer wanted speeches loaded with rhetoric and bombast. They wanted the facts and were prepared to face them. Camp realized that the average Canadian voter was more self-confident, venturesome, and creatively motivated than in the past. The centennial celebrations had shown that. "He thinks in broader concepts than the average politician. He is less security-ridden than many believe," Camp said.

Camp and his chief belonged to different generations. John Diefenbaker, born at the end of the Victorian era, was about to celebrate his seventy-second birthday; Camp would celebrate his forty-seventh. He was well aware of the change in voting patterns. Nine million Canadians— almost half the population—were under voting age. Soon these baby boomers would be storming the ballot boxes. Young people formed a plurality in the country. The biggest age group was between twenty-five and forty-five, which meant that its members were vital to the party. But Camp detected a tremendous amount of cynicism among them. There was no doubt in his mind that these younger voters wanted to feel real kinship with their leaders, a sense an earlier generation had not felt with Arthur Meighen, R.B. Bennett, Mackenzie King, or Louis St. Laurent.

Those were some of the reasons why Dalton Camp had boldly faced the possibility of political exile by insisting on a leadership convention. He had first explored the possibility in an off-the-record speech before the Albany Club, a Tory stronghold, in May 1966. He suggested then that potential candidates for the party leadership should come forward and make their views on policy matters known. Four months later he spoke in public about the need to reassess the party's leadership. Clearly, he was out to bell the cat. It was a lone crusade. He consulted with nobody because the party itself was racked by what he called "the conspiratorial view of history." And no one was more paranoid than the Chief himself. He was, as Camp said many years later, "an impossible man for anybody to get along with." He was "incapable of an adult human relationship. He could not abide criticism. He couldn't abide an opinion contrary to his own." Camp refused to be intimidated by Diefenbaker. "I was the only person in the Conservative party, I think, that wasn't afraid of him."

"People who disagreed with the leadership were not regarded simply as dissenters," Camp remembered when the campaign was over.

"They became conspirators. Since I knew that I was going to be branded, I thought perhaps I could be the capital "C" conspirator and involve no one else."

Diefenbaker, a politician who never forgot and never forgave, identified Camp as the vilest kind of traitor. The issued was joined in November 1966 at the party conference. Camp was re-elected national president by a slim margin and the party agreed to hold a leadership convention before January 1, 1968. This was, in effect, a dump-Diefenbaker resolution, but nobody said so. It was obvious that if the old Chief had been seen as a powerful vote-getter, as he had once been, nobody would have bothered to wrangle about a convention at all. The consensus was that before another election could be called, Diefenbaker would have to go.

Would he go quietly or face a humiliating rejection? To everybody's astonishment and to the dissidents' chagrin, Diefenbaker appeared on national TV to announce blandly that far from opposing a leadership convention, he'd welcome one—and then the kicker: "at the earliest possible date." Delay, he announced, would only "add to the confusion, general uneasiness, and harm the interests of the nation." It would also give the Camp forces more time in which to reorganize. Of course, Camp responded—a little weakly—that he welcomed the announcement, but he knew he needed more breathing space than Diefenbaker was willing to give him. The former prime minister was insisting on early spring, but the Camp forces won out, calling the convention for September and changing the rules so that delegates would be appointed on the basis of redistributed constituency boundaries. That gave the convention an urban cast. Dief's strength, of course, had always been in the boondocks.

But the Will-He-Run question remained unanswered and would not be answered until the opening day's deadline. No one seemed to know what was in Dief's mind. Nonetheless, his candidacy—or the lack of it—would have a powerful effect on the eight high-powered Tories who had placed themselves in contention. (Two others, John Maclean, a Brockville Hertz dealer, and Dr. Hugh Horner, an MP from Barrhead, Alberta, didn't have a chance. Nor did a later entrant,

Mary Walker-Sawka, a Toronto housewife, who got only two votes—those of her nominator and her seconder. She was, perhaps significantly, the first woman in the party's history to run for the office.)

Five former cabinet ministers had been glad-handing their way across the nation all summer. The first to bound out of the starting gate (and "bound" is the right verb) was smiling George Hees ("our man with élan"), who knew more delegates on a first-name basis than any other nominee. "I'm going like a house afire," declared the former minister of trade and commerce, whose strongest support came from rural Ontario. Some thought of him as a lightweight and a few as a clown. Duncan Macpherson, the *Toronto Daily Star*'s brilliant political cartoonist, always depicted him as a Regency rake, complete with embroidered coat and lace cuffs—an image that, no doubt, reminded some that Hees had danced on the periphery of the Gerda Munsinger scandal, in which the German-born call girl was found to have been inappropriately intimate with more than a dozen figures including at least one Russian official and Pierre Sévigny, who held the sensitive position of associate defence minister.

Davie Fulton announced his candidacy at the same time as Hees. Earnest and cerebral, the former minister of justice demonstrated his paucity of imagination by promising to "get this country really moving," a shopworn slogan borrowed from the Kennedy presidential campaign seven years before. Few expected much from Donald Fleming, the humourless former minister of finance, who looked a bit like a plump wind-up toy, or Alvin Hamilton, whose strength lay only in Alberta and Saskatchewan, or Michael Starr, the stolid former minister of labour, who didn't even bother to campaign, or Senator Wallace McCutcheon, who was doing his best to avoid looking like a Bay Street tycoon and failing miserably.

Why were all these singularly undistinguished politicians running for an office they hadn't a hope of winning?

Camp put his finger on it when he remarked that they were not running for election but for another reason. "They were running for redemption," he told Peter Newman.

By July Hees and Fulton were reckoned to be the front-runners, though Camp, among others, didn't believe that either had the ghost of a chance. The equation was suddenly disrupted by the possibility that Robert Stanfield, premier of Nova Scotia, might enter the contest. Stanfield agonized over the move, which would alter the complexion of the campaign six weeks before the convention. He had, that same year, won a landslide victory at the polls in Nova Scotia. Should he leave the running of the province to others? His image was that of a laconic, easy-going politician, but as his wife, Mary, remarked to Dalton Camp, "Don't fool yourself about Bob; he's the most ambitious man I know." Camp, who was being importuned by supporters of both Stanfield and the undeclared candidate, Duff Roblin, went to Halifax with other Tories to convince the Nova Scotia premier he should run.

"We talked it out and thrashed it out and so by midnight he said he agreed. He called me the next morning and said, 'I can't do it. . . .' He'd discovered a shortfall in the budget in federal support and one of his ministers was drunk and he had to fire him. He didn't want to leave that up to anybody and he didn't want to do it on the way out the door."

With Stanfield apparently out and Roblin playing Hamlet, Camp's people faced a choice between Diefenbaker on the one hand and the lacklustre crew of Tory has-beens on the other. In Fredericton they kicked around their idea of Camp himself as a candidate. Camp was about to make the leap, but that same day a call came from Stanfield saying he had changed his mind. He had once been quoted as saying, in his droll way, that he would consider running for the Tory leadership "in much the way I have considered ski jumping." Now the press wanted to know if they would be treated to the spectacle of him defying the slopes. Not at all, said the premier, "one bit of foolishness at a time is enough."

Stanfield emerged at once as the man to beat, even though he was not well known to the rest of the world. His entry on July 19 revived the Tory leadership campaign. Here was a fresh face, unscarred by political infighting, and a man with impeccable credentials—politically invincible in his own province, decent, unassuming, pragmatic, and certainly not flamboyant. His family had its roots deep in the Canadian frontier experience. From the windswept prairie to the snow-shrouded northern forests, the Stanfield family's long johns were as much a symbol as the parka and the moccasin. What voter was not familiar with the box-top image of two muscular wrestlers clad only in Stanfield's underwear?

Curiously enough, Stanfield's entry, rather than keeping Duff Roblin out of the race, inspired him to take the plunge. Now, to everyone's surprise and at a very late date, he threw his hat into the ring because, he announced, Stanfield's entry had made the contest "respectable." That backhanded slur on the qualities of his opponents was a political gaffe of the highest order and may well have cost him the leadership.

A broad-minded Conservative, fluently bilingual, and at forty-nine the youngest of the serious candidates, he was convinced that "we have to go as far as we possibly can to meet the views of French-speaking Canadians." If he had a political flaw it was his public image; more than one critic likened him to Tom Dewey, whose "man on the wedding cake" image had helped to lose him the 1948 U.S. presidential election against Harry Truman. Roblin's entry again changed the odds, damaging the campaigns of both Fulton and Fleming in Quebec and shattering Alvin Hamilton's plans to piece together a prairie coalition.

Camp had earlier tried to persuade a reluctant Roblin to run; now he was Stanfield's man. The two were old friends and campaigners. To Camp, Stanfield was the best possible choice to heal the party's wounds. But as the convention got under way those wounds were still visible. Peter Regenstreif, the pollster, taking the measure of the delegates for the *Toronto Daily Star*, reported that Camp's reward for forcing the convention on the party "appears to be political wilderness." His survey found that the delegates had almost as many unfavourable as favourable comments to make about Camp. Some sections of the party thought of him as a pariah. Even while admitting that Camp had done what had to be done in bringing the leadership question to a head, one delegate in four made "derogatory personal observations" about Camp, while a significant proportion accused him of causing dissension and questioned his methods. Diefenbaker, on the other hand, received more favourable comments than unfavourable. The Chief's charisma had not worn out. In the old days he had won a truly smashing victory, and it did not seem to matter that he had gone on to be one of the worst prime ministers in history, a man who found it impossible to make the kind of decisions that true leadership demands, who had alienated the province of Quebec with his blindness toward the reality of the Quiet Revolution, who had demonstrated a pettiness and a vindictiveness that did not become his high office. Yet, as Regenstreif reported, "When the pros and cons are watched, the 'index of favourability' shows Diefenbaker better than Camp." The old tiger might be in decline, but he could still bite. Stanfield's people so feared the wrath of the anti-Camp, pro-Diefenbaker forces that they used code names—Father for the premier, Mother for Camp.

Everybody waited to see which way the Chief would jump. By the end of August there was "a distinct possibility" that he'd enter the fray; but no one could say for sure, even though it was reported that thousands of *Keep the Chief* stickers were being readied by his supporters should he choose, at the last minute, to run. That would throw all speculation out of balance. On the eve of the convention it was rumoured that Diefenbaker would agree to abandon the contest if the so-called two nations policy and its pledge of special status for Quebec was dropped. There was little possibility of that.

The hoopla went on. As the delegates assembled, the cacophony in the hotel corridors and later on the convention floor, rose to a crescendo. "We've been out-razmatazzed," complained George Hees's campaign manager, Robert Macaulay. "Christ, we only have a couple of bands and buses. Roblin has more, and Stanfield had the whole damn navy down there tooting 'Anchors Aweigh' this morning in front of Union Station." Even Michael Starr, the non-candidate, had hired an empty garage opposite Maple Leaf Gardens just to stick his posters on. He also had a tame chimpanzee who held a sign reading "LEAD US OUT OF THE JUNGLE MIKE." The spectacle of a comic quadruped being used to garner votes at a staid Canadian political convention would be enough to cause Richard Bedford Bennett to revolve in his tomb, but that was before David Garroway, on NBC's popular morning television show, *Today*, had rendered chimps faintly respectable. This chimp was trained to dance an Irish clog to the tune of "McNamara's Band," an unfortunate bit of symbolism that did nothing to enhance the sluggish Starr campaign.

It is doubtful that all this contrived hullabaloo did anything to boost the prospects of the serious contenders; but it played well on the home screens, and all the candidates seemed to believe it was required of them. Hees was followed about by a group of hired musicians who called themselves the Metro Stompers. Stanfield had two bagpipers, emblematic of his Nova Scotia background. Fulton's placards read "VIVA FULTON!" Donald Fleming had folk-singers in his retinue. The least hip of all the contestants, he tried to modernize his image by holding a "happening" in the Westbury Hotel. Alas, only half a dozen teenagers turned up, and the happening didn't happen.

Diefenbaker's intentions were still not known when the convention opened, adding a little more spice to the proceedings. In June he managed to wangle a change in the program that would allow him to address the convention on Thursday night, September 7, whether or not he was a declared candidate. His opponents had not been happy with that. The evening was supposed to be a massive Hail-to-the-Chief extravaganza— more "farewell" than "hail." But it looked as if he might squeeze in a free campaign speech before the rest of the field was heard on Friday— an unfair advantage, perhaps, but one to which the convention committee had grudgingly agreed in order to prevent a mass walkout of his supporters.

Diefenbaker's public pose was that he had been "betrayed" by a mysterious cabal designed to thwart his leadership chances. All that summer his supporters had been urging that nominations not be closed until the morning after his Thursday night speech. Two weeks before the convention opened, the Goodman committee decided to go along with them, thus depriving Diefenbaker of the opportunity to cry stab-in-the-back.

As the convention opened, the wise money had been on Duff Roblin;

but Roblin had misjudged the importance of the series of ten-minute addresses the candidates were required to make before the policy committee. His short speech was far too preachy, and the press decreed that Stanfield had been the best performer of all. It wasn't content that mattered, it was credibility; and Stanfield had it. That was the turning point of the convention.

After Stanfield's speech, one French Canadian grabbed a reporter's arm. "Hey!" he said, "I believe that Bob Stanfield!" The reporter asked what it was that Stanfield had said. "Not much," came the reply, "but I *believe* him."

On Thursday night, at what was supposed to be a Diefenbaker love-in, it was noticed that when Eddie Goodman presented the old Chief with an appropriate John A. Macdonald silver tray, the recipient refused to utter one word, nor did he speak to Goodman again during the convention. By then, on that fetid September evening, the sweating delegates were tired and restive after two hours of introductions. Speaking in that vast barn was, to use Diefenbaker's own words, "like shouting down a rain-barrel." They cheered him, of course, as they had always cheered him, but Diefenbaker mistook those cheers for hosannas; what they were really cheering was the end of an era.

The *Globe and Mail*, in a impudent gesture, sent a drama teacher and producer, Eli Rill, to cover the speech. Rill treated it as a theatrical performance, which it was. "He was Mark Antony over Caesar's body, re-shaping a mixed collection of emotions and attitudes into a unified, loud-voiced People's Party, 'for all Canadians'—and conceivably all for Diefenbaker. With jabbing, emphasizing, accusing finger and head-thrusts that gave no hint of galloping old age, he built towards a passion suitable for defending the Monarchy.

"He quoted Scripture, touched lightly on his party's support of manly sports, invoking the unpolitical name of Bobby Hull. . . . He plunged on, the spellbinder stilling the applause-mad audience time and time again, holding them in check, playing them like a lyre. . . . His jowls quivered, as he repudiated the disaster-bound course of the Liberal government.

"Now he switched to schoolmaster tones and quoted poetry supporting the One Nation policy. . . . We listened, and listened, but he did not finish the drama—a drama that has been longer than the Oresteia and Hardy's The Dynasts combined. He left us longing for the final curtain—a cliff-hanger if ever there was one. The rest was silence, though Hamlet was not dead. Or was he? Was Lear dead—or was he still raging on the heath, conducting the winds and hurricanes as though they were the Ottawa Symphony?"

Speech over, it was becoming increasingly clear that Diefenbaker would enter the lists. He had no choice. If the party had reversed itself and accepted his one nation policy, he would have run because it would be obvious to him that he was still in charge. But if that policy was not accepted—and it wasn't—he would be compelled to run; the tenor of his speech made that clear. The following morning, just fifteen minutes before the deadline, Diefenbaker filed his nomination papers.

That changed the form charts. Donald Fleming, who saw the Diefenbaker campaign draining off his own votes, was beside himself. "The selfish monster!" he muttered. Later he would describe his former chief as "the most egocentric person I have ever met."

The tired campaigners had one more kick at the can. There have been times when a single inspired bit of oratory has changed the nature of a political convention (William Jennings Bryan's "Cross of Gold" speech at the 1896 Democratic convention springs to mind). It is doubtful, however, that any of their speeches that day made much of a difference. This was their brief moment in history. For all of that summer their faces had smiled confidently from the front pages and their names had popped out of the headlines—contestants in a race the newspapers treated as a sports event and that seemed so crucial at the time. Now most are half forgotten. Who, in Joe Batt's Arm, remembers exactly what it was that Alvin Hamilton did? And Wallace McCutcheon, who was he? Donald Fleming: where did he come from; where did he go? Does the name of Michael Starr mean anything outside of Oshawa or Sudbury? Unlike the hockey stars, immortalized on trading cards, in Halls of Fame, and in nostalgic sports columns, these names live on today only in remaindered memoirs gathering dust in the second-hand bookstores.

The balloting moved with agonizing slowness. Instead of speeding up the proceedings, the voting machines—another innovation borrowed from the Americans—slowed everything down, dragging out the television show and causing thousands of viewers to switch to another channel. TV reporters were everywhere, asking the standard "How do you feel?" question of harassed candidates, who replied with the usual optimistic answers.

The real contenders were the two provincial premiers, Stanfield and Roblin, who garnered 519 and 349 first-round votes respectively. Fulton, Hees, and Diefenbaker followed in that order. McCutcheon, trailing after the first ballot, threw his votes to Stanfield, who increased his lead. At that point one would have expected Diefenbaker, who had dropped down by one hundred votes, to bow out gracefully. Unable to make up his mind, as usual, he tried to quit but found he had waited too long. Now George Hees threw his support behind Stanfield. Diefenbaker, in fifth place, walked out of the convention a beaten man.

That marked the end of the Diefenbaker era in Canadian politics. He refused, of course, to accept the inevitability of defeat. Like the other has-beens in the contest, he suffered from that curious form of self-hypnosis that had convinced each one, in the face of all evidence to the contrary, that he was a sure winner. The Chief's leaving did not become him. Far better for his reputation had he retired gracefully before the convention and basked in the farewell tributes of his peers. But that was not his way. He insisted on nakedly displaying his incredible ego on the television sets of the nation, and that, from the public's point of view, hastened his downfall.

The previous November, when Dalton Camp was struggling to put a modern face on the Conservative Party, seventy-one Members of Parliament had signed a loyalty oath to their chief. But only sixteen stayed true to him on the third ballot. As he left the Gardens with his wife, the house orchestra struck up a familiar tune. Nobody seemed to catch the significance of that moment. For the band was playing

"Hail to the Chief," which was Diefenbaker's rallying cry—the sprightly march the Americans heard whenever their president appeared in public.

Robert Stanfield, confirmed as Tory leader after two more ballots, was about as far from the received image of the American politician as anybody could be. He was totally unpretentious. No chauffeured limousines for him; he drove himself around in a four-year-old Volvo. Generally, however, he walked to work in Halifax, a thirty-minute stroll that he sometimes had to do twice when he realized he hadn't taken out the garbage. When his longtime secretary was absent he answered his own phone. Before the convention his advisers tried to get him to have his hair cut, to buy a new suit, to shine his shoes more often. He wouldn't budge. "They will accept me as I am or not at all," he told his aides.

As one of George Hees's advisers (probably Robert Macaulay) put it ruefully, "He radiates pure innocence, intelligence, dignity, austerity, and dullness. What more can you ask?" He had what that old Tory warhorse Grattan O'Leary called "a civilized mind." During the leadership campaign, a reporter made so bold as to ask if Stanfield might be a bit too dull, too old-fashioned. "I don't want to sound presumptuous," Stanfield replied, "but Mackenzie King was a little dull."

He moved ponderously—some thought indecisively—but he refused to be hurried. Camp made a telling remark about his candidate. "If you hooked into Stanfield in 1000 B.C.," he ruminated, "and said, 'Look, Bob, I've got a great idea here. It's a circle and you put it on a cart and it's a wheel,' he would say in that slow voice of his, 'Well, I'm not going to make a speech about it until I see it. And until I see it, I'm not going to buy it.'"

"The way I make a speech," Stanfield had explained, "people know I'm not out to impress them, so I must be telling the truth." Believability and integrity—these were the strengths that had impelled Nova Scotia voters to give him four victories at the polls, the last a landslide in which he won forty out of forty-six seats. He could not be stampeded into indulging in any of the high jinks that characterized this most

106

American of campaigns. He himself was not cast in the American mould, even though, with his long, unsmiling face and craggy features, he was occasionally compared to Abraham Lincoln.

His was the only hospitality room at the convention that did not dispense hard liquor. The one time he went against the advice of his handlers was when they tried to persuade him to march down Yonge Street behind a band. He was utterly without side. At a Tory Thinkers Conference in Fredericton in 1964, he walked into the cafeteria and sat down beside Tom Hockin, a young professor doing postgraduate work at Harvard. "I hear you're at Harvard, my old Alma Mater," Stanfield remarked.

Hockin responded genially and asked, "What do you do now?"

"Well, I'm premier of Nova Scotia," Stanfield told him in his diffident way.

When some of the other candidates were forecasting victory during the balloting, Stanfield, who was absolutely certain he would win, kept his own counsel. "Let me shake the hand of Canada's next prime minister," an aging supporter greeted him on a Halifax street after he announced his candidacy.

"Oh, now," the premier warned him gravely, "let's not be presumptuous."

"Trying to define the real man inside the sober Stanfield," the *Vancouver Sun* wrote, "is a little like trying to tell what's happening in China by reading Peking wall posters. This rare politician knows how to keep his distance, how to maintain a space around himself that no one has been able to trespass. His main job will be to nurture national unity within his caucus with a majority who still feel bitter over Diefenbaker's downfall."

In Stanfield the Tory party felt it had the perfect candidate—the quintessential Canadian, a man with all the Boy Scout virtues, a proven vote-getter who seemed too good to be true, untarnished by the kind of scandal that had created headlines out of the misadventures of a fading German strumpet, the very epitome of family values who eschewed campaign glitter and was devoid, as Mackenzie King had been, of that new political quality called charisma, a word seldom heard until the sixties.

Looking over the threadbare list of fading politicians aspiring to the Pearson throne, the boys in the Tory back rooms might now feel that their future was safe and that the party of Sir John A., rejuvenated in the centennial year, could sweep into office with something that had eluded both Tories and Grits for three successive elections—a spanking majority.

The Liberals were tired in office, and frustrated. Stanfield looked like a clear winner over such candidates as Mitchell Sharp, Allan MacEachen, and Paul Martin. But the wiseacres failed to realize that something was happening in Canada. The response to the televised convention had shown that Canadians wanted the same excitement in their politics that they enjoyed in their hockey. Behind that fervour was the year-long love affair with the country engendered by thousands of centennial projects and the giddy triumph of Expo. What was wanted was a kind of political version of Bobby Gimby. And there, quietly waiting in the wings in his ascot scarf and sandals, was the man most likely to succeed to the throne. Here was charisma by the carload. But when the cheering died in Maple Leaf Gardens, no one thought of Pierre Elliott Trudeau as a candidate for high office—including the man himself.

THREE: THE BIG CHANGE

1

The end of the Dark Ages

2

The dawn of Women's Lib

3

A lingering sense of guilt

4

The seeds of Gay Pride

1

The end of the Dark Ages In 1967, Canadian manners and morals were on the cusp of change. The country was beginning to emerge as from the Dark Ages. The morality laws still belonged to another century. It was almost as difficult to get a divorce as it was to get an abortion. The law still made it a jailable offence to transmit birth-control information. As for homosexuals, they could be jailed—and were jailed, in one case for life—for simply being what they were.

All these attitudes and strictures were about to be thrown into the ashcan. The birth-control pill made a mockery of the law and helped change society's attitudes towards sex. A good segment of the public was well ahead of politicians by the time Pierre Elliott Trudeau was elevated to the cabinet in the spring of 1967. As the new minister of justice, he determined, with the Prime Minister's backing, to introduce a set of sweeping reforms to the Criminal Code that would make it easier for the citizens to get a divorce or an abortion. At the same time he moved to soften the harsh laws on homosexuality between consenting partners. As a result, the bedrooms of the nation would soon be safe from legal intrusion.

It would take the best part of two years to get Trudeau's 1967 intentions onto the law books. By today's standards, the Canada of the centennial year was still relatively straitlaced. Explicit public references to sexual matters were taboo. Dorothy Cameron, a Toronto art dealer who had dared to present an exhibition of mildly erotic paintings, lost her appeal to the Supreme Court against the police seizure of the exhibits that year. Members of a Ugandan dance group appearing at Expo 67 found they had to cover their traditional bare bosoms with net. Radio stations refused to play the Rolling Stones' hit, "Let's Spend the Night Together." In March the Montreal morality squad jubilantly announced that it had seized tons of girlie magazines whose only offence was the occasional depiction of a nipple. It was described as "the biggest ever" series of raids. In the same city, exotic dancers were deemed obscene, even if they covered their erotic areas. The judge ruled, "As far as I am concerned a dancer wearing pasties on her breasts and a G-string might as well be prancing around naked." Even belly buttons were taboo. A poster for a play showing a woman with a bare midriff was also banned in Montreal—though not at Expo 67.

We can see, in hindsight, that 1967 marked the beginning of a new understanding about how the law should be used to determine legitimate social behaviour and to what extent it ought to be employed to shore up what many considered old and outworn concepts. Should the government really be telling people how they should behave socially? Should the police be used to force the public to conform? In 1967, a growing number of citizens had come to believe that, after one hundred years, their country had achieved adulthood and the time had come to let its citizens behave as they pleased, as long as that behaviour did not harm their neighbours. By the end of the year, these new attitudes received official sanction as the government announced it would bring in progressive legislation to deal with divorce, homosexuality, abortion, and gambling.

Canada's social attitudes had historical roots: first, the frontier experience with its puritan values, and second, the protective colonial authority. This official paternalism was reflected in the great frontier institutions: the Hudson's Bay Company, the Canadian Pacific Railway, the North West Mounted Police, and the major churches. We were long used to being told from on high about how we could and could not act. Any kind of dalliance was frowned on because it diverted the individual or the community from the work ethic. Nobody could buy a drink within five miles of the CPR's main line during the construction days. Nobody was allowed to watch a kooch dancer on the Dawson City stage during the gold rush; the Mounties saw to that. The Lord's Day was sacrosanct; anybody caught chopping wood on the Sabbath faced arrest.

We emerged from the frontier stage long after the Americans, whose differing attitude to authority was shaped by the Revolution. Canadians, on the other hand, were used to deferring to their colonial masters. What had been mere questions of fashion in more open societies were, in Canada, hemmed in by "protective" strictures. The task of the police, apparently, was to save us from the damaging effects of salacious publications, lascivious motion pictures, prurient theatrical performances, and, of course, practising homosexuals. This web of social taboos, supported by the law, began to unravel in 1967. But another three decades would pass before a woman could legally appear topless on a Canadian street on a hot summer's day.

The lack of sexual knowledge was appalling, especially so because it was fostered by the religious establishment. Any discussion of birth control on television or radio had to be cleared in advance by the Board of Broadcast Governors. The word "condom" never appeared in the press, nor did the word "penis." The Criminal Code prohibited the sale or circulation of "instructions. . . intended or represented as a method of preventing conception." Fellatio was concealed as "gross indecency" and any married couple could be jailed for practising it. Because of the conspiracy of silence in the home, the schools, and the medical profession, cases of venereal disease were the highest in twenty years, flourishing at an annual rate of 25,000, far ahead of scarlet fever and tuberculosis. A two-year study by a University of British Columbia professor showed that most students knew a good deal about contraception, little about the structure and function of the sex organs, and even less about venereal disease. How could they, given the educational taboos? Prudery ran rampant. When the B.C. minister of education found a four-letter word in a textbook he moved to have it excised without even bothering to consult the province's secondary school English revision committee.

I Am Curious—Yellow, the first motion picture to put simulated sex on the cinema screen, was shown in New York but certainly not in Canada. Nor would the Ontario Film Review Board allow a film version of James Joyce's *Ulysses* to be shown because of Mollie Bloom's famous soliloquy. Thanks to a notable court case, people could *read* Bloom's frank monologue but could not hear an actor voicing it. That court decision, and another involving *Lady Chatterley's Lover*, marked the thin edge of the wedge that would lead to a more open society.

By 1967 most Canadians believed that the country's divorce laws

112

belonged to another age. The usual excuse for not scrapping them was that "the churches wouldn't stand for it." But by the centennial year even the Roman Catholic Church had come to the awkward conclusion "that since other citizens believe it is less injurious to the individual and to society that divorce be permitted in certain circumstances, we would not object to some revision of Canadian divorce laws that is truly directed in advancing the common good of civil society." The Anglican Church, the United Church, and the Canadian Jewish Congress were less circumspect. All three believed that there should be one legal reason for divorce, "marriage breakdown."

Such were the opinions advanced to the Parliamentary Committee on Divorce, set up in February by a prime minister whose government had been bombarded for some years by demands for divorce reform. At the same time Pearson promised to liberalize the equally antiquated laws on birth control and abortion. It was surely no accident that he made Trudeau minister of justice that spring to help carry out the promise.

The law was indeed being brought into disrepute because so many people were making a mockery of it. It was illegal to sell condoms, but every drugstore carried them under the counter. It was illegal to have an abortion, but people were having them anyway. In most of the country the chief and sometimes only legal way to obtain a divorce was to prove adultery. That meant that most of the sixteen thousand people preparing for divorce in 1967 were also preparing to perjure themselves in court.

A divorcée was a shunned woman. It's significant that the only Canadian woman willing to discuss her divorce in print that year insisted on concealing her identity behind a pseudonym. "Marilyn Selby" remembered going to a party in Christmas week just before the centennial year opened. The party was attended mostly by married couples.

"Everything was fine until I was identified as 'getting a divorce,'" she told the *Star Weekly*. "Then the wives' eyes went all narrow with alarm and suspicion. The husbands' eyes said 'Oboy! A divorcée! Fair game!' Because adultery was the only cause for divorce, the smear of sexual misconduct somehow attaches itself to both persons."

113

In British Columbia Marilyn Selby could have obtained a divorce if she'd been the victim of rape, sodomy, or bestiality. In New Brunswick, frigidity and impotence were grounds; in Nova Scotia, consanguinity (blood relationship), impotence, or cruelty. In Quebec and Newfoundland there were no divorce courts; she would have had to petition Parliament through a private member's bill. In the rest of the country she would have had to prove adultery, and that, in the end, is what she agreed to do.

To justify the degrading and expensive charade of hiring a professional co-respondent, the marriage had to be truly on the rocks. Marilyn Selby had married in 1958, and to her it seemed a perfect match. She and her husband came from similar socio-economic backgrounds, both were Anglicans, both were well-educated. She was nineteen; he was twenty-two. They'd been going together for two and a half years. They holidayed together with his family and dined often at her house. As her wedding day drew near she was ecstatic. She was achieving the goal that society set for women from the day they were born: to wear a white dress with a veil, carry flowers, and walk down the aisle. She loved her husband for better or worse—but it didn't work.

It was nobody's fault; it was both their faults. The truth dawned on her that they were incompatible. He was an introvert, kind and mannerly, but complacent. She was an extrovert who wanted to try anything. When she took him to the finest Chinese restaurant in town he ordered a club sandwich. His silences irritated her. She tended to ignore these apparently trivial differences, didn't want to admit to "the ultimate horror." She was raised with books, music, trips to art galleries and museums. He developed a passion for fishing, leaving her holed up at the lake with a mother-in-law who disliked her. When she wanted to go to the ballet, he'd say, "I'm not going to watch a bunch of fairies dancing around the stage."

As things began to go wrong, their sex life, which had once been lively, fell apart. Is it all my fault? she asked herself. When he was returning from a fishing trip she had her hair done, put on his favourite yellow dress, and met him with their three children at the plane. "I'll

114

be with you when I get my bags," he said casually. Tears started to stream down her face.

That night they talked it over. He agreed to be home more often; she promised to stay in more often. But things grew steadily worse. Finally one night, after a quarrel, he said bluntly, "I can't stand the sight of you any longer. I want a divorce."

A few months later he rented a basement apartment; she moved to the suburbs; and so the marriage died. In a later, more tolerant era, divorce would have been simple, but in 1967 it was so difficult that neither considered it. She was furious when she learned he had another woman, but soon came to see it was one more symptom of a bad marriage. A Toronto survey had shown that in sixty-five out of ninety-eight marital breakups, adultery was neither a cause nor a precipitating factor.

Like so many others, she found herself in a strange half-world. She had to find a job, and to get one she had to lie about her marital status. In those days employers considered a separated woman a bad risk; they reckoned she'd return to her husband and children. She couldn't even get a bank loan unless she had a relative who knew a banker. Marilyn went through a period of depression, wondering whether or not she'd done the right thing before slowly regaining self-confidence.

In March of 1967 she and her husband divorced after two and a half years of separation and a good deal of hocus-pocus. Like other couples in Canada—eleven thousand of them were divorced that year—the Selbys had to concoct a way of faking a case of adultery and lying under oath in court.

There was no chance that her husband's new girlfriend would bear the stigma of co-respondent. So a couple of private investigators went to a motel room and there, by previous arrangement, found her husband with a strange woman. In court he swore that he had committed adultery with her, a humiliating confession that was a fake. There he stood with his hand on the Bible, perjuring himself. There she was, the wife who had failed him to the point where he slept with someone else.

It was quickly done. Just ahead of her in court was a girl whom she knew. When it was over they went outside, laughed, cried, hugged each other, glad, sad, and most of all relieved. She could only hope that the law would soon make it possible for others to mend their marital mistakes with decency and dignity.

A raft of submissions persuaded the Parliamentary committee that a broken marriage couldn't be mended. In December 1967, the House of Commons passed the new divorce bill, which widened the grounds for divorce to include physical and mental cruelty, desertion, and, significantly, marriage breakdown. There was little political opposition. Pierre Trudeau steered the twenty-seven-clause bill through the House, and when it passed its third and final reading he was given a thumping ovation by all parties.

At the same time the new justice minister had been working fourteen hours a day to revise the Criminal Code. On December 21 he tabled in the House an omnibus bill that would, among other things, tighten gun control laws, make roadside breathalyzer tests mandatory, do away with capital punishment, allow federal and provincial governments to run lotteries, make homosexual relationships legal if they were carried on in private, and allow therapeutic abortions if the mother's life or health was threatened.

All year a number of organizations—the Canadian Medical Association, the Canadian Bar Association, the Federation of Women's Institutes, the National Council of Women, and the United Church, among others— had been pressing for a relaxation of the abortion laws, which the National Council of Women called "outdated, cruel and unjust." None of these high-profile groups went so far as to ask for abortion on demand.

Most Canadians would agree with Mrs. Lorne Perron, the president of the newly formed Association for the Modernization of Canadian Abortion Laws, that abortion on demand was unlikely in Canada even in the distant future. "We know that everyone would scream murder if we asked for that," Mrs. Perron said. But she was well aware of the ignorance about abortion. "Women just don't believe there isn't some drug they can take or some home remedy they can use that will terminate a pregnancy."

Statistics on abortion deaths weren't easy to come by. The best guess

116

was that one hundred thousand illegal abortions took place each year and that between five hundred and one thousand women died under an abortionist's ministrations. The city of Toronto, which recorded 22,698 births in one year, estimated that in the same period some 35,000 women underwent abortions.

It was virtually impossible for a woman to get a legal abortion. Although some hospitals performed a dozen or so therapeutic abortions a year, there was considerable argument whether or not these were legal because of the wording of the Criminal Code, which allowed abortions only to save a mother's life. It was far more unnerving (and also far more dangerous) in 1967 to get an illegal abortion than it was to fake a divorce. Years later a woman who had endured the procedure described the experience. Understandably, she too did not wish to identify herself except as "Louise," which was not her real name.

That August, after travelling through Italy with a girlfriend, she had gone back to Paris on her own only to discover that her suitcase containing her airline ticket home to Montreal had been lost. She went to the customs office in the train station and asked for help. A customs officer took her to lunch, where she drank too much wine, and then to his own quarters. When she came to her senses she realized that she was being raped. She did nothing to protest: she had no idea where she was and she needed that missing plane ticket. Eventually she got her suitcase back.

In Montreal she came to a dreadful realization: she was pregnant. She was working as a laboratory technician but living with her parents. She was twenty-one years old and knew that abortions were illegal (life imprisonment for the abortionist, two years in jail for the woman). Moreover, she had never known anybody who'd had an abortion and she had no idea what to do.

She felt petrified and ashamed. Intelligent, well-educated, she had no experience in such distasteful matters. She could not tell her parents but confided in a girlfriend, who suggested that she visit a doctor they'd had in residence during their university days.

Upset and crying, she told him her story. He suggested that a druggist

117

near the corner of Peel and Ste-Catherine streets might help her. He didn't say how.

She told the druggist that she was "in trouble." He told her to wait by the second pay phone in a bank. She phoned her lab and told them that she had been delayed at the doctor's and wouldn't be back that day.

Eventually the phone rang and a male voice told her to meet a man at eight o'clock the following Friday in front of a certain hotel. She felt like a performer in a sinister movie. He told her he would pick her up in a red Corvair and that it would cost her four hundred dollars—a fee equivalent to about two thousand dollars in 1997.

Her girlfriend drove Louise to the rendezvous and waited across the street. A little after eight a red car showed up and stopped. The driver, whose voice she recognized from the telephone, identified himself as "Louie," a name that increased her feeling that she was a character in a film. He was Belgian, about forty-five years old, and seemed friendly. He patted her reassuringly on the knee and drove her to the east end, where one of the cheap, "instant" Expo hotels had been thrown up.

He performed the abortion by dilating her cervix and poking about with a curette. The pain was excruciating. When she screamed, he threatened to stop and leave her if she didn't shut up. She chewed on the pillow.

Afterwards he gave her some antibiotics and proceeded to fondle her breasts and whisper to her. She was terrified that he was going to rape her, but he didn't. He dropped her off at a restaurant from which her friend drove her back home.

The abortion almost killed her. A week later she started to bleed heavily with huge clots. She told her parents that she was suffering through her period. For the next week she swallowed aspirins and 222s to deaden the cramps, changing pads almost every hour. Finally she phoned the doctor who'd recommended the drugstore. He was horrified when she told him she'd had an abortion. It is a comment on the times that he, in his ignorance, thought she'd be given a pill of some kind. But he told her to see a gynecologist, and she went immediately.

The gynecologist saw that she had anemia and was worried about the chance of infection. He admitted her to the Royal Victoria Hospital at once. She phoned her mother to say she had an ovarian cyst and that they were going to operate. Did her mother believe her? Perhaps. She asked no questions.

She had a D and C (dilatation and curettage) under anesthesia at the hospital, and when she went home a week later everybody figured she had "female problems," as they were called, and seemed to accept everything she told them. The gynecologist put her on birth-control pills, but she stopped taking them because she began to have wide mood fluctuations and panic attacks.

When she became pregnant again by her current boyfriend, the new law was not yet on the books. He suggested she see a doctor in the Côte des Neiges area. She had to wait a month for an appointment. At 6 p.m. she went to the doctor's office and waited until eleven, when the last patient had left. A Catholic, he proceeded to upbraid her about her behaviour until she was reduced to tears, but he agreed to perform an abortion in his office on Saturday morning. For the second time in her life she was scared to death.

The doctor was abrupt but efficient. His wife, who helped him, was clearly antagonistic. Again the pain was dreadful, and she found herself yelling and swearing until the wife told her to shut her filthy mouth.

The abortion was successful; she recovered and was able to go back to work in a few days. Years later she wrote down her experiences for the Canadian Anti-Abortion League. "I was single at the time," she wrote. "It never occurred to me to have the baby in either case. In the first instance I didn't know the father and in the second I was not in a serious relationship. I could not have told my parents because I didn't think they could help me and it would have upset them. Besides, I was too ashamed. I was lucky to have survived, and was able to have two children when I got married and was ready for them. The late sixties was a time of sexual freedom, but no preparedness for the consequences—just punishment."

2

When Hugh Hefner's Playboy Club, the seventeenth in the chain and the first in Canada, opened its doors on Aylmer Street off Sherbrooke in Montreal in 1967, it evoked a good deal of prurient interest. The club was far more inhibited than the magazine, but its very existence in Canada was news. Reporters wrote about the famous "bunny dip," a contortion that allowed the tightly garbed waitresses to bend down and serve drinks without revealing too much. Signs in the dressing rooms, so it was reported, warned that "Kleenex is not to be used for padding." Other signs made it clear that the customers could not touch the bunnies, much less date them. Reporters tracked down Hefner, head of the Playboy empire, who told them that in his opinion Canadians were indistinguishable from Americans. But beside the glitter of Expo, the critics found the club a little shabby and old-fashioned.

By this time *Playboy*, the magazine young men had once hidden under copies of the *Saturday Review*—or even under the bedclothes— had attained a new respectability, partly because of the changing times but also because its aura was different from its competitors'; it paid large sums to serious writers whose work was sandwiched in between the carefully airbrushed nudes. It was also a sign that times had not changed. The bunnies, with their little cotton-batting tails and rabbit-eared headdresses, were the subject of much banter, but no one suggested that likening them to a rodent noted for its breeding habits was in any way a libel on the female sex. The subtle message of the Playboy Club was that a cosy, upscale, all-male environment required sexy servitors, whose job was to pamper the male ego.

The age-old conviction that women should be subservient to men still prevailed in 1967. One could find it everywhere—in the advice given to the Women's Auxiliary of Mount Sinai Hospital, for instance, by Dr. Elliott Markson, a leading Toronto psychiatrist. Markson told his audience to stop competing with men and to seek fulfilment in motherhood (a euphemism for housekeeping), the supreme career to which every woman should aspire.

Judith Gault ran smack up against this prejudice when she was simultaneously cast in a leading role in Don Owen's National Film Board–CBC centennial program *The Ernie Game* and chosen by *Chatelaine* magazine to represent Quebec in their feature, "Women of Canada." Wife of a Montreal real estate broker, mother of three children, she discovered that "people are looking at me as if I'm doing something outrageous. I'm getting a lot of 'what's the matter, you can't stay home and mind the children? Are you sublimating?'"

Women were responsible for half the consumer spending in Canada, but 80 percent of the total earned income went to men. Married women who had no money of their own or didn't work for pay were totally dependent on their husbands. They could rarely open a bank account, apply for a credit card or even a library card without their husband's signature. In spite of equal pay laws in eight provinces, they were still paid less for work of comparable value. And that applied even to those who had a better education than their male counterparts.

Canadian women were poor. Two-thirds of all welfare recipients were female. The value of housework was underestimated and downgraded. A woman's contribution to the economy in the form of cooking, cleaning, laundry, and child care was not recognized in the Gross National Product. She was, indeed, regarded as a financial liability: the tax department allowed her husband a tax exemption for her.

Even in education, government, the church, and the press, women were paid less for doing work equivalent to that of a man. One might have expected Canada's leading university to have pioneered a progressive attitude towards the status of women in Canadian society. On the contrary, the University of Toronto made it difficult for any male to graduate without believing that women were not the equal of men. The evidence lay in the enclave of Hart House, to which no female student could belong. Thus women were barred from the famous Hart House debates. If they wanted to attend one of the Hart House concerts, they had to have a male escort. Noon-hour concerts were banned entirely, and the cafeteria was closed to them until 2 p.m.—after the men had eaten their fill.

The attitude that women were not on the same level as men was reflected in the statistics of the centennial year. The public service was three-quarters male, one-quarter female, and the women were not equitably paid. Six times as many women as men were making less than $4,000 a year. But almost three times as many men as women were in the $6,000-to-$8,000 bracket, more than five times as many in the $8,000-to-$10,000 bracket, and *twelve* times as many in the astronomical $10,000-and-over bracket. Elderly women were even worse off. The average income for males over sixty-five was $3,044; for women it was $1,556, some two hundred dollars below the poverty line.

The same imbalance was to be found in the church and in the press. Although the most progressive of the Protestant churches, the United, had ordained sixty women by 1967, few could find charges. The year before, the Presbyterians had accepted, by a narrow margin, the principle of women in the pulpit, but no one had yet applied for ordination. The Anglicans balked at the whole idea, fearing that it might slow down the ecumenical movement with the Roman Catholics who were, then as now, dead set against women priests. The situation was aggravated by the Anglicans' inability to attract men, let alone women, to the pulpit.

As usual, the Fourth Estate trailed behind. The male publishers thought they knew what women wanted to read about: food, fashion, children, and medicine. The headlines confirm this: "Eggs call for careful shopping"; "Two worlds blend in Italian fish sticks"; "Crested look is millinery news." Christina McCall, who dug up those headlines for *Maclean's* after studying a variety of "women's pages" for a week, wrote that these sections were unreal, outmoded, and insulting. "They propose a picture of women as an inferior sex, living inferior lives. They deny all the progress women have made in this century; all the victories we have won in the long war to be recognized as people." Between the articles about food, fashion, and family were columns devoted to the doings of "society," a word that was slowly losing its cachet. But many Canadian women's pages still covered engagements and weddings, sometimes with a page of photographs and a description of what the well-to-do guests wore. "Surely one of the silliest, oldest clichés in the newspaper business is the notion that there is some special way to write for women," McCall wrote. "Yet this idea is still being put forward in newspaper offices and journalism courses."

Because of the Newspaper Guild agreement, reporters working on women's pages were paid less than those on general assignment, and editors and publishers despised them. As one Ottawa newspaperman put it, "You can almost be sure that anybody in the women's department is either an old war-horse, too incompetent, or a young kid too inexperienced to move on. After working there for a few months anybody with half a brain starts to pester the editor to be transferred."

The exception to the general press blindness was *Chatelaine*, which, under its editor Doris Anderson, had for ten years been publishing a different kind of woman's magazine. A sample of article titles for 1967 suggests that it was pursuing new and controversial themes: "Do We Really Marry for Love?" "Is There Prejudice against Women on Juries?" "The Birth Rate's Down—What Happens Next?" "The Dangerous Disappearance of 'WOMAN'," "Troubled Marriages—Where to Get Help in Canada."

As the title of her autobiography, *Rebel Daughter*, makes clear, Anderson was always one to swim against the tide. She was born illegitimate to a mother who kept a boardinghouse in Calgary. Her father was an odd-job man she described as "a born rebel. . . anti-establishment, anti-royalist. . . a confirmed atheist. . . intolerant of foreigners . . . he considered politicians and members of the clergy little more than charlatans. . . distrusted lawyers, bankers, and even doctors. . . claimed to be a Communist [and] enjoyed drinking far too much." Eventually he married her mother who was, from that moment on, "entirely subservient to him."

From the beginning, Anderson was a confirmed feminist. In school she noticed with disdain that boys were treated better than girls. As a copywriter she learned that while her male counterparts rose to become department managers, she would be forever chained to her job. At

Eaton's she became part of a drive to unionize the company's workers and saw it fail after a year. At the age of thirty she joined the staff of *Chatelaine*, the sister magazine to *Maclean's*, whose male editors were soon tapped to run the distaff publication. That was not unusual. Most of the editors of women's magazines south of the border, such as the *Ladies' Home Journal*, were men. The *Journal* was constantly held up by the Maclean-Hunter hierarchy as the example for *Chatelaine*'s editors to follow, but Anderson considered it a relic from another era where "any suggestion that every woman wasn't jubilantly happy as a housewife and mother was, like most other unseemly matters, simply not discussed." Against this intransigent wall she continually battered her head. Her opinions counted for little; when she suggested starting an "advice" column she was greeted by bafflement. "Although all the men on the magazine. . . were married and all but [the editor, John] Clare, had children, they thought I was 'sick' for implying that women like their wives might not be perfectly contented."

More than once Doris Anderson found herself passed over for a man. In 1957, when she was informed by Floyd Chalmers, Maclean-Hunter's president, that Gerald Anglin, the associate editor, would be replacing John Clare, she dug in her heels. Chalmers was astonished when she declared, "Then I will resign." He asked why. "Because I have been carrying this magazine for the past year, and I know I would make a far better editor for a women's magazine than Gerry."

She would never forget Chalmers's response. "But," he said, "you are going to be married and you will become a hostess and a mother."

A hostess and a mother! Even today she is astonished by the emphasis on "hostess."

She remained adamant, and in the end the company grudgingly allowed her to run *Chatelaine* "against almost everyone's wishes." There was a catch, however. She was told she could have the job but would still be called managing editor, at least for the time being. "The message was clear. If you get pregnant, everything goes back on the table."

The night before Doris's wedding, her mother exclaimed to her fiancé, David Anderson, "I'm so happy. Now Doris has someone to look after her." She never understood, Anderson wrote, "that what I wanted more than anything was to be able to look after myself and make sure that every other woman in the world could do the same."

To the dismay of Maclean-Hunter management, Anderson did her job and had her babies as well. One month before her son, Peter, was born, she was made editor without any codicil. She was, in fact, so indispensable that her staff sent her articles for approval while she was still in the maternity ward. Her editorials ("Does our proposed divorce law go far enough?". . . "The snail-like battle for progress") established *Chatelaine* as the leading Canadian publication—indeed, the *only* publication—supporting the new women's movement, which most Canadians didn't realize existed. Words such as "feminism" and phrases such as "women's lib" had yet to enter the language in 1967. In the United States, Betty Friedan's trail-blazing book, *The Feminine Mystique*, published in 1963, had led to the formation in 1966 of NOW, the National Organization for Women. *Chatelaine* was well ahead of Friedan, who sent galleys of her book to the magazine, confidently expecting serialization. Jean Wright, the managing editor, read it and turned it down as too passé. "We've run most of this stuff in *Chatelaine*," she told Anderson. "In any case, it's far too American, and it's not very well written."

Early in 1967 Anderson noted all the gains and misses the liberation movement had made in the year leading up to the Centennial. Among the gains: the Presbyterians had approved the ordination of female ministers; two female judges and a female National Gallery director had been appointed; and the federal government had announced it would establish 250 offices across the country to counsel unemployed women.

The greatest miss was the failure of the new Bank of Western Canada to appoint a woman to its board of directors. Indeed, no Canadian bank yet had a woman director, although most U.S. banks did. As Anderson pointed out, more than half the wealth of Canada in stocks, bonds, mortgages, real estate, and savings was in the hands of women, but banking remained a male prerogative.

Anderson then took a slap at the Canadian government for its blindness to the rising women's movement: "The brief calling for a Royal Commission on the Status of Women in Canada, which was taken with high hopes to Ottawa last November and had the backing of thirty-two women's organizations, got as much attention at our nation's capital as if we had asked to have all the postboxes painted shocking pink.

"Yet in the last ten years in Canada we've had thirty-two royal commissions on such subjects as Gerda Munsinger and freshwater fishing. Half the population of this country—the female half—is undergoing great change. The effect of this change will influence the family, the economy, and all of our lives for the next century. Yet we're told the subject of women in Canada today doesn't warrant a Royal Commission. If this is the final decision, it's a setback for the nation—not just for its women."

During her twenty years as editor, Doris Anderson became convinced that the all-male hierarchy at Maclean-Hunter didn't even read *Chatelaine*. "If they had known what I was going to do with that magazine," she says, "they would have had a collective heart attack." Her biggest (indeed, her only) asset was that the magazine was Canadian. It could exist only by taking a bolder approach than its American counterparts, who, she felt, were short-changing their readers. By the end of her first decade, one Canadian in three was reading *Chatelaine*, which was making money, while its American counterparts—*Ladies' Home Journal* and *McCall's*—were losing.

While *Chatelaine* was showing a profit, *Maclean's* was in the red. Yet, in Anderson's phrase, "we were the Cinderella and *Maclean's* was the crown prince." At one point she discovered to her chagrin that the editor of *Maclean's* was being paid an annual $35,000 when she was getting only $23,000. She was finally able to squeeze a seven-thousand-dollar raise out of a reluctant management. Only later did she learn that the editor of *Maclean's* was actually being paid $53,000 a year—an increase over her own stipend as great as her own original salary. And *Maclean's*, unlike its feminist counterpart, was, in her own phrase, "leaking money."

In spite of *Chatelaine*'s strong editorial stand, there was no women's liberation movement in Canada in 1967. The phrase was unknown to me, among others. When I launched a five-part series of half-hour television programs on the subject, I referred to the feminists (a noun not yet in general use) as the New Suffragettes.

But there *was* a women's movement, and it *was* revolutionary, even though that was not its image. Its proponents did not wear tattered jeans, carry placards, or make shrill speeches. They were upper-class matrons, collectively known as "club women," who were affluent enough not to need to work and who had, through a number of women's groups, learned something about organization and leadership. They were well-educated, informed, and doggedly mainstream. It was impossible to dismiss them as wild-eyed radicals; many had husbands high in social and financial circles. But all were linked by a common concern—a vague feeling of helplessness, a dissatisfaction with their inability to control events, and a concern for their children's future growing out of their fear of a nuclear holocaust and the continuing pollution of the environment.

Lotta Dempsey, a flamboyant *Toronto Daily Star* columnist known for her choice of hats and her long cigarette holders, put that feeling into print in May 1960 when she wrote a column with the title "What Can Women Do?" The response astonished her. She followed with a second column quoting from the avalanche of letters and phone calls that poured into her office. "Can we live with ourselves," she asked, "if any children suffer the effects of even one atomic bomb?. . . Let's scream for the preservation of children all over the world."

Dempsey's office became a clearing-house for women's concerns and for the first attempts to unite women in their worries about the future of the world. A mass meeting in Toronto's Massey Hall followed, and out of that an organization known as the Voice of Women was born. Its founders sought a more respectable image than that of the anti-war and ban-the-bomb activists. As Cerise Morris explains in her doctoral dissertation, "No More Than Simple Justice," VOW leaders were usually described as "prominent" or as "the wife of the well-known. . . ."

VOW's aims were soon broadened beyond the original anti-nuclear stand to encompass a range of environmental and "quality of life" issues that were part of the bubbling activism of the decade. Though it was in decline by 1967, VOW served as a link between the passionate left and the middle-of-the-road groups that helped to generate the ideology and program of the burgeoning women's movement.

At this point, a powerful new figure emerged as the leading advocate of women's rights in Canada. In 1964, Laura Sabia, a big, handsome Italian Canadian from St. Catharines, Ontario, became president of the powerful and respected Canadian Federation of University Women. She began at once to lobby for a royal commission on the status of women. More than anyone else, she deserves the credit for forcing a reluctant government to acknowledge the women's movement in the centennial year and forcing an equally unwilling prime minister to establish the desired commission—or face the consequences.

Though no one would describe Laura Sabia as typical—she was, after all, a *force majeure*—she did represent the winds of change that were sweeping across Canada in the late sixties, climaxing in the centennial year. The little girl in the convent dress and black stockings who managed in the end to terrify the Canadian government into submission was always her father's child. He was a remarkable immigrant who had arrived from Italy an orphan at the age of thirteen. With no more than a Grade 4 education and burdened with the sole support of his brothers and sisters, he went to work with a shovel and wheelbarrow and by the age of twenty-two owned his own construction business.

Laura was his favourite, and he was a dominant figure in her life. He drilled into her his creed that "there's nothing a man can do that a woman can't do better." When she was thirteen he started taking her from the Villa Maria convent to the stock exchange to watch the tickers. (The nuns, on learning this, would go down on their knees to pray for her immortal soul.) On these occasions he'd hand her a ten-dollar bill and ask, "Now what do you want to invest in?"

Both her parents thought she should have been born a boy. She hated dolls, preferred slacks to dresses, and looked after her younger brother

128

Above: *Bowsman's burning biffies lit up the sky on Centennial Eve — a quirky but memorable way to launch our big birthday party. By July 1* (below) *the country was rejoicing. On Parliament Hill* (overleaf) *the crowd went wild.*

Judy LaMarsh couldn't always appear in the same outfit when she greeted every VIP who came to Ottawa. A man, of course, could make do with a dark suit. In spite of Judy's problem, the Prime Minister refused her a clothing allowance.

*To most Canadians, John Fisher was "Mr. Canada" thanks to his long-
running series of CBC radio broadcasts that fairly dripped maple syrup.
As chairman of the Centennial Commission he travelled the country making
hundreds of speeches to jolt Canadians "out of their apathetic rut."*

Bobby Gimby became the personification of the Centennial, playing his jewelled trumpet, wearing his piper's cape, and leading gaggles of youngsters down the byways of the nation, all carolling a new national anthem: "Ca-na-da."

In 1967, the country was given a year-long history lesson, not all of it accurate. Yes, there was an Indian Princess pageant, but aboriginal history doesn't disclose any evidence of actual "princesses" among our native tribes. The Voyageur pageant (below) *had far more authenticity, recapturing the great days of the fur trade. Most of the time the Manitoba canoe was in the lead.*

The Confederation Train was one of the big hits of 1967. The terrific response it got was unexpected. Whole families cheerfully queued for hours to view the exhibits. An astonishing ten million Canadians visited the train and the caravans that were sent to communities not served by rail. That represented half the population of the nation.

at school. She was quite capable of taking on three bullies and beating them all up. Nor was she abashed when people told her parents about "that awful daughter of yours." She met her husband at McGill and, like so many Canadian women of those days, was still a virgin when she married him. Later, she told an interviewer, "I think, really, I married with the idea sex was something revolting you put up with. I would say it took me all of ten years, maybe more, to realize—'What the hell! This is fun!'"

She moved with her husband to St. Catharines, where, as a young bride, she put in her time cleaning house and polishing floors—"all the traditional terrible things." As she later explained, in those days "your husband was just your *ideal*, and you looked after him. He went from the arms of his mother to the arms of his wife—that kind of protective custody." Years later, Laura Sabia wondered how she had managed to exist under those conditions.

Children came. She loved them, but never looked forward to motherhood and hated pregnancy. "I felt contaminated by it. I found the act of birth disgusting." When the first baby came, she didn't want a second. When the second arrived, she thought, "I can't go through with that again," and when the fourth was born, all she could think of was "What can I do so I can't have another?"

After ten years of marriage, while she was suffering from a severe illness, a young hospital intern said to her, "You're intelligent. Why don't you do something, *really*, besides raising children." That decided her: she wasn't going "to do the traditional thing" any more. She began to join various organizations just to get out of the house. She was already a member of the Catholic Women's League, but since it was not politically active she started the first parent-teacher organization in the Niagara Peninsula. She realized that it wasn't going to force any changes, and it came to her suddenly that the only way to make changes was to get into power. The easiest method was to become a member of the Separate School Board, a closed corporation that hadn't bothered with an election in eighteen years; prospective board members were invited to join and elected by acclamation. Laura Sabia forced an election and "alienated immediately the whole status quo." She led at the polls even though, or perhaps because, there had been no woman on the board to that date. For four years she fought to make meetings open to the press and public, but then she realized she didn't really believe in a separate school system at all. And so she quit.

Still, she missed her battles within the board. Politics, she decided, was everything. She was well known by this time, having been on the board of the YWCA, president of the local University Women's Club, and a member of the national executive of the CFUW. She decided to run for the local town council and found her knees almost giving way under her when she stood for nomination. In seven successful elections she always led the polls.

This was the most enjoyable time she'd ever had. Her house was bedlam—between thirty and forty phone calls a day. She strongly believed that the average person should have a voice in government and often brought delegations to council to put forward their views. "Here comes Laura and her delegation," they used to say. Her style was flamboyant, she knew how to attract headlines ("even a bad press is a good press as far as people are concerned"), and she learned, as she matured, that she had to be flexible, that you can't just push established structures away. As the Centennial approached, she found herself growing increasingly fed up with the government's attitude towards women. Now the national president of the most respected women's organization in the country, she was tired of traipsing to Ottawa year after year to bring her organization's resolutions to the political leaders. "There would be a big fanfare and the government would flatter you to death and then say: 'Thank God, that's over for another year!'"

She decided to write to every national women's organization and ask, "Are you tired of this nonsense?" It turned out that they too had reached a saturation point as far as appeals to Ottawa were concerned. On April 18, 1966, on behalf of the CFUW, Sabia invited delegates from all established women's organizations to attend a meeting to discuss the status of women in Canada.

"For many years the women of Canada. . . have been disturbed and concerned by the increasing prejudices found in every facet of our society against women's full participation. . . . Just recently we read of the Prime Minister's appointments to the Senate. Not one woman was appointed, despite the fact that Canada has ratified the Convention on the Political Rights of Women. . . . The questions of domicile, divorce, appointments to the Senate, to federal civil service, judgeships, C.B.C., Royal Commissions. . . and present antiquated discriminatory legislation should be aired, discussed, and rectified. . . . A Commission on the Status of Women has become mandatory. Some organizations are pressuring the government for such a Commission. *We could be far more effective if all women's organizations would come together. . . .*"

A meeting in Toronto on May 3 was attended by fifty women representing thirty-two organizations. Sabia herself was elected head of a nine-member steering committee charged with producing a working resolution for future action. On May 27, the committee met and recommended that the thirty-two organizations demand that the federal government set up a royal commission. Doris Anderson backed the recommendation in a *Chatelaine* editorial in July. At a second meeting a committee on the equality of women in Canada was established to increase the pressure on the government.

The committee wanted a meeting with the Prime Minister. It finally got one on November 19 after two months of promoting the cause in public appearances and interviews with the media and individual politicians. Pearson, who didn't want a commission, didn't turn up, sending his justice minister, Lucien Cardin, in his place. Judy LaMarsh, who had been pressing for a royal commission for several years, also came on her own initiative. "In a state that prides itself on being free of organized discrimination, to turn away from the recommendations, which represent half the people, could cause this half to feel very strongly that there *is* discrimination," she said. "This is a luxury that can't be afforded."

LaMarsh herself got nowhere with the Prime Minister. When she mentioned the possibility of a royal commission to a national women's meeting, "there was an immediate and scathing reaction from some of the responsible press," while the Prime Minister "backed off as if stung with a nettle." In her memoirs, she said that the royal commission was the most difficult achievement in all her years in the Pearson cabinet and would not have been possible without Sabia and her pressure group.

Cardin was receptive but noncommittal to the women's requests. Pearson had already described his own attitude in response to the NDP's Grace MacInnis, in the House the previous July. He promised to look into the matter "and as a result of my investigations have decided to be very cautious."

As the centennial year opened, it appeared that the government had no intention of caving in to what many of LaMarsh's cabinet colleagues thought of as "Judy's pet concern." A *Globe and Mail* reporter called Sabia with the news that Pearson had turned her down. It was eleven o'clock at night and, as Sabia later described it, "he kept pushing me."

"I was tired of talking to him, so finally I said, 'Ah, I can march two million women to Ottawa.'"

The following day, she opened her morning paper to be greeted by the headline: "Women's march may back call for rights probe." The story reported that "two million Canadian women may be asked to march on Ottawa if the federal government fails to announce by the end of the month a Royal Commission on Women's Rights. . . . Mrs. Michael Sabia. . . has given an ultimatum to the government to establish a Royal Commission or face the consequences." Sabia was quoted as saying: "We're tired of being nice about trying to get an official inquiry into women's rights in Canada. If we don't get a royal commission by the end of this month, we'll use every tactic we can. And if we have to use violence, damn it, we will."

When she read this, Sabia recalled, she "nearly died." She immediately phoned her old friend Margaret Hyndman, a prominent Toronto lawyer and an early activist. Only the second woman in the Commonwealth to be named King's Counsel, the first Canadian woman to appear before the Privy Council and the first to sit on the board of a trust company, Hyndman had an international reputation. Kenneth Mackenzie, her opponent in several legal actions, called her "the most distinguished self-made woman in Canada." Now she listened as Sabia, disturbed by the militancy of the newspaper article, asked, "Have you seen the headlines?"

"Yes," Hyndman replied. "I'm having a nice cup of coffee. Sit back and relax. You'll get your royal commission now."

But Sabia was worried. *Two million women?* "I wouldn't have been able to get *three* women to march on Ottawa," she confessed later. The CFUW was being held together by a thread. Her slogan was "Pacify, pacify, pacify." She tried to quench the fires by resorting to the old political dodge that she was quoted out of context. Still, some organizations telegraphed the government dissociating themselves from her remarks. One club wondered whether any action would be "in good taste." Judy LaMarsh managed to delay transmitting these messages to the cabinet.

LaMarsh told Sabia that there was consternation in Ottawa because of the *Globe* story. Two million people in the nation's capital?—pouring off planes and specially chartered buses, holding mass demonstrations on Parliament Hill, attracting worldwide attention from the media, especially from television! The government did not relish that prospect. LaMarsh herself moved to control the situation fearing that it might only serve to antagonize her cabinet colleagues.

"I am very much afraid that if the strident tone that has been used in the last couple of days continues, it will constitute pushing too hard on an open door and will undo all the good that has been done. The Prime Minister and the cabinet are men as other men and if you have harpies harping at them, you will just get their backs up and they won't do anything. . . ."

In fact, the pressure on the government convinced Lester Pearson that the time had come for a royal commission. But who should chair it? The last thing he wanted was a woman of Sabia's character in charge. He needed somebody with stature who could not be considered in any sense an activist. He settled on Mrs. John Bird, wife of a Parliamentary Press Gallery columnist and herself a journalist who wrote under the pen name Anne Francis. An American who had immigrated to

Canada at the age of thirty-one and was a graduate of Bryn Mawr, she had been trying to arrange an interview with the Prime Minister when he called her. No, he wasn't calling about the interview, he told her; he wanted her to chair the new commission.

"Oh God!" she said.

He needed an immediate answer. Sabia had insisted on a decision by the end of the month and that date had already passed. Pearson wanted Mrs. Bird in his office the following morning so that he could make an immediate announcement in the House.

"You look awful," a friend told her at tea that afternoon.

"I've had a shock," said Florence Bird.

She was of two minds about Pearson's offer. Her career as a freelance writer was going well and she was enjoying life. Two outlines she'd submitted to the CBC for documentaries had been approved. As a result she could look forward to trips to the United States and Sweden. She had friends who'd chaired previous commissions and knew how exhausting, demanding, and endless their work had been. "My mind boggled at the thought of taking on a job charged with so much emotional dynamite," she confessed in her memoirs. She knew her personal life would suffer. The job would be especially hard on her husband ("J.B.," she called him), who was a correspondent for the *Financial Post*.

But as she added up the pros and cons of the offer, she had to admit that for twenty years she had been writing with concern and dismay about the way women felt about themselves. She had supported Sabia and LaMarsh. She had written and lectured on the need for women "to stop being shrinking violets." She had inveighed against women who used the excuse of "family obligations" to avoid promotion, since most men had family obligations too. Now her bluff had been called.

She knew that if she refused to serve she would be haunted by guilt for all her remaining years. She thought of all the women who were stuck in badly paying jobs; of intelligent women passed over again and again when men were promoted over them; of a girl who committed an abortion on herself and who cried for help in the night: how could one small body lose so much blood?

134

When her husband came home she asked him what she should do. He told her it was a decision she'd have to make herself. She bombarded him with questions. Was her health up to it? Wouldn't somebody else be a better choice? Was she not more useful as a TV or radio commentator? Finally he spoke: "There is just one question you should be putting to yourself. If the Prime Minister of Canada asks you to take on a tremendous, difficult job to help half the people in the country, can you say no to him?"

That did it. On Friday morning, February 3, 1967, the Prime Minister announced in the House that the government was setting up the Royal Commission on the Status of Women in Canada and that Florence Bird would chair it.

Within half an hour French and English television teams were at her door. A succession of reporters followed. Most of the women asked serious questions, but she found many of the men "ill-informed and self-consciously flippant." Next morning the phone rang at six o'clock. An angry truck driver was on the line demanding that something be done about the rights of men.

These attacks continued for about ten days, then tapered off. One woman became a regular cocktail-hour caller. She kept telling Bird how normal she was and how normal her husband was and always ended up by shouting, "Drop dead! Ha-ha. You won't be able to trace this call. Drop dead!" There were many calls from women asking for help and also from those who maintained that there was no need for any change in the status of women. They were comfortable and satisfied.

A spate of newspaper comments followed. The mainstream press generally took the commission seriously, but with reservations, hoping sceptically that it might perhaps do some good. But the consensus was that the resultant report would be pigeon-holed and forgotten. Some columnists clearly viewed women as sex objects. Others believed their place was in the kitchen. Several used the occasion to try to be funny. Many TV and radio broadcasters viewed the commission as a great joke.

There was evidence, Bird wrote in her memoirs, "that many news-papermen regarded women as garrulous fools incapable of agreeing about anything or bringing out a sensible report." Frank Tumpane of the *Toronto Telegram* urged his male readers: "Now let's sit back, fel-las, and see if they can agree on just what it is they do want." Charles Lynch of Southam News wrote of the commission: "They need have nothing to fear but other women. If they can get over the mistrust, if not loathing that they feel for one another, our national life will be enriched beyond measure." Other writers were supercilious. "I believe that the Royal Commission is ill-conceived, superfluous, and may have ominous results," F.S. Manor wrote in the *Winnipeg Free Press*. "It should be disbanded before a lot of bossy, ugly women spoil our lovely world."

It is difficult for those of us who have lived through the post-centennial period to absorb the truly revolutionary change of attitude brought about as a result of the government's decision to give Cana-dian women a commission of their own. Royal commissions have long been a subject of satire. As I once wrote in verse for a stage revue: "When all's done and said/there is nothing so dead/as a Royal Com-mission Report." It is contended that the reports gather dust on gov-ernment shelves, that the commissioners' deliberations have little effect, and that their recommendations, at best, are watered down. Even if that were true, those who sneer at this most Canadian of institutions forget that its real purpose has been not to recommend but to educate. That was the great legacy of the Status of Women commission. Since 1967 we have seen a total reversal of attitudes towards women and largely because of the drip-drip-drip effect of those months of headline-making public sessions.

Consider, for example, the mocking and patronizing editorial reac-tion of the Ottawa *Journal* on February 4, 1967: "The reaction of Cana-dian men to news that a royal commission on women's rights has been appointed is what one would expect of a tough, hard-working, straight-talking male: fear. Everyone knows what commissions are like at their worst. Everyone knows what women are like at their worst. Put the two together—well, we could end up with the longest established permanent royal commission in history. Somebody once said that individually, women are something, but together they're something else. . . . What makes these girls think any Canadian man in his right mind would sit on such a commission? By all means let the girls gather facts and see how they can be strengthened where they need it. Bosh! But we suggest to them, for their own good, of course, that they do it in the same way that they have advanced their cause in recent years—quietly, sneakily, and with such charming effectiveness as to make men wonder why they feel they need a royal commission. . . ."

No newspaper would publish such an editorial today. But the *Journal*, on its front page, thought nothing of accompanying it with an unscientific man-on-the-street survey, which depressed Florence Bird. It included such comments as: "Incredible"; "Won't change my wife's status"; "It's ridiculous, expensive and a waste of money." Seventy percent of those polled by the newspaper said they felt the commission would accomplish little. A minority of respondents—mostly women—thought it a good idea.

Some prominent women pooh-poohed the project. To Charlotte Whitton, the gadfly mayor of Ottawa, it was "the most fantastically inexcusable thing I've ever heard." She'd been against it from the outset, declaring that "the door was open to women if they weren't sissy-prissies making sandwiches for political meetings." The president of the Vancouver Council of Women declared that "women have been around for a long time, and if they haven't managed to establish themselves by now, I can't see the point of energy being expended on the Royal Commission." In spite of these less-than-heartening comments, Bird went to work immediately with the six other commissioners chosen to sit with her to lay the groundwork during the centennial year for a series of public hearings that would take place over the next four.

While they waited for the briefs to come in, the commissioners had to absorb a mountain of material. One managed to get through fifty books in the space of four months—this in addition to the massive pile of published papers that had to be studied and digested. Many of the briefs that poured in were enormous. That of the Manitoba Volunteer Committee on the Status of Women ran to more than two hundred pages; another, from the Corrections Association of Canada, to seventy. The hearings that followed were, in Bird's words, "mind-expanding, exciting, always exhausting." She found that, as a result, many of her original ideas were either modified or changed for the better. The hearings were widely covered, underlining the truth that the real value of any royal commission is educational. Long before the commission's report was tabled in December 1970, many minds had been changed, and the movement known as Women's Liberation, which had scarcely existed in the centennial year, was being discussed and argued about in the media, a powerful influence in modifying public attitudes that had been frozen only a short time before.

3

A lingering sense of guilt Something was stirring in Canada that year, something that contrasted with the general feeling of euphoria that marked the birthday celebrations. In the midst of all the drum beating and the flag waving, some people were beginning to experience a lingering sense of guilt.

The phrase "human rights" was being bandied about in the press like a ping-pong ball. Some provinces had set up human rights commissions to process complaints, although these were generally handled privately and without fanfare. In the spring of 1967, however, the Ontario department of labour in its annual report revealed that formal complaints of discrimination had doubled in the space of a single year.

The visible minorities who faced discrimination in Canada were the blacks and the native peoples. The blacks were burdened by what might be called the "our-record-is-better-than-yours" syndrome. History made Canadians look a lot more tolerant than the segregationists below the border. After all, weren't we on the northern end of the Underground Railroad that brought fleeing slaves safely to Canada? And indeed, the handful of American blacks who came north were often loud in their praises when they compared the situation here to the one that had driven them out of the United States.

Much of the smugness was shattered in May when a University of Toronto anthropologist, James Anderson, published the results of a thirteen-year study of Toronto children whom he had watched grow from the age of three into their teens. The study showed widespread and bitter racial prejudices among the twelve hundred children in the study. Eighty percent of the youngsters, for instance, said they wouldn't attend a dance with a person of a different colour.

By 1967, the number of black faces seen in the streets of Toronto, the Mecca for most English-speaking black immigrants, caused the media to take notice. In just six years the population of blacks in York County had ballooned from 4,247 to an estimated 20,000. Most of these came, not from the United States, but from the United Kingdom and the Caribbean. In August the *Toronto Daily Star*, noting that for the first time blacks formed a sizeable minority in the city, published a well-documented, multi-part series dealing with the new immigrants. It revealed, among other things, that there was a quota system for most jobs and that blacks were forced to pay higher rents than whites.

The prejudice against blacks extended to the Canadian Football League, which had forty-odd black players in 1967 compared to more than two hundred and forty white players. On most teams, the black players found themselves segregated because accommodations were arranged so that blacks boarded together, two to a room, while white players boarded with other white players.

When Lovell Coleman of the Calgary Stampeders started to date a white woman, his coach, Bobby Dobbs, advised him to take the romance underground. Eventually the two married. Coleman's wife, who knew very little about race relations, couldn't believe there was discrimination against blacks in Calgary, but then, apart from members of the football team, there were few in that city. "She thought I was too sensitive," Coleman recalled. "She couldn't see how any of my teammates could consider me anything but an individual."

He had already explained to her that there were half a dozen players on the team who made sure their black teammates didn't hear about their parties. That she refused to believe, so Coleman suggested they throw a party themselves and invite everybody. To her chagrin, only ten players showed up. A few responded with excuses; others acted as though they had never been invited. After that, Mrs. Coleman began to catch on.

The native Indians, of course, were far worse off than the blacks, although the prejudice against them was rarely overt except in some of the small prairie towns. The facts, which were published over and over again, seemed to have had little effect on the general public. Only a tenth of native teenagers were in school in 1967. Thirty percent of native babies were so undernourished that their chances of survival were doubtful. Three-quarters of all native Indians were paying less than $2,000 annually for shelter—half as much as more comfortable whites. Thirty-eight percent were on relief. The life expectancy of an Inuk at birth was fifty years, of a native Indian, sixty-six years, of a white Canadian, seventy-six years.

Drunkenness was a continuing problem, a situation that bothered Mr. Justice William Morrow, in charge of another of those seemingly endless commissions the government periodically convened to examine native problems. "What worries me," he said, "is that a young girl, not even twenty-one yet, has put in more time in jail over a period of two years for being drunk than someone who has perhaps almost killed a person."

Morrow's comment was made in a Slavey village near Hay River—the first time, it turned out, that anyone had visited the community to ask the people what could be done about irregularities of justice in the Territories. And something certainly needed to be done. Members of the RCMP, it developed in testimony, were taking the law into their own hands by barging into the Slaveys' homes without warrants to make arrests or conduct interviews.

One might have expected the young activists who were demonstrating in the streets against nuclear war and racial discrimination to

140

have taken notice of the appalling conditions faced by aboriginals in the Canadian North and the larger cities. But the glamour of the Selma March and the clarion voices of Martin Luther King and Stokely Carmichael had diverted their interests south of the border.

The underground press, notably Vancouver's *Georgia Straight*, tried occasionally to focus on the Indians' plight. The recently organized Company of Young Canadians sent a few of its naïve young volunteers into native enclaves, though with limited success. This was also the year that Gene Rhéaume, a former MP for the Northwest Territories and himself a mixed blood, issued the report of a task force on Indians and the law. And Howard Adams, the Métis Ph.D. and most visible native leader in the country, organized a jamboree at Duck Lake, Saskatchewan, largely for the benefit of the media. Something was undeniably stirring—a desire for self-expression, a rejection of white culture, an attempt to instil a sense of pride in the native peoples based on their heritage.

The Rhéaume report, *Indians and the Law*, was another attempt by the department of Indian affairs to grapple with an apparently insoluble problem. Commissioned by the department at a cost of sixty-five thousand dollars, it was the result of seventeen months of research; when it was leaked to the press, it made instant front-page headlines. It declared that racial hostility between Indians and whites in several Western Canadian cities had reached explosion point. It did not, as some previous studies had done, urge the dissolution of the department; how could it? But it did call for yet another conference to launch a fifteen-point program aimed at creating a better life for the native peoples.

Some of the statistics that Rhéaume's task force had gathered were shocking. The Indians of Canada were filling the jails—there was now no doubt of that. An incredible 35 percent of all men, women, and children in custody were of Indian ancestry. There were ten times more Indians in jail than there should have been in proportion to the population. The population of women's jails in The Pas and in Kamloops was *100 percent native*, in Kenora, 95 percent. Most were behind bars for trivial offences, and no attempts were being made to rehabilitate them. They got into trouble because they were poor, discouraged, and resentful over discrimination, scanty social services, and intergovernmental muddles. As a result they drank, and when they drank they were jailed.

They were bedevilled by two sets of attitudes. "When Indians drink heavily at carnivals and rodeos, people call them worthless drunks. When non-Indians get drunk, people call them 'real swingers,'" the report pointed out.

Predictably, the politicians in the communities named by Rhéaume took umbrage. "A lot of nonsense," cried the mayor of Kenora.

"Unwarranted and exaggerated," declared the mayor of Kamsack, Saskatchewan.

Howard Adams's powwow at Duck Lake was more upbeat, staged in the hope that similar events would follow in which the natives themselves could realize how many problems they had in common. The choice of Duck Lake was, of course, no accident. There, in 1885, Louis Riel's Saskatchewan rebellion had begun. This was a very sixties occasion. Even the Indians referred to it as a talk-in. "McLuhan talks about tribalism," one young Indian dancer told the press, "and that's what we, the real tribes are experiencing." His attire might be described as psychedelic and indeed was; it seemed as much a part of the present as the past—the loud purple costume with the bands of intricate beadwork around his arms, waist, and leggings, and the brilliant feathered headpiece atop his shoulder-length hair.

Peter Gzowski, then on the verge of a career that would establish him as the best broadcaster in Canada, visited the powwow and saw the celebrants "not only as a people with a past, but as a people who feel that they too have a place in the twentieth century McLuhanistic world."

Adams's purpose was to emphasize the strengths and values of the aboriginal culture. A whisper of that culture was evident at Duck Lake that summer, in the throbbing of the giant tom-toms and the powwow dancing of the participants, an indication that in spite of the white man's attempts to ram his own culture and sense of values down the Indians' throats, something of their own past had survived. Gzowski, a child of his times, professed to see in this a link with the psychedelic movement of the sixties—the colourful dances, the drug peyote, the pounding music. As a journalist seeking an angle, he was stretching matters a bit. The Indians at their powwow and the young upper-middle-class children cavorting to hard rock had only a superficial similarity. At a time when Canada was assembling space rockets there were people at Duck Lake who still considered a ration of bannock and tea a satisfactory meal.

There was nothing psychedelic about the alcoholism in the community, as Gzowski himself reported. "Sodden drunks are as common on the unpaved dirt streets of Duck Lake as used and dirty cars." The local beer parlour, where the bartender was a grandson of Riel's great general, Gabriel Dumont, was a place of uncommon squalor. "Drunks lurched from table to table. Beer was spilled and chairs overturned. . . . The point was, apparently, to drink oneself into oblivion and many of the native people succeeded."

That scene was in no sense unique; it would be repeated all across the nation in northern towns and larger southern cities. The Centennial Commission was attempting, in a variety of ways, to include the natives in the country's one-hundredth birthday party by emphasizing the strengths and values of their culture. That was not an easy task. The various tribes were not really organized to hold a birthday celebration, nor did they seem to want to. Most, living in squalid shacks on remote reserves, didn't know much about the Centennial. In fact, they didn't have a word for it in their many languages. And those who did know about it didn't care, as a working paper in January 1965 had made clear. Ralph Steinhauer, co-chairman of the Indian Advisory Council on the Centennial and later lieutenant-governor of Alberta, pointed out that the Indians of Canada weren't at all sure that the year 1867 and the period surrounding it were anything they wanted to rejoice in or celebrate a century later. In approaching the matter, the Indian leaders concluded variously that they should abstain from participation, or that they should participate to please the white man, or that they should seek to exploit the anniversary for whatever financial or recreational gains were available.

It was, of course, unthinkable that the aboriginal peoples should not be included in the birthday festivities. As early as 1965 the press was commenting on the lack of Indian participation. The Centennial Commission realized that some public statement had to be made "in order to prevent a second round of poor publicity." To appease the Indians the commission adopted two stances: first, to look forward into the future and not the past, and second, to acquaint all Canadians, and indeed the Indians themselves, with their own culture through pow-wows, tours, Indian days, arts and crafts exhibits, and pageants such as the Indian Princess contest that had been launched in 1963.

Bolstered by centennial funds, the pageant was held near Qu'Appelle, Saskatchewan, and pronounced a huge success. Marion Meadows, the co-chairperson, wrote to the commission that "society, both Indian and non-Indian, has benefited by the projection of a new kind of intelligent, articulate, friendly, sophisticated, and ambitious personality, as compared with the old drunk, lazy, etc." The purpose of the pageant was "to bring pride and interest to native culture. . . . The hardy pioneers who first discovered and settled this great land should not be forgotten, especially during our centennial year. The Canadian Princess pageant is a welcome reminder of our heritage and most certainly does bring pride and interest to our Canadian Indians."

"Heritage"? *What* heritage?

The nine princesses who toured Canada included a telephone operator, a communications worker, a disc jockey, a nursing student, a dressmaker: nobody at the government level is recorded as asking how an American-style beauty contest (sans bathing suits) fitted into Indian heritage. Nor did anybody seem bemused by the fact that the Hollywood concept of an "Indian Princess" had nothing to do with native culture.

The Indian pavilion at Expo was a different proposition entirely, possibly because the Indians themselves were responsible for it. Those

144

Expo visitors who went expecting to encounter the Noble Red Man stereotype and the usual baskets-and-beadwork displays were shocked out of their skins. It was perhaps the most controversial pavilion on the grounds, and it angered a great many visitors. "It's horrible, I'm not going to stay here," one Montreal woman exclaimed to a group of fellow visitors as she encountered a large panel reading: "The white man's school is an alien land for the Indian child." As evidence, an accompanying display demonstrated some of the books the native children were being given to read, including several about those highly urban palefaces Dick and Jane, not to mention their dog Spot and their cat Puff.

The pavilion was one of the most striking at the Expo site, and also, I think (though no one mentioned it at the time), the one whose influence was the most lasting, for it literally changed the attitudes of many who visited it. A colourful, gigantic teepee of steel and timber, it fitted Expo's architectural theme of joyous celebration. But the story it told was one of white exploitation. No paleface entering those precincts could fail to be startled and ashamed. In the midst of pavilions so proudly paying tribute to Man the Explorer and Man the Creator, this one, boldly and coldly, told the story of Man the Exploiter. The message was explicit: "When the white man came we welcomed him with love, we sheltered him, fed him and led him through the forest. The white men fought each other for our land. We were embroiled in the white man's war. Many Indians feel our fathers were betrayed."

"Give us the right to manage our own affairs," one huge sign pleaded. Photographs of tattered, unhappy Indian children were placed beside pictures of white children playing in the comfort of the suburbs.

"We are stating the case as the Indian people wanted it stated," a deputy commissioner general, T.R. Kelly of the Haidas, told the press. "We are trying to tell the truth, not to please anybody."

Surprisingly, the Indian pavilion was one of the most popular at the big fair, perhaps because of some "masochistic paleface quirk," as Neil Compton, a Montreal critic, wrote. Certainly it was impossible to leave the premises without a tingle of guilt, and that, of course, was the Indians' purpose. This unique pavilion, with its blunt, uncompromising message, was widely publicized and probably had more to do with a change of attitude on the part of the public than all the seminars, task-force reports, and white papers combined. Like the women's movement, the Indian movement that emerged in the decades that followed had its roots in the centennial year.

4

The seeds of Gay Pride In the late fall of 1967, when gaiety reigned unconfined, one minority group remained joyless. The Supreme Court of Canada had just upheld the conviction of one of their number, a young man named Everett Klippert, to life imprisonment. His crime: homosexuality. He was not being put behind bars for the rest of his years for what he had done but for what he *was*. It sounds incredible to us today and it sounded incredible then, but not just to the "gays," who weren't gay at all and who had not yet publicly adopted that oddly inappropriate code word (an adjective turned into a noun). It also jarred the consciences of a good many others, including the justice minister, Pierre Trudeau, who moved, in the dying days of the centennial year, to keep the state out of the nation's bedrooms.

The natives and the blacks were highly visible groups, but in the Canada of 1967 homosexuals were not. Apart from a small minority of cross-dressers and drag queens who camped it up in the clubs and on the city streets on Hallowe'en night, they were indistinguishable from the straight community. They wanted it that way. Only a very few, such as the activist James Egan, who allowed himself to become the subject of a CBC documentary, dared to come out of the closet. The reason was understandable. It was a crime to be a homosexual.

Yet here again something was stirring—a subtle change of attitude on the part of the *straight* community, a slowly growing realization that most homosexuals did not belong to the mincing, campy stereotype that had been imprinted on the subculture by countless stage skits, cartoons, films, and even newspapers. The breakthrough can be traced

146

to a more enlightened attitude in the media and notably to two articles by Sidney Katz in *Maclean's*.

Katz, who held a Master's degree in sociology, spent considerable time in Toronto's gay world—in clubs, bars, and restaurants, most of which, he discovered, were invisible to outsiders. His conclusion, that the average homosexual was "a much maligned individual, unfairly discriminated against by our laws and by society" and "rarely the weird sex monster so often depicted in psychiatric case histories, police records, and lurid fiction" was supported by the appalling professional ignorance uncovered among lawmakers, physicians, and clergymen. Some of the examples of medical advice reported by those who sought help from doctors seem unbelievable to those of us who have forgotten how attitudes have changed since those times:

"The doctor told me to lie on a couch and loosen my clothing. Then he passed his hands over me telling me to think beautiful thoughts and to forget my evil actions."

"He said I was a namby-pamby. He told me to get a piece of paper and draw pictures of nude women."

"He advised me to get more exercise."

"He told me to pull up my socks, find a nice girl, and get married."

Many homosexuals who turned to the church for help and comfort left feeling wicked and doomed to eternal damnation. One young man was told by his minister that his desires were "evil and sinful. He said I must come to church regularly and ask God for strength. In time this would help me forget all about my unpleasant impulses and experiences and I'd meet a nice girl and marry her."

Another who appealed to a clergyman for counsel was told: "You can't be a homosexual if you're an engineer. Only artists and actors and people like that are queer." With that kind of ignorance rampant at the professional level, the public attitude towards sexual inversion is understandable.

Katz's articles appeared in 1964 and were widely circulated among the homosexual community, whose members gained some confidence from the fact that a straight publication had tried to dispel some widely held myths. *Maclean's* then had a readership of more than a million, and that undoubtedly meant it affected the straight world.

An even greater influence was the acceptance in 1967 of the Wolfenden Report in Great Britain, which decriminalized homosexual acts between consenting males. That left Canada as the western country with the most draconian laws dealing with homosexuals. Among other straws in the wind were the formation of the short-lived Association for Social Knowledge "to studiously confront Canadian society with the fact of its homosexual minority and challenge Canadians to treat homosexuals with justice and respect," and the publication of two homosexual magazines, *Gay* and *Two*.

All this activity was devoted primarily to law reform. Section 149 of the Criminal Code stated that "everyone who commits an act of gross indecency is guilty of an indictable offence and liable to prison for five years." What was "gross" and what was "indecent" were not defined in the code, nor was homosexual activity specifically mentioned. The law could be used to indict a straight male for urinating in public or a young woman for swimming in the nude; in practice, it was used by the police as a weapon against homosexuals.

A homosexual act between two adult males was gross indecency, even if carried out in private, as a Vancouver court case in May 1967 made clear. The lawyer appearing for two men argued that, since the act of which they were accused was not performed in public, the "gross indecency" argument could not be used against them. The magistrate overruled him. "Even agreeing that society is generally, as it is in so many other cases today, adopting a more broad-minded attitude or a more condoning or accepting attitude toward these deviant behaviours" he still found them guilty, handed out a two-year suspended sentence, and imposed a bond of one thousand dollars.

That mild sentence suggested that attitudes were softening. Acts between consenting homosexuals came before the courts less often. No police force in the country was making much effort to detect homosexual activity unless some public element was involved—a public washroom, a park, a parked car.

148

In Vancouver that year police spotted a man and a woman apparently indulging in oral sex in a taxi and thought that they had discovered a case of prostitution. They trailed the couple to a hotel, listened at the keyhole, broke into the room, and found them both in bed, nude. One was Jean Lupien, vice-president of Central Mortgage and Housing Corporation and a deputy commissioner general of Expo 67. The other was a male prostitute, Serge Boisvert, who had been dressed in women's clothes complete with blond wig, nylons, and high heels. Lupien tried to escape the charge of gross indecency by insisting he thought his partner was female. He even presented psychiatric evidence to show he had an aversion to homosexuals. But the police description left no doubt in the court's mind as to what was going on. Both men were found guilty. Lupien was fined $750, Boisvert a mere $100. Neither went to jail.

The police did their best to foster the impression that it was illegal for men to wear women's clothing, and a good many gays believed this. But there was no such statute on the books. It was only illegal to dress as a woman to commit a crime. The police harassed the gay clubs, looked for illegal drugs, sneered at the female impersonators as "faggots" and "queers," but didn't charge them because they couldn't.

The image of the homosexual as outrageously effeminate was still held by many Canadians. These "drag queens" belonged to a small but highly visible subculture within the larger gay culture. For the most part they were shunned by the mainstream, who felt they were giving homosexuality a bad image. One homosexual explained to a newspaper reporter, "I think it's a throwback to playing dress-up when you're very young. You put on high heels and lipstick and your mother says 'you make such a pretty lady.'" Whether or not that was true, there was certainly a measure of defiance in breaking society's rules. As one man put it, "In the gay clubs you can do whatever you want—wear a dress, mince, and act affected. You don't have to pretend any more."

Because it wasn't easy to prove gross indecency, and because you couldn't arrest anybody for reasons of fashion, some policemen simply harassed homosexuals and let them go. In the summer of 1967,

Russell Alldread, a thirty-six-year-old bisexual, left Toronto's gay cabaret, the Music Room, where he was performing in drag, and drove off with a friend in a red sports car. A police car followed them, and when they parked at a coffee shop on Bloor Street, it pulled up beside them and Alldread was asked to produce his driver's licence. The two were ordered out of their car and driven around the block, where more policemen crowded in and began to threaten them. "We're going to drive you down the street and each of us is going to give you a swim," one of them said. They could not charge either man, nor did they make good their threat. Instead they took them to the College Street police station and sat them down in the outer hallway where an older policeman walked back and forth, kicking them in the legs and trying to pull off their false eyelashes. Finally they were released and driven back to their car.

For Alldread it wasn't a big deal. He was used to being hassled. And sometimes it wasn't a hassle, it was an invitation. One cop followed him home and asked to see his driver's licence. "Nice night, isn't it?" he said. "Aren't you going to invite me in for tea?"

Russell Alldread cheerfully complied. "There were a few policemen that were in the closet themselves in those days," he remembers.

Alldread was one of a small minority of gays who got a thrill out of entertaining in women's clothes and was known as a featured performer in the gay nightclubs. Despite the hassles, he remembers this period as a happy time. He was living a double life as a straight shoe salesman during the day and as "Anita," an extrovert in his own circle of drag queens, evenings and weekends. He was young, he had a host of friends, he even won an award in the Music Room in a Miss Gay Community contest. Now, he looks back on the period with a certain nostalgia. One gets the impression that the continual presence of danger from the police excited him. He still performs as a female impersonator, but some of the thrill has gone. He no longer lives a double life.

In 1967, George Hislop remembers, "life was okay as long as you kept your head down." In Toronto, homosexuals had their own beverage rooms, such as in the old Ford Hotel on Dundas Street, and their own cocktail bars, such as Letros on King and the St. Charles on Yonge

(Alldread was once elected Miss St. Charles). The gay steam baths, such as the Golden Baths on Bay, were just beginning to flourish. Two hotels on Queen Street near York were such good areas for cruising that they were known as the Chamber of Commerce and the Board of Trade. Montreal, however, was a desert in 1967 because the Expo authorities closed the obvious homosexual establishments so that the city wouldn't get a bad name.

There were well-established cruising areas in Toronto, known to the police as well as homosexuals. One was Philosophers' Walk in the Queen's Park area behind the Royal Ontario Museum. George Hislop, when asked if he had a university degree, would say he was a Ph.D.— Doctor of Philosophers' Walk. There, in the summer of 1967, while having sex with a young Australian, he was arrested by a sharp-eyed policeman. It proved to be doubly embarrassing because they knew each other. The cop had been a classmate of Hislop's and was in a quandary about arresting his friend. The law took its course, however, and for Hislop, who had just turned forty, the experience was traumatic.

He was held in the bull pen of the College Street police station, "where you were made the lowest of the low." It was a big, barred area with an open toilet in one corner and a number of wooden benches occupied by sleeping drunks. When he was taken upstairs to the court-room he was handcuffed to another prisoner who didn't want to be attached to a "queer." This suggestion that he was some kind of leper angered Hislop, who was also concerned that his Australian friend might be deported. He remembered an incident when another immi-grant he knew had been charged with gross indecency, sentenced to six months in prison, and then put on a boat and sent back to Europe. Now it was 1967, and judges tended to be more lenient. The Australian wasn't deported, only fined.

Hislop's regular lover bailed him out the next morning, at which point he was plagued by a dilemma that faced many homosexuals. He needed a lawyer and got one—an ambulance chaser who cheerfully took him on as a client but who, it turned out, preyed on men like him. He invariably pleaded his clients guilty, and so Hislop, who had paid him five hundred dollars, found himself also paying a five-hundred-dollar fine.

Before the end of the decade Hislop would be out of the closet, acting as unofficial spokesman for the gay community that was slowly organizing itself into an activist role.

There were no Gay Pride marches in 1967 (the phrase itself was in the closet), but the seeds were being sown that year, especially in a newly awakened media. The TV program *Sunday* came under attack in Parliament for two episodes on homosexuality. They showed gay men dancing cheek to cheek in a gay bar, young homosexuals defending themselves, and female impersonators putting on makeup and dresses. Scott Symons's *Place d'Armes*, which dealt with a man who tries the gay life, was widely reviewed in the press, and John Herbert's Canadian play, *Fortune and Men's Eyes*, which, in Nathan Cohen's words, "pushes freedom of speech and frankness of behaviour to new extremes," couldn't find a backer in Toronto but was given a regular off-Broadway production in New York.

The major newspapers were beginning to publish sympathetic articles on the homosexual lifestyle. A leading editorial in the *Vancouver Sun* on July 10 is typical of the changing attitude: "Whether it thinks it's ready for it or not, this country will have to face up to the question of homosexuality and the law before much time has passed. . . . The fact is that our social climate is changing and we can no longer abide laws and codes of conduct of Christian origin or earlier which do great harm and precious little good."

But the real breakthrough came in December, when the Supreme Court handed down its decision on Everett George Klippert's appeal against a lifetime sentence for homosexuality.

Until the case was aired, few Canadians realized that Canada had the most severe restrictions on homosexual practice in the world. But when the court, in a three-to-two decision, upheld a lower court ruling condemning Klippert to prison for life as "a dangerous sex offender," the editorial pages erupted. Dangerous? It was clear that Klippert was no more dangerous than a pet rabbit.

152

The *Toronto Daily Star* called the decision "a return to the middle ages." The *Winnipeg Free Press* said it was possible to deplore such homosexuality "without treating its practitioners as if they were monsters." In the mild words of the Calgary *Albertan*, "The aspect of a possible life sentence seems to us to be a little severe."

Klippert was now, to quote the Montreal *Gazette*, "the most publicized homosexual in Canadian history." That was the last thing he wanted. In fact, his desire to save his large, respectable, middle-class family from embarrassment had been his downfall.

When he was thirty-four, the Calgary police investigated a claim that Klippert had had homosexual relationships and charged him with gross indecency. Everett Klippert made no attempt to defend himself, co-operating blindly in the naïve hope of avoiding a scandal. He even let the police thumb through his little black book containing the names of consenting adults with whom he'd had sexual relations. At no time did he consult a lawyer. He pleaded guilty in court and was sentenced to four years in the penitentiary.

His second error, on being released in 1960, was to flee, not to a big city with a large homosexual population where he might easily have escaped notice, but to Pine Point, Northwest Territories. A northern community of four hundred people scarcely constituted a hiding place. The RCMP had his record, of course, and warned him to watch his behaviour. Klippert got a job as a mechanic's helper and tried to keep his head down.

On August 15, 1965, Corporal James Armstrong called in Klippert for questioning about an arson case. Klippert clearly had nothing to do with setting a fire, but Armstrong used the interview to quiz him further about his activities in Pine Point. According to Klippert, he was told that unless he pleaded guilty to homosexual activity he would be charged with arson. Once again, without legal advice, he told the police everything needed to convict him.

There was no shred of evidence that he had anything to do with the three cases of arson the police were looking into. Nor was there any evidence that they had investigated any of the four homosexual encounters to which he confessed. They had got all they needed by using the arson investigation as a cover to bully him into compliance. He was charged on four counts of gross indecency and sentenced— again with no lawyer present—to three years in prison.

Three months later, an RCMP officer visited Klippert in the Saskatchewan penitentiary and handed him an official notice that the Crown was proceeding with a hearing to have him declared "a dangerous sexual offender." Klippert was shattered. He went back to his cell and began leafing through his Bible for the Twenty-third Psalm. He stopped at the Twenty-second when he noticed another passage: "For he has not hid his face from him but has heard when he cried to Him."

The picture that emerges from the court record is that of a quiet, sensitive, unobtrusive man—a good worker, well liked, who did his best to stay out of trouble. He came from a large family. His eight brothers and one sister were all married with children. Everett, the oddball, lost his mother when he was six and had been brought up by his elder sister. Apart from that there was nothing in his early background to explain his sexual pattern. By the time he was fifteen he knew he was a homosexual. His aversion to the opposite sex was more than passive; the idea of relations with a woman revolted him. His sexual contacts were discreet and only with consenting adults; he preferred men in their thirties. His affairs were all short term; there were no lasting relationships.

In both his penitentiary terms he worked in the shoe shop. One inmate who worked with him described him as a good worker who minded his own business, a sensitive man who kept to himself. Dr. Donald Griffith McKerracher, a psychiatrist who testified for the Crown, said that Klippert "informed me he found life in the penitentiary extremely painful. . . because I think he is a sensitive man." Some of his fellow prisoners, he said, made life "considerably rough and difficult for him." The garage foreman for whom Klippert had worked in Pine Point testified that "he got along with everybody in the shop very well. There was no dissension at all." He described him as a man "who was never violent. . . very gentle. He would never pick a fight. . . he doesn't seem to be the type."

At this point Klippert found himself in a catch-22 position. The psychiatrist said he felt the penitentiary was "not a good place for the accused. It increases his anxieties and tension. It certainly increases his homosexual drives, urges, or stimulus." On the other hand, Dr. McKerracher said, Klippert would be well advised not to leave the penitentiary without counselling or follow up. "His pattern of behaviour is not well understood by the public, there is a tremendous ignorance about this. There is the question of shame. . . . He cannot go to the usual person for advice—to the minister or the physician—because they are not equipped to give this advice." He was unable to control his sex drives, the doctor said, and should only be released on parole "on a very strict arrangement where he was entitled to and would get follow-up advice."

The appeal court found, and the Supreme Court agreed, that Klippert was a dangerous sexual offender under the law and should be kept in preventive detention for life. The Criminal Code defined a dangerous sexual offender who might be detained for preventive reasons as "a person who by his conduct in any sexual matter has shown a failure to control his sexual impulses, and who is likely to cause injury, pain or other evil to any person through failure in the future to control his sexual impulses or who is likely to commit a further sexual offence." Two of the five judges dissented, including Chief Justice John R. Cartwright, who said he refused to believe that it was Parliament's intention to incarcerate harmless homosexuals for life. But the majority concluded that although he was unlikely to cause pain or damage, he was likely to commit further sexual offences and should, therefore, stay in prison.

The ramification was not lost on the public, which realized for the first time that any practising homosexual could now be liable for life imprisonment. As the *Globe and Mail* declared, "it is strange to the point of being unbelievable that conduct in Britain, which would not even bring a criminal charge, can, in Canada, send a man to prison for life."

The response was so strong that the law was changed. On December 2, 1967, in the House of Commons, Pierre Trudeau tabled amendments to the Criminal Code that would make it impossible for any court to sentence a man to indefinite imprisonment for indulging in homosexual practices with consenting adults. Trudeau told the press that the Klippert case had strongly influenced him. Though he had intended to make some changes in the law regarding preventive detention, "the Supreme Court decision enables us to go a step further." The police, of course, were opposed. The Calgary chief, Ken McIver, said the new law represented a decay in Canadian society. He described homosexuality as "a horrible, vicious and terrible thing. We do not need it in this country."

For Everett George Klippert, however, the wheels of justice ground with agonizing slowness, partly because of the impending Liberal leadership race. It was two years before Trudeau's amendments were incorporated in the Criminal Code. And for all that time, the man most responsible for the big changes continued to languish in durance vile.

FOUR: THE GENERATION GAP

1
Hippieville

2
The Children's Crusade

3
Banning the *Georgia Straight*

4
Mark Satin's choice

1

Hippieville

In the early months of 1967, a visitor to Toronto's Bathurst Heights Secondary School could scarcely be unaware of a fifteen-year-old boy sitting at a desk—not in the classroom but in the hall next to the principal's office. He had been there every school day since the previous September when the school opened, a virtual prisoner who could not attend class discussions, could not enter the classroom, could not involve himself in the give-and-take of normal student-teacher relations, could not even visit the school cafeteria for a meal or a Coke. There he sat, in splendid isolation, reading science fiction paperbacks and books on the philosophy of Santayana.

What terrible crime had this precocious Grade 11 student done to merit such punishment? It seems incredible, but Howard Szafer's offence was that he insisted on affecting a Beatles haircut! By later standards, his hair was not very long, reaching no lower than his ears. But that was much too long for those who made the rules and demanded conformity in everything, including matters of taste and fashion. Alone of all his classmates, Howard Szafer refused to toe the line.

A more perceptive teaching staff might have noticed that this was an unusually promising young man—a bit of an oddball, perhaps, but one whose own interests and enthusiasm suggested the kind of restless curiosity that an ideal educational system ought to encourage. The previous summer he had hitchhiked around Ontario alone, an adventure that contributed to his sense of independence. But the standard educational system of that time did not encourage independence. Here was a natural musician who had taught himself to play the saxophone and whose main interest was, of all things, biology. An enthusiastic amateur naturalist, he had collected and preserved scores of specimens of moths, butterflies, and other insects. In his basement at home he also bred delicate and rare tropical fish and made pocket money selling them.

None of this, apparently, mattered to the school authorities. Howard Szafer didn't fit in. He had defied the adult world by refusing to cut his hair in the style of the older generation, and so he must be punished.

When the first term opened, early in September 1966, the school tried to expel him. As soon as he arrived in class, one of the teachers collared him and took him before the vice-principal, who told him he could not enter sporting a Beatles haircut. But Szafer knew the law: everyone under the age of sixteen must attend school. He went home and called the truant officer who took him back to Bathurst Heights and explained the statute to the principal. Szafer was clean, well-groomed, and, after a cursory inspection, found to harbour no lice. Unable to throw him out, the school placed him in isolation in the hall. There he would stay until he conformed to authority's conception of how a young student should look.

Everybody expected Howard Szafer to cave in and let the adults reassert their control. His father, Samuel, a Polish immigrant who made men's pants in a suit factory, threatened to whip him. His mother, Betty tried to change his mind, first with tears, then with scorn. She poked fun at his "horrible, girlish hair-do" and appealed to his pride: "Howie, you're going to fail. You averaged 75 percent last year and this term you've dropped down to the fifties. Why can't you go along with convention like everybody else?" But Howard Szafer was not moved.

His principal, J. Wilkie Davey, tried another tack: "Would you expect us to tolerate boys coming to school wearing Nazi swastikas or reading 'North York Breast Stroking Team?'" Szafer thought these analogies ridiculous. There was nothing fascist about his hair style. The principal kept on: "Education must develop followship as well as leadership. . . the qualities insisted on by business and industry." Szafer found that even more ridiculous. He didn't intend to go into business or industry; he intended, in the phrase of the day, "to do his own thing"—to pursue his interests in music and biology. He didn't want to be either a leader or a follower. He was that *rara avis* in the regimented high schools of the time—a rigorous nonconformist.

The school board superintendent, Dave Tough, vowed that Howard Szafer would be isolated until he conformed to Regulation 98, Section 70, laid down by the Ontario department of education, which stipulated that a student must be "clean in his person and his habits." What had that to do with hair lengths? Girls wore their hair long and were thought of as neat and clean; why not boys?

Something unusual was happening in Canadian society, and Howard Szafer was a symbol of it. All across the country in 1967 the older generation was making war on the younger generation, and the youth of the country were in rebellion against their elders. Young men were taunted because of the length of their hair; young women were taunted because of the length of their skirts. It made no sense. Hair styles and skirt lengths have always been matters of transitory fashion. From Jesus Christ to John A. Macdonald, long hair has been in and out of style. Girls at private schools, from Norfolk House, Victoria, to Havergal College, Toronto, wore pleated skirts that were shorter than the minis of 1967, and no one raised a whisper because that was a uniform. The issue, of course, wasn't fashion; the issue was control. The new generation of baby boomers refused to be controlled, as Oscar Wilde did when he insisted on shaving his face in a bearded society.

Howard Szafer's treatment was not unique. Everywhere in Canada adults who should have known better were attempting to shape intelligent, independent teenagers into square pegs and plug them into round holes. At St. George's private school in Vancouver, a student who wore a Beatles haircut was told, "You may continue to wear it if you also wear short pants to show how juvenile you are." At St. James Collegiate in suburban Winnipeg, the principal, Lawrence Bernard Friesen, set his own equally arbitrary rules for hair styles: "Eyebrows exposed, ears uncovered, and hairline above the collar." In Montreal's Baron Byng College, Principal Marcel Fix refused to admit any boys until they snipped their locks. "Messy hair reflects a messy attitude toward life," he declared.

In Ottawa, the principal of Lisgar Collegiate, James Wright Beil, ordered four boys with long hair to stay home until they realized they were "oddballs" who would never get a decent job on graduation. When Wayne Marshall, a fifteen-year-old organist with the musical group Rockers, repeatedly turned up with a ponytail at St. Andrew's Junior High in North York, Principal Eric Runacres was affronted. Rebuking

160

Marshall for his "flagrant and insolent refusal to obey orders to get it cut himself," he wielded a pair of scissors, and while two teachers held the boy down nipped off the offending locks.

Some of the brightest and least compliant spirits among the younger generation were refusing to obey orders they thought silly. From time immemorial lazy parents had been responding successfully to the childish question, "Why?" with the equally childish answer, "Because I say so." No more. The world of 1967 was a world in which everything from sex to religion was being questioned, and the old answers weren't working. To say there was no love lost between the two generations is to put the situation too mildly. A portion of the adult world hated the younger generation (the word is not too strong)—hated and feared it. In turn, many young people despised their elders.

Their response was fuelled by a cynicism that leaked across the border from the United States, where establishment values were held in contempt by college students facing the Vietnam draft. The continuing colonial war, the human rights struggle by black Americans, and the pollution of the environment by multinational corporations who put profit ahead of human health—all these convinced the baby boomers that anybody over the age of thirty was, in Jerry Rubin's words, not to be trusted.

But why was *this* generation so different? After all, young people have always been wide-eyed idealists, bent on changing the world for the better and getting into trouble with their elders. Certainly television was one reason for the gap. Everybody under the age of twenty had been brought up with TV. The Vietnam War was fought in the living rooms of the nation, and Martin Luther King's struggle to achieve his dream was visible to all. Television is a marvellous medium for activists. All you have to do is make a few signs, march around a building, and you're on the air. By 1967, the protest march, along with the love-in, the be-in, and the happening, took its place with the Ban-the-Bomb and Stop-the-War campaigns that enlivened the nightly news.

The generation gap had another root. There had rarely been another time when life for middle-class youth had been so easy. Unemployment was at a new low. Jobs were easy to get. Canada was at peace. A young man or woman could pack a guitar and hitchhike across the country, crashing with friends or in the summer sleeping in the parks. It was this casual denial of the Calvinist work ethic that, I think, most infuriated the older generation.

Anybody over the age of forty was a creature of the Great Depression, wounded by it, scarred by it, shaped by it. In the hungry thirties, "job" was the deity that the people worshipped. If you had a job you were somebody, and you fought to hang onto it. If you were jobless, you were nobody. The country was divided into these two groups. Not to have a job was somehow shameful, even though a quarter of the population was jobless. Municipal "relief," as welfare was called, was treated as charity, and to accept charity was humiliating. (I remember my Sunday School teacher doing the "workfare" of that day, digging in a ditch; I averted my eyes because I was too ashamed to speak to him.) A man who had a job—any job—could hold his head up in society. The idea of suddenly quitting work and "taking off" would have been incomprehensible in the 1930s. In that miserable decade the only people who moved about the country were despised as hoboes and bums. Hence members of the older generation could not understand young people who quit work on a whim and spent their time strumming guitars in the so-called hippie havens.

By 1967 the word "hippie" was well entrenched in the argot of the day, being used as a pejorative by most adults. Anybody in jeans who wore long hair, played the guitar, and had no visible means of support was a hippie and, by definition, an alien. The fear of the outsider, which lies behind the virus of anti-Semitism and other forms of racism, was rampant in the centennial year. Like the Jews and gypsies of Europe, hippies were beyond the pale—foreigners in their own country who looked different, acted unconventionally, and hewed to a credo that was the antithesis of establishment values. Like Howard Szafer, they refused to conform and so waved a red flag in the faces of those who, in an earlier era, had been forced to toe the line for economic reasons.

The mean-spirited attitude towards hippies that reached a peak in 1967 was much like the feeling of an earlier generation about strangers who talked, dressed, and acted differently from what was then acceptable. These were the so-called Galician immigrants—Poles and Ukrainians, mainly—who poured into the prairies in the first decade of the century. The same adjectives—"filthy," "lazy," "unkempt"—were applied to these Slavic farmers. A former prime minister, Mackenzie Bowell, wrote that "the Galicians, they of the sheepskin coats, the filth and the vermin, do not make splendid material for the building of a great nation." Frank Oliver of Edmonton, a leading Liberal, called them a "servile, shiftless people. . . the scum of other lands." These familiar epithets, which have also been used against the blacks in America, seem to pop up in the language whenever the establishment feels itself threatened by the Stranger.

When Howard Szafer turned sixteen in March 1967, he walked out of school, never to return, and went straight to Yorkville village, a two-block enclave in central Toronto, where he met and worked with his own kind. Here he found a refuge from the hassles of the adult world and an environment where he felt safe, valued, and respected. If hippiedom could be said to have a capital in 1967, Yorkville was it. That spring thousands of young men and women like Szafer descended on the village and made it their own, to the discomfiture and rage of the adult world, especially some of the businessmen and women in the area.

Why Yorkville? Probably because here flourished a cluster of coffeehouses with names like the Riverboat and the Inn on the Parking Lot featuring poetry readings, folk songs, and a popular new beverage: espresso coffee. The original Yorkville hippies were genuine middle-class drop-outs who, having decided that the rat race was not for them, were obsessed with finding an alternative lifestyle. They were products of the new discontent, concerned with the issues of the day—pollution, Vietnam, race, the Bomb. When the university terms ended, a new group of "summer hippies" arrived. These were young people caught up in the glamour of Yorkville who thought it chic to affect poverty, wear ragged clothes, and go barefoot in the streets. Their costumes made them indistinguishable from the genuinely poor hippies—

163

children, really—who came from places as far off as Sydney, Nova Scotia, and Corner Brook, Newfoundland. These were largely working-class kids who had sometimes been subjected to sexual abuse and had fled their homes, were half starved, and slept in apartment lobbies and stairwells. They survived by begging, or selling drugs, or, in the case of some young girls, selling their bodies.

It was this strain of poverty that opened the eyes of June Callwood to the real Yorkville. A well-known journalist, she had thought of the village as a magical place until her nineteen-year-old son Barney changed her perception. He began bringing kids to their house, and Callwood remembers what a sad lot they were. "It was before fluorides and most of them had dental problems—teeth rotting. They were strung out on drugs and they were scared. They had left school. They had no skills. And the community was united against them. They would go into hospitals with injuries or drug overdoses and they'd be ignored. The hospitals wouldn't treat them. They'd sit out in emergency and they'd be overlooked. They'd been thrown out of school for having long hair and they certainly couldn't get welfare of any kind, so it was a desperately sick culture."

Yorkville seemed to swallow up missing children, especially young girls. Frantic parents roamed the village seeking their daughters. Berserk fathers smashed down rooming-house doors and started fights in coffeehouses. Mothers walked the streets in tears holding up photographs of a lost child, buttonholing passersby who might recognize her. More than eighty girls between the ages of thirteen and twenty were arrested in Yorkville that year on charges relating to marijuana—either having it or dealing it. Another 125 were arrested on vagrancy charges, the outdated and infamous law that made it a crime in Canada to be poor.

The story of Mandy Mandrill, a fourteen-year-old lost in the Yorkville jungle in the late summer of 1967, is typical. She lived a snug, sheltered life with her parents in a forty-thousand-dollar house in Etobicoke until one day she suddenly packed up and disappeared into the village. What had gone wrong? Why had she fled? The Mandrills had not suffered any sort of marital or financial crisis. Yet here was John

164

Mandrill (whose name I have changed), tramping the streets, slipping dollar bills to seedy youths who might have some knowledge of a little girl who had seemed so happy at home only the day before.

Based on the previous year's figures, the police estimated that more than a thousand runaways would land in Yorkville in 1967. The Reverend Tom Smith, the minister of St. Paul's–Avenue Road United Church just north of Yorkville Avenue, reckoned that at least three-quarters of these came from middle-class families without apparent problems. But the media had made them aware—more aware than their parents—that the world was fraught with danger. They were haunted by an urge to get their kicks before they were destroyed. Home had become a disenchanting place, their parents dull, unexciting people.

Mandy Mandrill's parents had had no hint of her inner restlessness during the summer at the cottage. Back home she spent her evenings playing Beatles records and painting "mod" pictures that her art teacher thought showed great promise. She sulked a little when her parents grounded her for the weekend for breaking the 9:30 curfew they'd imposed. They found she'd been frequenting a local park with boys two or three years older than she and suggested she bring her new friends home. To that she agreed. Then, after an apparently happy holiday weekend with her family and some friends, she went off to school one morning, came home when she knew nobody would be around, packed up, and left.

Her parents were stunned. John Mandrill, a popular Boy Scout leader who thought he understood teenagers, now spent his nights searching the village and learning things he never would have believed. "I'm willing now to try almost anything," he'd say. "I'd throw the house, the car, and the boat in the pot if it would mean getting out of this agony."

Mandy knew from the Yorkville grapevine that her father was searching for her. When he got too close, she and a fifteen-year-old runaway, Sue, would hitch a ride out of town. In their gym bags they carried the phone numbers of people who would help in the hippie colonies of Montreal, Rochester, and Buffalo.

165

In her hurry to leave home, Mandy had left behind a list of items she planned to take to Yorkville. It provided clues that led Mandrill to a Yorkville apartment frequented by prostitutes. He learned that the two runaways had recently spent a couple of nights there. At that point they were on their way to Buffalo, having hitched a ride with a holidaying couple and two small children. By a lucky chance, an off-duty policeman spotted the pair begging for the price of a cup of coffee outside a café. And so John Mandrill caught up with his daughter and brought her home.

He and his wife sat down with her and tried to find out why she had run off. All they could get from her were some vague references to "strictness." They asked her to work out a set of family rules that would be acceptable. She did that, but as her father said, "The incredible thing is that the new set is hardly different from the old. All we've really done is relax a few little things, like how often she tidies her room."

So the Mandrills were left with doubts. Were they to blame in some way they couldn't know? Did their daughter actually believe they couldn't be expected to understand? Instead of making some effort to meet them halfway, was she just waiting for an opportune time to go missing again? One thing they realized was that they would have to learn to be parents all over again, go to counselling classes, and question all the values and standards that had once made them "model" parents.

To help confused children like Mandy, an informal group of older hippies made it their business to see that no young person arriving in Yorkville went hungry. The Diggers took their name from a similar group in San Francisco's Haight-Ashbury district who modelled themselves on a seventeenth-century movement of revolutionaries who dug in the common land for agricultural purposes. The major activists were Brian "Blues" Chapman and Don Riggan, two artists, Hans Wetzel, a dishwasher, and, most important of all, David DePoe, son of a prominent CBC newscaster.

The Diggers' first home was the basement of St. Paul's United Church. It was there that Howard Szafer, whose hair was growing longer by the month (until it reached his nipples), found a cause. Every day he scrounged around for day-old vegetables, chopped them up, threw them into a huge pot, and made borscht. "I thought it was very cool. I liked being a public servant a lot. I saw people eating the food. It really did something for me."

Winter was approaching. June Callwood realized that the homeless children sleeping in Yorkville's streets were soon going to need some shelter. She found an old empty house on Spadina Avenue being held by the city in the path of the proposed Spadina Expressway—the one that was never built. She put up the first month's rent herself—six hundred dollars, a considerable sum in those days—and set out to raise more from the churches. As she put it, "I still had some concept that maybe religions would put their money where their mouths were about caring for lost sheep." She asked the Anglican Church for a month's rent; they gave her two hundred dollars. The Presbyterians gave one hundred. The Roman Catholics gave nothing. She went to see the controversial rabbi Abraham Feinberg at Holy Blossom Temple; he gave her two thousand dollars. Finally, Ray Hord of the Board of Evangelism and Social Service of the United Church responded with five thousand.

But the city did not want to rent the big house to Callwood. There were protests from taxpayers, and she was told that, as a woman, she would need a co-signer before any deal was cut. Callwood was then ghost-writing a book for Dr. John Rich, a well-known psychiatrist, who agreed to put his name on the lease. Finally, the house opened just after the end of the year.

Meanwhile, solid citizens were demanding that something be done about Yorkville. Sylvanus Apps, a former hockey great and now chairman of the Ontario Legislature's select committee on youth, called it "a festering sore in the middle of the city" that was corrupting young people and should be wiped out. He didn't say how that could be accomplished, but he did admit that his knowledge of the village was based on a half-hour walk through the area. George Ben, a Liberal MPP, demanded that the legislature "break up" Yorkville, whatever that meant. Herbert Orliffe, a city controller, wanted to place the Yorkville hippies in "work camps," an idea that had been tried during the Depression with spectacularly unsuccessful results.

David DePoe and his fellow Diggers realized that something had to be done to turn public opinion around. Why not a love-in at nearby Queen's Park? The idea, like so many others, was borrowed from the United States. The first love-in or "be-in" (the name was derived from the lunch counter sit-ins of the previous decade) was held in San Francisco's Golden Gate park on January 14, 1967. A new organization, the Yorkville Cultural Activities Committee, was organized with Hans Wetzel of the Diggers as president. He applied for a permit to hold the love-in on Victoria Day, May 22, and after considerable bureaucratic stalling he got it.

What followed baffled the police and intrigued the public. Harry Boyle, then supervisor of features for CBC Radio, turned up on the fringes of the crowd of five thousand and was accosted by a girl in a miniskirt with flowers stencilled on her cheeks who danced by and said, "Do you love me? I love you. Here's a flower for you to carry." Boyle watched her approach a man in country tweeds holding a nervous show dog on a leash. "Do you love me?" she asked, blowing him a kiss. His face reddened; his moustache quivered. "I say," he asked a policeman, "what's all the fuss about?" He had been used to walking his dog in the park. Now here were young girls distributing flowers and talking about love, young men and women in strange attire chanting Buddhist prayers, burning incense and blowing soap bubbles, and two rock bands enlivening the proceedings. One twenty-one-year-old who called himself Psychedelic Peter had bells on his trousers; a young girl named Beverley David had painted half her face with a silver-blue eye makeup; the leader of the Evolutionary Church of Man wore a slip cover turned into a robe. Leonard Cohen turned up and sang "Suzanne" for the crowd, and Buffy Sainte-Marie, the folk-singer, stopped by on her way to Saskatchewan.

The demonstration itself was peaceful, naïve, and winning. The young people formed a human chain and invited older ones to join them. The hippies were on their best behaviour, and the police almost self-consciously tried to avoid trouble. It wasn't as spontaneous as love-ins were supposed to be, but it wasn't overorganized either. As David DePoe said: "What kind of overorganization can you have with an expenditure of twenty-one dollars? For twenty-one dollars we managed to get these five or six thousand people in Toronto talking to each other and making their own entertainment. Is it any wonder we're pleased with it?"

As the summer moved on, Yorkville became a kind of circus. Everybody in town, it seemed, wanted to come down and look at the hippies, as if they were strange creatures in a zoo. The parade of cars crawling along Yorkville Avenue, their passengers hoping to get a glimpse of drug-mad youth, slowed almost to a stop. Soon the two-block, one-way street became a gigantic traffic tangle.

To the Diggers, the answer was simple: close the street and turn it into a mall. DePoe agreed to propose this idea to Controller Allan Lamport, who had walked through Yorkville in early August and decided it was a haven for criminals and psychotics. Although one newspaper, the *Toronto Daily Star*, supported the idea of closing the street to traffic, the rest of the establishment was against it. The city's planning commissioner, Matthew Lawson, declared that such a move could ruin the entire area. It was a vital lifeline to "one of the city's most thriving and colourful business districts." A traffic ban would be ruinous to boutiques, coffee shops, restaurants, and other businesses that required daily deliveries. The police also opposed the idea because they felt the movement of traffic helped control the crowd. "The motoring public should have every right to sightsee," the deputy chief remarked.

Controller Lamport himself initiated a "talk-in" at the city hall in August. What followed was a demonstration of the unbridgeable gap between the generations. Lamport, a former mayor, had enjoyed a reputation as a trail breaker who had fought the established churches in Toronto the Good and introduced Sunday sports and Sunday movies to an uptight city. He invited David DePoe and the Diggers to city hall because he genuinely wanted to understand them. But he could not communicate with them or they with him. To Lamport, at sixty-five, the hippie way of life was so far removed from his own ethic as to be incomprehensible. "There is no way, there must be no way that you can survive in society without working," he told the hippies. But his definition of work bore no relation to theirs.

What followed was high farce. When I referred to it in a book published at that time, I set it up in dialogue form, using the actual words of the participants and editing it only slightly.

LAMPORT: What do you want—recreational facilities, educational facilities? What are your aims and objectives? [*Groans from the hippies.*]

BLUES CHAPMAN: We don't need facilities. I don't think anyone thinks it's a crime to sit there [in Yorkville] and talk to someone.

LAMPORT: But what is it that makes you not want to be a productive member of society?

CHAPMAN: That's the very attitude I resent.

LAMPORT [*A bit testily*]: Now I'm prepared to accept your attitude no matter how invalid it may be, and I'll ask you to accept mine no matter how invalid it may be.

CHAPMAN: I don't think that's anything you have control over. We're fed up with a social system that puts the stress on production and money and places individuals in pigeon-holes, when the most important things are people's dignity and pride.

LAMPORT: A number of them haven't been washed for weeks. Now they're not seeking dignity, are they?

CHAPMAN: What's cleanliness got to do with dignity?

CONTROLLER FRED BEAVIS:What's your objective in life? Where are you going?

CHAPMAN: My object is to engage in something that would effect some sort of change. . . to try and find a way that would give us a more effective way of life.

BEAVIS: But what *is* a hippie way of life?

CHAPMAN: Dropping out of society for a way of life that means more to them.

170

ALDERMAN DAVID ROTENBERG: If you want to be allowed to live your sort of life your way then you have to adjust and let older people, your neighbours, live the way they want to. The city has been receiving complaints about noisy parties, motorcycles, and couples going into people's backyards and doing what comes naturally [*he pauses*]. . . *and on private property.*

CHAPMAN: Is it all right on public property?

DAVID DEPOE: Most of that comes from outsiders—tourists who come down to the village to look at us.

LAMPORT: But why don't these people want to work? Because the greatest happiness in life is derived from working! [*More groans from the hippies.*]

LAMPORT: I don't say it's a crime not to work if you can't work. [*Laughter from the hippies.*]

[*Pleading*]: Will you please tell us what we can do?

VOICE FROM THE REAR: Practise leaving us alone!

LAMPORT: That's nice but society doesn't work that way.

SAME VOICE: Well, what do *you* want for Yorkville?

LAMPORT: I'd like Yorkville to grow up as a shopping centre. . . [*hoots and guffaws from the hippies*] and as a place for artists to display their work and coffeehouses to operate. [*Defensively*] It's to be desired. It gets a lot of tourists.

The discussion, obviously, got nowhere. The city council turned down the suggestion of closing Yorkville Avenue. The confrontation with Lamport so infuriated David DePoe and the others that they decided to stage a sit-in on the street on Saturday, August 20. At three o'clock that morning, three hundred Yorkville residents walked out into the middle of the street and sat down, blocking all traffic. Thirty police arrived and arrested fifty people, including a seventeen-year-old girl, a sixty-seven-year-old man, Robert "Pops" Gilgou (who called himself the "oldest living hippie"), and DePoe himself.

He didn't expect to be arrested. He was not sitting down but walking along the street, intending to organize a demonstration in front of

171

No. 52 police station, when he was recognized. He was thrown in the back of a police cruiser and charged with creating a disturbance and obstructing traffic. He was shocked. He had done his best to stay out of trouble, and now he was making headlines. He was, for one thing, the son of the best-known broadcaster in Canada—the CBC's Norman DePoe. But there was something more serious. He was a paid worker for the Company of Young Canadians, a highly controversial group under heavy criticism from politicians and press. And here was the company's most conspicuous member behind bars for organizing a violent demonstration against constituted authority—and doing it on the taxpayers' money!

2

The Children's Crusade The Company of Young Canadians!

What promise lay in that phrase when it was first mentioned in the Speech from the Throne back in April 1965! What hope it engendered! The government was going to come to grips with the generation gap by giving the youth of the nation the opportunity to perform community service on a voluntary basis. Nothing like it had ever been tried before. It was, to quote one of its analysts, "the most daring and imaginative piece of social legislation in North American history." Its inspiration had been John Kennedy's Peace Corps, but the Peace Corps was tightly controlled by the American government. The Canadian company, on the other hand, would be controlled by the young volunteers who were expected to flock to its banners. They would elect ten of the fifteen-member governing council, and they would be at arm's length from the government—enthusiastic members of a newly minted Crown corporation that reported to Parliament through a single cabinet minister, Marc Lalonde.

Nobody realized it at the time, but the government, hungry for the youth vote, was actually subsidizing revolution without knowing it—and without really pausing to ponder its implications. Who else but the young radicals and idealists did it expect would volunteer? The company's objectives were "to support, encourage, or develop programs for social, economic, and community development in Canada and abroad through voluntary service." That vaguest of manifestos was an open invitation to the activists on the cutting edge of the youth revolution to try to change the face of Canada. And the government had given them carte blanche to do it. Ian Hamilton, who "suffered and bled with the Company for more than two years," has called his personal narrative *The Children's Crusade*. The CYC "leaves scars on people," he wrote. Its mandate was so broad it was virtually meaningless. "It could sponsor a revolution or help old ladies across the street."

When the company was created by Act of Parliament in July 1966, all three parties enthusiastically backed it. They had seen the CYC as a kind of support group, helping underprivileged children in summer camps, candy-striping in hospitals, teaching personal hygiene on Indian reserves. But the CYC as it developed was far more radical; its purpose could be defined by that hackneyed revolutionary phrase "Power to the people." It was going to teach the disadvantaged how to organize and take power. Here could be discerned the germs of a new political movement.

It is no wonder, then, that by 1967 the Company of Young Canadians was in deep trouble. The story of Barbara Hall, who was considered one of the most stable in the odd and often weird mélange of volunteers attracted to the CYC, is instructive. By the summer of the centennial year she realized that she had reached the end of her tether. There she was, sitting in her van on a wet Halifax street, tears pouring down her cheeks, a slender twenty-one-year-old with a freckled face and jet black, shoulder-length hair. She had wanted to change the world so badly, but the world—the real world—was changing her. And she was more than three thousand miles from home.

She came from Victoria, B.C., and here in Nova Scotia she felt completely isolated, shut off from the world she knew, unclear about what she should be doing or what she was able to do. The previous summer she had been assigned by the CYC to work with a black community at

173

a place called Three Mile Plain, but apart from six bizarre weeks of sensitivity courses and instruction in community organizing tactics—an experience that sent more than one volunteer to a psychiatric hospital—she had no practical training whatsoever. In the spring of 1966 she had graduated from the University of Victoria, which, as she said later, "was not a hotbed of activism." Once, when she wore slacks to a Saturday class, her professor admonished her: "Miss Hall, young ladies in my class do not wear trousers." She was concerned about the usual issues of the time—American issues, mainly—civil rights, poverty, racism. When she heard about the Company of Young Canadians she was excited and decided that on graduation she would apply.

In response to her application, Barbara Hall received a lengthy questionnaire—twenty-five questions, no less, with a full page provided for each answer. Her mother, a social worker, and her father, a naval officer, helped her with the document. At one point her father suggested she get commendations from some of his political friends, but Hall told him, quite correctly, "I don't think that's what they want."

She was accepted immediately as one of the fifty-six volunteers who would take six weeks of sensitivity training at a resort called Crystal Cliffs near Antigonish, N.S. "The Company is yours," an executive staff member told them at the opening session, "you will run it." That was a strange welcome for a group of young people who were, by and large, cynical about any kind of structure. It was an adult concept, an establishment concept. The dichotomy would plague the company for all of its brief existence. These were not hardened and experienced organizers of the Saul Alinsky variety—though the sacred name of Alinsky, the hugely successful American activist, was invoked time and time again. These were high school and college kids, for God's sake, wet behind the ears, with no understanding of how to organize anything and philosophically opposed to any kind of structured organization.

Margaret Daly, who also chronicled the company's up and downs at the time, called the Antigonish experience "a disaster." It was, she said, "a hastily arranged, unco-ordinated, ill-conceived and utterly

174

bizarre training session that was to prove useless for most [and] mentally destructive for a few." Seven volunteers quit the course and sixteen needed psychiatric treatment by the time it ended. (The CYC picked up the doctors' bills.) Barbara Hall, known as one of the "strong, sensible" volunteers, told Daly the course was a complete waste of time that still gave her the shudders when she thought about it.

Thirty years later, when she was mayor of Toronto, Hall recalled the experience. "Virtually everybody had different ideas of what this organization was about. There were some very political people with very set agendas. There were a lot of very naïve, idealistic people. There were some very disturbed people. We were supposed to have sensitivity training, but nobody knew what that was. Some people said, 'It's just like LSD,' but none of us knew what LSD was like, really."

One of the people Hall encountered was "a very spacey, vague woman." Nobody could figure out why she was there or how she'd been let in. Apparently she'd answered one of the questions, "What do you like to do in your spare time?" with a single sentence on the long answer page: "I like to watch leaves drop in the fall." She'd been admitted at once, Hall remembered, because somebody had said, "Oh, this is a wonderful, whimsical person! We'll have her come."

Another was "a very angry, frustrated man from Toronto who was part of a gang, and who sort of lived in poverty, who would bang on the table and scream about his life, living in the gutter. A very violent, inarticulate man."

Hall had originally planned to work for the CYC in Toronto, but towards the end of her session at Antigonish she changed her mind for reasons that can only be described as altruistic. By the summer of 1966 the company had not yet delivered any results. It was still in the planning stage. Nothing was happening. Questions were being asked in Parliament. There was a sense of real political pressure to do something. A young reporter from the *Globe and Mail*, Michael Valpy, had been assigned to write an article on the CYC, and Hall, who was convinced the paper was planning a hatchet job, remembers sitting with him for hours in an orchard, pleading, "Michael, if you write an exposé, the social revolution won't happen in Canada." Indeed, Valpy himself was seduced by the concept. He quit the *Globe* and spent six months as the company's public relations director. Hall knew that the CYC had promised to initiate programs in the Maritime provinces and was worried that if those promises weren't kept it would lose national support. And so she agreed to work as a volunteer at Three Mile Plain with a monthly stipend of eighty-five dollars.

Until very recently she had never known anybody who wasn't white. At Antigonish she met several blacks including Rocky Jones of SUPA, the Student Union for Peace Action, a Canadian branch of an American group concerned about the Vietnam War. Jones, one of the best-known activists in the Maritimes, offered to drive her to Windsor, the town nearest to Three Mile Plain, on his way to Halifax. They found a small hotel; she went in and registered; he offered to help her with her bags. *Consternation!* A white girl with a black man! The hotel was about to throw her out until Jones explained he wasn't staying. Off he went, leaving her alone and terrified.

She had no idea what she was supposed to do. That night, almost sick with worry, she got very little sleep. She thought about her home in Victoria but didn't call her parents; long distance was a little-used and expensive luxury in those days. The next morning she boarded a bus for the four-mile trip to Three Mile Plain. She knew she was supposed to organize the community in some way but hadn't a clue as to how to do it.

The bus dropped her off at a gas station. She saw some black youngsters playing ball in an adjoining field and walked over to chat with them. She took the bus back to Windsor for lunch, returned for the afternoon, watched the game, and went back to Windsor when it was over. The next day when she returned, a remarkable thing happened. One of the boys walked up to her and said, "My mom says do you want to come to lunch?" And that was how she met Maddie Simpson, a black cleaning woman.

"Are you going to Association on the weekend?" Maddie asked her over lunch.

"I'm not sure," she replied hesitantly. "Are you going?"

Maddie Simpson said she was and so was her eldest daughter Caroline, and several others. Hall said she'd go too. "Well," she was told, "Deacon Upshaw's driving and there's room for you in the car."

She now learned what "Association" was—a black Baptist annual get-together, held in Truro. She turned up in the same tasteful little dress she'd worn to parties at Royal Roads, the naval training centre in Victoria. "Don't you have a hat?" Maddie asked her. "You got to have a hat." She found one, slapped it on Barbara's head, and off they went. Thus did Barbara Hall get a toehold in the community.

She was still an outsider. The Simpson family was supportive and generous, but the rest of the community regarded her with suspicion. Everything she did or tried to do came under careful scrutiny.

She had no real plan of action. She'd been taught at Antigonish that the first thing one did was to go out and meet people, talk to them, find out their concerns, and organize around those issues. That was a tall order for an inexperienced girl who hadn't yet reached voting age.

She did her best. The company paid its volunteers a small allowance to cover rent, but there was nothing to rent in Three Mile Plain. She decided to buy an old trailer and live in that but found the company rules didn't cover purchases. She borrowed three hundred dollars from her mother and set up the trailer in a field. The young people, she realized, had nothing to do except play baseball. The trailer became a rallying point as she developed a relationship with the teenagers and the younger children. Not far away was a vacant schoolhouse; she co-opted it as a headquarters where she could work with some of the parents to organize programs after school and on weekends. She even persuaded some students from Acadia University to come down and do some tutoring.

The social workers from the Hants County Family and Children's Services knew little about the CYC. To them, Hall was an intruder and a potentially dangerous one. Their main fear was that she would start some kind of demonstration. At the same time, the company's Ottawa headquarters provided no support and when it did try to help, in its innocence, made things worse. There was, for instance, the matter of transportation. Somebody at headquarters had heard that the RCMP was selling off some of the horses used in the famous Musical Ride. Why not buy one of these horses for Hall? The prevailing view at Ottawa, apparently, was that everybody in rural areas rode about on horseback, but the only people in rural Nova Scotia who actually did were the students at Edgehill, the private school in Windsor. What Hall wanted was a cheap, used Volkswagen that wouldn't look ostentatious. Because the company ruled that cars could not be bought, only leased, she ended up with a brand-new and very flashy Chevrolet van that contributed to the local belief—also held by the Mounties—that she was a prostitute. Otherwise why would she live in a trailer and invite black boys to visit her? Where did she get the money for the car? What were all those trips to Halifax about?

The trips to Halifax were to confer with the staff directors of the regional office, who never came out to Three Mile Plain. One eventually did turn up before he quit the company. Hall drove him around the area to show the kind of community she was working with. They were just starting to talk about the problems she faced when he looked at his watch and exclaimed, "Oh, my God! It's a quarter past five. It'll take an hour and a half to drive to Halifax, and I never work after six." That was the only trip he ever made to the community. His successor made none. Sometimes senior staff came from Ottawa, but "they wanted to talk about issues, as opposed to what was going on there."

Hall was shocked by the housing conditions she encountered at Three Mile Plain. There wasn't a house in the community with indoor plumbing except for the one belonging to the white gas-station owner. Maddie Simpson bathed her eight children with water from a pail. When she established her trailer in the park, Hall realized she was going to need an outhouse but had no idea how to solve that problem. Where do you get an outhouse, especially if you have no money? She had to search about, find some men, and figure how to get them to help her. It was a painful, frustrating process, but in the end she solved the problem and got the job done. It was, for her, an important learning experience. In later life these acquired skills were of enormous value.

She did not feel safe in her trailer. One night a bunch of young white

178

men, clearly drunk, arrived in their pickups, circled her trailer, and remained for some time shining their lights on it. The systemic racial prejudice frightened her. She had made friends with a VON nurse in Windsor, but when she visited her with a group of young blacks, the nurse was evicted from her home.

So there she was, in the centennial summer, about the same time that another CYC worker, David DePoe, was organizing the Yorkville hippies, sitting in her car in Halifax in the pouring rain, sobbing her heart out. Nothing had worked, really, except for the tutoring sessions at the school, and those had petered out. She had tried to do something about housing, something about agricultural prospects, but it had all fallen through. I'm coming apart, she told herself.

She found a phone booth, looked through the Yellow Pages for a psychiatrist, called the first number on the list, and told the woman who answered that she needed to talk to somebody. "I'm with the CYC and I'm on a project by myself and I feel totally alone," she said. By sheer good luck the woman had a summer home near Crystal Cliffs and was a good friend of the psychiatrist who had been called in to the training sessions. She steered Hall to a doctor who agreed to see her that very day. She had several daily sessions with him and followed his advice to the letter. "You need to go home," he advised. "You need to go some place where you feel safe."

Looking back, she did not regret the experience. In fact, after she recovered, she returned to Toronto as a street worker for the Central Neighbourhood House. Nor was her work at Three Mile Plain entirely fruitless. When the Nova Scotia government introduced its first public housing program shortly after she left, the people of Three Mile Plain, led by the indefatigable Maddie Simpson, were among the first to avail themselves of it. Barbara Hall had taught them how to organize.

Three decades later, in the mayor's office in Toronto, she looked back on those days as a painful but perhaps necessary learning process. "It taught me an incredible amount. The kind of skills I learned, the kind of things I had to figure out were, on a much larger scale, the kind of things that got me here."

Proper organization of communities of the dispossessed using Saul Alinsky tactics required tough, experienced militants who were prepared to stand up to the establishment. Some volunteers—David DePoe was one—had the stamina to attempt this. Others, such as Harvey Stevens, crumbled under pressure.

Stevens, a twenty-one-year-old, joined the CYC because, he said, "It was my obligation as a Christian." More than that, he said, he was there "because the whole thing smacks of freedom. Here, I think, I've encountered the truth of Christianity—the concern that people have for one another. . . . This community is the most moral I've ever lived in." That was all very well, but the mild-mannered Stevens wasn't up to it, nor was his fellow CYC worker, Doreen Jarvis. They had been assigned to do inner-city work in Winnipeg's Logan Avenue district, a rundown neighbourhood of impoverished Métis. One of the great buzz phrases of the period was "urban renewal," a euphemism obscuring the fact that the original residents were about to be thrown out of their homes. And Logan Avenue was slated to be "renewed."

Stevens wasn't cut out for the kind of door-knocking required to organize a community. He made a halfhearted attempt, then turned his apartment into a drop-in centre for teenaged boys. Jarvis started out knocking on doors, too, but it terrified her, and she vowed never to do it again. "My idea of community development," she said, vaguely, "is just to be a friend of the people."

"The Company wants supermen—ya, ya," Stevens wrote in the CYC's internal magazine in January 1967. "Where are the natural training grounds in our society for producing this tough, mature, radical person? Personally, I can't work in a vacuum. I need to relate what I'm doing to other efforts." That sounded very much like a call for a more structured program—something the early volunteers had resisted.

Stevens put his finger on another problem the company faced. "This 'hip, radical' bit alienates the power structure of the country," he wrote. "And it is naïve to think that successful change is going to come about by organizing the masses. . . . Ultimately it is the power élite who make the policy decisions, which create the social climate of the country. . . ."

180

That was a long way from the anti-establishment attitudes that had inspired the CYC. Stevens quit in 1967 to go back to graduate school. Doreen Jarvis quit, too, to become a teacher.

Unlike Stevens, David DePoe had no feeling for the CYC when he joined. To him, the company was there merely to further his aims in Yorkville. Bored by high school, he did badly until he reached Grade 13 and realized that he had to use the system to get to university and achieve what he wanted to do. As he confessed later, "I sat down and memorized and was a good boy and got honours and got the hell out." He hoped to find something challenging at the University of Toronto's University College. He didn't. "Everybody was marking time and nobody was interested in teaching *me* about anything. The professors were concerned with maintaining an orderly system and the students were concerned with figuring out that system and then going *around* it." He got through on bluff, standing 480th in a class of 500. To his father's dismay and irritation, he cut classes, started hanging out in Yorkville, bought the mandatory guitar, and began to listen to the words of the songs he was singing.

For the first time, David DePoe had become involved in something outside himself. He didn't bother to write his university exams, again exasperating his father. He took a job on Bay Street as an assistant to the manager of a trust company—a cynical act that gave him entrée to "the System" (or so he told himself) to look at it, to explain it, to understand it, to be able to change it. He had entered the job with a feeling of horror—"all those people working there, it was destroying human potential." Just before they fired him, he quit. For the next six months he did nothing but sit around and read books. Then, in May 1966, he got a job driving a cab, "the greatest job I ever had," meeting hundreds of kinds of people and finding out what they thought.

After the CYC was formed he volunteered for Yorkville because he thought "nobody had been paying any attention to these people" and he thought he had the background to do something. There he became a familiar figure, long-haired and short-bearded, in a black gaucho hat that made him easily identifiable to the press and to the police and instantly recognizable on television. By 1967, he had unwittingly become the symbol of the CYC.

He joined the Student Union for Peace Action. Frustrated by their inability to get their ideas across to the general public at a meeting in Waterloo, 150 SUPA delegates decided to demonstrate as a sure way of grabbing media attention. They would gather in front of the U.S. Consulate on University Avenue in Toronto carrying the usual placards protesting the Vietnam War. DePoe came along with some other CYC members including Lynn Curtis, another striking figure with his long, unruly hair, flowing beard, and huge overcoat, several sizes too large. DePoe even brought his guitar and was immediately labelled as the "leader" of the demonstration, which, because of the anarchical style of the hippie movement, had no real leader at all.

The demonstration lasted three-quarters of an hour (plenty of time for the press to arrive) and gave the CYC an instant and unwanted image. Within twenty-four hours every front page, every radio program, every TV clip made it clear that the taxpayers were footing the bill for an anti-American demonstration in Toronto. It is debatable whether the affair did much to raise SUPA's image, but thousands who had never heard of the Company of Young Canadians were now familiar with the black-hatted, guitar-playing DePoe and his friend Curtis.

"The actions of CYC pair: disgrace," one headline read. "Kooky carryings-on crumbling Company of Young Canadians," read another. It was useless for DePoe to insist that his presence at the consulate had nothing to do with the company. That wasn't the way the media, the politicians, or the public saw it. Nor did the new hippie image help the work that other members of the CYC were trying to do across the country.

On January 7, the CYC's council called an emergency meeting to deal with the problem. When they learned that the worried prime minister planned to send a representative to the meeting, Alan Clarke, the executive director, reacted angrily. He said that he would resign on principle if the company's independence was threatened by politicians, and he insisted that Pearson say so publicly.

Marc Lalonde, who had cabinet responsibility for the CYC, moved

182

in to paper over the crisis before it became public. That in itself was ironic, for Lalonde was generally thought of as the Enemy—a political hatchet man. As Michael Valpy remembered, "he was literally hated. Any time he came to our office, we all hid and refused to speak to him." But Lalonde was moving to save the CYC. He helped the Prime Minister draft a statement to be read in the House announcing that the demonstration had nothing to do with the company and that the two high-profile members who took part in the picketing had acted privately and as "citizens of a free country." The company, the statement made clear, acted with a maximum of independence and "I don't think the government should interfere with the details of their operations."

The incident, however, had alienated the politicians and disturbed the press. DePoe's stipend was modest, but it was paid by taxpayers. The company's image had suffered badly, and the media were now alerted to the news value of long-haired "hippies" on a government payroll. DePoe himself symbolized not only the CYC but also the hippie community in Toronto. In the press, he was "the Mayor of Yorkville."

Then came the so-called Hippie Revolt of August 20, and DePoe found himself in jail along with some fifty other Yorkville sit-downers. It had been an ugly confrontation as police waded in to disperse the three hundred or so young people sprawled across the street. They used nightsticks to strike down the village types and then kicked the fallen, who, in the time-tested technique of peaceful protest, had gone limp and had to be physically dragged away. At least one man was knocked unconscious, one young girl was hit in the face, and a dozen walk-in patients were treated in hospital, two with broken arms.

DePoe, who had tried to calm the crowd when it was threatening to attack the police, was charged with two counts of creating a disturbance and released on bail of one hundred dollars the following day. After their court appearance on August 21, the entire group sang folk songs, then dropped to their knees to recite the Twenty-third Psalm.

DePoe continued to make headlines. The *Toronto Daily Star* reported that "David DePoe, bearded 23-year-old leader of the Yorkville hippies, threatened another sit-down tonight on Yorkville Ave. if the road between Bellair St. and Avenue Rd. is not closed today."

The news stories again tied DePoe to the CYC, and Alan Clarke again came to his defence. DePoe's job, he explained, was to "get involved with young people in Yorkville and try to help them resolve their problems."

That night the sidewalks were jammed with people from curb to doorsteps as a line of cars turned off Bay Street and inched along Yorkville Avenue. Seven film camera crews and dozens of news photographers turned up. Reporters were trapped in the crush as police vainly struggled to keep the street clear. Eight more people were arrested.

This latest demonstration did one thing for David DePoe. It brought about a reconciliation with his father. Norman DePoe had become enraged at the police action the night before on August 20. For two years, father and son had engaged in an ongoing and often vituperative debate about David's attitude. Now, suddenly, Norman DePoe decided to get himself arrested. There he was in the crowd with a phalanx of police standing by, some on horseback, others near paddy wagons.

"Cossacks!" DePoe shouted. "Cossacks! Arrest me! Arrest me!" His son watched as a staff sergeant pointed to a young constable and ordered: "Follow that man and make sure nobody arrests him." The last thing the police wanted was to have their image flaunted on the ten o'clock news tossing the country's favourite newscaster into a paddy wagon. Canada's favourite newscaster was infuriated by this special treatment.

Nineteen sixty-seven was the year in which the CYC began to crumble. Five programs were abandoned, another ten were doomed, forty-five volunteers quit. Many of the others were in a state of shock. At Antigonish they'd been told that if they loved and trusted the people they were sent to help, everything would work out. Instead, they found themselves attempting to pull off miracles in a hostile environment. Long hair was only just accepted in the big cities; in the smaller communities it was totally unacceptable. Yet the CYC's young volunteers refused to cut their hair or shave their beards.

Equally serious was the rift developing between the volunteers in the field, existing on pittances, and the salaried staff at Ottawa spending big money, hiring consultants and researchers, and flying about the country on CYC credit cards. Michael Valpy was frustrated by the endless discussions—all talk and no action—in the Ottawa headquarters where nobody seemed to know quite what the others were doing. He would never forget one discussion when the group leader simply lay down on the floor, curled up in a fetal position, and refused to speak. In the end Valpy grew tired of writing press releases that he did not believe and went back to his old job on the *Globe and Mail*.

Despite its flaws, the company chalked up the occasional success. In the backwoods Alberta community of Faust, two volunteers, Al Burger and Jeremy Ashton, had been trying since the previous fall to improve relations between the whites, who controlled the economy, and the larger community of Métis, who were mainly on welfare. When, in February, a group of forty-five white residents met to discuss running Burger and Ashton out of town, the Métis rallied to support the pair because no one else had ever taken the trouble to address their needs. In April the white community did succeed in driving them out of town; but the success of the project was ensured when the Métis circulated a petition asking them to come back, and they did.

Canada was undergoing a transformation. People at the grass roots were beginning to learn that you *can* fight city hall. The CYC was part of that new attitude. In many ways, the company was even ahead of its time, practising participatory democracy before that became a buzz phrase. It can now be seen as one of the catalysts in the struggle for human rights, native rights, women's rights, and grass-roots politics— all new concepts in 1967. The rise of the various citizens' groups that enlivened the post-centennial years grew directly out of the CYC experience. In their fumbling fashion, the crusading children prepared the road for some of the advances that were to follow. One CYC volunteer, for instance, was George Erasmus, the future Indian leader.

It was also no accident that the young separatists in the province of Quebec found a home in the Company of Young Canadians. How could it have been otherwise? The CYC was using government money to preach revolution elsewhere in Canada. Did the government expect that the youth of Quebec would ignore what was going on around them? The company attracted activists everywhere, and naturally it attracted them in French Canada. Some of the liveliest of these were Quebec nationalists.

Martin Beliveau, the company's regional director in Quebec, moved to separate the Quebec wing from the rest of the company. He even wanted to change its name to the Company of Young Québécois. It would be, he said, "a social action movement with a clearly defined goal: democratic participation," and in his manifesto there was more than a whiff of Marxism. "We constitute an independent organization of Quebec volunteers," Beliveau said early in 1968, "independent of the federal government, independent of the provincial government." That was too much; Beliveau was forced to resign. In March 1970, the government moved in. The company would no longer be controlled by volunteers at arm's length from Ottawa. It would, instead, be controlled by an appointed council of nine, picked by the government and responsible to the government. Ottawa would even pick its executive director. In short, the CYC would become just another government bureaucracy. For all practical purposes, the original company was dead.

3

Banning the Georgia Straight The idea of launching a counter-culture paper in Vancouver was first floated in late January 1967 at a party after a reading by Leonard Cohen at the University of British Columbia's poetry festival. Why not, somebody suggested, start a political/cultural journal to offset the bias of the mainstream media?

Nobody can remember who had the idea first; it seems to have developed out of a casual group discussion. Milton Acorn, a poet whose work became increasingly well-known, Pierre Coupé, an artist and writer, and another poet, Dan McLeod, who would eventually become publisher and editor of the proposed paper, were among those present.

186

It was christened, appropriately, over a beer at the Cecil Hotel. The name was a joke based on the weather reports that were always issuing gale warnings for the Strait of Georgia. It would be subtitled *The Vancouver Free Press* and based loosely on the *Los Angeles Free Press*, the best-known of the underground papers south of the border. The time was right for a new kind of publication in Vancouver. The long-haired youths clustered along Fourth Avenue West, a counterpart of Toronto's Yorkville, were being hassled by police and attacked by the mainstream press. The *Georgia Straight* would be their advocate.

Dan McLeod didn't look like a flaming radical. Nor could any stranger, on first encounter, have imagined he was the moving spirit behind a newspaper that much of the adult world considered politically subversive, dangerously radical, and scandalously pornographic. Jack Webster, the *Sun*'s top reporter, remembers him as "shabby, short, sickly-looking, and beaten down." The *Straight* was invariably called a hippie paper, but he never thought of himself as a hippie. He preferred an earlier term, "beatnik," for its literary associations with Kerouac and Ginsberg. A shy, quiet, even hesitant young poet, he had taken honours mathematics at UBC. But like so many of his contemporaries, he was disturbed by the intrusion of the U.S. military into Canadian life. He had worked briefly in oceanography while a summer student only to discover that he was actually doing submarine research for the department of national defence, apparently on a subcontract from the Pentagon. That soured him. He had expected to enter the academic world but now felt that would be unconscionable—a form of complicity with those who were supporting the Vietnam War.

At university he had written poetry for *Tish*, a literary magazine, which he eventually edited. On a trip east he'd been exposed to the alternative press in Ottawa and Detroit, and the energy he found there excited and also frustrated him. *Tish* wasn't enough. He wanted something bigger and more influential. Once the *Straight* was launched he found himself shouldering much of the work of putting out the first issue, which was produced on a typewriter and printed by the offset process by a firm called College Printers.

The paper quickly established itself as the voice of Vancouver's hippie district, a four-block-long stretch of Fourth Avenue West. Lined with one-storey shops and vacant lots, it had become home to the rebellious young men and women who lived in dilapidated low-rent houses on the side streets that circled the area. As in Toronto, and in lesser Yorkvilles in smaller Canadian cities, these so-called hippies were a mixed lot. They included originals who took their cues from San Francisco's Haight-Ashbury district and rejected the conventional work-oriented society, poets who espoused similar values, painters who chose to live in the area because the rents were low, teenyboppers in revolt against their parents, and draft evaders from the United States. They hung out in a number of coffeehouses and shops catering specifically to the counter-culture with such names as the Psychedelic Shop, the After-thought, Phase IV, and the Advance Mattress, a coffeehouse that saved money by simply retaining the painted name of the previous tenant.

Harry Rankin, a maverick alderman, later tried to define the word "hippie" in an article in the *Straight*: "Hippies are rebels even if rather unconventional ones. They are rebelling against the widespread violence and war in our society. They are disillusioned with false middle-class values and standards, with status-seekers, with people living beyond their means, with the vulgar materialism and the bitter competition so prevalent today. They are suspicious that automation will make man into a workhorse, a cog in an immense machine. 'Hippies' want a more rational world, with the emphasis on the freedom of each individual to develop his own personality." There were only some twelve hundred hippies in Vancouver in the spring of 1967. Still, as Jack Batten wrote in *Maclean's*, "in a city that records more suicides, more heroin addicts, and more Grey Cup riots than any other in Canada, the hippies are emerging as the prime civic menace."

Cafés such as the Arbutus, at Fourth and Arbutus, refused to serve them. Halford Wilson, a local alderman, wanted to move them all to a rundown east-end section of the city, though how that could be accomplished he didn't say. The president of the Kitsilano Ratepayers' Association, Harold Kidd, said he believed they were all Communists. "At least they talk like Communists. I am sure they never take their clothes off when they go to bed. They're driving business down by fifty percent in Kitsilano." Police harassment was constant. "Some nights," said Jamie Reid, a young Vancouver poet, "there are actually more cops in sight than hippies."

The city's daily newspapers, especially the *Vancouver Sun*, led the outcry with headlines such as "Psychedelic slum feared" and "Lice on long-haired hippies?" That reflected the attitude of Stuart Keate, the paper's publisher. When the *Sun* assigned a reporter, Arnold Myers, to explore the Fourth Avenue scene in a ten-part series, Keate handed it back because it was too sympathetic. Myers quit and sold the story to *artsCanada*.

The police used every kind of excuse to harass so-called hippie enterprises. Three cafés were told to stop burning incense on their premises on the grounds that "incense smells almost like marijuana and covers the smell, making it harder for the police force." An art gallery proprietor who refused to take down a painting the police insisted was obscene was hustled into court so swiftly he hadn't time to call a lawyer. On June 10, somebody fired a one-inch ball bearing through the window of the Advance Mattress and another through the window of the Psychedelic Shop. The police remained indifferent. "What do you expect us to do about it?" the complainants were asked.

The Advance Mattress suffered constant pressure from the police. Milton Acorn wrote in the *Georgia Straight* that the Vancouver dailies were doing their best "to give the impression that these attacks on non-profit coffee houses are part of a much trumped-up LSD campaign. As a matter of fact, the Advance Mattress is the centre of opposition to this sometimes useful, sometimes dangerous drug—especially against the morbid [Timothy] Leary cult. For those who know that this alleged complaint is a vicious lie, it is possible to believe the Advance Mattress is being attacked by 'Communists.'"

Acorn pointed out that the café ran a Thursday night "blab" session "in which anyone can get up and say anything that he or she likes. In this society, free speech is much talked about but little practised. . . .

The deliberate, cynical persecution of the Advance Mattress seems to be only part of a co-ordinated attack on the Kitsilano neighbourhood as a whole. The fire department has started enforcing laws which have been ignored for years—though there's not been a single fire in Kitsilano. A prominent. . . activist has been given less than one month to vacate his house. The rent of one artist's studio has been raised from $40 to $125." In the end, the Advance Mattress was forced to close. Acorn wrote that the most subversive aspect of the coffeehouse was that the people in it worked without pay and prices were conveniently low.

One printer after another refused to print the second issue of the *Georgia Straight*. The manager of College Printers said that if he'd read the first issue before printing it, he'd never have done so. He refused to print the second issue even though it was cleared by a lawyer. "You know how people think," the manager of the *Columbian* in New Westminster explained, when he turned the job down. A spokesman for Broadway Printers said his firm would not print it and nobody else would either. McLeod offered to pay in advance, but that offer did not succeed. "It's not the money," he was told. Finally a small shop that would do the job was found in Victoria.

The most effective tool the police had was the vagrancy law of the time, especially "Vag A," which ruled that any person without a fixed address and having no visible means of support would be jailed. In Vancouver as in Toronto, it was a crime to be poor.

Thus, on May 3, a seventeen-year-old girl was arrested for "hanging posters." When the police discovered that she was actually licensed to hang posters, they changed the charge to vagrancy. She was jailed for five days before the case was heard. The charge was dropped, but nonetheless she was ordered to get out of town and return to Toronto, an extralegal bit of magisterial justice reminiscent of the Old West but used more than once in Vancouver.

The *Straight* publicized such cases and tried to forestall others. When eighteen-year-old Andrew Broersman was arrested on a charge of vagrancy in front of the Kitsilano Theatre on May 12, McLeod was present with a photographer, Terry Musciuch, who photographed the scene.

Musciuch had found a death-threat note slipped under his door the night before, but the police pooh-poohed it. They could not charge the photographer with vagrancy since he had an obvious means of support—his camera—but they demanded McLeod produce identification. He refused to give anything but his name and address, which was his right, nor would he answer any questions. Instead, he continually asked the police, "Am I under arrest?" No, was the reply, "but you soon will be if you don't answer the question." Five such exchanges followed, after which McLeod was arrested. "On what charge?" he asked. The policeman said there was none but that McLeod was being held "for investigation." At that time McLeod didn't know the police had no right to take such action; unless one is charged one does not have to go to the police station. He was held for three hours, refused his right to make a phone call, and then released. Broersman was found guilty of vagrancy and held on a five-hundred-dollar bond and told to get out of town. If he didn't leave, he was told, he'd lose the five hundred.

As a result of this incident, McLeod decided to fight harassment with harassment. The *Straight* prepared to fight back by telling all those who were stopped by the police to insist on their legal rights. A long article explained that nobody had to answer police questions except to identify themselves and give their address. The paper then printed a form to give to the police:

"I am only required by law to give you the following information: my name and address. If you ask me politely, I will justify my presence by telling you either (a) where I am going or (b) that I am merely going for a walk. I might tell you whether I have a job or I might not. I am not obliged to, and will not answer any additional questions, wishing to preserve the rights and freedoms held by individuals in Canadian society."

McLeod was learning about the law. When police persuaded the Arbutus Café to put a sign in its window reading "WE DO NOT SERVE HIPPIES OR BEATNIKS," he and Pierre Coupé made a point of monitoring the restaurant. When they were refused service, McLeod left, returning an hour later with a copy of city bylaw No. 386, which prohibited discriminatory business practices. That evening the owner removed the sign.

The White Spot, a chain of hamburger restaurants owned by a popular sports figure, Nat Bailey, was another target. On the evening of Saturday, June 10, two teenagers, Kurt Reichel and Pete "Zip" Almasy, entered the restaurant at Broadway and Larch streets and ordered a chicken dinner, a hamburger, and coffee. Although they were dressed cleanly if casually, they were refused service "because they dressed like hippies." The place, of course, had no dress code. In Vancouver's hamburger joints, people dressed as they liked.

The following evening the pair returned, this time with members of the *Straight*'s staff, some dressed casually in jeans, sandals, and beads. Others wore white shirts, sports coats, and ties. Some had beards, some wore their hair short. All were refused service and asked to leave. The owner called the police, and when the group stayed put they were forcibly ejected. The scene was reminiscent of the lunch counter sit-ins in the U.S. South.

Reichel and Almasy were charged under a city bylaw with disorderly conduct, "unlawfully loitering in a public place," and "obstructing persons who were there," crimes that now seem archaic. Bail was set at $750, and since the court was due to close in fifteen minutes, they spent the night behind bars. Next morning their bail was reduced to $35 and the charge changed from "loitering" to "creating a disturbance." Later *that* charge was upgraded to "common assault." The police apparently believed the earlier vague charges would be thrown out.

The following Monday a large crowd demonstrated in front of the White Spot. The *Straight* reported that service had been refused not only to so-called hippies but also to Indians, Jews, and even Vancouver *Province* reporters, the latter because of their association with the demonstrators. By Wednesday, a mass of spectators had caused a traffic tie-up at the corner of Broadway and Larch, and the restaurant was forced to accept mediation. The White Spot finally agreed to serve "hippies" as long as they dressed cleanly and caused no disturbance. The assault charge against Almasy and Reichel was dropped, but each

Walter Gordon was back in the news for most of 1967. He believed the Prime Minister had given him a free hand to battle for Canada's economic independence. But he found he had been seriously misled.

In 1967, as Canadians lost control of their economy they lost control of their national game, too. Toronto's Leafs won the Stanley Cup that year but the NHL expansion meant they could never again play Montreal in the playoffs unless they met in the finals.

*The Old Guard goal-
tenders,* Terry Sawchuk
(left) *and* Johnny Bower,
*celebrated the Leafs'
victory in the final game
for the pre-expansion
Stanley Cup. Below left:*
Toe Blake *vainly
egging his boys on.
At right:* Punch Imlach
*in his trademark hat,
complete with feather.*

The American influence was to be seen in the hoopla that enlivened the Tory convention in September. Robert Stanfield's big win was engineered by the ultimate backroom boy, Dalton Camp (right), *who knew that the party needed a new face to succeed at the polls. The other hopefuls didn't have the ghost of a chance.*

Youth was on the rise, and the establishment was not amused. When Daryl Duke (left) *used McLuhanesque techniques to transform the* CBC's *flagship program,* Sunday, *the higher-ups cancelled it. David DePoe (below, with black hat) turned up at an anti-war rally before the U.S. Consulate leaving the Company of Young Canadians inadvertently embroiled in controversy.*

Barbara Hall (right) *was a naïve but enthusiastic member of the Company of Young Canadians. She soon learned that enthusiasm was not enough. Still, her CYC experiences helped her become mayor of Toronto thirty years later.*

With Doris Anderson (left, foreground) *at the helm,* Chatelaine *paved the way for the feminist revolution in Canada.* Below: *Dan McLeod organized a protest after Vancouver's mayor banned the street sale of his* Georgia Straight.

In the summer of '67, the so-called flower children staged "love-ins" (an American phenomenon) in the open spaces of the big Canadian cities—from Stanley Park, Vancouver, to Queen's Park, Toronto— much to the discomfiture of the adult world.

was fined fifty dollars on the original charges of loitering and obstruction. The magistrate, Douglas Hume, remarked that although they had the right to dress as they pleased, individuals were also bound to respect the civil rights of a business establishment.

By midsummer the *Georgia Straight* was a roaring success. Its circulation had passed sixty thousand. Seven hundred vendors hawked it on the streets at fifteen cents a copy. The vendors received half the cover price, and so it could be said that the paper, by employing hundreds of otherwise unemployable youths, was making a considerable contribution to the local economy. Vancouver had always had newsboys on the streets, but these unkempt, long-haired boys and girls were different. They didn't wait passively for customers; they approached passersby with a sales pitch. Indeed, a critic might well say that they were joining the very world they'd rejected by acting as aggressive salespeople, though their lifestyle was markedly different. Each night scores of them "crashed," to use a new word in the lexicon of the sixties, in the paper's warehouse and even on the stairs of the *Straight*'s office.

In September the *Straight* started taking advertisements. One full-page ad, signed by sixty readers including two doctors, announced that "The Law Against Marijuana is Amoral in Principle and Unworkable in Practice." The personal ads were more intriguing: "Amateur photographer applying for contract with United States 'Girlie Magazine,' wishes models for nude and semi-nude sets". . . "Horny chick, 20, with baby wishes to meet young man, digger, 21–?, object common law marriage". . . "Swinging road-minded couples and single girls only! Exciting new club in the making."

Some Vancouverites were disturbed by the spectacle of youths with unconventional clothes and weird hairstyles hawking a paper that advocated legalizing marijuana (but not LSD, which the *Straight* opposed), welcomed U.S. draft evaders to Canada ("the Vietcong never called me a nigger"), urged school children to organize unions at school to pressure teachers and principals, and, in its classified column, came close to advocating free love.

To many collar-and-tie citizens scurrying down Granville Street, the newspaper being waved in their faces was advocating revolution as surely as the so-called Reds who were still scaring the pants off Cold War politicians and journalists. "Make school interesting by taking it over," the paper advocated. "Organize love-ins in school yards. During fire drill act as if there were a real fire. If you don't like a textbook, lose it. If any teacher or principal hits you, charge him with assault. Insist that schools be left open at night so you can have a place to sleep in case conditions at home become unbearable. Plan out your own courses and teach them yourselves. Ask sympathetic teachers to help you. Start a school newspaper, let your imagination run wild with new ideas."

On August 3, Kenneth Reid was selling the paper on Granville when two policemen placed him under arrest for those catch-all crimes, disturbing the peace and vagrancy. They testified later that they'd received a complaint over their intercom about "a hippie selling newspapers." Because Reid looked like a hippie, they arrested him and seized one hundred copies of the paper as evidence. Reid was driven to the public safety building on Main Street, fingerprinted, photographed, and incarcerated until 9:30 next morning in the "holding office," a large room without beds where the prisoners outnumbered the mattresses on the floor. The case, of course, was thrown out. Quite clearly, Reid had means of support—selling the very paper that had got him in trouble. Nonetheless, he was ordered to leave town.

If a newsboy peddling the *Vancouver Sun* had been arrested for doing his job, the paper would have run a front-page account with an accompanying editorial about freedom of the press. But the mainstream newspapers were virtually ignoring the continuing story that was under their noses. One university professor who heard about Reid's troubles offered to sell the *Straight* on the street and get himself arrested. "Then," he said, "I'll challenge them in the courts." He discovered, of course, that a short-haired man wearing a suit and trench coat had no more chance of getting arrested than the mayor himself.

The mayor, Tom P. Campbell, sardonically dubbed "Tom Terrific," had ideas of his own. He was determined to suppress the *Straight* with or without due process; after all, it was being sold in the vicinity of the city's schools. Into the paper's offices marched a man from the licensing commission. Did the *Straight* have a business licence? It was the first time anybody had had an inkling that a newspaper needed a licence, but the *Straight* was happy to buy one. The editors paid their money and hung the licence on the office wall. A day or two later—on September 28—the paper was told that its licence had been revoked. It was, the mayor declared, "a filthy, perverted paper." He put his feet up on his desk and announced, "They're out of business."

Again, one might speculate on what would have happened had the mainstream press been harassed. Canada's dailies, which invariably denounced any attempt to bring newsboys under the minimum-wage laws as an infringement of the freedom of the press, ran no trenchant editorials defending the *Straight*'s right to publish. Apart from Allan Fotheringham, then a *Sun* columnist, nobody uttered a peep.

McLeod fought back. His lawyer filed a writ seeking a declaration from the B.C. Supreme Court that the suspension was without legal authority. When Mr. Justice Thomas Dohm refused McLeod's application for a restraining injunction, he went out of his way to describe the paper as "filth."

McLeod responded by distributing a free one-page flyer that explained the paper's side of the case. More to the point, McLeod's research showed that the mayor himself owned some property in the Fourth Avenue area—property whose values, according to the Kitsilano Business Association, were deteriorating because of the hippie presence.

On November 10 the *Straight* reappeared, apparently without any objections from a city council that was becoming increasingly nervous over the controversy. In its next issue, November 24, the paper published a mind-boggling letter from Milton Harrell, the city's licensing inspector. "In view of the contents of the most recent issue of the *Georgia Straight*, which I have examined. . . the suspension of your publisher's license is no longer in effect." Had this city bureaucrat taken it upon himself to decide what the content of a newspaper should be? Or, as before, was he operating under orders from the mayor? One way or the other, it meant that either a civil servant or a politician—or both—was telling a newspaper what it could and could not publish.

On the surface, the *Straight* had managed to fight city hall and win. But had it? The summer hippies who formed much of the sales force were back in school. The circulation was dropping. McLeod realized that to make a profit the newspaper would need to sell advertisements. That led to an open break between McLeod and four of his editors, who walked out to form a new, short-lived, counter-culture paper. Although the *Straight* pledged to help the new paper, the break was so bitter that Milton Acorn, one of the dissidents, shattered the glass as he slammed the door on his way out.

The *Straight* became the only survivor among more than four hundred underground newspapers that flourished in North America during the late sixties. It survived because it adapted. It transformed itself from an underground newspaper into the largest entertainment weekly in Canada, with an audited circulation of almost one hundred thousand and a readership of close to five times that—more than the weekly edition of the *Vancouver Sun*, more than Toronto's popular *NOW* weekly.

It was not, of course, the *Georgia Straight* of old. "We specifically avoided politics," McLeod explains today, "because of all the problems we got into in the past." Problems cost money and bring expensive lawsuits; the *Straight* had had its fill of those in the months that followed its resurrection. These included one hilarious case that hinged on the origin (or lack of it) of the colloquial phrase "muff diving" (slang for cunnilingus), which had appeared in the *Straight*. Because a UBC English professor testified that it had no established meaning in English, the judge threw the case out. But Dan McLeod soon concluded that he couldn't afford the legal grief and expense. He is now over fifty years old, has two kids, lives in a house in Vancouver's fashionable Shaughnessy Heights, and drives an Infiniti to work. He is no longer an angry young man—"young, stubborn, immature, angry, and foolhardy," to use his own words. Recently he turned down a classified advertisement that showed two lesbians in bondage gear. The old *Georgia Straight*, the paper that fought city hall, is no more; but then, neither is Tom Terrific.

4

Mark Satin flew into Toronto in January 1967, his hair purposely cut short "to look nice and square," and by the end of the year had become the best-known draft dodger in Canada. Born in Minnesota and raised in Wichita Falls, Texas, he was in no sense typical of most draft evaders, many of whom were beginning to trickle into the country that year. They usually still retained a grudging affection for the United States, whose policies they were opposing. Some even risked jail to sneak back briefly for a family wedding or a funeral. "It's still my country over there," one long-haired twenty-year-old told the press that year. "I do want to go home, once more, like this summer. But, man, it's five years in the pokey if I do, and Dad would be the first to turn me in. So I can never go home." *Mark Satin's choice*

Unlike most of his fellows, Mark Satin detested his native land. "That godawful, sick, foul country; could anything be worse?" he asked rhetorically when a *New York Times* writer interviewed him. "I've cut all bridges with it. I don't care if I never go back. My old man wouldn't either. You don't know what s.o.b.s they are in Wichita Falls."

Clearly, he wasn't the sort of youth to fit easily into a conformist Texas oil town. He felt out of place—an oddball who preferred listening to opera to going to high school. As he said, "People thought I was crazy." There was no one of his own age he felt he could talk to; such subjects as racial discrimination and the Vietnam conflict were taboo. Young men were so unquestioning about the war that most volunteered for service before they were drafted.

It wasn't until he arrived at the University of Illinois that Mark Satin realized he wasn't such an oddball after all. There he met a number of campus radicals who had decided to "remake filthy America together." He took courses in urban planning, believing he'd be drawing up blueprints for beautiful cities, but was disillusioned when he found that was a naïve notion. "You had to conform, deny your individuality, fit into a big, amorphous team, like any corporation slave." He tried other colleges and quickly dropped out. Then a girlfriend gave him a copy of a pamphlet published by SUPA in Toronto, the same group that would shortly picket the U.S. Consulate. It was titled "Escape from Freedom," and Mark Satin decided to escape.

He could have registered as a conscientious objector, but he reasoned that he would still be serving the war machine in a non-combatant role. "The only thing I wouldn't be doing was pulling a trigger." As for jail, the United States made no distinction between political prisoners, murderers, drug addicts, and rapists.

His father had tried every tactic to stop him from defecting. Both his parents refused to admit that their son was a "draft dodger" because they were afraid that would affect his father's career as a member of the faculty of Midwestern University. "I cannot condone what he's done," his mother told Gail Cameron, a writer for the *Ladies' Home Journal.* Her next remark underlined the generational gap in the family: "Oh, Mark, my sweet little Mark, why don't you grow up and become a big boy?" As Cameron wrote: "Probably no two people understand Mark's decision less than his own parents."

Satin threw himself obsessively into a job at SUPA, working seven days a week, from nine each morning often to midnight. Out of this grew the Toronto Anti-Draft Program. It was Satin who put together a ninety-page *Manual for Draft Age Immigrants to Canada* that contained all the information any draft resister would need to know about moving north of the border.

Most draft evaders did not know how to apply for landed immigrant status. Very few knew anything about the country at all—its political system, its historical background, how it differed from its neighbour. Doug Fetherling, who was later to achieve recognition in his adopted country as a poet and literary figure, was an exception. As soon as a friend put the idea of a possible exile in Canada into his head, Fetherling began subscribing to Canadian periodicals and monitoring the CBC. He established a daily routine, going up to the main New York library on Forty-second Street to study Canadian politics, culture, and economics. In time, he began corresponding with a handful of Canadian writers. Fetherling later wrote that "the abiding tradition of anti-Americanism, always present deep down in the lay public if not always pursued by cowardly governments, was one I found especially attractive."

Satin's pamphlet was badly needed. Some immigration officers at the border were hostile to draft evaders. Prospective applicants for landed immigrant status were sometimes told that they needed five hundred dollars and a job to go to before they could enter the country. That was hokum.

Actually, these young, well-educated Americans were among the best immigrants that Canada could attract. Once they had filled in the necessary papers and taken a medical examination, it was a matter of routine. Most had a college education; the average Canadian hadn't got past Grade 12. Though plenty of jobs were available for university graduates, some immigration officials were turning them away for flimsy reasons. When one nineteen-year-old black immigrant from Philadelphia arrived at Fort Erie with his papers in order, he was put off by an official who told him he would have to apply by mail. He hopped a bus to Niagara Falls and was admitted without any hassle.

Mark Satin's profile was so high that he became the virtual spokesman for his fellow countrymen in Canada, especially in Toronto. Others deliberately concealed their status as draft evaders. One twenty-seven-year-old from Cleveland went to great pains to disguise his background. Oliver Clausen, who made a study of draft evaders in 1967 for the *New York Times*, referred to him only as "Colin." After the Cuban missile crisis, Colin decided he would not answer a draft call and wrote to the Cleveland board making that clear. Back came "the nastiest letter I've ever received practically calling me a criminal and a traitor." By then he had his landed immigrant papers and was safe in Canada. The board issued a bench warrant and the police made repeated visits to his parents to pressure him to return.

Colin did so well in Canada that he was offered a senior advertising job with a large corporation. He took it without realizing the trap into which he'd fallen. The company was entirely American owned, and, like so many other firms in Canada, required its executives to make frequent trips across the border. As a result, his life became a nightmare. Over and over again he was urged to make a trip to head office in New York. He didn't dare. For all he knew, a warrant for his arrest awaited him at the airport. He made excuses, pleaded sick, created extra work to keep him in Toronto.

Then one day the Toronto police arrived at his office to tell him an FBI agent wanted to see him. He asked them to keep their voices down. It was well known that the Mounties were co-operating with the FBI but not generally realized that local police forces also had reciprocal arrangements. The rule was that the FBI could not interrogate a landed immigrant without a Canadian policeman present, so Colin was taken out to a squad car where a member of the bureau questioned him. He was civil enough, but Colin "had a hell of a time making people in the office believe that the cops had just come to ask about a parking ticket." It was obvious that he would have to find work with an all-Canadian company. Unless there was an amnesty sometime in the future, New York was barred to him.

The exiled Americans found Canadians generally easygoing and tolerant. As Mark Satin put it, "They take you as you are and don't beef about it. My landlord disagrees with me all the way but he accepts me without argument." The attitude of the American establishment ranged from bewilderment to outright anger. Pierre Salinger, the former White House press secretary, visited Toronto and called the draft evaders "contemptible." General Wayne Clark appeared before the Senate foreign relations committee to demand it call on the Canadian government to ship them all home. United States radio and television stations along the border sneered at them. "They are not the kind of people we want here, and Canada won't want them either," one Buffalo broadcast declared. But as Paul Martin, the secretary of state for external affairs, made clear, "We don't feel under any obligation to enforce the laws in that regard of any other country." Conscription in peacetime was against Canadian tradition; draft evaders were to be treated like any other immigrants.

Many of the young men who came to Canada in 1967, before the

Vietnam War became so disliked, were vilified by their parents. Doug Fetherling's mother phoned him one night to tell him he was a disgrace to her family, to her dead father's memory, to the United States, and to the entire white race. She ended by slamming down the receiver. The peer pressure on families back home could be brutal. When the local newspaper in a small Ohio town damned the family of one sensitive twenty-year-old as "un-American," he responded to their entreaties, went home, and ended up in boot camp. He couldn't endure it. While on leave at Christmas, he killed himself.

Some Americans opposed to the Vietnam War felt that fleeing to Canada was a cop-out. Joan Baez, the folk-singer who had gone to prison for her views, declared in Toronto that year that "these kids can't fight the Vietnamese madness by holing up in Canada. What they're doing is opting out of the struggle at home. That's where they should go, if only to fill the jails." Stokely Carmichael, the Black Power advocate, echoed her words in his own vernacular. "Those cats can't kick the bastards in Washington from here," he declared during a Toronto visit. "They oughta come on back and go to jail with me. If racist McNamara has the guts to draft me, I'll even accept white power to help take over the jails and then we'll see how smug America remains."

But very few black evaders came to Canada in 1967. Oliver Clausen, whose research was extensive, could track down only one in Toronto. It was the affluent and the best-educated whites who crossed the border. Many were high school or college drop-outs, like Dale Hayman, who'd been to six different colleges. He was twenty-four years old, a blond, clean-cut Californian with a pretty girlfriend, a good job, and a love of tinkering with things mechanical, including a broken-down 1965 Porsche. Ten days before his draft notice arrived, he piled everything he owned into the back of the car, drove north, rattled through the border point at Blaine, Washington, and told the immigration officials that he was a visitor, planning to stay only three or four weeks. They gave him a permit to remain for a month and nobody looked through his baggage.

Hayman checked into a room at the Vancouver Airport Inn and there, for the first time, felt the loneliness that almost every draft evader experienced. It struck him forcibly that Canada was a foreign country, full of strangers who wore similar clothing and spoke the same language but whose personalities didn't quite mesh with his. He had one phone number—belonging to a friend of a friend who, unfortunately, happened to be in Hawaii when he called. He sat down disconsolately and wrote to his parents explaining that he had no idea where to go, what to do. Eventually he thought of UBC and headed out to the campus, seeking kindred spirits. There he met a long-haired hippie pushing pot on the side, members of a motorcycle gang wearing black leather jackets, and some of the would-be journalists in the offices of the *Georgia Straight*. He began to wonder where all the normal people were.

At last, a social worker took him to a lawyer who explained that he could stay in Canada as a temporary visitor or as a student or as a landed immigrant. This advice did little for his emotional problems. He knew he would have to find people with whom he could communicate at his own social and intellectual level. The lawyer introduced him to a couple of earlier draft evaders. They found him a boardinghouse and suggested he get in touch with the Committee to Aid American War Objectors.

This group, formed by a twenty-seven-year-old university mathematics professor, Benson Brown, had become part of a loose network in Vancouver, Toronto, and Montreal. Like Mark Satin's group, Brown's committee was not yet a year old, but the need for it was becoming obvious. The centennial year was the first in which a trickle of draft resisters began to take on the proportions of a flood. No one knew for sure, but an informed guess places the number at some three thousand in 1967. By 1970 it would swell to an estimated twenty-five thousand.

By late spring, the Vancouver committee had encountered 250 visitors with Dale Hayman's problems. Its volunteers put him in touch with other Americans who offered solid advice on housing and jobs. By December he was living in a fifty-five-dollar-a-month, share-a-bath apartment in Kitsilano, making about seventy dollars a week, and beginning to think like a Canadian.

That year the Canadian government adopted a point system for immigrants—a great boost to war resisters because it limited any subjective appraisal by bureaucrats. No longer would personal prejudice conspire to keep a draft evader out of the country. The new rules made Mark Satin's pamphlet, when it was published at the end of the year, virtually essential. To get landed immigrant status, the applicant needed fifty points—so many for being the right age (between eighteen and thirty-seven), so many for job offers, so many for being bilingual, so many for having adequate funds, so many for skills and education. A prospective immigrant could also receive ten points for "personal assessment," something that the two committees underlined when they urged applicants to cut their hair short.

With a few exceptions Canadian government officials welcomed the draft evaders. Roger Neville Williams in his book *The New Exiles* wrote that "in literally hundreds of cases, young exiles-to-be told the officer they were deserters or dodgers and they received maximum points for the interview. Indeed, many were allowed in with only forty-eight or forty-nine points when their plight as refugees was made clear."

And Mark Satin, one of the first and most diligent of the refugees— what of him? After a couple of years, the seriousness of his exile in Canada began to sink in. "Unless there was an amnesty I'd be stuck there forever." That revelation, accompanied by "pain and regret," made him something of a footloose wanderer in his adopted country. (He hitchhiked across Canada sixteen times.) He rejected his earlier Marxist rhetoric, published an autobiographical novel and a highly successful pamphlet, *New Age Options*. When President Jimmy Carter granted an amnesty to American expatriates, he returned to the land he had once called a "godawful, sick, foul country." He founded a respected and award-winning national political newsletter, *New Options*, which was later published in book form by the California State University Press, whose stable of writers included Frank Lloyd Wright, Federico Fellini, and William Saroyan. He also made peace with his family. "I would have proposed publication of *New Options for America*, whether or not Mark Satin was my son," wrote the Press's founder, Joseph Satin. He added, "But I am very glad he is."

FIVE: MEN OF THE WORLD

1
The guru of the boob tube

2
The boy who broke the rules

3
The barber's son from Timmins

1

Early in the centennial year, the Canadian academic world was startled to learn that Fordham University in the Bronx had offered its Albert Schweitzer Chair to Herbert Marshall McLuhan, a professor of English at the University of Toronto. The fee would be $100,000—an enormous sum at that time. Worth more than the Nobel Prize, it was the equivalent of half a million in 1997 currency.

This was to be McLuhan's year—a year in which he sprang from relative obscurity to international fame. A bona fide Canadian from Edmonton, Alberta, who never betrayed his roots, he was actually the invention of two offbeat advertising men from San Francisco who, having discovered his early works—*The Mechanical Bride*, *The Gutenburg Galaxy*, and *Understanding Media*—plotted to promote him as an original thinker. They succeeded so well that by the time the year was half through, McLuhan had become the best-known Canadian in the world.

In 1967 twenty-seven articles in magazines as diverse as *McCall's*, *Family Circle*, and *Catholic Trustee* carried his byline, and no fewer than ninety-seven periodicals, including the *Nation*, *Look*, *Forbes*, and the *New Statesman*, published articles about him, his theories, and his writings.

It was impossible to escape the McLuhan image that year. Cartoons in *The New Yorker* and the *Saturday Review* joked about the McLuhan craze. NBC-TV presented an hour-long documentary about him. CBS (Columbia) interviewed him at length on its top-rated Sunday night public affairs program. His early, out-of-print books were back on the shelves in new editions, all hot sellers. The Dial Press produced an anthology of thirty articles about him—*McLuhan: Hot and Cool*. And his newest work, *The Medium Is the Massage*, a pun on his famous aphorism, was being reviewed in all the major media. "The medium is also the massage," he told *Playboy* magazine in a desperate attempt to justify the pun. "It literally works over and saturates and molds and transforms every sense ratio." *Every sense ratio?* That's what the man said.

The image conveyed by his work was that of a psychedelic prophet in tune with his times—the guru of the electronic age, to use the current buzzwords. But McLuhan in the flesh was a disappointment—a tall, tweedy, fifty-five-year-old professor with pallid features, thinning hair, a slightly dishevelled look, and an abiding interest in the Renaissance, of all things. He didn't look a bit like a guru; he looked like a Canadian.

Robert Fulford wrote that McLuhan had an air of distraction about him, as if he was listening to several conversations at once. Real conversation with him tended to seem one-sided, for McLuhan was a man who loved to talk. Ideas, quips, puns, insights, epigrams, and prophecies poured from him in a steady stream, dazzling and often confusing his listeners, who were hard put to unravel the meaning of one outrageous pronouncement before being hit by another.

McLuhan did not argue. He insisted that his pronouncements—many of them "far out," in the vernacular of the day—were not dogmatic but only "probes" to stimulate discussion. "Don't explore my statements," he'd say. "Explore the situation. Statements are expendable. Don't keep on looking in the rear-view mirror and defending the status quo, which is outmoded the moment it happens." That year he and his University of Toronto colleague Edward Carpenter launched a new magazine whose influence far outdistanced its circulation. It was called, naturally, *Explorations*.

By inventing the idea of the "probe," McLuhan neatly got himself off the hook. He could make the most outlandish assertions and deflect any criticism by explaining that he was merely "probing." "People make a great mistake trying to read me as if I were saying something," he told a group of reporters. "I poke these sentences around to probe and feel my way around in our kind of world."

He preferred conversation to the more difficult act of writing, which explains why so much of his work appeared as a collaboration with others, often in the form of an interview. "Conversation has more vitality, more fun and more drama than writing," he remarked, glossing over the fact that it's also a lot easier to ramble away while somebody else takes notes than it is to sit down at a desk and compose a series of literate and graceful sentences.

McLuhan's own works were dense and murky, "horrendously difficult to read—clumsily written, frequently contradictory, oddly organized, and overlaid with their author's peculiar jargon," in the words of one critic, Richard Kostelanetz. McLuhan was an acknowledged expert on communications, but, as many a critic said, he couldn't communicate very well. He didn't really write; he dictated his works, and he never bothered to rewrite. When he became a media darling, he did not have the time or the inclination to commit his thoughts to paper. He disarmed his critics by agreeing with them. Of his abstruse theories he said: "I don't pretend to understand them. After all, my stuff is very difficult."

Attacks by critics bothered him not all. A less self-assured man might have taken umbrage at Malcolm Muggeridge's review of *The Medium Is the Massage*. "There is scarcely a sentence which does not contain some schoolboy howler," Muggeridge said. "Professor McLuhan's writing, I should say, is a sort of low-brow Joyce at his most incoherent and H.G. Wells at his silliest." Another critic, Christopher Ricks, described his style as "a viscous fog through which loom stumbling metaphors." To all of these quibbles McLuhan remarked blandly and a little wickedly, "Most clear writing is a sign that there is no exploration going on. Clear prose indicates the absence of thought."

In the centennial year, with some misgivings I interviewed him on television. He was in full flight soon after the first question, and I could hear, in my mind, the dismaying click of hundreds of television sets changing channels. I tried, with limited success, to assume the role of an interpreter, as if I were facing, say, the ambassador from Outer Moravia. I'd try to zoom in and put his pronouncements into simple English. "What you're saying, Professor McLuhan," I'd begin, trying to get the essence of it across to the unseen audience. But before I'd finished he was off on another tangent.

He was, at that time, attracting huge fees from business concerns such as General Motors, who paid him handsomely to tell them that

208

the automobile was obsolete, or Bell Telephone, to whom he explained that they didn't understand the function of the telephone.

There is an amusing conversation in Donald Brittain's National Film Board documentary on Roy Thomson, *Never a Backward Step*. Thomson is told that he, the king of communications, should meet the philosopher of communications. By the time McLuhan arrives, Thomson has done some homework. But he's clearly baffled by McLuhan's theories.

"It's about the telephone companies don't know the business they're in," he says to his son, Ken. "Because they've never asked themselves the question."

He looks up owlishly over his thick spectacles.

"Well, I have a pretty good idea what business I'm in," he says, "and I think they have, too." He's still chuckling when McLuhan enters the room and is introduced.

"Did you say the Bell Telephone Company, for instance, has never asked itself what business it's in?" Thomson asked McLuhan.

"No," says McLuhan with that certainty that marks all his pronouncements. "It has never asked itself what sort of an image people have of their bodies and their friends as a result of the telephone."

"How would that affect your profit?" Thomson interjects in what seems to be a non sequitur but isn't. "Frankly, I'm interested in profit."

"And the body image," McLuhan continues, moving blithely on and changing the subject, "of course the body image is changing so rapidly right now that people are beginning to have their doubts about motor cars. The American for thirty years had an image of himself as part of a motor car. Now he's losing this image. And the motor car industry is on his side."

Thomson looks baffled. "You see," he says, "to really absorb what you're telling me I need it written out. I have to read it."

"This is the talk of a literate man," says McLuhan, "a literate man who's all for absorbing things. The new sort of electric man doesn't want to absorb anything."

"You mean in the future that people aren't going to be as literate?"

"Oh, indeed, yes. Literacy is on the skids."

Thomson grins. "Now I understand where you got the reputation. You're a shocker."

McLuhan takes his leave and Thomson turns to his son. "He's way out, you know. I mean, talking about these things. If he ain't, then, by God, I am! The only thing that impressed me was that he went to Cambridge."

The scene was obviously arranged by the producer, and since both men were ham actors, each in his own way, it worked. Many of McLuhan's quoted remarks seem to have been uttered on the spur of the moment for effect or to give him a chance to indulge in his weakness for puns. James Joyce, after all, was his hero and *Finnegans Wake* his Bible. Yet his two most famous epigrams—the ones that are still current—are crystal clear. Both express the essence of McLuhanism. When he coined the phrase "the Global Village" everyone knew exactly what he meant. Modern communication had caused the world to shrink to the point where it seemed that everybody knew everybody else. When he said that the medium was the message, he conveyed in just five words his point that it's not the content that matters, it's the *form*— the method by which it's conveyed. Movable type made the world think on logical and linear lines. It moved us out of the pre-literate, tribal age into the age of the individual. Television, McLuhan believed, would create a new tribalism. "The media works on you much like a chiropractor, or some other masseur, and really works you over and doesn't leave any part of you unaffected; it is a surround that is a process. It is not a wrapper, it is a process and it does things to you. The medium is what happens to you and that is the message."

McLuhan's two pronouncements were the essence of what the French were already calling *McLuhanisme*. On close examination some other declarations seem less profound. When colour television came to Canada in 1966, McLuhan predicted "a return of hot sauces to American cuisine." But was it colour TV that affected our taste buds, or was it the jet airplane that brought new and exotic foods from the outer limits of the global village or the great postwar immigration boom that brought lovers of hot foods—Hungarians, Cubans, Szechuan Chinese, Puerto Ricans—to these shores?

210

McLuhan pretended to be embarrassed by the intense light of publicity that shone on him during 1967. "My only complaint at present," he wrote to the poet John Wain, "is the excess of adulation and attention that has been blizzarding my life. When you go into the public domain by the media route, everybody develops the illusion that they own you. They resent even the slightest efforts at privacy." In fact, he was happiest when he was the centre of attention. Certainly he doesn't seem to have turned down a single request from *Playboy*, *Mademoiselle*, or the myriad of popular publications that clamoured to interview him.

In his speeches he liked to toss in references to Flaubert or the Symbolist poets because, he said, he found it useful to put the audience in its intellectual place. He was a master of the dogmatic statement, declining to qualify his opinions in the approved academic fashion. "If I make a cautious, measured statement," he once remarked, "somebody might mistake me for a stable character." Thus did he disarm his critics in advance. "Unless a situation is startling," he said, "no one will pay attention; they will put it down as a point of view." He likened his work to that of a safecracker: "In the beginning I don't know what's inside. I just sit myself down in front of the problem and begin to work. I grope, I probe, I listen, I test—until the tumblers fall and I'm in."

His byline often appeared on articles that he inspired but didn't write, like the two-parter that appeared in *Look* in 1967 and was really written by George Leonard, one of the magazine's editors. Such articles contained several far-out predictions. Were they his or Leonard's?

"By the time this year's babies have become 1989's graduates (if college 'graduation' still exists), schooling as we know it may only be a memory." A second article on the future of sex suggested that homosexuality would fade away. "If a new, less specialized maleness emerges, it is possible that the need to turn to a specialized homosexuality will decrease. There is a striking absence of it among the communal-living young people of today."

On the other hand, the articles did forecast the effect the birth-control pill would have on romantic love and sexual restraint. The articles were typically McLuhan (although he later declared he had had no part in writing them), a mixture of shrewd forecasts and wild-eyed assumptions. *The Medium Is the Massage*, the hottest "non-book" of 1967, was put together by Jerome Agel, who had interviewed McLuhan in 1965, and Quentin Fiore, a book designer. It was a kind of anthology of McLuhan's work, illustrated by photographs developing McLuhan's point that "the media acts like a masseur and really works you over." The title was pure McLuhan, the lover of bad puns, which he liked to call the jokes of the present day, supplanting the old, structural humorous stories. Already waning in popularity, the pun was further enfeebled by efforts such as McLuhan's "Alexander Graham Kowalski was the first telephone Pole."

He was a consummate performer. The Canadian writer B.W. Powe has written a brief description of a McLuhan seminar:

An eager voice blurted: "Dr. McLuhan, your colleagues think you're the most ignorant man on campus."

"Yes, almost as ignorant as they are."

"But they think you pander in half-truths. . . ."

"Now look," he sat forward, "a half-truth is an *awful* lot of truth! Most people never get that much!"

"But," the voice persisted, "you've only lived your whole life on a university campus."

"Well," McLuhan responded, "if you've lived on a university campus, you know a lot about stupidity. You don't have to go outside the university to understand the human condition."

There was laughter.

"You can't always recognize stupidity at first sight," he continued. "Or immaturity. Very few people go past the mental age of eleven now. It isn't safe! Why—they'd be alienated from the rest of the world!"

By 1965, when McLuhan was "discovered" by the California advertising men, he had enjoyed a rich academic career. Born in Edmonton (his father was in real estate, his mother an elocutionist), he had enrolled

212

in engineering at the University of Manitoba but after a summer of light reading switched to arts and literature. Those were the days when ambitious young students pursued graduate degrees in Europe, and McLuhan followed that pattern, attending Cambridge on an IODE scholarship. He returned in 1936 to teach in the American Midwest and three years later made two decisions that changed his life. He married a beautiful Texan actress, Corinne Keller Lewis, and, prompted by the works of G.K. Chesterton, converted to Roman Catholicism. After that he taught only at Catholic institutions—Assumption College at Windsor and St. Michael's at the University of Toronto. In 1942 he completed his doctoral dissertation, earning a Ph.D. from Cambridge in medieval education and Renaissance literature—odd preparation, some might say, for the future apostle of the psychedelic age.

McLuhan's first book, *The Mechanical Bride*, published in 1951, was largely ignored and quickly remaindered. Later it became a collector's item, seen in retrospect as the first serious attempt to examine the effects of mass culture on individuals. During the McLuhan boom of 1967 it came back into print.

His second book, *The Gutenberg Galaxy*, published in 1962, was heavily influenced by the University of Toronto's noted economic historian, Harold Innis, whose own insights pointed McLuhan towards the revelation that the medium is the message. In his introduction, McLuhan wrote that Innis was "the first person to hit upon the *process* of change as implicit in the *form* of technology. The present book is a footnote of explanation to his work."

In the book, McLuhan argued that for a long time, without actually understanding it, we had been living in a culture in which our whole way of looking at the world had been determined by typography—by the successiveness of print. One source of McLuhan's notion was J.C. Carruthers, a psychiatrist who had described the startling effects of the printed word on the African population.

McLuhan's third book, *Understanding Media*, published in 1964, was the work that helped create the McLuhan boom. It was here that he developed his theory of "hot" and "cool" media—radio is hot, TV cool—and his contention that television is tactual rather than visual. It was here, too, that he propounded the thesis that the media are an extension of human organs—as the wheel extends the foot, radio extends mouth and ear, and electric technology extends the entire nervous system.

Understanding Media was read by a San Francisco surgeon and business consultant, Gerald Mason Feigen, who alerted his partner, Howard Gossage, a brilliant, if eccentric, advertising man (he plugged Rainier Ale by offering sweatshirts printed with the faces of Bach, Beethoven, and Brahms). Gossage and Feigen ran a business consulting firm and as a hobby indulged in what they called "genius scouting." Feigen's scouting had paid off. Up in the wilds of Canada, a genuine genius was waiting to be discovered. They promptly phoned McLuhan to say they were coming to Toronto to meet him.

They took him to dinner at the Royal York's Imperial Room and immediately hit it off (Feigen's weakness for puns endeared him to McLuhan). The pair returned to San Francisco to plot a McLuhan Festival. They plugged it by papering the town with a phrase that Henry Gibson would later use on one of the most popular TV shows in the country—*Rowan and Martin's Laugh-In*—"Whatcha doin' Marshall McLuhan?" Soon the San Francisco *Chronicle* was referring to McLuhan as "the hottest academic property around."

To introduce McLuhan to New York's media elite, they set up a series of meetings and lunches in some of the city's poshest caravansaries, leading off with a Monday cocktail party in Gossage's suite at the Lombardy Hotel. To Gossage's bafflement and despair, McLuhan didn't show up. Gossage phoned him in Toronto and asked what the hell he was doing. McLuhan said he was grading papers.

"Grading papers?"

"And waiting for the excursion rate."

"The excursion rate! What excursion rate?"

McLuhan explained that he could save twelve dollars round trip if he waited to come to New York on Tuesday morning.

"But Marshall," Gossage expostulated, "you're not even paying for it!" He added that there were so many people willing to invest money in his work that he'd never have to grade papers again.

Now, suddenly, the man who had been viewed in Toronto as a campus eccentric—a bit of a clown, really—found himself being wined and dined all over Upper Manhattan and offered free office space by both *Time* and *Newsweek*. The Luce press went all out in gushing over the new phenomenon—a pop star, albeit an academic one—"the oracle of the electric age" (*Life*), "one of the major intellectual influences of our time" (*Fortune*). The New York *Herald Tribune* pushed the blandiloquence up a notch, proclaiming that McLuhan was "the most important thinker since Newton, Darwin, Freud, Einstein, and Pavlov."

McLuhan was not accustomed to such adulation in his native land. Why hadn't his fellow Canadians responded as the Americans had? Because, said McLuhan, "Canadians are mildewed in caution." But he also paid tribute to his Canadianism. "Canada," he remarked more than once, "is a kind of cultural DEW-Line, a cultural counter-environment. The Canadian is an outsider to the United States. You must live outside an environment to understand it; to participate in it is to blind yourself to all the hidden effects it may have on you."

He was no expatriate. After his stint at Fordham he would go right back to the University of Toronto. Nor did the Americans adopt him as one of theirs as they did so many Canadians, from Lorne Greene and Jack Kent Cooke to John Kenneth Galbraith. It was as if McLuhan's very Canadianness contributed to his image—that of a strange savant from a frozen world, a messenger from an unknown country. One is reminded of the patent medicine ads in the pulp magazines that featured a bearded Viennese doctor promoting yeast or mouthwash, the implication being that this foreigner was more expert and knowledgeable than the local talent. The smallest press notices invariably identified McLuhan as a Canadian, as if the word carried a special cachet.

Probably the biggest fish that Gossage and Feigen lured with the McLuhan bait was Tom Wolfe, one of the hottest journalists in the Big Apple. Wolfe was assigned to write about McLuhan by *New York*, then a Sunday magazine of the New York *Herald Tribune*. Wolfe went out to San Francisco in August 1965, and his subsequent article, which asked "What if he's right?" written in the style of the New Journalism, introduced McLuhan to a wide audience. In his article, Wolfe described how he took McLuhan, along with Gossage, Feigen, and Herb Caen, the widely read San Francisco columnist, to a topless restaurant. The other men, Wolfe reported, seemed faintly embarrassed, but the guru from Canada calmly proceeded to fit the scene into his own theories.

"Well!" he said. "Very interesting!"

"What's interesting, Marshall?"

"They're wearing *us*!". . .

"I don't get it, Marshall."

"We are their clothes," he said. "We become their environment. We become extensions of their skin. They're wearing *us*!"

Wolfe's lively profile, which later appeared in book form, inspired other magazines to examine the McLuhan phenomenon. By spring 1967, with his picture on the covers of both *Time* and *Newsweek*, Fordham University's $100,000 award in the headlines, and *Understanding Media* on the best-seller lists, McLuhan was on a roll. He was "the Dr. Spock of pop culture," "Canada's intellectual comet," "the guru of the boob tube," "the high priest of pop think."

Large corporations vied to pay him fancy fees to address seminars. Magazines pleaded for articles. Television stations demanded interviews. At one point he was receiving three invitations a day, from all over the world, to write or to speak. He cheerfully obliged.

What if he's right? Tom Wolfe had asked. Sometimes he was. He told IBM that they should move into software. They ignored that advice and wished they hadn't when the CD-ROM revolution hit them in the wallet.

He said that "the mini-skirt is the ultimate act of violence," whatever that meant; but he had also been perceptive enough to announce, as early as 1966, that "within fifteen years an actor will be elected president." He predicted that "goods will be sold in bins," a forecast soon realized by the new bulk food stores. Late in 1967, he wrote to Hubert Humphrey that it was plain that the Vietnam War was "our first TV war, just as World War 2 was a radio war and World War 1, a railway war." The big change, he said, "is that there is no more division between soldiers and civilians. In the TV age, the entire public is participant in the war." That observation has become a commonplace today, but in 1967, with Vietnam only heating up, it was prophetic. Two decades before the video cassette explosion he wrote in *Understanding Media* that "at the present time, film is still in the manuscript phase, as it were; shortly it will, under TV pressure, go into its portable, accessible book phase."

His off-the-cuff statements plunged him into controversy. His remarks that advertisements were the greatest art form in human history and his predictions that we had come to the end of the book-oriented world infuriated the literati, who rushed into print to point out that there were more books and magazines being published than there were before TV invaded the living room. McLuhan's short aphorisms were easier to follow than his longer, convoluted essays, but then McLuhan himself had made that strange remark about "clear prose indicating the absence of thought." That was nonsense, of course; obscurantism was the method of defending himself that he wore like a suit of armour. "I don't pretend to understand everything I've written," he once remarked. Nor did he agree with all of everything he said. Thus did the critical bullets ricochet off the psychological chain mail he had fashioned for himself.

His one-liners were widely quoted, for they not only sounded clever but also hinted at some deep revelation: "People don't actually read newspapers; they get into them every morning like a hot bath." He dressed up his aphorisms with contemporary allusions: "The Middle Ages were the Late Show for the Renaissance." "Money is the poor man's credit card." "*Bonanza* is the perfect instance of the rear-view image. It is the latest suburban world seeing itself in terms of the previous nineteenth-century environment."

Often he was ludicrously wrong: "Twiggy is a geometric abstraction. She's not a real person. The age of Sophia Loren is kaput. Twiggy is not a picture. She's an X-ray." But Twiggy has faded and Sophia Loren has not.

McLuhan was always announcing that certain institutions were obsolete. The big-breasted Playmate in *Playboy*, he said, "signals the death throes of a departing age." Large cities were doomed because "people would no longer concentrate in the great urban centres for the purposes of work. New York will become a Disneyland pleasure dome." Here, McLuhan was onto something; thanks to the fax and the personal computer, middle-management executives no longer need to commute to downtown offices. Yet the fact that they still do suggests that the desire to congregate outweighs the quest for solitude. Human nature has belied McLuhan's prediction. In 1996 demographers reported that, as more people are being drawn into the world's cities, urban dwellers now outnumber rural residents.

The enormous wave of adulation visited upon Marshall McLuhan brought the expected reaction. Dwight MacDonald was one critic who was less than enthralled by *Understanding Media*. One defect of the book, he wrote, was that the parts were greater than the whole. "A single page is impressive, two are 'stimulating,' five raise serious doubts, ten confirm them, and long before the hardy reader has staggered to page 359, the accumulation of contradictions, non-sequiturs, facts that are distorted and facts that are not facts, exaggerations, and chronic rhetorical vagueness has numbed him to the insights. . . and the many bits of new and fascinating information. . . ." McLuhan's response to such criticism was that it was the product of linear thinking.

Another critic, Theodore Toszak, took a jaundiced view of McLuhan's probes: "What is a 'probe'? It is apparently an outrageous statement for which one has no evidence at all, or which, indeed, flies in the face of obvious facts. This is, no doubt, the hip version of what Washington these days calls a 'credibility gap' and what the squares of yesteryear used to call a falsehood."

The London *Observer* devoted an entire page to an assessment of McLuhan by Rudolf Klein, who called him "a man of genuine perception"—a prophet indeed, but a dangerous one because "he relieves us of personal responsibility. . . . No wonder that he is the centre of a new cult—which demands no effort and apportions no responsibility." To Klein, McLuhan was "a master of the brilliant half-truth and the dogmatic overstatement."

That judgement would no doubt have delighted McLuhan. Much of it he would have agreed with; as we have seen, for him a half-truth was better than no truth. And since he publicly disclaimed any responsibility for his insights or aphorisms, he was impervious to scholarly analysis. Certainly his influence was felt during his lifetime. Architects, filmmakers, and television producers took inspiration from him. The plan of Scarborough College in Toronto, considered to be one of the most modern designs in the world, was McLuhan-influenced, according to its architect, John Andrews. TV programs, from *The Monkees* to *Laugh-In*, bore his stamp, for they consisted of a series of commercial-length bites, thrown together with no beginning or end. Expo 67, held in the year of the big McLuhan boom, was called "McLuhanesque." Certainly most of the films shown at the big fair—multiscreen documentaries, totally nonlinear in format—were pure McLuhan.

Is that influence lasting? Certainly, some movies have lost their linear pattern, starting in the middle or at the end, and working back and forth towards, say, the beginning; but that trend may owe as much to the influence of George Orson Welles as that of Herbert Marshall McLuhan. The same can be said of some novels, but their models, too, precede McLuhan. The mainstream media are still relentlessly linear, although McLuhan might riposte that interrupting a television narrative with a series of commercial non sequiturs changes the traditional way of telling a story. But the video cassette has yet to replace the wide-screen epic; it has simply replaced the second-run neighbourhood cinemas. And books are more in demand than ever; readers have not been persuaded that it is easier to read words on a screen than on a page.

On the other hand we are quite clearly moving into the global village that McLuhan (among others) foresaw. And nobody can take away from him the insights expressed in the epigram "the medium is the message." His influence has waned since those psychedelic days when he burst like a rocket into the firmament of the sixties. Has the rocket sputtered out? Not entirely. But as Michael Bliss, a historian and political critic from McLuhan's own university, has said: "To a handful of true believers, he is passing into history as an interesting product of a strange moment in Western culture."

In retrospect, he appears as a classic victim of hubris. In the 1950s he was noted, like Northrop Frye at Victoria College, University of Toronto, for his English literature courses. His lectures were full of illuminating insights. But where Frye is revered for his sagacity and his scholarship, McLuhan is dismissed for his flashy hit-and-miss pronouncements. He was a victim of the emerging cult of Celebrity, with its new emphasis on pop stars in every field from music to philosophy. McLuhan was tempted out of his own discipline into a sphere beyond his capacity; he was too clever by half, but not smart enough to realize that he was becoming ridiculous, rather as if Einstein had tried to do a stand-up turn in a comedy club.

2

The boy who broke the rules

In the summer of 1967, Glenn Herbert Gould, the one authentic musical genius this country has produced, embarked on his own centennial project. It would be called "a play documentary for radio," and it would be unique, unlike anything that had been produced before, the creation of a brilliant, eccentric concert pianist who had left the stage forever and who had never produced a radio documentary of the kind he proposed.

It would be called *The Idea of North*, and its godfather would be the CBC, which aired the finished product in late December. The subject fitted Glenn Gould's austere temperament. He had never crossed the Arctic circle or seen the North West Passage. The closest he had been to the North was a trip he had taken a year earlier aboard the Muskeg Express to Churchill on the shores of Hudson Bay. "I have come away from it," he wrote at the time, "with an enthusiasm for the North, which may even get me through another winter of city living, which as you know, I loathe. . . ."

"What I would like to do," Gould wrote to a friend that centennial summer, "is to examine the effects of solitude and isolation upon those

220

who have lived in the Arctic or sub-Arctic. In some subtle way, the latitudinal factor does seem to have a modifying influence on character."

That phrase, "solitude and isolation," neatly summed up Gould. The pianist, it has been said, is the most cloistered of musicians, for he does not have to depend upon an accompanist or an orchestra to achieve his effects. And Gould was the most isolated of all pianists, especially when he quit the concert stage for the recording booth. "The recording experience," he said, "is the most womb-like experience that one can have in music. It is a very cloistered way of life and indeed I've given up all that was non-cloistered in my musical life."

No wonder that the solitude of the North appealed to him. He had been fascinated by it since childhood. As a boy, he would pore over maps of the Northwest Territories, learning to distinguish Great Slave Lake from Great Bear, intrigued by "the idea of the country," influenced by the romantic paintings of the Group of Seven and, later, by aerial photographs that made him realize that "the North was possessed of qualities more elusive than even a magician like A.Y. Jackson could define with oils."

He felt himself at one with the dull, low skies, the wild terrain, and the very emptiness of the land. He saw the North as a puritan realm, separated from the urban world by the barrier of latitude, the puritanism increasing as the latitudes went higher. This austerity, which appealed to his temperament, was matched by the austerity of his playing—his keyboards rendered tight and crisply puritanical by his own constant tinkering.

He equated the idea of North with morality and rectitude, which perhaps explains his affinity for the Scandinavian and German composers and his disapproval of the French, such as Debussy and Ravel. Nor did he care for the ebullience of Italian opera. He was very much in tune with the Northern monochrome—sullen skies, dun-coloured rocks, gunmetal lakes. His abnormal sensitivity to bright colours and bright light appears irrational until one recalls that it is also the hallmark of a certain type of genius. Nikola Tesla, perhaps the most extraordinary scientist of the nineteenth century (who arrived at the concept of

221

alternating current while reciting Goethe in a Budapest park), was so sensitive that he could detect the presence of an object at a distance of twelve feet by a sensation in his forehead. The sound of a watch ticking in a distant room disturbed him, and in moments of danger or elation he was subject to inexplicable flashes of light over which he had no control.

"The only colours I can tolerate," Gould said, "are blue and grey. . . . I never wear anything else but blue or grey. Every wall I have is painted grey. I cannot bear bright colours." As a small child he was presented with a red toy fire engine. The colour caused him to fly into a tantrum from which it was difficult to calm him down. "I wouldn't have, as a child, any toy that was coloured red at all," he recalled. "I hate clear days, I hate the sunlight, I hate yellow. To long for a grey day was, for me, the ultimate one could achieve in the world."

According to Andrew Kazdin, the Columbia Records engineer who worked with him, Gould's socks *never* matched. One was dark blue, the other grey or black. Kazdin was convinced that this was on purpose; the dictates of probability suggested it. To Kazdin that indicated the presence of control "just as much as if he wanted them to match."

Kazdin reported that Gould's productivity at recording sessions was very much influenced by the state of the weather. "He made it a point to show me that he could sail through the most difficult of compositions with great spirit and determination if it was grey and raining outside." One of his favourite covers for an album (of three Beethoven sonatas) showed a photograph of him in very bleak, snowy surroundings. He liked the image for what it represented. "It's very *me*," Gould said.

The Idea of North was Gould's first "contrapuntal documentary," in which he treated his compositions like pieces of music. Robert Hurwitz, in the *New York Times*, attempted to describe listening to one of them by comparing it to "sitting on the IRT during rush hour, reading a newspaper, while picking up snatches of two or three conversations as a portable radio blasts in the background, and the car rattles down the track."

Gould's centennial program begins with a babel of overlapping voices, as at a cocktail party, each saying something about the effect of the North, some of it lost in the crowd, much of it retained by the listener. Gould eventually comes on to introduce the five Northerners featured in the work by name and occupation; they then proceed without further identification or interruption. Again the voices intermingle, trail off, overlap, reassert themselves, fade away and return, while in the background we hear the sound of a train—the Muskeg Express heading towards Hudson Bay. The voices are all distinctively Canadian, and, as the show progresses, the listener begins to identify with the speakers.

The entire program was created in the recording studio by Gould, who likened it to a piece of music. Each of the speakers had been interviewed separately by Gould. None had ever met. "Taking. . . an interview. . . chopping it up and splicing here and there and pulling on this phrase and accentuating that one, throwing reverb in there and adding a compressor here and a filter there. . . it's unrealistic to think of that as anything but a composition."

It was painstaking work. In one of his contrapuntal documentaries, Gould later revealed that one woman's speech had required sixteen hundred edits. He started editing *The Idea of North* on Thanksgiving Day, often working as late as 3 a.m., and was still at it until the very evening of its radio debut.

The Idea of North reinforced Richard Kostelanetz's assessment that "he was a radio artist of the first rank, if not the greatest in North America." Radio production "was as much a part of his life as was music." In the years following his departure from the concert stage, Gould later noted, he spent roughly half his time working on radio and television programs that had nothing to do with music. The nation owes a debt of gratitude to the CBC, which indulged him in a manner that no other North American network would have countenanced. Gould happened to be born at the right time and in the right place to give full play to his singular talents.

Radio had always fascinated him. An early influence was the CBC's "Stage" series in which Andrew Allan's brilliant repertory company helped give Canada an international reputation as the leading producer of high-quality and often experimental radio drama and documentaries.

Radio was meant for a loner like Gould. As one of his biographers, Geoffrey Payzant, has written, "there was something about that medium itself, something about hearing a disembodied voice trying to make a connection, that interrupted and delighted the lonely school boy. Radio brought him the outside world and yet it did so without violating his strong sense of privacy." His first experience of a voice coming in over the airwaves was, Gould said, "something quite special. . . that original human contact, that incredible spine-tingling sensation of awareness of some other human voice and persona."

Yet he viewed his earlier radio work for the CBC with some dismay. "I was always dissatisfied with the kind of documentaries that radio seemed to decree. You know they very often came out sounding—okay, I'll borrow McLuhan's term—linear. . . . They came out sounding 'over to you, now back to our host, and here for the wrap up is—' in a word predictable. . . it seemed one had to accept the linear mold in order to pursue any kind of career in radio." Marshall McLuhan's influence is easily detectable in *The Idea of North*. Gould and McLuhan were acquaintances and often conversed, usually on the telephone in the dark hours of the night, a time that suited them both.

Gould came from a musical family. His father was an amateur violinist; his mother was a relative of Edvard Grieg, the Norwegian composer. She bore him at the age of forty-two after several miscarriages, and played the piano during her pregnancy in the hope that the newborn would turn out to be a classical pianist. He amply fulfilled her ambitions for him. As soon as he was old enough to be held on his grandmother's knee, he would explore the keyboard, never pounding it with his fist as most young children do, but pressing down on a single key and holding it until the sound died away. The vibration fascinated him. By the age of three he was marked as a prodigy, a boy with absolute pitch who could read music before he could read words. At five he was composing and at six was taken to his first live concert. By then he had decided that he wanted to be a concert pianist.

He was miserable at school. "It has been my conviction for some

224

time," he told *The New Yorker*'s Joseph Roddy, "that my great interest and enthusiasm for music is in large measure the result of my disagreements and dissatisfactions with my schoolmates. At any rate, by my tenth birthday I was not only absorbed in the acquiring of keyboard skills—both piano and organ—but in such pursuits in counterpoint as would have left my poor teacher speechless." Robert Fulford, the Toronto journalist, who grew up next door to the Goulds in the Beaches district of Toronto, remembered him as a puritanical child who "couldn't stand to hear blasphemies or use obscenities and would actually beg you not to." Fulford remembered that "even as a child Glenn was isolated because he was working like hell to be a great man. He had a tremendous feeling and loving affection for music. . . . It was an utter complete feeling. He knew who he was and where he was going."

He was quite aware that he was unique and separate from the rest of the schoolboy world. Even in his childhood his sensitivity was so great that he would not indulge his fingers in play. His cousin, Jessie Grieg, has told a touching story of him standing by and watching as she and her brother played marbles. He was seven or eight at the time. He watched for a long time with his hands in his pockets and finally said, "I'd like to play." But he could not play. "He just put his hand down once in the cold earth and withdrew it *so* quickly—and he put his hands back in his pockets and said, 'I'm afraid I can't.'" The scene helps to explain the later "eccentric" Glenn Gould: the mittens in July, the scalding hot water treatment before a concert. As a child he had few close friends and in later life rationalized that by saying he liked animals better than people.

He was his mother's pupil until the age of ten, then studied under Alberto Guerrero at the Toronto Conservatory of Music as it was called then. At nineteen, he quit high school before matriculating, much to his mother's chagrin. He decided he no longer needed a teacher and in later days always referred to himself as "self-taught."

Gould had begun his concert career before that at the age of fifteen under the guidance of the impresario Walter Homburger. His first American appearance in 1955 (he was twenty-two) drew a rave from the

Washington Post's critic, Paul Hume, who wrote that "Gould made some of the *most* glorious music I have ever heard from any piano." A subsequent recital at New York's Town Hall brought an immediate contract from Columbia Records, the first time that such a contract had ever been awarded after just one Town Hall appearance.

Those who were fortunate enough to attend those early concerts were as transfixed by the spectacle of the young Canadian at the piano as they were enchanted by the quality of his music. And what a spectacle it was: the eyes screwed shut as if in prayer, the head tossed back over the left shoulder, the undisciplined hair flaying the contorted brow, the torso twisted as if in anguish, the gaunt young face exalted as if in supplication, and the abandoned fingers capering up and down the keys as if to celebrate their release from the body.

He broke the rules. Everything he did seemed wrong by traditional standards. He crouched seven inches too low beneath the keyboard, sitting cross-legged on a sawed-off kitchen chair, humming loudly and occasionally making wild conducting motions with his left hand. He did not practise heavily, and he seldom played scales. Any music teacher would despair of him, for everything was quite obviously out of kilter—everything except the music; and the music seemed to have been made in heaven.

The Columbia executives were startled and a little dismayed when Gould, deaf to all objection, insisted on choosing for his first recording Bach's difficult and rarely played *Goldberg Variations*. They were just as surprised when he arrived at the recording session with an armload of paraphernalia: his personal chair, which allowed him to sit just fourteen inches off the floor, his collection of sweaters and scarves (this was, after all, a steamy June in New York), five small bottles of multicoloured pills, a batch of towels, and two large bottles of spring water because the pianist couldn't abide what came out of Manhattan's taps.

Gould proceeded to boil water on a hot plate until it was scalding and then immersed his hands it. "This relaxes me," he explained. Before he commenced the session, a small Oriental rug was placed under the pedals because Gould did not like to rest his feet on bare wood. In spite of the mild weather, an electric heater was set up to keep him warm. He began to play but suddenly flung his arms up. "I can't," he said. "I can't. There is a draft. I feel it. A strong draft." A covey of workmen was dispatched to track down the offending draft and at last the session got underway.

What emerged after a week, was, in Otto Friedrich's opinion, one of the greatest recordings ever made. "Here we learned," he wrote, ". . . that Gould could play the piano like nobody else in the world." Friedrich, who wrote the best biography of Gould, explained that "we who had not been present at the Town Hall. . . now had our first chance to discover Glenn Gould. Here, we learned for the first time that Bach's Variations (and, by implication, all of Bach) was not a cerebral construction to be respected from a respectful distance, but rather a creation of passionate intensity and immense beauty." It is rare that any performer can establish his reputation on the basis of a single recording, but Gould did. His version of the *Goldberg Variations* remains his masterpiece.

It took a week of splicing and editing for him to get the effect he wanted. The music begins, in Gould's words, "with an ingenuous little saraband," the theme on which Bach based his variations. Gould recorded it last after all the variations were on tape to his satisfaction. Only then did he work on the theme. "It took me twenty takes in order to locate a character for it which would be sufficiently neutral as not to prejudge the depth of involvement that comes later in the work." The theme he used on the recording is Take 21.

More and more that became Gould's approach to music. By taking the raw material of his own work, by splicing, editing, fiddling with controls, by choosing one of many takes and experimenting with others he became the creator of something new. There was a time when a pianist played a composition through from beginning to end, and that was the way it was recorded, but not Gould. He was a child of the postwar electronic revolution. Like the conductor of a symphony orchestra, he was in total control of his own performances, which by 1955 he was able to shape on the new audio tape. He looked forward to the day when a music lover, returning home from the office, could spend his leisure hours splicing tape in a Gouldian studio. "The listener," he predicted, "can ultimately become his own composer." That would be the culmination of the technological revolution in music, a revolution that, thanks to new recording techniques, was making celebrities out of long-forgotten composers. As Gould saw it, technology would bring about the transformation of the listener from a passive to an active participant. "I'd love to issue a kit of various performances and let the listener assemble his own," he once said. Even "dial twiddling," he pointed out, "is in its way an interpretive art."

I enjoyed two long sessions with Glenn Gould in the late fifties. He had returned from a European tour, the highlight of which was his triumph in the Soviet Union. The first North American pianist to appear on a Russian stage, he had been greeted with wild enthusiasm and choruses of bravos, cheers, and rhythmic hand-clapping as audiences demanded more encores. He responded with equal enthusiasm. "It was a sensation equivalent to that of perhaps being the first musician to land on Mars or Venus," he remarked.

I met him first at his home in the Beaches district along with Budge Crawley, the Ottawa filmmaker, and his musical director, William McCauley. Crawley wanted to produce a film of "The Shooting of Dan McGrew," based on the Royal Winnipeg Ballet's dance version. Though the idea came to nothing, the discussion provided a glimpse of Glenn Gould in action.

"Do you ever improvise?" McCauley asked him after our business was concluded.

"Why, it's my favourite pastime," Gould said. "What do you want me to try?"

I suggested Chopin. "I never play the composer," Gould said, "but— all right."

He sat at the piano and invented on the spot a Chopin nocturne that, had we not known, could have come from the pen of the composer himself.

"Give me something harder," Gould suggested. I was not then aware of Gould's lifetime fondness for games of all kinds, especially games

228

at which he could excel and that gave him a sense of power—such as identifying every piece of music played on the radio, or the "I'll be Mozart, you be Beethoven, and we'll have a philosophical discussion" game.

When McCauley suggested that Gould could improvise a bit of Mozart, the pianist was delighted. "I'll do you a Mozart opera," he said. The result could have been written by Mozart. Gould not only played it but also *sang* it in a kind of bastard Austrian, the sort of eerily familiar gobbledygook that Sid Caesar and Carl Reiner indulged in on television.

Shortly afterward, on the last day of December 1958, I paid him another visit to try to discover what made him tick. I found him in a snow-covered cottage on Lake Simcoe, sitting alone with his dog, Banquo, in the shadow of an eighty-year-old Chickering Grand, which he had been tinkering with all morning.

Some concert musicians (Rubinstein was one) were content to play any piano they were offered. Gould was more particular. He was cheerfully prepared to pay $250 to ship his favourite Steinway from Toronto to Detroit for a single performance. He kept pianos that he loved in two or three cities about the continent and tried to use them exclusively. Otherwise he might spend three or four days working on a strange piano, tearing it apart, changing the action, and lowering the keys a sixteenth of an inch to help the light, crisp style that had become his trademark.

To Gould, every piano had a different personality. By simply reading a musical score he could conjure up in his mind the tactile sensation of a piano a thousand miles away and ten months in the past. Thus he could, in a sense, practise on any piano he wanted to, without touching it. That explains why he practised so little on real ones. The secret, he once revealed, was not to move his fingers. The fingering was all in his mind. His wrists actually ached when he heard one particular recording of himself playing a piano he disliked, and he tried not to hear that record on the day of a concert for fear it would affect his performance.

"Do you mind if I don't play?" Gould asked. He was lounging in an easy chair, dressed as always in shapeless old clothes, shoes half kicked off. "I'd really rather not, because the action on this piano still isn't right and I don't want it to put off my performance in Minneapolis on Friday."

To Gould, a performance was a terrifying and at the same time exalting experience. Everything he did—all his odd quirks, his so-called mannerisms, bouts of hypochondria, his almost fanatical struggle with the physique and mystique of the piano—was tied to his fierce insistence that a performance be nothing less than perfect.

He took that impossibly low kitchen chair to every concert and even jacked the piano another inch higher so that, in defiance of all rules, he could get his fingers *below* the keyboard. That was no mannerism; by doing so he found he could eliminate the excess movement of his shoulders and elbows and control the keys entirely from his fingertips, caressing them rather than hammering them.

"Feel this shoulder," he said, suddenly levering himself from the chair. I reached over and felt an awesome hump on the right shoulder blade. "I wasn't born with that," Gould said. "I developed it over the years. I need it, you see, to keep my shoulders and arms rigid so that the fingers don't have to do the work of supporting them on the keys."

It was this freedom of the fingers that had helped him master the *Goldberg Variations*, where one hand is spread directly above the other, the fingers interlocking—Gould's tour de force.

It was to achieve this control that he went to great lengths to keep his body (slung exceptionally low) in proper balance: the legs crossed for better equilibrium, the head thrown over the left shoulder to balance the right hand, which was the weaker since Gould was left-handed. Often, again in the interests of equilibrium, he swung his left hand in the famous conductor's motions—the habit that caused critics and conductors alike to assail him for his "mannerisms"—like a pitcher winding up.

And he *hummed*—again to the dismay of the critics, for this was, to him, a psychological aid, an attempt to forget the piano completely, to drown it out of his mind. Was this pure rationalization on Gould's part— an attempt to excuse his odd contortions at the piano? Perhaps; but who cares when the results were so magnificent?

230

"It is very easy to let the piano become your enemy when you have lived with it and worked with it," he told me, "especially when the majority of pianos are ones you don't like. The piano symbolizes all the terrors of the performance and the only thing you can do is hypnotize yourself so that the actual ordeal is less great."

This genuine terror of performance was, in effect, the terror of failing in public. When he was a boy of eight, he said, a schoolboy standing near him was physically sick. All eyes turned on the wretched child, and from that instant, Glenn Gould was haunted by the spectre of himself being ill in public. That afternoon he returned to school with two soda mints in his pocket, a small, tousled boy on guard against the moment when he might lose face.

The soda mints were soon supplemented by aspirins and then by more pills. In school, Gould literally counted each second until lunch hour (ten thousand seconds at nine o'clock; a comforting nine thousand, one hundred at nine fifteen) and prayed that nothing might happen to humiliate him.

Nothing ever did. He had never been ill in public or anywhere else to speak of, although he had recently cancelled one more concert. By the time I talked to him, the soda mints had become two jammed pill cases, with an incredible potpourri of medicaments that he always carried about with him. Their use, I think, was exaggerated, but their presence comforted him, as the presence of a mother in a nearby room comforts and relaxes a sleeping child. Before a performance he sought more relaxation in a final attempt to "play with newborn fingers" by soaking his hands in scalding water. At other times he protected them from drafts, encasing them in gloves and mitts, eschewing the hearty handshakes of strangers, and massaging his arms with a high-frequency sound machine. One can scarcely quarrel with this supersensitivity, for without his hands Gould would have been a cipher.

I left him that afternoon alone with the piano he would not play. He gave me an autographed copy of the *Variations*; I gave him a copy of *Klondike*, which, for all I know, may have in a small way piqued his interest in that cold and rugged land to the north. How odd, I think now, that Gould, who hated and feared the cold, who wore mitts, muffler, overcoat, and a wool hat on the hottest days of summer, should become intrigued by a land where the summers can be chill and the winters are eight months long!

I bade him farewell, for this was New Year's Eve and revels awaited me. For Gould there would be no party, no New Year's kisses when the clock struck twelve. He would sit there all alone until late in the evening, when he would drive into town and board a plane for Minneapolis. There, once again, he would break all rules and make music that seemed to come straight from heaven.

Gould's remarks about the fear of failing in public came back to me after he gave his final concert on March 28, 1964. It wasn't billed as a farewell performance; he had not announced that he was quitting, and it took some time for his public to realize he would not appear on the stage again. There is little doubt that the fear of making a fool of himself before an audience had something to do with it. That, of course, is the essence of any "live" performance—the tension brought on by the possibility that something may go wrong. Will the pianist hit a wrong note? Will he stumble or even collapse? It is unlikely, but it *could* happen, and it is this quality of the unexpected that gives such a performance an edge. The Flying Wallendas knew it when, to their disastrous dénouement, they worked without a net.

But Gould needed the net. He wanted complete control over every phrase, every note. To him the concert stage implied a kind of competition. Throughout his teens, he once said, "I rather resisted the idea of a career as a concert pianist. . . . Performing in the arena had no attraction for me." I find it revealing that Gould saw the concert hall as an "arena" where prodigies competed as matadors and the audience was consumed by what he called "blood lust." At live concerts, he once said, "I feel demeaned, like a vaudevillian."

"Even from what little I then knew of the politics of the business," he said, two years before his retirement, "it was apparent that a career as a solo pianist involved a competition, which I felt too grand ever to consider facing. I couldn't see myself as ruthlessly competing against other seventeen-year-olds who quite probably played the piano much better. The spectator in the arena, who regards musical performance as some kind of athletic event, is happily removed from the risk."

To a man who popped pills into his mouth almost by the handful, the stage was a risk. "A performance," he said, "is not a contest but a love affair," and for the audience to treat it otherwise was to miss what was really going on: the performer's attempt "to form a powerful identification with the music." Later Gould, who liked to make forthright and striking statements, told an interviewer, "I happen to believe that competition rather than money is the root of all evil." Yet, as Otto Friedrich has pointed out, he had thrived on competition since his childhood. In other areas, he certainly liked to compete; on the croquet lawn it was desperately important for him to win.

Gould rarely attended a live performance. "I'm extremely uncomfortable at concerts," he said, "and, for me, the real approach to music is sitting at home. . . listening to recordings." When he was obliged to attend, he stood in the wings rather than sit in the best seat in the house. During a Rubinstein concert in Toronto in January 1960, he lurked in the broadcast booth, much to the soloist's puzzlement. "Surely, you can't enjoy the sound back here," Rubinstein remarked. "Maestro," said Gould, "I always prefer to listen in the wings." He found audiences claustrophobic. Only on stage did he feel he had room to breathe. He did not care to sit among people "with the perspiration of two thousand, nine hundred and ninety-nine others penetrating my nostrils." It was part of his monasticism. To an interviewer who asked if he ate very much, he replied that he ate very little and felt guilty when he did. The interviewer followed with a question about his need for people—or lack of it. Gould replied, "People are about as important to me as food. As I grow older, I find more and more that I can do without them. I separate myself from conflicting or contrasting notions. Monastic seclusion works for me."

Human contact, especially the physical kind, distressed him. On one notorious occasion in 1959, William Hupfer, the chief Steinway technician, engaged in what Gould, in a court deposition, called "unduly strong handshakes and other demonstrative physical acts." Winston Fitzgerald, a Steinway official who was present, insisted later that "Mr. Hupfer just laid his hand gently on Gould's shoulder, and Gould suddenly went into a state of gloom."

"He *hurt* me," Gould said. He sued Hupfer, claiming that Hupfer had approached him from behind and "recklessly or negligently let both forearms down with considerable force on the plaintiff's neck and left shoulder, driving the plaintiff's left elbow against the arm of the chair in which he was sitting," and ignoring the fact that the pianist was a man of "extreme and unusual sensitivity to physical contact." Gould sued Steinway for $300,000 and cancelled all concerts for the next three months. In the end, to placate its superstar, Steinway settled for something under ten thousand.

Gould had another reason to quit the concert stage: his fear of flying, which was as grave as his fear of failing in public. Even before he retired from public performances he had decided never again to set foot in an airplane. That would make further European engagements impossible and stretch his North American tours to the point where they detracted from his composing, writing, radio work, and tape recording.

To retire at the peak of his powers when he was only thirty-one was a radical act. More than one critic predicted he was risking his future. They were wrong. He had no regrets about leaving the concert circuit. Indeed, a remark he made in 1967 suggests he was proud of it. "Except for a few octogenarians, I'm really the first person, who has, short of a nervous collapse or something, given up the stage."

Now Gould had time to devote to his other interests. He did radio recitals, he interviewed guests in front of the microphone, he headlined regular programs, playing records and talking about his interests, and he worked on his major radio compositions, each of which took hundreds of hours to produce. Only a man of Gould's prodigious talents could have achieved what he accomplished in a recording studio. Otto Friedrich wrote that "he seemed to have heard and perceived and taken in sound in a way that was quite different from the way these things are done by ordinary people." His failure to practise—he went for

234

weeks without touching a piano—stunned many of his contemporaries.

Gould liked to tell the story of the time a housemaid interrupted a Mozart fugue on which he was working by running a vacuum cleaner. He was thirteen at the time, but the experience stayed with him. In the louder passages "this luminous music became surrounded by a halo of vibration." In the softer passages he couldn't hear the piano at all. He could sense the tactile relation to the keyboard and could imagine what he was doing without hearing it. "But the strange thing was that all of it suddenly sounded better than it had without the vacuum cleaner and those parts which I couldn't hear actually sounded best of all." In later years, when he was in a great hurry to imprint a score upon his mind, he said, "I simulate the effect of the vacuum cleaner by placing some contrary noises as close to the instrument as I can. It doesn't matter what noise, really—TV westerns, Beatles records, anything loud will suffice—because what I managed to learn through the accidental coming together of Mozart and the vacuum cleaner was that the inner ear of the imagination is very much more powerful as a stimulant than any amount of outward observation."

Gould liked to play two radios at the same time, listening to music on FM and news on AM, and discovered that he could learn a difficult Schoenberg piano piece by using this technique. Similarly, he could carry on a phone conversation while reading a magazine. Friedrich compared this talent with that of someone who plays chess blindfolded.

It was Gould's memory for each "take" of a piece that served him well in the recording studio and became a legend among the musicians, technicians, and producers with whom he worked. Sometimes others couldn't detect the difference between two takes, but Gould's sensitive ear never failed him. After recording several versions of the A minor fugue from Bach's *Well-Tempered Clavier*, "upon more sober reflection I agreed that neither the Teutonic severity of Take Six nor the unwarranted jubilation of Take Eight could be permitted to represent our best thoughts on this fugue." Gould then discovered that both takes, despite their difference in character, were performed at an almost identical tempo. His solution was to alternate the two takes.

235

This combination produced "a performance of this particular fugue, far superior to anything that we could at that time have done in the studio."

Old-time composers and concert performers would undoubtedly have sneered at this artificial mixing of different performances to create a new one. But, Gould would say, they belonged to another era. What was wrong with making use of new technology to create a work? The Beatles were doing much the same thing with their new album *Sgt. Pepper's Lonely Hearts Club Band.* Gould was convinced that the idea of a public performance was a nineteenth-century concept outmoded in an era when, thanks to audio tape and modern sound equipment, a performer could "compose" his own work. Evan Eisenberg, in his book *The Recording Angel*, puts his finger on what may be Glenn Gould's major contribution. "History may conclude," he has written, "that Gould was the one sane musician of the century; and his colleagues who work the continents, packing their hearts from Altoona to Vancouver, may seem as pathetic to our grandchildren as all the bowing and scraping geniuses of the eighteenth century seem to us."

It may well be that Glenn Gould, the outsider, the denizen of lonely places, the philosopher of North, will himself be seen one day as a pioneer, worthy to be ranked with Champlain, Mackenzie, and Hearne, explorers all in the Canadian tradition of experiment and inquiry.

3

The barber's son from Timmins

As 1967 dawned, Roy Herbert Thomson, first Baron of Fleet, achieved his greatest triumph. At the age of seventy-three, the one-time radio salesman took control of the world's most prestigious newspaper, the venerable *Times* of London. That audacious move confirmed him worldwide as one of the three best-known non-political Canadians, and one who, like Marshall McLuhan and Glenn Gould, was always identified as Canadian. Thomson had "Canadian" stamped all over him. Once snubbed by the aristocracy of Great Britain as a crude and unsophisticated hick from the Ontario backwoods, he was now at the top of the heap, the world's most powerful newspaper proprietor, wined, dined, and sought out by the leading statesmen everywhere. All of his life he had craved prestige. Now he had it.

It had cost him a great deal of money. British peerages don't come cheap, and Thomson hated to part with a shilling. He called his acquisition of *The Times* "the oddest deal I ever made," for there was no profit in it. He was forced to agree to merge the paper with his immensely successful *Sunday Times*, which he had acquired some years before, and to rule himself out of the new company because, as he himself put it, "the main obstacle [to the purchase] was undoubtedly me." He wouldn't have any say in its management. He wouldn't even be on the board of directors. He doubted that Lord Astor, *The Times'* proprietor, "could stomach the idea of giving some control of his paper to a roughneck Canadian." Thomson got his way by agreeing to pay for the losses of the newly acquired paper out of the *Sunday Times'* profits—if there were any profits after this drain on his resources. *The Times* was hemorrhaging money; it would eventually cost Thomson a million pounds a year. Yet he wrote in his autobiography that "this deal was the greatest thing I have ever done. It was the summit of a life's work." He was quite willing to pay through the nose in order to be known as the greatest press baron in the world. Even to a man who still insisted on cramming his bulky body into tourist-class seats on national and international airlines, one million pounds a year was more than chicken feed; but to him it was worth it. As proprietor of *The Times*, he had entrée into every private club and palace in the realm where he could rub shoulders on an equal basis with the international statesmen.

It wasn't money that mattered, though he sought it as feverishly as any Klondike gold-seeker and held onto it as tightly as an alpinist clinging to a cliff. What he cared about was his long-sought and newly attained eminence. He believed, and not without reason, that in the twentieth century a self-made millionaire was the subject of veneration. I remember asking him about it during a television interview in London. He replied that since the making of money was the yardstick by which the world judged success, he had been determined since childhood to make a lot of it.

To him every dollar counted. A few days before that program he phoned me to ask what he was being paid. When I explained that it was not our policy to pay for interviews, he wanted to make certain that the rule applied to everyone. "You're sure, now, Pierre," he said. "I wouldn't want, you know, to be exploited."

To say that he was not a philanthropist is to put matters too mildly. He was firmly opposed to charity. Although he was prepared to lavish great sums on certain institutions, it was always with the expectation of a payoff—such as his eventual peerage. He did make an exception in 1967 when he gave $110,000 for a swimming pool in North Bay, the town that gave him his start. But that was his centennial contribution; he could scarcely escape it. Asked to sign the guest book during the community's centennial celebration, he responded cheerfully, "I'll sign anything but a cheque."

His affinity for the buck was legendary. Sir Denis Hamilton, who edited his *Sunday Times*, remembered being involved "in some tremendous deal with lawyers and accountants huddled round a table" when suddenly Thomson looked at his watch and left. He was away for about an hour, and when he returned Hamilton couldn't resist asking the reason for his absence.

"Oh," Thomson replied, "I'm on the board of the London regional branch of the Royal Bank of Canada and it meets every Tuesday. I get paid out in dollars for attending and I never miss it."

"It was incredible," Hamilton wrote in his memoirs. "We were involved in a deal worth tens of millions and he risked it all to collect $75 in cash."

Hamilton also watched with considerable astonishment a scene in the dining room of a Malta hotel when Thomson's son, Kenneth, entered with a copy of the *Sunday Times*. Roy Thomson put down the paper he was reading and said, "Ken, take that back to the bookstall. You can have mine when I'm finished with it."

It was Hamilton's lavish spending, however, that put Thomson's

238

Sunday Times into the black. Thomson winced at the sums Hamilton was paying for memoirs and serials. "Denis," he told the editor, "do what you want—do anything, but never tell me."

Once he asked, "Is it true that you paid one hundred thousand pounds for Khrushchev's memoirs?"

"Yes, Roy."

"Jeez, Denis, thank God you didn't ask me!" Thomson couldn't even bring himself to approve his directors' salary increases. He left that to his general manager, James Coltart, whom he had stolen away from Lord Beaverbrook.

Surely no other tycoon has been so disarming about his fortune. In a world where it is considered vulgar to refer to one's personal wealth, Thomson flaunted his. "My fortune," he told one journalist, "is as large as my credit rating. . . and my credit rating is limitless." Newspaper libraries bulged with his candid remarks about his wealth: "Primarily, I'm a money-making man". . . ; "I love big figures". . . ; "I'm not open handed". . . ; "For enough money, I'd work in hell". . . ; "I'd rather read a balance sheet than a book."

What was editorial content, he once asked rhetorically, and answered himself, "the stuff you separate the ads with." In his early radio days, when asked what his favourite music was, he replied that "the most beautiful to me is a spot commercial at ten dollars a whack." His most outrageous gaffe, the description of his television venture in Scotland as "a licence to print money," haunted him for life. Once, seated next to Princess Margaret at a fashion show in Scotland, he commented on a model's lamé gown. "My favourite colour," he told the princess. "Gold!"

As a well-heeled penny-pincher, he had no peer. Hamilton found him one morning prepared to fly to Newfoundland from London. He had two open suitcases near a pair of weighing scales. "I've paid four hundred bucks for this passage," he said, "and I'm not going to pay another cent." He began taking out socks and other personal articles and stuffing them into his overcoat pockets until he reduced his baggage to the weight allowance. Usually, all he took aboard was a small suitcase containing two shirts and a pair of pyjamas. He refused to fly first-class, because, he said, all it offered was free champagne—and he didn't drink.

There was the memorable Monday morning—the day after New Year's, 1964—when for the first time in his career he was not at his desk. By ten, his staff was frantic. Where was he? It developed that the new baron had been queuing up at Burberry's for a sale of overcoats. He returned to the office jubilant that he'd got a seventy-five-pound cashmere coat at almost half price. "Anyone who doesn't buy at a discount sale should have his head read," he remarked.

He dieted so often that his Savile Row suits never seemed to fit. He didn't care. Once, his fellow press baron Cyril Lord gave him several yards of Irish poplin. He took the cloth to Moss Bros. and ordered three shirts. On the trip back to his office he hesitated, turned around, went back to the shop, and reduced the order to two.

At one point he had trouble walking. His feet hurt so that Hamilton persuaded him to see a celebrated orthopedic surgeon, who made an instant diagnosis. "You wear your shoes too tight," he told him. Hamilton offered to take him at once to a first-rate shoe specialist in St. James Street, but Thomson demurred. "Not likely," he said; "these ones aren't worn out yet."

He didn't care what he ate as long as it was cheap. When he was negotiating with Lord Kemsley for the entire Kemsley chain of newspapers, including the *Sunday Times*, he stayed at the Savoy, where the room rate did not include breakfast. He bypassed the famous grill room and took his general manager, Coltart, to a lorry drivers' café in Covent Garden that he regularly frequented. For three and six they had orange juice, eggs, and coffee. At that point, Thomson and Kemsley were deep in negotiations involving more than ten million pounds. Kemsley wanted six pounds a share; Thomson drove him down to five. That night he bought a bagful of plums and apples, ate them for dinner in his room, washed his drip-dry shirt, and went off to sleep.

When he went north to Edinburgh to buy Thomas Nelson & Sons, an important British book publisher, he was prepared to bid £2,600,000, but Gordon Brunton, head of Thomson newspapers, argued that the earnings justified an offer of only £1,750,000. Thomson got the company at that price and turned gratefully to Brunton. "That was a very good suggestion of yours," he said magnanimously. "I'll buy you supper for that." Brunton's hopes for caviar and champagne vanished as Thomson, who had just been saved close to a million pounds, took him to an Italian restaurant for spaghetti and meatballs.

In spite of this, Thomson was known for the lavish banquets he held for VIPs. He had started them in North Bay and continued them in Edinburgh and London. Leading politicians, journalists, and members of the aristocracy were flattered to accept his invitations, for these were bounteous repasts on which no expense was spared. Well, perhaps not quite. He was once heard suggesting to his staff, "If we cut out the fish course, we could maybe get it down from forty-two and six to thirty-five shillings a head."

One colleague would always remember a trip Thomson made to Ireland for a conference. "Lord Thomson got a free ride over there. He disappeared in the morning, turned up for the free lunch, vanished again when the boring speeches started, and turned up for the free ride back. There was no car waiting for him at the London airport; he shared the bus with us and I thought this remarkable. I said that to one of the fellows with us and he said: 'You don't know half the story. What do you think he was doing in the afternoon? He was buying the *Belfast Telegraph* for two and a half million pounds.'"

If Thomson understood the value of a dollar it was because he was born poor, and proud of it. In his autobiography, written without the help of a ghost, he continually refers to himself as "the barber's son from Timmins." Actually, his early years were spent in Toronto, where his mother kept a boardinghouse to supplement the family's meagre income, and later North Bay. Young Roy was a shy, introverted boy— plump and myopic. A lifelong regime of forty separate diets did nothing for the former; glasses as thick as the bottoms of mason jars helped the latter, though he was never able to drive a car. From the age of seven he couldn't read a word held farther than nine inches from his pale eyes. Still, he managed to read a good deal, as introverted boys often do; not surprisingly, his favourite author was Horatio Alger.

Financial disaster dogged his early years. At nineteen, married with two children, he invested his savings in a Saskatchewan farm and lost everything. With his brother-in-law he became an auto parts salesman and went broke again. By this time he had shed his shyness. "My name's Thomson," he'd say. "Call me Roy." For the rest of his life that was his standard greeting to all, princess or pressman.

In North Bay he tried selling radios. Reception was so poor he decided to open a station himself and did so on borrowed money. Since he couldn't afford to hire anyone, he himself did all the announcing, conducted interviews, sold advertising time, and continued to peddle radios.

To open his new station, CFCH, on March 31, 1931, he threw one of the extravagant dinners for which he would soon be known, inviting the town's leading citizens. This was the turning point in his life, for that little station set the pattern that would, in 1967, lead him to the proprietorship of *The Times*.

Who, in North Bay, would have imagined it? There he was, a shabby, bulky two-hundred-pounder in an unbuttoned overcoat, shambling about town, a fedora pushed back on his head, munching continually on a pocketful of candies. He ran for the town council and was elected. Mort Fellman of the *North Bay Nugget* noticed that when he stood up in the council chamber, there was a patch visible on the seat of his pants.

In 1976, while doing research for a book, I visited him in his Toronto office to talk about those Depression days, when the Dionne quintuplets were the big news in North Bay. He was then in charge of dispensing relief. He looked at me candidly with those pale blue eyes, enlarged by the impossibly thick spectacles, and told me that the experience had prejudiced him against relief. "I don't believe in relief at all, you see," he said. "I'm probably the most right-wing person you've ever met. I believe that you should look after yourself. . . . I think we've ruined the calibre of our people with handouts. . . . Before anybody should get any help from the government they should suffer a little

. . . it's probably better to try like hell to get a job and fail than to just walk in and take a handout. I did it, you know."

This was the creed of a self-made man who ran for mayor, was defeated, ran for council again, was elected, and in the midst of campaigning managed to borrow enough money to buy two decrepit radio stations in the mining towns of Kirkland Lake and Timmins. Since the *Timmins Daily Press* was in the same building as the station, he bought the paper too. From that point on he collected newspapers as other men collect stamps or old coins. He had over 150 in his stable when, more than thirty years later, he acquired *The Times*.

Somehow he managed to turn the *Press* into an eight-page daily; when there wasn't enough type to fill it, he solved the problem by printing the same story twice on different pages.

He was chronically short of cash and working sixteen hours a day, but he continued to acquire more radio stations and newspapers, always on borrowed money. A brash young salesman, Jack Kent Cooke, himself a future multimillionaire, joined him as a sales representative, and the two became close friends. They faced each other at the same desk, joked together, took meals together, even talked to each other on the phone in pseudo-Chinese accents that could reduce both to tears of laughter. Between them they acquired radio stations, newspapers, and a magazine, *New Liberty*. They agreed to split everything they owned, but Cooke reneged on the deal when he wangled a hundred-thousand-dollar-a-year contract from Southam Press. The breakup was as painful as a divorce.

Thomson was not welcomed into the charmed circle of Canadian newspaper magnates. Conservative families such as the Southams and the Siftons were coldly hostile at the Canadian Press meetings when Thomson attended—and no wonder. This was a man who showed his balance sheet to anybody interested and remained unfailingly cheerful in the face of snubs.

But he worked so hard in committee that in 1950 the Canadian Daily Newspaper Association named him president. At that year's Imperial Press Conference he asked everyone he met, "Got any newspapers to sell?" He bought three more that year, and when in 1952 he became president of Canadian Press, he bought another eight. It was not the best time for newspapers. One publisher stood up at a CP meeting to complain that circulation was down, radio newscasts were stealing his stories, labour demands were endless, costs were rising, advertising revenue was falling. He talked for ten minutes, then gloomily resumed his seat. Thomson rose, eyes twinkling behind his thick lenses. "Want to sell?" he asked amid a chorus of laughter.

By this time he had changed banks. Although the president of the Bank of Nova Scotia told him his credit was unlimited, he balked when Thomson, in hock for half a million, wanted another $750,000. Thomson's response was to walk across the street to the Royal. "Do you want my business?" he asked. They certainly did, to the chagrin of Scotiabank. A loan from the Royal enabled him to buy the Guelph *Mercury* and the Chatham *Daily News*. When he was asked how many papers he wanted, Thomson replied, "Fifty-two, one for each week of the year."

All these small-town dailies—he owned no major Canadian newspaper—were subjected to strict budgets that covered everything from salaries to such minor items as glue, tape, and string. One of Thomson's obsessions was to compare the price the *Timmins Daily Press* spent on paper clips with the expenditure of the Guelph *Mercury*. The system was inflexible. No salary could be exceeded. No matter how brilliant a reporter was, if he asked for wages over and above the budget, he was turned down. Nor could any editor steal a hotshot reporter from a rival paper if the offer exceeded the budget.

Roy Thomson boasted that he never interfered with the editorial policies of his newspapers, even the pro-segregation opinions of one of his newly acquired properties in the American South. Short of attacking God or the monarch, his editors were free to write what they liked. A newspaper could support the political party of its choice, but if it spent a dollar a month more on typewriter ribbons, it had to answer to him. Even when he stood as a Tory candidate in York Centre in 1953, he refused to harness the power of his nineteen Canadian papers to

244

his political ambitions. They remained independent. Thomson lost.

This penny-pinching did not help the reputation of the Thomson chain. The country's journalists considered Thomson newspapers a cheap rip-off. Their contempt so irritated Thomson that he published his "Creed" in the *Globe and Mail*: "I can state with the utmost emphasis that no person or group can buy or influence editorial support from any newspaper in the Thomson group."

The real "influence" came from another direction—the bottom line. Thomson papers did not rock the boat; that wouldn't be profitable. They did not attempt the kind of tough investigative reporting that might anger not only the subscribers but, more importantly, the advertisers. They swam with the tide, not against it. They were bland, not trenchant. According to Thomson's published creed, they had the interests of the community at heart, but those interests were always the interests of the establishment. No editor could afford to take a radical or unpopular stand. Thomson was quite right when he declared he didn't oversee or influence his papers' editorial policies. He didn't have to.

Susan Goldenberg, in her study of the Thomson empire, has suggested that there were two Roy Thomsons. There was the young Roy who made his mark in Canada with a string of small-town papers and radio stations where the emphasis was on profits from advertising, not editorial comment—the man who insisted on financial controls so tough that reporters were told to use scrap paper rather than notepads for interviews. Then there was the second, older Roy Thomson who, at fifty-nine, moved to Great Britain, bought some of the country's greatest newspapers (more for prestige than for profit), and never demurred when reporters spent thousands chasing a news story around the world.

Denis Hamilton, though scarcely unbiased, summed up the general attitude to his boss in Great Britain—one that was totally at odds with his Canadian image. "Perhaps there will never be another Roy Thomson, a man with an insatiable appetite for ownership but without interest in exercising power. Behind his absurdly thick spectacles lurked neither envy nor spiteful ambition. He wasn't in any way religious, and yet his character was open and sincere. I never met a man less trumped-up or simpler in his tastes and joys. He radiated a sort of good-will, a confident courage, an almost childlike enjoyment in challenge. Beside the Maxwells and Murdochs of this world, he was like an innocent. And unlike Kemsley, he knew how to delegate."

Compare that with a Canadian assessment by Jack Scott, the *Vancouver Sun*'s best-read columnist: "This self-centred little creature. . . driving with relentless fury towards his Buckingham Palace goal. . . casting his businessman's blight on every property he touched."

In his sixtieth year, when most men are preparing for retirement, Roy Thomson left Canada and set out to conquer the United Kingdom. He has described it as "a bleak period in my life." His wife had died of cancer; his closest friend, Cooke, had broken with him; his two daughters had married; and his son, Kenneth, was "still too young to appreciate what made the old man tick." There was no one in whom he could confide or on whose understanding he could count. His solution was to uproot himself and begin afresh in a Scottish city, Edinburgh, which had a reputation for aloofness and where he knew hardly a soul.

Why? "Because. . . I was always afraid of standing still, of stagnation." Equally significant, a prestigious prize was being dangled before him—the *Scotsman*, a newspaper with an international reputation that bore no relation to anything he owned. He confessed to "a curious urge to step into the top class, probably due to nothing more complex than the loss of my wife." But there was more to it. Cooke had left him to get into the big league. Thomson was determined to show his erstwhile partner what the big league really meant.

The *Scotsman* was losing so much money that its financial adviser urged the board to sell it. The only stipulation was that it must not be sold to an Englishman. Thomson headed for Scotland having advised the Royal Bank that he'd be needing money to buy it. "Nonsense," said the bank's Scottish president, James Muir. "It can't be bought. It's an institution. If he thinks he can buy it, he's crazy." It was, he said, like asking a gentleman how much he wanted for his wife.

Muir was wrong. After three hours of hard bargaining, Thomson got three-quarters of the stock by promising to become a resident publisher and never to sell out to Fleet Street. "If my name had been spelt with a 'p' [the English spelling]," he said later, "I'd never have got it."

The Scottish establishment soon became aware that a strange breed of cat had landed among them—a man who insisted on putting everybody on a first-name basis, who could read a balance sheet as well as Glenn Gould could read a score, who answered every letter he received, took his own telephone calls ("you never know if it's some guy who's going to offer me a newspaper"), whose candour was disarming ("I'm frank, brutally frank. And even when I'm not frank, I *look* frank"), and who was, to the dismay of his new acquaintances, devoted to the hard sell with an almost religious intensity.

He candidly admitted that what he really wanted was a knighthood. His acquisition of the *Scotsman*, he believed, would help him get one. The paper was piling up colossal losses, but Thomson, looking it over, was not disturbed. "You'd have to be crazy not to make money on this deal," he said. "The real estate and buildings are worth a million pounds" (a quarter million *more* than he'd paid). "My God," he continued, "you'd wonder how they could run a business like that. They wouldn't last six months in Canada."

He was impervious to snubs, and there were snubs aplenty. Edinburgh's upper crust closed its doors to him. He accepted all invitations indiscriminately and turned up at all the functions, where he was urged not to change the newspaper—not a paragraph, not a line. But he knew there would have to be changes if only to improve the paper's coverage. "Edinburgh's idea of stop-press news," he said during one of his many visits to Canada, "is a picture of some mouldy old ruin with a description of what it was like two centuries ago!"

He moved warily, but firmly, to replace the *Scotsman*'s front page with news instead of advertisements. It took him three years. To announce the big change, he hired London's Festival Hall and invited every prominent Scot in the city. It wasn't fitting, he told them, for the leading Scottish paper to introduce itself with advertisements. When the first reorganized edition came off the presses he invited the cream of Edinburgh society to the *Scotsman*'s offices. Each guest got a copy of the paper with news appearing for the first time on the front page. Next day the paper was swamped with calls from angry readers cancelling their subscriptions.

Though he now owned a chauffeur-driven Daimler, he offended his peers by queuing up outside his office each night to take the bus home. He did his best to buy goodwill by giving large sums to various Scottish institutions. Meanwhile, he publicly announced his intention of bidding for an independent Scottish television station. "It's going to be a money maker," he told his colleagues. Few agreed. Had Thomson gone mad? In England, commercial TV was losing five million pounds a year. How could a brash Canadian with no experience get a Scottish charter?

But he plunged ahead. In his application he listed his twenty-five years of radio experience and his shared ownership of two Canadian TV stations, gave details of his programming policy, and pledged to support the venture financially.

He found little backing. Those he approached seemed to agree with Sir Alex King, who said, "It will be a failure, and I will not be associated with failure." Everybody from Clifford Sifton in Canada to Lord Beaverbrook in London—both seasoned journalists—refused to contribute a cent. In the first months of 1955, Thomson sent out a blizzard of letters to all the Scottish peers and heads of clan, even to the Scottish Co-operative Movement and the Labour Party, but the Scots wanted no part of Thomson's mad venture; nor did the English. One of the problems, as he candidly admitted, was Thomson himself, the parvenu seeking to break through the establishment's crust.

He needed £400,000 to build, open, and sustain the new television station. All he was able to raise—from some show business personalities, his own employees, and a smattering of commoners—was £80,000. The remainder would come out of his own pocket.

He got his licence in spite of the fact that he had no studio, no artists, no announcers, no producers, no technicians, no musicians, and no programs—only a contract to found Scottish Television Limited, with himself as chairman.

"What do we do first?" Jim Coltart asked him.

"I haven't any idea."

Coltart was taken aback. "Roy, I get a certain impression that you know nothing about running a TV station."

"That's quite correct."

"But you said in the application to the Authority that you were a part owner of two stations in Canada!"

"Well, I am. But I only took a share in them to give Rupert Davies—Senator Rupert Davies—some financial backing when he needed it. I've never had anything to do with the running of them."

Coltart could only close his eyes and laugh. "That's fine," he said. "So we both start from scratch."

From the beginning Thomson kept a keen eye on the new operation. He got copies of every order for advertising time on the new station and carried these folded up in the pocket of his coat to be able to refer to them repeatedly whenever he paused for a cup of coffee. As a result, he was the first to know how much money was being spent and where he stood financially. It quickly became apparent, as he himself blurted out, that he'd been given a licence to print money.

During the first eight years, Thomson's share of the television profits ran to £13 million. Within two years the take was such that he could buy the Kemsley publishing empire, the largest in the United Kingdom, which included the *Sunday Times* and twenty-two other Sunday, daily, and weekly papers. It was the biggest takeover in British newspaper history and for Thomson a sweet deal in more ways than one. Five years before, when he had tried to purchase Kemsley's *Aberdeen Press & Journal*, the patrician press lord had delivered a calculated snub by jacking the price impossibly high. Now Thomson had it all.

Fleet Street's reaction was predictably sour. Sir Beverley Baxter, a fellow Canadian, implied that Thomson must acquire "polish and grace" to operate the *Sunday Times*. An executive of the *Observer* called him "a vulgar North American whose only virtue seems to be that he knows it." Kemsley himself claimed he sold out to Thomson because he knew the Canadian wanted a title and would pay through the nose to become a Fleet Street press lord.

As a member of the Big Four—with Lords Beaverbrook and Rothermere, and Cecil King of the *Daily Mirror*—Thomson now found himself accepted everywhere. When Donald Brittain made the National Film Board documentary about him, he wanted to show his subject at lunch with some prominent figures. Thomson simply picked up the phone, called the prime minister, Harold Wilson, and asked him to come over and bring some bigwigs. Wilson dutifully turned up with a covey of diplomats, including both the Russian and the American ambassador. After Wilson left, Brittain said he'd like to film Thomson in the Communist zone. "Where do you want to go?" Thomson asked. Brittain suggested Czechoslovakia. Thomson's influence enabled Brittain to photograph the newest Fleet Street magnate interviewing Antonin Novotny—the first interview the Czech dictator had ever given.

At this point Thomson had two goals: first, to increase his newspaper holdings; second, to gain a peerage. He was, in Denis Hamilton's words, "absolutely obsessed by his desire for a title. He had assets worth millions of pounds, but only one thing counted in his mind—to become Lord Thomson."

In spite of his antipathy to charity, but in the interests of a peerage, he put up five million pounds—an enormous sum equal to some twenty-five million dollars today—to fund the Thomson Foundation to train senior newspaper and television staff. He buttonholed everybody, including the Prime Minister of Canada, to get what he wanted. John Diefenbaker couldn't do much because no Canadian could accept a peerage, though he did offer the governor-generalship of Canada. Other honours were heaped upon Thomson. He became Honorary Colonel of the Toronto Scottish Regiment, and Chancellor of Memorial University, St. John's ("I am the only Chancellor of a University who quit school at fourteen and had no further education," he announced proudly). Thanks to prodigious research, he acquired his own Thomson tartan and his own coat of arms with the motto "Never a backward step."

He had the temerity to ask the then prime minister, Harold Macmillan, about the prospects of a peerage. Macmillan said he couldn't recommend it to the Queen unless Thomson became a citizen of the United Kingdom, which he promptly did. The *Sunday Times* attacked Macmillan editorially, but Thomson, true to his creed, did not interfere. Fleet Street, used as it was to titled newspaper magnates dictating the editorial policy of their papers, found this both refreshing and astonishing.

"Why not a life peerage, Roy?" Diefenbaker asked him. Not good enough. Why? "Because an hereditary peerage is the best way I can prove to Canadians that I'm a success."

To his consternation, Harold Macmillan—his best hope of getting a title, now that he had rejected his Canadian citizenship—fell ill. His successor was Alex Douglas-Home—Lord Home now—whose appointment the *Sunday Times* had bitterly opposed. But Macmillan had told Home that he wanted Thomson to have a peerage, and Thomson got it.

Baron Thomson of what? Ontario? Toronto? The Canadian government suggested Mississauga, where he had his Canadian home. Thomson held out for a more impressive title. He discovered that the River Fleet ran directly beneath Fleet Street, so Thomson of Fleet it would be. At Beaverbrook's eighty-fifth birthday dinner, held by Thomson, the aging press lord called him "the cheekiest fellow who ever lived. . . . You tell us how to run our business more efficiently and then right in front of our noses, you take the title of Fleet—when we all should have thought of it before you."

For Thomson this was the pinnacle. It had been, he said, an even greater ambition than owning a hundred newspapers "because it seemed such an unreasonable one—a hundred-million-to-one chance."

Now the new peer rubbed shoulders with the world's crowned heads, from Haile Selassie of Ethiopia to the Shah of Iran, as well as the most important world leaders from Khrushchev to Nasser. He began to diversify, moving into magazines, books, publishing, and even packaged holidays. His great triumph had been his insistence on producing a colour supplement for the *Sunday Times*, an expensive gamble that cost him £100,000 in the first eighteen months but which, by the time he received his peerage, was a formidable success. The paper's circulation had been less than a million when he bought it; when Thomson merged the *Sunday Times* with *The Times* in 1967 it had reached a million and a half.

A new Roy Thomson had emerged, a man who could afford to spend vast sums of money to acquire status and prestige, which was all *The Times* could give him. He told the Monopolies Commission that taking over the highly unprofitable paper was the most difficult task he had ever accepted. If any handicaps were placed in his way, he would not undertake it.

Given *The Times*' appalling losses, no one but this newly minted citizen was willing to save Britain's pre-eminent newspaper. Reckoning that he might lose at least eight million pounds to keep it afloat, Thomson was at last prepared to publish a newspaper for reasons other than profit and to step aside and watch its progress at arm's length.

He had told me that he went after money because, in the twentieth century, money was the yardstick by which people judged success. Now he had it. He had said that he wanted to own fifty-two newspapers, one for every week in the year. By 1967 he owned more than one hundred and fifty and he couldn't stop, for he was more than a businessman, he was a *collector*.

In his remarkable career, one can find proof for the old adage that if a young man wants something badly enough, he can, if he is single-minded, eventually achieve it. The young Thomson had studied his Horatio Alger intensively. His temperament was such that early financial disasters didn't faze him. He was too shrewd to permit himself the luxury of anger or revenge. He remained cheerfully impervious to personal attacks, vicious criticism, and calculated snubs. He was clearly convinced that he could surmount them and do so without cutting his cloth to fit the style of his times. There wasn't a pompous bone in his body; he continued to be "Roy" to all. He said what he thought, often to his personal disadvantage. Frankness was part of his style and also part of his charm.

Business was his life; he knew few other pleasures. His only indulgence was collecting hundreds of cheap rings. In moments of boyish

252

abandon, he would sometimes lie down on the floor and fling them over the carpet. He had few vices other than his celebrated stinginess. No scandal besmirched his name. He did not drink and he did not take pills. Whenever a headache threatened he tried to out-think it. He was convinced that this ability to concentrate was the secret of his success. Everything—triumphs, failures, problems solved—was neatly filed in his brain, as in a computer, for future use.

"Thinking is work," he wrote. "In the early stages of a man's career it is very hard work. When a difficult decision or problem arises, how easy it is. . . to give up thinking about it. . . . Sloppy and inconclusive thinking becomes a habit. . . . If one wants to be successful, one must think; one must think until it hurts. One must worry a problem in one's mind until it seems there cannot be another aspect of it that hasn't been considered. . . . There are few people indeed who are prepared to perform this arduous and tiring work."

The time would come, Thomson said, when the work would become less arduous, when "one's mental computer arrives at decisions instantly or during a period when the brain seems to be resting." He called this "a bank of experience" that one builds up in the early days and draws on heavily in later years.

Thomson's whole career, which still had almost a decade to run and would include his exploitation of North Sea oil, was certainly testimony to that.

SIX: TERRE DES HOMMES

"A man's reach should exceed his grasp, or what's an EXPO for?"

1

We look back today on the miracle of Expo 67 with feelings of pride and nostalgia. "Miracle" is the proper word. How did we manage to pull off the greatest world exposition in history with about half the start-up time that most world's fairs require?

It is salutary to remember that, at the outset, very few Canadians thought it could be done. Montreal's ebullient mayor, Jean Drapeau, was almost alone in his belief that such an ambitious project was possible. We see it now as one of the shining moments in our history, up there with the building of the Pacific railway or the victory at Vimy Ridge. As I well know, both of these, like Expo, took extraordinary efforts by remarkable people to make them succeed. And all three were launched in the face of widespread pessimism about the country's ability to mount a project so fraught with pitfalls.

There was, indeed, a growing feeling that this kind of universal exposition was passé. "The world's fair is a tired institution," wrote the leading American urban critic, Ada Louise Huxtable, in 1960. "It is a long time since it startled the world with its products or offered stimulating or controversial ideas. No longer an instrument of genuine intellectual exchange, it has been reduced to an expeditious economic shot in the arm and an instrument of national propaganda."

The Russians certainly didn't believe that one was feasible or desirable. Seven years earlier they had won the right to mount a world exposition in 1967, but their enthusiasm waned when a French fashion show held in Moscow in 1960 produced staggering attendance figures. A three-mile queue just to visit a hairdressing salon! How could they cope with such crowds over a six-month period? Nor, it was hinted, did the secret police really want tens of thousands of Westerners traipsing through the city, spreading the gospel of free enterprise.

Whatever the reason, the Soviet Union bowed out in 1962, leaving the field open to Canada. Thanks largely to Drapeau's intensive international lobbying, the new exhibition would mark not the fiftieth anniversary of the Russian Revolution but the one hundredth anniversary of

Canadian Confederation. Canada received the official go-ahead on November 13. The time was short: the Russians had eaten up two years, leaving Canada with less than five to mount the project. An additional ten months were lost through politicking. Montreal municipalities and real-estate developers squabbled over the merits of six possible sites while the rest of the country argued about the cost of the "Montreal Fair," as it was termed then.

"Canada cannot be expected to underwrite wild extravagances—Canada cannot be expected to provide to Quebec, under the guise of fair costs, services which Quebec should provide for itself," thundered the *Globe and Mail*. The exhibition was certainly not a priority for the Diefenbaker government in that winter. George Hees, who tended to see events through rose-coloured glasses and who sat on the board of the newly created Canadian Corporation for the 1967 World Exhibition, was uncharacteristically pessimistic. Hees didn't think there was "the slightest chance for Expo." To Prime Minister Diefenbaker, it was nothing more than a glorified trade fair. The background of his two choices to head the Expo team suggests his attitude: Paul Bienvenue, the new commissioner general, was a spaghetti manufacturer, and C.F. Carsley, his deputy, was in the vinegar business. These were patronage appointments. Both men were party stalwarts from Montreal.

The political tangle that followed—and that the Pearson government inherited when it came to power on April 22, 1963—resulted in more delays. Apart from the three-day thinkers' conference at the Seigneury Club at Montebello in May that established the theme of the exhibition, very little was accomplished. Yet of all the shilly-shallying that complicated the early planning stages of the great exhibition, none was more significant or more important than the decision reached at this conference. The artists, intellectuals, scientists, and administrators who sat down together to set the Expo theme had loftier ideas than Diefenbaker or his political successors.

The participants included such respected Canadians as Alan Jarvis, director of the National Gallery, novelists Hugh MacLennan and Gabrielle Roy, J. Tuzo Wilson, geophysicist, and Claude Robillard, town planner. It was they who decided upon the unifying conception "Man and His World," taken from Antoine de Saint Exupéry's *Terre des hommes*: "To be a man is to feel that by carrying one stone you can contribute to the building of the world." Robillard, who had once spent an afternoon with Saint Exupéry, championed the idea at a meeting in the Windsor Hotel in Montreal. Drapeau, who was also present, took to it. As Robillard said, "I thought the time was over when we could have world exhibitions showing gadgets, mechanical devices, the latest automobiles and the latest screwdriver, and that it was time the accent was placed on man rather than his inventions."

The Montebello Conference developed this keynote over its three-day session. One of the most active participants was Gabrielle Roy, who insisted that the fair's planners constantly recall Saint Exupéry's words. The theme pavilions (Man the Explorer, Man the Creator, Man the Producer, and so on) all reflected this humanist view. "The entire development of the Exhibition on the site shall reflect the primacy given to human values and aspirations in the theme Terre des Hommes," the report of the conference read. "It must not be presented as a Terre des Nations or a Terre des Machines." With those words, the conference set Expo 67 on a dramatically different course from all previous world fairs.

The big question, as Gabrielle Roy later wrote, was "Could a world exhibition, an exchange of displays on a mass scale, take its inspiration from such an ideal? Could it hope to evoke reaction in the multitudes that would come, drawn much more, let us admit, by the desire to be entertained than the desire to be 'provoked'? We were then led to ask ourselves: What is a world exhibition? Here it was necessary to distinguish between a fair, where man brings the products of his activity to sell, and an exhibition where his purpose is to compare, to show with pride, to emulate. In simpler words, an exhibition might be interpreted as a gathering in the public square of the world to show what we have done and to see what others have done. . . .

"At Montebello each of us made recommendations: where possible the participating countries should consider the same philosophy in their

258

plans for national pavilions; the Canadian Corporation for the 1967 World Exhibition should devote its efforts to making the theme the central core of all its pavilions and in all its other projects. This would be its distinct and personal share in the common effort of the seventy-odd countries that would join with us to create Expo 67. The theme pavilions with constant emphasis on human interdependence would then form the hub of the great wheel of men and nations. . . . We thought it desirable that contributions to the project should blend, complement one another, forming one complete whole, like the perfectly balanced instruments in an orchestra."

As a result of his meeting with Robillard, Drapeau was very much in tune with the thinking at Montebello. Without his push in the early stages, there would have been no Expo. Hard-driving, incorruptible, visionary, even dictatorial, he put his stamp on the venture. He could not be deterred, in spite of vigorous opposition, from his plan to build the exhibition on two man-made islands in the St. Lawrence. On August 13, 1963, he went so far as to arrange an official ceremony at which the Prime Minister tilted twenty-five yards of earth onto Île Ste-Hélène, even though the site had not yet been officially chosen. Pearson sounded remarkably lukewarm. "I would be less than frank," he said, "if I did not add that I feel we all have cause for concern over the magnitude of the tasks that must be accomplished if the fair is to. . . be the success it must be."

A week later both Bienvenue and Carsley resigned. The continuing political squabbles between three levels of government had soured them, or so they said. Certainly the Liberals made little effort to retain them.

At this point, Expo had no top management, no sure site, and, many thought, no future. If the Prime Minister sounded sceptical, he had reason to be. How could Canada manage to mount a first-class international fair at this late date? It would be a black eye for the country if the only official Class 1 world exhibition ever to be held in North America was a bust. One group of experts hired to assess the problem reported that Expo 67 would have to become Expo 69. "The simple solution is to call off the whole thing," the *Toronto Daily Star*'s financial editor wrote that September. But Jean Drapeau knew, and Pearson also realized, how devastating it would be to the Liberal Party's prospects in Quebec if the event failed.

Drapeau was adamant about the site. A lesser politician might be forgiven for knuckling under to the opposition he was encountering. The proposals alarmed some downtown Montrealers, who foresaw an unruly tourist invasion. Others objected to the idea of enlarging one island, the Île Ste-Hélène park. One Westmount housewife was photographed picketing the island with a placard urging Montrealers to "PROTECT THIS RECREATION PARK FOR CHILDREN." The Quebec Society for the Protection of Birds mounted a protest against the destruction of the mud flats, which were the nesting places for thousands of ring-billed gulls. The mayor of St. Lambert on the South Shore waged an anti-Expo battle that even reached the Quebec legislature. "How would you like a Coney Island on your doorstep?" he asked.

But Drapeau saw it differently. It would not be a Coney Island, and it would not be a "fair," a word he despised, with its connotations of livestock displays and Ferris wheels. New York was planning something of that sort for 1964. Drapeau wanted no part of it. Expo 67's theme, as defined by the Montebello Conference, would be on a higher plane.

Pearson admitted in his memoirs that Drapeau's plan to hold the exhibition in the middle of the river was, at first, "one of the silliest things I had ever heard." He assumed that "with four million square miles of land in Canada, we would be able to find a plot some place." But the eloquent mayor, whose powers of persuasion were legendary, won him over. Twenty-five million tons of fill would double the size of Île Ste-Hélène and create a second island, Île Notre-Dame, just as big. In one move, Drapeau had outflanked the bickering municipalities and real-estate firms that expected to make a killing if they could get the fair in their backyard. His neat solution also made it impossible for speculators to profit from adjoining real estate.

Pearson was so taken with Drapeau that when he became prime minister he wanted to make him commissioner general to replace

Bienvenue. The mayor declined and suggested Pierre Dupuy, the dean of the diplomatic corps. Pearson didn't believe Dupuy would take the job; he was nearing seventy and on the verge of retirement. Drapeau then promised that if Dupuy refused, he'd take over the task himself until a suitable candidate could be found. What Pearson didn't know was that the mayor had already been on the phone to Dupuy—his wife's cousin—in Paris and talked him into it. When Pearson phoned Paris himself, he was amazed that Dupuy enthusiastically agreed to do the job.

When Dupuy, a charming man with a friendly, crinkled face, arrived in Ottawa, Pearson asked him three questions: "Pierre, I would like to know if the exhibition is possible on the site recommended to us? Second, is it possible in 1967? Third, have we the financial resources to do it?" He gave Dupuy a month to come up with the answers. Dupuy was back in three days with three yeses.

By October, the new commissioner general had put together an impressive team of top executives. The dredging of the St. Lawrence channel began that same month. But many members of the government remained dubious. The cost would be phenomenal—the estimated $167 million grew to a staggering $439 million by the centennial year of 1967. Walter Gordon was one cabinet minister who flinched at the price tag. When the newly appointed general manager, Andrew Kniewasser, arrived with a preliminary budget, Gordon looked at the figures, then threw his arms around Kniewasser. "Thanks very much, that's marvellous," he said. "That's the end of the fucking exhibition." But the next day the cabinet approved the budget by a narrow margin. The scales were tipped by the French-speaking ministers.

As for Pearson, according to Kniewasser, "he loathed the exhibition. He loathed it to the last, until opening day. He didn't believe in it." When the fair opened officially, a minor strike of security men briefly threatened to hold up the ceremony. Pearson turned to Kniewasser. "I told you this wouldn't work," he said. Perhaps he was joking. The strike had already been resolved so swiftly and efficiently that few realized anything had happened.

From the outset, the Expo planners were refreshingly open-minded, prepared to toss out old concepts and proceed on their own instincts. The Japanese, who were planning a world exposition in 1970, sent a team to study the Canadians' plans. "Where did you get your foreign advisers?" a Japanese advance man asked discreetly. He was startled to learn that the corporation had none. It had discarded the idea after spending several millions on misleading data supplied by the Stamford Research Institute, a Connecticut firm. The institute's studies estimated that no more than sixteen million people would pass through the gates and that the average age of the visitors would be twelve years. The idea that the entire fair should be designed for sixteen million children did not sit well with the Canadians. They threw out the studies and proceeded on their own. In the end, of course, Expo 67 was an adult fair that attracted fifty-two million customers.

Few Canadians took issue with the name. Indeed, the word "expo" became the accepted name for future world's fairs from Osaka to Vancouver. The phrase quickly entered the language, to be used by entrepreneurs from automobile manufacturers to shoe salesmen.

The Expo symbol, designed by the Montreal artist Juline Hébert, had a rougher reception. The House of Commons spent hours of debate trying to kill it. Members of all parties, sparked by an enraged John Diefenbaker, went on a rampage. "Artistic monstrosity. . . weird. . . sickening. . . . A combination of a tractor 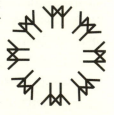 wheel and a bunch of power poles. . . beatnik. . . it hurts every time I look at it. . . . It will bring ridicule to Canada." Politicians are not art critics. What the new symbol brought was one million dollars in licensing revenues.

"Montreal," Jean Drapeau declared, "will not be plagued by a lack of imagination." A sixteen-mile subway (eventually twenty-one miles long) with twenty-two stations, its cars riding silently on rubber tires, would be completed in time to carry the crowds to the festive islands in the St. Lawrence. Every four minutes, day and night for seven months, truckloads of fill, much of it from the subway excavations,

262

rattled over the single access bridge to provide the twenty-five million tons needed by June 20, 1964, the date on which the city was to hand over the property site to the exhibition corporation. The cost of creating one island and enlarging another, together with building a second bridge, an ice boom, and a pier, soon exceeded the amount spent on the St. Lawrence Seaway.

During this period, Gabrielle Roy visited the site. "In the light of a sombre grey day, it looked more like a soggy field, its edges trailing away into the mists of the river—nothing but acres of mud and the whining of the dump trucks. Could anything as glittering as a world's fair rise from this mess?" she asked herself.

Of course it did rise, and it is relevant to pause here and consider what might have happened if, say, the Diefenbaker government had remained in power after 1963, or if Drapeau's predecessor, Sarto Fournier, had won his bid for a world's fair in 1958. At the best, I suspect, we might have got a pale Canadian copy of the mishmash that Robert Moses created at Flushing Meadows in New York. Diefenbaker's famous "vision" was blurred as far as the exposition was concerned. He thought of it purely in commercial terms. Lester Pearson was not wildly in love with the idea, but he was flexible enough to listen to Drapeau, who was. The two Tory bagmen from the food industry, Bienvenue and Carsley, were incapable of handling the kind of extravaganza that Drapeau envisaged. When they resigned (or were pushed), the mayor got his way. Now at last Expo 67 was truly under way.

It has been said that Canada is not a country of salesmen. The men who designed and built Expo modified that stereotype. Pierre Dupuy, the consummate diplomat, acted like an international Fuller Brush salesman, hammering on doors in 125 countries, peddling his wares. He went about the task like a whirling dervish, travelling more than a quarter of a million miles over the next three years. He spent more time outside Canada than he did in Montreal—six weeks abroad for every month on the Expo site. He saw ninety heads of state, spent a minimum of three days in each country, and revisited a good number. They called him Mr. Energy. Every Canadian diplomat abroad was conscripted to support him—to push the idea of Expo with his opposite number. But Dupuy, accompanied by a single aide, made the major approaches himself, using charm, flattery, appeals to national prestige and self-interest to convince every country from Cuba to Pakistan that it could not afford to stay away.

"I've never seen anyone with such stamina," said Jacques Asselin, his executive assistant. "He would be played out and then recuperate during a one-hour flight. He eats the national dishes of each country without the slightest qualms." In the end, sixty-two nations signed up to attend, a number that broke the previous record of forty-six, set in Brussels two decades before.

Dupuy's right-hand man, Robert Shaw, the deputy commissioner general and vice-president of the corporation, ran the show when Dupuy was absent. He came reluctantly to the job, his arm twisted by Ottawa, but once drafted he became the corporation's anchor man. A down-to-earth pragmatist who'd had a brilliant career as a professional engineer and builder, he had started out working for the Foundation Company as a day labourer and risen to become its president. To him, Expo was a mammoth construction job. Tall and imperturbable, he was named the most distinguished pipe smoker of 1966 by the Pipe and Tobacco Council of Canada.

Once Dupuy and Shaw were chosen, the key managers for the Canadian Corporation were appointed. Pat Carney, then business editor of the *Vancouver Sun*, called it "possibly the most exciting and most successful corporation ever created in Canada." The management team met formally every Tuesday morning, complete with secretary to record its minutes, but the real decisions were arrived at by consensus on Wednesday evenings when the members met informally in each other's homes. Here they ate, drank, argued, beefed, and pressured each other in language that no secretary would ever record. Here red tape was slashed and immovable obstacles pushed aside.

They called themselves, rather proudly, *Les Durs*, the tough guys, the hard-nosed ones. Together they were the men who built Expo. As Yves Jasmin, director of public relations, a former P.R. man for Air

Glenn Gould's train trip on the Polar Bear Express was the basis for his centennial project, The Idea of North. *In 1967 he was one of three Canadians with towering international reputations. The others: Roy Thomson, shown signing a cheque (left), and Marshall McLuhan the guru of the sixties.* (ovcrlcaf).

Without Jean Drapeau, the imaginative mayor of Montreal, it's doubtful that Expo 67 would have become a reality. Colonel Edward Churchill (below), the exhibition's master builder, refused to tolerate bad design.

Above: *Philippe de Gaspé Beaubien, the "mayor of Expo," devised the passport system that evened out the crowds.* Below: *Israeli-born Moshe Safdie based Habitat's design on his McGill thesis. It became the most talked about exhibit at the big fair.*

Charles de Gaulle was lionized in French Canada when he cried *"Vive le Québec libre!"* a clear indication of the growing separatist movement. The FLQ was on the rise in 1967. When one of its founders, Pierre Vallières, returned to Canada in handcuffs, he brought along the manuscript of his influential polemic, White Niggers of America, written in New York's notorious Tombs.

The end of an era: René Lévesque (left) *resigns from the Liberal Party in the fall of 1967 to launch a movement that will become the Parti Québécois.*

Below: *The Bi-Bi Report is delivered at last by Davidson Dunton* (left) *and André Laurendeau. Had history passed them by?*

As 1967 passed into history and a band of Liberal has-beens contended for Lester Pearson's crown, few paid much attention to Pierre Trudeau. All that changed in a matter of weeks. But without Expo 67, would Trudeaumania have come to pass?

Canada, Molson, and Ford, put it, "We really felt close, one to another. If one was under fire, the rest would rally round. It was a great feeling to know that if you were having difficulty you could count on the solidarity of the others." This informal, lively, and often contentious way of blowing off steam undoubtedly saved the sanity of more than one key executive. It was an all-male affair; women's lib had not yet made much impression on the Canadian scene. At each of the host homes, the wife cooked the dinner, then discreetly retired.

Two of *Les Durs*, Jean-Claude Delorme, general counsel, and G. Dale Rediker, director of finance and administration, were holdovers from Bienvenue's regime. The new directors included Kniewasser, the general manager—a tall, tough troubleshooter who'd been a commercial counsellor in Paris; Pierre de Bellefeuille, former editor of the French version of *Maclean's*, in charge of theme pavilions and credited with much of Expo's success in keeping the exhibits non-commercial; Philippe de Gaspé Beaubien, director of operations, known as the corporation's Billy Graham, a dynamic speaker whose main job before the opening was to sell tickets; and Colonel Edward Churchill, director of installations.

Churchill, a retired permanent army officer, had helped Montgomery build airfields during the war. When Shaw tapped him for the job, Churchill exclaimed, "Me? Go to Expo? You're out of your goddamn mind. I've a soft job here in Ottawa and I'll kill myself at your ridiculous project." But he later told his fellow *Durs* that he was leading too easy a life and so took the job, mainly because he believed in Shaw more than he believed in Expo. A short, broad-shouldered, red-haired officer with a bulldog face and a raspy voice, Churchill belied the Colonel Blimp image of the permanent force officer. A Winnipeg-born Jew, he was an atheist who cared as much about the look of Expo as its designers did. "We didn't tolerate bad design because it scratches at you; it's an abrasive quality," he recalled. "People always feel locked in when they travel a road lined with billboards. But they feel joyous if they see a beautiful vista. So we set up an aesthetics commission that would rule on everything. . . . No corporation should avoid aesthetics;

if they do not have it, they can't be a corporation with any long-term success."

Churchill could also be tough. It was claimed that he was perfectly prepared to call a bulldozer and push a partly finished building into the river if it was not completed on time. His reputation was such that the threat never needed to be enforced. He was a man who, in the hyperbole of his chief engineer, "could pack five million things in his mind and remember them all." One of his colleagues was startled to encounter a display of this uncanny ability at a cocktail party. "I wonder if you remember when we first met," he asked Churchill, harking back to a casual encounter four years earlier.

"Sure, I remember," Churchill shot back, "and the bar bill was twenty-two dollars."

He worked a seven-day week, often up to midnight, until in November 1965, in the middle of a conference, he collapsed from exhaustion. Sent to hospital, he began giving pep talks to doctors and nurses about how Expo was shaping up. As one colleague said, "He did a bigger selling job for Expo in the hospital than our salesmen have done in the field." Recuperating at home, he had people running in and out with maps, blueprints, documents, and letters. Back at the office, he was ordered to lie down and rest on a newly installed couch for half an hour every day. He never used it; it was always covered with blueprints and charts.

A cutter of red tape, Churchill borrowed the "critical path" method from the U.S. space program, expanding and adapting it for Expo. Under that system, every task is broken down into stages. A pavilion, for instance, could be charted through a dozen stages, from "intention" and "talk" to "working drawings" and "start foundations." Each stage was allowed a specific number of working days on a calendar that began on Day 1 and ended on Day 878—the start of Expo. This method enabled supervisors to co-ordinate one project with another so that Churchill could, for example, order concrete for several buildings and know they'd all be ready to take it. Crews installing sewer lines would be told they could block off a road on a certain day because building crews were scheduled to work around that interruption. Without the critical path, the big fair could not have been finished on time. Expo's builders could not afford to wait to do things in a logical sequence. It was Churchill who realized, for instance, that pavilions could be landscaped while construction was still proceeding and that trees could be transplanted and survive in forty-below weather, something that had never been done in Canada before.

The critical path method had another advantage—a psychological one. It was used to goad two levels of government, federal and provincial, into hasty action. As Kniewasser said, "I would go to these governments and say, 'Now here's the critical path. If you fellows don't deal with Submission No. 1024, which we sent you two months ago, the exhibition will not open in April. And I'll make it perfectly clear to the whole world why.'"

Churchill built the fair; his opposite number, Philippe de Gaspé Beaubien, ran it once it opened. A thirty-two-year-old whiz kid, scion of one of the most illustrious Quebec families whose progenitors had sailed up the St. Lawrence three centuries earlier, he was quickly dubbed the Mayor of Expo. A Harvard graduate, salesman, management consultant, and marketing expert, Beaubien had sold his successful potato chip business and was independently wealthy. Darkly handsome, dapper, and a dynamic speaker, he was part manager, part promoter.

Beaubien was hired in November 1963 by Shaw, who said he needed a crazy French Canadian—crazy because no one in his right mind would take the job, and French Canadian because he needed a Quebec presence at the top level of executives. Beaubien debated the offer with his wife, the former Nan-bowles O'Connell, a beautiful Boston blonde. The two were turning over all the possibilities of failure when Beaubien suddenly exclaimed, "Look, I've been talking about Expo for hours. It's the most fascinating thing I've ever heard of. Imagine what it could do for this country. There's no choice. I must take it."

Three days later he was in Paris, defending Expo before the Bureau of International Expositions. It was very late in the day. The general attitude was cool; how could the Canadians do the job in half the time

267

usually allotted? Beaubien was sitting on the steps of the bureau when he overheard a conversation between two Frenchmen. "Wait till you see those Canadians really flub the deal," one told the other. "They don't have any idea of what it is to do something intelligent and competent on an international scale. This is going to be a disaster and we'll have a good laugh and the next one we'll bring back to Europe." That got Beaubien's dander up. "That's what kept me going day and night," he recalled, "to show those bastards that we could do it. That was the driving force: to show the world."

After he went to the unofficial world's fair held in New York in 1964 and 1965, Beaubien was haunted by worry based on the problems he'd witnessed there—bottlenecks, long line-ups, people frustrated by delays. How could he equalize the crowds at Expo so that everybody didn't queue up at the most popular pavilions—Soviet and American—and nowhere else? How could he get people to visit, say, the Thailand pavilion? Beaubien struggled with the problem until the proverbial light bulb went off above his head. Why not provide every Expo visitor with a passport? Visitors could buy a passport and get the booklet stamped whenever they visited a pavilion. Once inside, Beaubien figured, they might stay awhile.

This ingenious idea for evening out the crowds seems obvious now to those of us whose souvenirs of Expo include these keepsakes, squirrelled away in a bottom drawer. But the idea met with fierce opposition at the time. The commissioner general for France declared that Beaubien's proposal was an insult. The additional costs of having a hostess stamping passports at each entrance would be prohibitive. Beaubien went to see the commissioner general of the U.S. pavilion and reminded him of the New York fair's problems. "You're going to be swamped," he warned the U.S. official. "Will you be able to handle the crowds?"

He won his point. At a meeting of the commissioners general in Moscow, the Americans gave the passport idea their vote. It passed by a narrow margin and turned out to be the most popular piece of gimmickry at the entire fair. People became obsessed by the need to have their passports stamped at as many pavilions as possible. Later world exhibitions copied the idea.

To entertain the crowds waiting in the longer queues, Beaubien hired buskers and troubadours; he even had figure skaters performing on portable rinks towed around by a jeep. To keep the crowds moving he installed six electric signboards giving such messages as "Lots of room and no waiting line at the British Pavilion. Go there now!"

Even without these touches the people in the queues were content, perhaps because the environment was so serene. This was not a raucous fair. The planners had managed to keep the decibel count down by actual measurement. Automobiles were barred from the site. Visitors moved about on several levels: on a monorail overhead, on the "people movers" and pedicabs at ground level, and aboard gondolas that slid silently along the canals below.

Beaubien suggested the idea of canals, which elicited an exasperated response from Churchill, who thought he'd gone out of his mind. By God, he said, in effect, I've just taken the water *out*. I'm damned if I'm going to build a canal. But in the end he did—not canals, as it developed, so much as "spines of water," in Dupuy's words.

It struck Beaubien that this kind of co-operation was the secret of Expo's success—"the Québécois flair, the English-Canadian pragmatism." Churchill wouldn't have thought of canals, but Beaubien couldn't have cleared the way to build them. "I look at my country and I say—who gives a damn?" he said later. "Who gets the credit? The fact is we did better together than alone. It's probable that we've been closer together, English and French, in Montreal and in Canada than anywhere in the world."

The Expo experience has often been used to extol the idea of French-Anglo co-operation. That, perhaps, is making too much of national stereotypes. In truth, the Anglo-Canadians at Expo also showed a good deal of "Gallic" flair while the Québécois demonstrated considerable British pragmatism. In the two centuries since Wolfe fought Montcalm, the characters of both peoples had been shaped and tempered by two powerful influences: the Canadian weather and the Canadian environment. The Montrealer skiing on the Laurentian slopes has more in common with the Torontonian snowmobiling on the Muskoka lakes than with the Parisian lolling in a Montparnasse café. That being said, it can also be noted that this was really the last time that both peoples were able to work together on a great national project without a hint of politics. The result was harmony.

The New York fair had been a jumble of buildings, some astonishing, others tawdry. There seemed to be no uniformity, no theme to tie them together. The Expo planners were aware of that. Everything, including the triangular trash cans and bench supports, bore the stamp of a single designer. Signage was uniform throughout and generally appealing, even though the skirt on the woman's figure on washroom doors was at first too short, confusing the image with its male counterpart. The Expo planners thought of everything, from repair bars for women who had broken their shoe heels in the queues to machines that provided a one-minute leg massage for tired trudgers.

The colour schemes, the architectural design, and the landscaping were all blended to create a unity and an eerie serenity that reflected the Canadian North. Lighting was indirect so that the light flowed upward, not downward, and was softer on the eyes. At no other time in this century was the Canadian passion for order more firmly and effectively demonstrated—and also, one might add, for neatness: double the number of workers were hired than the estimates had called for just to keep the site clean. Because so many people were living on site, especially at Habitat and the marina, the park could not close. It operated twenty-four hours a day. At midnight a whole new world opened. After the pavilions shut, the gardeners arrived and worked through the night on the lawns and flower beds.

In all his days at Expo, Beaubien was never able to attend a single event without being interrupted by his beeper about another problem. Seventeen times during the run of Expo heads of state or their wives received death threats, a fact that the security forces managed to conceal from the press to avoid panic. Beaubien did set out to attend the one event he had planned and wanted to enjoy from beginning to end—the Bolshoi Ballet. Two minutes after he and his wife were seated at Montreal's Place des Arts, his beeper went off: the transport workers had gone on strike! My God, Beaubien thought, I've got seventy-eight thousand people on site and now they can't get home. Using loud hailers, his staff started to move the entire crowd to the amusement park, La Ronde. There everybody partied before walking over the Jacques Cartier bridge to the mainland.

La Ronde was the most popular area on the site, especially after dark. It was also one of the few that made money. At the outset, Dupuy did not want it. It was too commercial, he said, out of keeping with the Expo idea. The matter came up before Montreal's executive committee, whose chairman, Lucien Saulnier, told Beaubien the amusement park didn't fit in with an international exhibition. At forty million dollars, he said, it was a waste of money. Visions, perhaps, of the sleazy Conklin midway at Toronto's CNE: *Laff in the Dark. . . Strange People All Alive. . . Wild Mouse.*

"With all due respect," Beaubien told him, "you're talking without knowledge. Before you make that decision, you should have knowledge. I defy you to come with me to the Tivoli Gardens in Copenhagen. After we've gone together, if you still feel that way, then I'll go along with your decision. But until you've gone there, I don't think you can rightly say it's a waste of money."

"When?" Saulnier asked.

"Tonight!"

"You're kidding."

"No. It's four o'clock. We'll take the seven o'clock plane and be back on Monday."

"You're on," Saulnier told him.

Beaubien escorted Saulnier through the Tivoli Gardens, where they visited pavilions, drank Danish beer, and met people. They were back in Montreal Sunday night.

"You bastard," said Saulnier, laughing. "You're on."

Beaubien badly needed experts to build La Ronde. He and Churchill flew off to see Walt Disney in Hollywood. Disney asked what they wanted. Beaubien said he needed two of Disney's people for two months. Disney supplied them immediately.

The press, which at that time had been generally unenthusiastic about Expo, pounced on this development. Americans running Canada's big fair? And *Disney* Americans, at that! But these two had an expertise no Canadians had achieved. They didn't charge a nickel for their two months' worth of advice.

Canadian apathy was also apparent when Beaubien launched a big press conference in Toronto to match the one that he'd held in Montreal. Only three reporters turned up. Canadian restaurateurs were equally blind to the possibilities waiting to be exploited. By opening day, not a single Canadian had applied for a food concession at Expo 67.

To the astonishment of many, the fair opened on time. On April 27, seven thousand VIPs attended the formal inauguration at the Place des Nations. Beaubien, who had to settle a minor strike on that day, was late for the opening ceremonies, arriving just as the Canadian flag was being hoisted. Fireworks exploded, jets roared over, the entire audience sang "O Canada," and, as Beaubien said, there wasn't a dry eye in the crowd, including his own. My God, he thought, we've done it, we've pulled it off. We haven't slept, we've scarcely seen our wives and families, we've faced up to a host of challenges, but we've made it. Then he thought of the two Frenchmen sneering at Canada's inability to do anything so magnificent. "We'll have a good laugh," they'd said to each other. Now the laugh was on them. His people—English- and French-speaking enthusiasts—had brought off a miracle. We showed them, he thought, as the balloons soared into the sky; we showed them!

2

The Expo 67 officially opened to the public on the morning of Friday, April
dome and 28. The first man officially through the gate was Al Carter, a forty-one-
the tent year-old jazz drummer from Chicago who already had a reputation as
"the first man at world's fairs." Four years earlier he had written to Jean

Drapeau about Expo, but failed to get an answer. That didn't dismay him. He began to bombard Expo officials with requests for the No. 1 ticket to the fair. "If Expo ever issues a certificate for the most persistent and tenacious visitor to the site," Expo's admissions sales manager, J.P. Lussier, wrote to him, "the name of Al Carter would be inscribed in gold."

So Al Carter was there on opening day, brandishing ticket 00001 for a seven-day Expo passport. "I just thought I couldn't retire without a true national effort," he told Richard J. Kaufman, assistant area manager, at the main gate. Kaufman heard his story and agreed to sign an unofficial document: "This gentleman was waiting at Place d'Accueil this morning at 9:30 for the general public opening. To our knowledge, this man is the first in line at Expo."

Carter joined a group of twenty-five young people from as far away as Vancouver who wanted to be able to say they were the first visitors to the fair. The group included two women who sensibly brought hot coffee, a radio, sandwiches, playing cards, a guitar, sleeping bags, and woollen blankets. They and the others were joined the night before the fair opened by two youths from British Columbia who had hitchhiked across Canada—and by Carter. They were all happy to give Carter first place in the line-up because they admired his stamina and dedication. So did Beaubien, who presented him with a gold watch for his feat.

The crowds were so thick that morning at the Île Ste-Hélène Metro station that the gates, scheduled to open at 9:30, were unofficially opened forty-five minutes early. As the atomic clock completed the official countdown, the waiting throng at the Place d'Accueil began to cheer the rhythmically bilingual voice on the loudspeakers: *Quinze. . .* fourteen. . . *treize. . .* twelve. By the time the count reached *onze*, the voice was drowned out.

As the gates opened, an enormous and enthusiastic crowd, reckoned at between 310,000 and 335,000, surged into the grounds, far exceeding the 200,000 visitors the Expo authorities had expected. Sunday's attendance soared to 569,500, a total that surpassed every one-day world's fair record ever set. On its best day (which was its final day), the New York fair had pulled in no more than 446,953.

Montreal's subway was so jammed with crowds heading for the fair that one station had to be closed because of the crush. The specially designed refuse bins couldn't handle the unexpected litter; workmen had to rush five hundred extra receptacles to the site. The unprecedented attendance caused other problems. The sewage system broke down twenty-seven times during the weekend. Water supplies failed at several points. Dust clouds stalled mechanisms in some of La Ronde's rides. There was such a shortage of footpaths that plans were quickly drawn up to cut through the grass to allow more walking space, paved with asphalt to alleviate the dust stirred up by thousands of pairs of feet.

None of these snags seemed to quench the enthusiasm of the visitors or to dampen the professional critics, whose reviews bordered on the ecstatic. Without exception the major U.S. newspapers, TV networks, and slick magazines agreed that Expo was a smash hit—one that couldn't be considered in the same league with the New York fair.

The *New York Times* said "the fair bids to be one of the great international shows of the century. . . . The sophisticated standard of excellence. . . almost defies description." *Newsweek* predicted that Expo "may well be. . . the greatest international exhibition in the history of the world." *Time* called it "the greatest international exposition ever" and devoted eleven pages of colour to its cover story. Practically every other major American magazine gave Expo a similar spread. "Its very existence," *Time* wrote, "is a symbol of the vigor and enthusiasm of the Canadians who conceived an impossible idea and made it come true."

The country basked in this surfeit of praise. For the first time in years the Americans were not only noticing Canada but even looking at the country with awe and enthusiasm. "The Canadians whose ego, individualism, and sense of personal worth have long suffered in the shadow of the colossus of the south, will take a prideful look in the mirror and exclaim: 'We did it!'" wrote the *Washington Post*. The *Economist* pointed out that "the acclaim won for the show on the man-made islands in the St. Lawrence may have done more for Canadians' self-confidence than any other recent event." To Americans, Expo was as startling as it was unexpected. "What's Got Into Our Good Gray Neighbors?" asked a *Look* headline.

The Canadian media, which had been decidedly lukewarm in the early days, now fell all over themselves to haul out superlatives. "How. . . can we ever be the same again?" Peter Newman asked his readers. "This is the greatest thing we have ever done as a nation (including the building of the CPR) and surely the modernization of Canada—of its skyline, of its tastes, its style, its institutions will be dated from this occasion and from the fair. . . . The more you see of it, the more you're overwhelmed by a feeling that if this is possible, that if this sub-Arctic, self-obsessed country of 20 million people can put on this kind of show, then it can do almost anything."

The Prime Minister forsook his earlier caution to call Expo "one of the most daring acts of faith in Canadian enterprise and ability ever undertaken." It was time, Pearson declared, "that we stopped beating our breasts and did a little tub thumping." Pat Carney in the *Vancouver Sun*, the paper that had once wanted Expo scrapped, compared the euphoria she felt on the site to that she had experienced when given a drug for medical reasons. "The world of Expo, like that of heroin, is very real, only more, well, pleasant. The colours are brighter and the air is cleaner, and the flowers are lovelier and the things that normally irritate you don't."

Expo brought out that kind of self-revelatory response in usually blasé journalists. Writing in the *Toronto Daily Star* as "Max MacPherson," Harry Bruce returned for a second trip and again experienced "the silly-headed glee that, for lack of a more original phrase, I must describe as the spirit of Expo. It is a feeling that under certain circumstances, anyway, people really can be good to one another, straight forward, kind and noble. I was no longer tired of myself at Expo. I felt good about me. Mrs. Max felt better about herself, and my kids, who feel pretty good about themselves all the time anyway, they were ecstatic for hours at a time."

When I covered Expo for *Maclean's*, I confessed in print that "I fell captive to an unexpected emotion: a moistness in the eyes and a huskiness in the throat of the kind one usually experiences only in moments of national stress. . . . It was nationalism unabashed and I discovered later that others had felt it too."

Expo obsessed me. I made five trips to the fair including a stay in Habitat and another memorable week parked in a boat at the marina with my family. For me, as for the children, it was a walk through fairyland. I was reminded on each occasion of my first visit to Toronto as a child of eleven, after almost a dozen years spent in a Yukon village. At that time—the year was 1932—I had never seen a neon sign, ridden in a streetcar, or tasted a milk shake. Roller skates were as novel as traffic lights, and the Sunnyside amusement park on the lake shore, with its Dodgem cars and its thrilling roller coaster, was truly for me a magic kingdom. Now, at Expo, the magic returned, making my memories of Sunnyside seem a little tawdry. At Expo we were all children, wide-eyed, titillated by the shock of the new, scampering from one outrageous pavilion to the next, our spirits lifted by the sense of gaiety, grace, and good humour that these memorable structures expressed.

If Expo made visitors feel good, it was partly because it had a unity of design that other exhibitions failed to achieve. In lesser hands it could have been chaos—jarring and cacophonous—as the New York fair had been. As more than one commentator noted, the order and unity imposed on the site by the strict control of street furniture and signage was almost puritanical. Yet the result wasn't sombre, and it certainly wasn't sterile. It was exuberant in a way that few Canadian cities were. After Toronto (good, grey Toronto now), whose antiseptic main drag, University Avenue, I had once dubbed Tombstone Alley, Expo was a revelation. Gondolas, of all things, sliding along the canals! A whiff of Venice on Île Notre-Dame. In many ways it was a McLuhanesque fair, for very little about Expo, from the films to the buildings, could be described as "linear." Each pavilion, by its architectural style, tried to convey something about the sponsoring nation. Though Expo looked back into the past and forward into the future, it was very much in the mood and the mode of the sixties.

The contrast between the U.S. pavilion and that of the Soviet Union

276

was remarked on by almost everybody. The American exhibits, at their best, were playful, nostalgic, and entertaining, but rarely boastful. Housed in Buckminster Fuller's marvellous geodesic dome, the most visible landmark on the islands, they conveyed a mood rather than information. The Soviets, who spent twice as much as the Americans on their awesome, glass-sided pavilion, were obsessed by technological gimmickry, much of it oppressive. Where the Americans were ironic, the Soviets were grandiloquent, offering a formidable statement of technological achievement (a working model of the largest hydroelectric station in the world). The Soviet films were like old-fashioned travelogues, uplifting but dreary. The American film, a three-screen portrait of children's games, was hailed as a documentary breakthrough. Many American visitors were angered at their country's soft sell, with its huge, specially commissioned canvases of pop art, its gigantic photographs of Hollywood stars, and its nostalgic collection of ingenious and well-loved artifacts from the past, such as apple peelers and cherry pitters. Yet there was an implicit message: the United States did not need to shout about its technological achievements. Its exhibits radiated confidence. Its theme was Creative America and its subject was pop culture.

The geodesic dome that housed the U.S. exhibits came of age at Expo. Originally conceived in 1947, when Fuller was an outsider and considered a bit of a nut, it became so popular and so visible (standing 187 feet above the fairground) that it spawned copies everywhere, from Toronto to Vancouver. Its see-through, plastic-and-glass hexagonal sheets, twenty storeys high, gave the pavilion a light, fairy-tale feel in contrast to the huge, glass-sided Soviet behemoth that faced it across the water. At night, lit from within, the dome was sheer fantasy.

The British, who had the tallest building at Expo, topped by a three-dimensional Union Jack, also caught the sixties mood, striving to banish the image of stuffy Englishmen and concentrating on pop groups, long-haired youths, and miniskirts. It was swinging London transferred to Montreal, and no one bothered to note that the swinging image was really the invention of *Time* magazine, hungry for a different kind of cover story. One message, outlined in moving lights, asked: "The

British—are they dignified. . . stuffed shirts. . . chivalrous. . . hum-bugs. . . just shy?" Or maybe lighthearted. As one observer wrote: "There is more gaiety and humour. . . in the British pavilion than in the majority of others."

The West Germans, who had embraced democracy just as the Czechs were forced to abandon it, came up with the most inventive, and, with Fuller's dome, the most influential design of all—"an enormous sur-realistic circus tent," as one reviewer, Neil Compton, called it, as open to the outdoors as the new Germany was to fresh ideas. The great tent was supported on a number of raked masts, the tallest rising more than 120 feet, over which a network of wire mesh was stretched, and open on all sides except where the supporting masts were anchored to the earth. By day it was lit by sunlight filtering through the mesh; by night, it glowed romantically. Conceived by Otto Frei, an expert in suspended structures, it would be widely copied in the days ahead.

The cult of extravagance, which was the hallmark of the period, reached a kind of peak at Expo. Pavilions often identified themselves in terms of statistics. Ontario revelled in the fact that it had imported 12,292 tons of Precambrian rubble for its pavilion—all of it quarried in Quebec. Two of the theme pavilions—Man the Producer and Man the Explorer—were made up of truncated tetrahedrons that required, so a breathless public was informed, no fewer than two and a half million nuts and bolts (made necessary because there weren't enough riveters in the country to do the job). The Netherlands' portable, three-storey pavilion boasted thirty-three miles of aluminum tubing. Quebec's con-tained forty-two hundred two-foot cubes, all painted in bright colours.

Those figures hint at the wild and wacky architecture that was Expo's glory. Expo was an architectural three-ring circus in which designers indulged themselves with every conceivable shape, size, texture, and colour. From this disunity—isosceles triangles painted green (pulp and paper industry), columns that looked like rolled Persian rugs (Iran), gigantic boxes in primary colours (Venezuela)—came a kind of unity. Since every structure represented a radical departure from accepted standards, the unconventional became the norm.

In 1967, the Toronto-Dominion Bank had commissioned Ludwig Mies van der Rohe, the innovative modernist, to design its new headquarters on King Street in Toronto. The Toronto-Dominion Centre incorporated two austere black slabs, the taller one rising fifty-four storeys. Measured against the new concepts realized at Expo, that much-praised complex would be seen as a dreadful bore. It took time for the exuberance at Montreal to filter down, but certainly a case can be made that the exhibition spelled the end of the International Style. James Acland of the University of Toronto's school of architecture, who railed against "monotonous cubes towering into our skies," declared that "something of the virility and sensuous delight, which has been appearing here and there in Canadian architecture, will have a chance to flower in the prismatic structure of the fair." The public agreed. In June when the Expo corporation asked several thousand visitors what they liked about the fair, architecture topped the list.

The Expo influence was not always an improvement. In the major Canadian cities some really dreadful buildings (often in really dreadful colours) sprang up, their architects apparently determined to prove their works could be as different and as spectacular as the ones on display in Montreal. And so we got semi-circular buildings, round buildings, spiky buildings with *faux* battlements and arches. Some of these were hailed as "post-modern," but many seemed only to echo the wacky geometry of the world's fair.

To a large extent Expo was about "image," an old word that had taken on a new meaning in the age of television and political pollsters. Many pavilions were intent on projecting a new image—not the one they had of themselves but the one they hoped others would gain from the exposition. Both Quebec and Ontario undertook market research in this area. The Ontario marketers discovered that most respondents expected the province to stress business and technology. Quebec found, on the other hand, that people wanted its creativity displayed in the form of traditional arts and crafts. Both then decided to do the opposite; in each pavilion, predictable characteristics were reversed. Ontario's was swinging—rock music and electric guitars, op art, endless television (dancing teenagers), talking robots (bilingual, of course), campy displays showing nineteenth-century Ontario. The Quebec pavilion was austere and cool on the outside, belying the *habitant* image—a high-style structure of tinted glass entirely surrounded by water. Inside, the theme was all about challenge, struggle, and drive. Ada Louise Huxtable called it the sleeper of the fair. "It says suddenly and stunningly what a 1967 fair exhibit should be." Quebec gave its visitors an immediate tactile experience in circular elevators that rose from total darkness through a fluorescent forest of infinitely reflected stylized trees and icicles. Its message came through loud and clear: *Forget that rural parish bunk; Quebec is as modern as a discothèque.*

Just as the British strove to show they weren't really stuffy, so did the dictators of the world pretend they were cheerfully freewheeling. The best example, the Czech pavilion, was the hit of the fair, doing its best to prove, through a series of ingenious films and displays, that it wasn't the drab Iron Curtain regime that had chucked democracy overboard after the war.

The huge Canadian pavilion turned architecture upside down. Surmounted by a gigantic inverted thousand-ton, blue-green glass pyramid known as *Katimavik* (Inuit for "meeting place"), it sprawled over four acres and cost twenty-one million dollars, far more than either the Russians or the Americans had spent. The press of Canada, which since Expo's opening had become more and more enthusiastic, revelled in this example of uninhibited Canadianism.

Harry Bruce let his hair down and gave vent to his enthusiasm in the *Canadian* magazine. "The Katimavik is more than striking architecture; it is a celebration. It celebrates the idea of Expo 67. It accelerates the gathering of nations to show their pride in human achievement and to demonstrate that, on remarkable occasions like this one, they can really manage to be nice to one another. The spirit of the Katimavik is the reason why there is a subtle quality to the good times at Expo—a quality that lifts *these* good times to something better, something more, like fine wine, than the pleasures of ordinary world's fairs."

280

Katimavik, like so many of the buildings at Expo, was sculpture as well as architecture. Sculpture dominated the fair, and the public approved. Much of it was outside, in the open air, where passersby could see it and even touch it, like Alexander Calder's sixty-seven-foot stabile *Man*, a piece of art that required forty-six tons of stainless steel; or Gerald Gladstone's *Optical Orbital No. 9*, set in the same waters in which people bathed their aching feet; or the 110-foot steel wall, designed by another Canadian sculptor, Gord Smith; or the three-thousand-square-foot mural constructed over a four-month period by two Cape Dorset Inuit for the La Toundra restaurant. Canada alone commissioned twenty-two outdoor sculptures, all destined for Canadian museums after Expo closed. And these did not include the eleven polished stainless steel figures, all identical, that the Canadian artist Michael Snow carefully arranged in various places around the grounds of the Ontario pavilion.

Expo provided the kind of showcase a sculptor like Snow could not ordinarily command. His remarkable collection, *Walking Woman Works*, each piece cut from the same stencil, was one of the most attractive, and yet mysterious, sculptural installations on the site. It served to enhance his growing international reputation as an imaginative and resourceful artist. Like Gladstone's cleverly placed footbath, Snow's stainless steel women were *used*. You could see your face reflected in them. You could look through the cut-out image of one and see another. They were not placed haphazardly. Snow arranged them so that they worked together. He did it himself, left nothing to chance—even designed the concrete bases on which the walking women stood.

The cut-out women were always seen in profile, caught, in Louise Dompierre's phrase, "in mid-stride, alert, advancing, arms poised perfectly to balance a compact frame." Dompierre, who produced a book on the subject, wrote how the shining figures "flared in the sun, turned dark against sparkling water, were clothed in an ever-changing range of colours and patterns from the trees, sky, river, rocks and passing people. They disappeared entirely in the reflections of dense crowds." They were all larger than life—more than ninety inches tall. One "negative" figure was created when others were cut out of a steel slab. In a "crossing" figure, two of the walking women overlapped. Three figures dominated the entrance plaza, so subtly situated that they influenced the traffic flow. One was isolated down by the water and half hidden by a building so that those who happened upon it experienced a sense of surprise.

This show would be the swansong for Snow's Walking Woman, which had dominated his life and career for five years. The first Walking Woman exhibition, held in Toronto in 1962, was hailed by the art critic Paul Duval as "among the important contributions in Canadian art." That summer Snow began to place life-sized cardboard cut-outs of his figure at bus-stops and in Toronto's subway, where he then photographed them. That year he and his first wife Joyce Wieland, the artist, moved to New York and began to paper the town with the Walking Woman. Manhattan was vibrating with new and radically different kinds of art—pop and op—featuring Andy Warhol's Campbell's soup tins and Claes Oldenburg's gigantic hamburgers. Stimulated by this atmosphere, Snow produced his subtler, more intellectual work. He would creep out in the middle of the night with a pot of glue and a pile of Walking Woman posters and stick them up on hoardings. To his delight, when he retrieved them they'd be frayed and covered with slogans. "That's the start of a new painting," he remarked. The woman image was everywhere, always the same, always walking, always personally intent on her own business as the passing crowd rushed by intent on theirs.

Snow used stencils to make tiny paintings and put them on subway advertising panels. He made a set of rubber stamps of the Walking Woman on different coloured papers, took them to bookstores, and slid them into volumes that he thought might have some relationship. He cut the Walking Woman into pieces like a jigsaw puzzle, put them into envelopes, and mailed them to friends. Soon her shape became familiar to thousands who knew nothing about art.

Through all this period, he was interested in the relationship of the woman to her background. He photographed her in a variety of environments and even gave cut-outs to travelling friends who photographed her against backgrounds as diverse as Ecuador and Russia.

In 1966 Snow entered a contest to choose artists for the Ontario pavilion. Along with Josef Drenters, an entirely different kind of sculptor, Snow got the official nod and a cheque for more than twenty thousand dollars. At Expo he had the perfect venue—thousands of people passing by his work, examining it, touching it, and being photographed against the polished steel figures in which other similar figures were being reflected. Using a plan of the pavilion, he placed his subjects as in a Japanese garden so that one saw only part of the exhibit at a time; to see more, you had to turn a corner.

His work, which he always saw as a single piece, covered a larger area than any other sculpture on the Expo grounds. It was hugely successful. Most people who visited the fair retained only a few images in their minds: the big U.S. dome, the German tent, Habitat, the Czech movies, Calder's stabile, perhaps. But it was not possible to forget those shining steel figures. The Walking Woman, striding purposefully forward against an ever-changing background, belongs to us all.

Expo seemed to be a turning point for Snow. His other medium was taking over. He produced his first major experimental film, *Wavelength*, in the centennial year.

Film in all its manifestations dominated Expo; for many visitors it was the crowning glory of the fair. Everywhere you went there was a film. They surrounded you, wrapped you inside them, bounced off walls, were projected on cubes, prisms, and cruciforms. There were films that moved around the audience and others in which the audience moved around the film.

Here on the islands of the St. Lawrence, a gigantic film festival of the avant-garde ran night and day. No pavilion was complete without at least one film. A cinema addict could have spent every minute of 183 days at the fair just looking at the screen and still not have seen every frame available.

Three thousand films! And most bore little or no relation to anything that had gone before. These were not "movies" in the traditional sense. The majority were non-linear, in the McLuhan definition: bereft of any narrative line, appealing to the eye—experiences rather than chronicles. They were devised, of course, for people whose attention spans would necessarily be short. Some were indistinguishable from architecture. They came with their own building.

The concept of the multi-image or multiscreen film was not new. It went back to the days of Abel Gance's silent masterpiece, *Napoleon*. That inventive couple Rae and Charles Eames pioneered a multiscreen mix of film stills and live action at the 1964–65 New York World's Fair. At Expo, filmmakers from Anaheim to Prague grabbed hold of the idea and ran with it.

The most highly touted film adventure at Expo—and also the spookiest—was *Labyrinth*, created by the National Film Board's Roman Kroitor. It was more than a film—a windowless, five-storey theme pavilion dedicated to Man the Hero and based on the ancient Greek myth of Theseus and the Minotaur. Kroitor likened the experience to a vivid dream that you don't really understand. In the first of three chambers, the audience, hanging over one of four galleries, stared down at a swimming-pool-sized screen on the floor, or peered across at a gigantic vertical screen thirty-eight feet high. In the twenty-minute film that followed, the screens worked together so that a trapeze artist swinging through space somersaulted onto the bottom film. Following that, the audience made its way through an eerie series of narrow corridors and chambers, punctuated by pinpricks of light—the labyrinth. In a second theatre, multiple moving images were projected on five screens arranged in a cruciform. The ultimate shock came when man faced the beast—an Ethiopian in a canoe, who killed a crocodile with a spear thrust. At the climax, the huge central screen showed the animal lashing about in its death throes while the other four screens suddenly lit up with startling still photographs of grotesque African masks. The effect was unnerving, especially when it became apparent that the real beast was man himself. "Conquer it," a voice boomed, "and you can truly join the world."

Graeme Ferguson's *Polar Life*, made for Man the Explorer, featured four slowly revolving theatres on a huge turntable with twelve projectors all running simultaneously. In Ferguson's hands the split screen, often used as a gimmick, became an enormously effective instrument. No better film on life in the polar regions has ever been made; no other has been able to convey the unique experience of living in a polar community.

The wide screen was in constant use at Expo, but one film turned the idea on its side. The screen in Man the Explorer was thirty feet high and only thirteen feet wide. It used three films, stacked one above the other, to show man's ability to cope with hostile environments—deserts, jungles, cities. Entitled *The Earth Is Man's Home*, made by Nick and Ann Chaparos, it ran eleven minutes, about the average time for an Expo film.

To make a multiscreen presentation of this kind required miles of film. The Toronto filmmaker Chris Chapman produced a highly popular film for the Ontario pavilion, *A Place to Stand*, that ran seventeen and a half minutes, but was really ninety minutes long because it contained as many as fifteen simultaneous images on the screen in various geometrical shapes. Most of the films at Expo had a short life, being created specifically for the exhibition. No ordinary theatre could show them. But Chapman did not use separate screens; he edited everything into a single strip of 70mm celluloid so that any projectionist could show it, as many later did.

The Telephone Association provided another spectacular—a vast circular auditorium in which a gigantic 360-degree film surrounded the audience. It was the perfect medium, one wag said, for those fortunate people born with their eyes in the back of their heads. It was also the most nationalistic show on the grounds, complete with Niagara Falls, a hockey game, the schooner *Bluenose*, the Canadian Rockies, and the Mounties' Musical Ride. Far too jingoistic, perhaps, for any Canadian producer, it was the work of the elves at the Walt Disney Studio.

The sleeper at Expo was Kaleidoscope, a building sponsored by Canada's chemical companies and not strictly a film so much as an experience. In its own building devoted to Man and Colour, in a series of mirrored chambers, a bustle of brightly coloured abstract shapes and patterns of colour whirled, flared, and swooped. Flowers suddenly burst open, firecrackers exploded, birds changed colour, providing what many reviewers referred to, in the argot of the day, as a psychedelic trip.

It remained for the supposedly sombre Czechs to add a sense of fun and a great deal of ingenuity to the Expo film festival. They had already captured first prize at the Brussels World's Fair with their imaginative *Laterna Magika*, a combination of film and live action (which also ran at La Ronde). The Czech filmmakers scrambled to outdo themselves in their own pavilion. The most popular of their several films was the *Kino-Automat*, where the audience was invited to contribute to the plot of the film. At a dozen or so points, the frame froze and the leading actor came on the stage offering everybody two choices—a moral one and an immoral one. Should the hero whack an obstructionist doorman on the head with a wine bottle? The audience could decide the outcome by pressing a Yes or No button on the arms of the chairs. Since the immoral decision made for a better plot, the majority usually pressed the Yes button. "What we are doing here really is making a sociological study about group behaviour," the *Kino-Automat*'s creator, Raduz Cincera, explained. "It is fantastic. We are learning that people decide not on a moral code but on what they like to see." Was that so surprising? Hollywood had long known that bad guys and immoral women were the essence of successful movie making.

It is chastening, three decades later, to read the prophecies about the effect that Expo's mixed media would have on future filmmakers. "No one who makes movies," wrote Joseph Morgenstern, *Newsweek*'s film critic, "and wants to make better ones, will ever be the same once he sees the sights and smiling audiences at Expo." Frank Kepplar, in *Life*, suggested "if it is true [that] members of this post-Gutenberg generation absorb knowledge largely through their senses, the mixed media may bring a real breakthrough in education." Kepplar believed that special theatres would dot the cultural landscape, showing multiscreen films, and that the Czechs' *Kino-Automat* "could make a profitable career by asking housewives which wash is whiter."

Graeme Ferguson predicted that Expo would change filmmaking

more than any other event in history. It certainly changed it for Ferguson, who, with Roman Kroitor, created the big Imax installations that were Expo's chief film legacy. (There are now 150 Imax theatres in twenty-two countries and the number is growing.) Apart from that, the kind of movie that awed and titillated Expo 67 visitors has remained a phenomenon confined to amusement parks and to later Expos. Robert Fulford, in his book *Remember Expo*, suggested that the new multi-screen techniques could be and probably would be adapted to feature movies. In a melodrama, for instance, he pointed out that simultaneity might replace cross cutting. A safecracker and the policeman coming to catch him could be shown on twin screens at the same time. That hasn't really happened. At Expo the popular motion picture experiments put technique ahead of content. But in the real, post-McLuhan world, producers and audiences alike have opted for content every time.

3

The most controversial, best-known, most talked about theme pavilion at Expo celebrated Man and His Environment but was far better known as Habitat. It was remarkable in many ways, but the most singular thing about it was its creator. Some of the world's most original architects produced buildings at Expo. But Habitat was the inspiration of a totally unknown twenty-eight-year-old Israeli Canadian named Moshe Safdie. *Moshe Safdie's dream*

No one could miss Habitat. Stretched out on the north shore along Mackay Pier, it looked like a cluster of building blocks scattered about by a Brobdingnagian child. Actually, it was the much revised result of a graduate thesis written by a young student who, when he advanced the proposition, had never built anything in his life.

Safdie was no ordinary student, and, as it developed, no ordinary architect. A gold medallist at McGill, where he won a fistful of awards, he stood first in his class. But to turn his thesis into a vast, avant-garde, $13.5-million-dollar complex housing more than one hundred and fifty families! That took nerve, not just on the part of the architect but of the Expo hierarchy, notably Colonel Edward Churchill.

The times were right, and Habitat was very much a product of the times. Builders and architects were rejecting the past and looking to the future. Historic structures were neglected and often demolished; 1967 was a year dominated by the apostles of the new. "It was," Safdie has recalled, "the period of new towns, the great society, urban renewal, and housing. . . . It was a heroic, optimistic period of looking ahead. The sky was the limit and the future would be rosier." City real estate was growing scarcer; people were fleeing to the suburbs or living in impersonal downtown high-rises. Habitat was seen as a way of asserting the family's identity in its dwelling place while at the same time meeting the pressing need for scarce urban land. The complex, the *Montreal Star* wrote, "is all that is exciting about the city itself, a blending of the past, present, and future that takes one's breath away. Its location and view caught the essence of Montreal's past, while its design caught the city's 1967 spirit—the headlong rush not only to catch up with the twentieth century, but to push eagerly into the twenty-first."

Habitat, in its final, scaled-down form, consisted of 354 modular units organized into suites for 158 families. These were precast in concrete and manufactured in a huge, temporary, barn-like building adjacent to its site. Once each concrete box was formed, cured, and sandblasted, it was moved to the finishing yard where ready-made components were put inside it. Complete bathrooms of moulded fibreglass were installed, very much as in an automobile assembly line. Kitchens were inserted in the same way. Prefabricated partitions were fitted into place along with plumbing, wiring, and glazing. When each unit was complete, it was hoisted into its place in the cluster by a gigantic crane, then bolted, secured, and connected up. At that point the fine finishing, such as painting exterior doors, was done.

The three Habitat clusters rose in irregular pyramids to a height of twelve storeys, so that the roof of one served as the garden terrace of another. Three elevators stopped at every fourth floor, which allowed access to the covered walkways. Safdie called these walkways

288

"streets," and he called the dwelling units "houses." And they were, in a sense, houses, so arranged that each family could enjoy maximum privacy and its own unique outlook, even though living cheek by jowl with its neighbours. Every house had a private terrace and garden—some had two—and a front door that opened out onto a street. Each main street dipped periodically to widen out into a fully protected playground park. The feeling of space was enhanced by the floor-length sliding windows that led into the garden from every room and was magnified in those houses that were spread over two storeys. Thanks to carefully constructed balustrades, nobody could look down on any of these gardens. All the public areas were automatically cleared of snow by electric heating, and all the gardens were automatically irrigated to prevent plant roots from drying up, as they would tend to do in a mere two feet of soil.

Some visitors to Habitat were reminded of a Mediterranean village, which was not surprising, given Moshe Safdie's background. He was born in Haifa, where he felt very close to nature. It is a hilly town where the roads follow the contours and are connected everywhere by steps. He and his family spent their lives walking up and down stairs rather than driving. Even though they lived in an apartment, it was, like others in Haifa, arranged with its own private entrance on the hill. The Safdie family kept fifty chickens, two goats, and two beehives—a little farm in the heart of a bustling city, where, as in other Mediterranean communities, the lines between rural and urban are slightly blurred. Here were sown the seeds of Safdie's philosophy.

By the time he was fifteen, the family had emigrated to Canada and settled in Montreal. Young Moshe had already decided to become an architect and in 1955 registered in architecture at McGill. There he came under the influence of Douglas Shadbolt, who talked about the problems of mass production and about industrializing the building industry. Safdie and his fellow students were assigned to plan a housing project in Vancouver—an actual program of the Central Mortgage and Housing Corporation. It was typical of its day: two apartment slabs with one- or two-bedroom units and some row houses at the base. The more Safdie thought about this monotonous conformation, the less sense it made. He began making drawings, models, and cardboard cut-outs and came up with an unresolved model of terraced units piled one on top of the other and "set back in some way." But the final solution eluded him.

While still an undergraduate, Safdie was chosen as one of a group of students from every architectural school in Canada sponsored by CMHC to travel about the United States looking at public housing and suburbia. Two things stood out: high-rise apartment buildings that didn't work for families, and suburban developments that, though preferable to high-rises, didn't work either. Single-family developments were choking the cities.

In the formal presentation required of each student, Safdie announced that in a high-density environment, the amenities of the house and the village must be recreated. Humphrey Carver, who was on the advisory committee of CMHC, said it couldn't be done. "Well," said Safdie, "I'm going to try and do it." He abandoned his proposed thesis, an apartment building in Jerusalem, and decided instead to plan a housing system. Student theses were supposed to involve single buildings. Safdie wanted to design a complex that would not apply to any one particular site. After some negotiation, he was given reluctant permission to go ahead. He called his idea "A Three-Dimensional Modular Building System." As he wrote later, "It had all the ingredients that were eventually to make up Habitat."

Although everybody was sceptical at first, his thesis eventually won the highest marks at McGill and a gold medal for Safdie. In 1961, after graduation, he went to work for a Montreal firm headed by Sandy van Ginkel, a colourful, red-headed architect whom Churchill called "the best recognizer of talent I've ever known." Safdie, who continued to work on his plan, found van Ginkel "an inspiring and ebullient critic; words come out like eruptions in a fencing match, waiting for a chance and charging again. . . ."

He completed his plan in a year, and then decided to try to work for the world-famous architect Louis Kahn. Since Kahn was in a

Philadelphia hospital awaiting an operation, Safdie used the time to travel through Arizona and Mexico to hone his ideas on urban planning. The ruins of Indian cliff-dwellings in the Grand Canyon, the adobe clusters on the desert hilltops, and the villages surrounding the causeways and pyramids of the Mayan and Aztec cities had a tremendous influence on him. He was overwhelmed by Taxco, a Mexican town sitting on a hill with walkways and connecting stairs, and "a unity that seems to have been achieved by cobblestones, whitewash and planter-boxes all like lace work on the steep hills." This village was more meaningful to him than any work by individual architects. "I can't think of very many buildings that have moved me as the little hill town of Taxco did," he wrote.

His roundabout route eventually took him back to Philadelphia where Kahn, newly released from hospital, put him to work. But the idea of a Habitat-like structure was never far from his mind. It was 1962, and planning for the New York World's Fair was well under way. While working on one of Kahn's projects, Safdie sent a careful sketch and letter to the Portland Cement Company Institute in Chicago, showing how to build half a dozen houses as a pavilion. They were never acknowledged.

The following year, van Ginkel, who was now deputy to Claude Robillard, Expo's master planner, urged him to return to Canada. Safdie had three conditions: he wanted time off to work on his Habitat housing plan, he wanted to develop it within the Expo structure, and he needed ten thousand dollars a year to live on. He got them all and was back in Montreal that August.

Van Ginkel had assembled a group of imaginative young architects. Their first move was to extend the exhibition site back to Mackay Pier so that the city as a whole could enjoy long-term benefits from Expo. But what was to go where? Everybody had an opinion. Dupuy wanted the "noble nations"—Canada, the United States, Great Britain, and France—to be together on Île Ste-Hélènc. The young architects had other ideas. They felt La Ronde should be off by itself because, as an amusement park, it kept longer hours; the Canadian pavilion should not be at the entrance; as host country, Canada should be at the end of a circular path. The Soviet Union and the United States should be at opposite ends of the circular pattern—like two big shopping centres anchoring a mall—with smaller pavilions in between.

But something was needed to give the fair site unity. To quarry enough rock to build the dykes needed to extend the area, the city had dug enormous holes on the island, 150 feet deep. Safdie suggested filling them with water, making a sort of canal—"spines of water," he called it. That was the idea that Beaubien took to a sceptical Churchill. Water would become the visual link, the unifying element for all the diverse pavilions.

Meanwhile, Safdie continued his work on Habitat. The name had come from Jean-Louis Lalonde, a Montreal architect who represented the cement companies of Canada at Expo. It had the advantage of meaning the same thing in both languages. Lalonde was prepared to offer money for a feasibility study, but where would the cash come from for the finished project? Safdie hoped to get it from Central Mortgage and Housing Corporation.

When Ian Maclennan, CMHC's vice-president, heard Safdie's proposal to build a totally urban structure to house two thousand families on Mackay Pier, he was bowled over. "If this is built it will set housing in Canada fifteen to twenty years ahead," he said. But there was still no budget for a project that was simply marked as Habitat 67 on the completed master plan. When Shaw wanted to take it off the plan, Churchill argued for it. "I think it's a good thing," he said. "I can see that it would make the difference between a real exhibition and just a fair. I insist that it stay on." Shaw went along with that.

Safdie worked on the feasibility study at a hectic pace. He took his sketches and drawings to Dr. August Komendant, an engineer who had done most of his work for Louis Kahn. "We spread the sketches and drawings on the floor," Safdie recalled. "Komendant took out his pipe and started sucking on it. Three hours later, in his old Prussian style, he said, 'Yes, it can be done.'" Komendant stuck to his guns in the face of continued criticism from a stream of engineers. "Without him," Safdie said, "Habitat would not have been there."

CMHC gave Safdie eight weeks to work out his plan in detail and prepare estimates with a team of young architects and a hard-headed developer, Bud Andrews, from Webb and Knapp. They worked day and night to meet the deadline. The proposal called for nine hundred and fifty housing units on inclined planes, with a complete commercial and cultural centre on the ground floor. It would cost forty-two million dollars.

Safdie's feasibility study, with a set of colour drawings and a model, landed on Churchill's desk on February 21, 1964. He studied it over the weekend and on Monday morning stuck his head through the architect's door. "That's a fantastic thing," he said. "We've got to make it go." The cement companies, who had paid for the study, were furious. They had wanted the right to vet the plan before sending it to Expo. Churchill stood firm. "Are you prepared to build it?" he asked. "Are you prepared to finance the whole project?" They weren't. "When you give money to the government," Churchill reminded them, "you give it without any strings attached." This was a tense moment. A lesser executive might have crumbled. But not Churchill. "Right there he saved the project," Safdie wrote.

In the end Habitat was built of concrete and the cement companies were mollified. This would be the most spectacular concrete structure at the fair, one of the most spectacular anywhere. But now the steel companies were affronted, insinuating that the cement people had been given the job because they paid for the feasibility study. To that Churchill responded: "They spent some money, why don't you? Why don't you show us how to do it in steel?" Forty thousand dollars later, they concluded that precast concrete was the most appropriate material for Habitat.

Again, the financial question nagged. Habitat was a prototype, like the model of a futuristic car. It would cost forty-two million, but its market value, in terms of revenue generated, would be only half that. Where would the rest come from?

One plan was to call Habitat "research," which it was, and benefit from the 150 percent deduction that federal laws allowed. But the National Research Council, which did not want to set a precedent for other nonconformist buildings, turned it down. Without detailed engineering and architectural drawings and more cost estimates, no private firm could afford to make the commitment. Expo thereupon undertook to finance and organize this phase of the operation. Since Safdie could hardly handle the task alone, Churchill decided he should resign from his Expo job and open an office in a joint venture with an experienced firm. "Moshe," he said cheerfully, "you are fired." The same day Safdie was appointed consulting architect to Expo. "We never would have had Habitat if Churchill hadn't done that," Kniewasser remembered. "Safdie was incapable of completing Habitat on his own."

Safdie needed a partner. The firm he chose, John B. Parkin Associates of Toronto, thought the project too risky and backed out. But a Montreal firm, David, Barott, Boulva, accepted the partnership on the same terms.

For two months in 1964 Safdie made daily presentations to the presidents of every large corporation in the country, from the Royal Bank to General Motors, seeking funding. Three conditional offers came in, and Safdie set off for Ottawa with Churchill and Shaw to make a presentation to the cabinet committee. This was a defining moment and they knew it. "You're twenty-five and you're going to make a presentation to the Cabinet of this country," Churchill told the architect. "Isn't that absolutely wonderful?"

The concept was well received, but the problem was cost. Robert Bryce, deputy minister of finance, asked if the job could be done for ten million dollars. Safdie said it was impossible to reduce the size of the project. "Well, that's too bad," Bryce replied, "because that may mean the thing is dead."

So it was—in its original form. Two months later Safdie got the final word from Treasury Board: ten million for construction, an additional million and a half for design and development, and not a penny more. Safdie was in a state of shock. For three days he stayed home, unable to work. His staff had been toiling at a furious pace, preparing the final working drawings. Safdie couldn't bring himself to break the news to them.

Safdie's problem was compounded by Jean Drapeau, who had opposed Habitat from the beginning. Drapeau, who tended to think in monumental terms, was obsessed with the idea of building a thousand-foot tower as the symbol of Expo. The idea harked back to the Eiffel Tower, which had been the crowning glory of the Paris Exposition of 1889. Drapeau's first plan was to borrow the Eiffel Tower from France, bring it to Montreal, and reassemble it, bolt by bolt. When that seemed impracticable he opted for a modern tower, almost one hundred feet higher than Alexandre-Gustav Eiffel's creation. This scheme was in direct contradiction to the decision of the Montebello Conference. Safdie's supporters had always felt that Habitat would be the symbol of Expo 67. To have a second symbol would be not only redundant but also unaffordable. The tower would cost almost as much as the housing complex.

The city called for bids on the tower at the same time Expo called for bids on the first phase of Habitat. Most contractors bid on the tower. It was an unfortunate situation. Drapeau, who had been farsighted enough to locate Expo on the St. Lawrence islands, was now obsessed with a borrowed symbol that echoed the past. In the end, the tower was never built.

After a great deal of inner deliberation, a disheartened Safdie agreed to scale down his dream, thus tripling the unit costs. His decision would haunt him in the years ahead when his critics said that Habitat was too expensive. Habitat could work efficiently and economically only if the cost was spread over a large number of units, bolstered by revenue from commercial enterprises on the ground floor. He realized that a mere 158 families isolated on Mackay Pier couldn't qualify for a public school, let alone retail shops.

He faced another problem. The Camus Company, the largest prefabricated system builders in France, were interested in Habitat, possibly as precast contractors. At their request, Safdie gave them all his drawings, feasibility studies, and cost estimates. They offered to make a study and get back to him a month before he presented his revised plan to the government. Only at the last minute did he learn that Camus was planning to submit its own design to replace Habitat and had tried to hire some of his key men as consultants. This was barefaced theft, but instructions came down from Ottawa that the Camus plan was to be looked at carefully. Safdie learned that the French ambassador had made a special presentation to the minister of trade and commerce. Moreover, Camus had scheduled its own presentation for November 1, several days ahead of Expo's. To get their plan before the government first, Safdie and his team would have to move their own deadline ten days forward. It seemed impossible; they had already been working fourteen or fifteen hours a day, including weekends. But they had no choice, and so, in Safdie's words, "worked like dogs."

Somehow they made the deadline. When the representatives of CMHC, the Treasury Board, and Expo met in his Montreal office, Safdie had a new model and new drawings. It wasn't what they had expected, since they had thought Safdie would simply lift a ten-storey section from his original scheme. This was a different concept, and they liked it. On October 28, 1964, Safdie was given the official go-ahead to proceed with the new plan for 158 suites.

That left Camus out in the cold. When the French firm made its proposal in a glossy, two-and-a-half-inch-thick book, the text looked like a paraphrase of Safdie's own feasibility study. Expo's project architect for Habitat, in a comprehensive report, called it inappropriate, and the proposal was rejected.

On a bitterly cold fall day in 1965, Nina Safdie broke a bottle over the first of her husband's concrete boxes. Soon the site was swarming with visitors. But in January 1966, Mitchell Sharp, who had been the federal minister in charge of Expo, left to become the new minister of finance, and Robert Winters took over. This almost sounded the death knell of Habitat. Safdie noted a total change in attitude in Ottawa. Winters was one of a group of Liberal hopefuls with an eye on the coming change in leadership of the party. With the convention in mind, he could pose as the taxpayer's saviour. He launched an intensive examination of Expo's finances with special attention to Habitat. The project was being questioned from first principles, and there was talk of abandoning it altogether—of paying off the contractors and dismantling the building. A study was even mounted to see if the modular boxes could be dropped into the river.

Habitat was built as three clusters of houses. By 1966, the south and centre clusters were complete; the foundations for the northern cluster were also finished. Now came the order from Winters to abandon the north cluster, even though the houses were already cast, and to see what credits could be negotiated from the contractor. With the help of structural engineers, Safdie was able to show that the north cluster had to be built to balance the entire complex. Winters responded by ordering that all the interiors in the north cluster should remain unfinished and that Expo should try and get some money back from the contractors. But they had already purchased much of their material and equipment, and Expo would lose the rental revenue. It turned out that half a million dollars could be saved by these moves, but the cost of completing the work after Expo closed would increase by more than twice. Winters, however, insisted that the contract be changed.

The pressure on Safdie increased to cut back on "frills." The garden irrigation must go; some of the lighting in public areas must go; surely cheaper materials could be substituted! At one point it was even suggested that the whole elaborate landscaping plan—retaining walls, terraces, and so on—should be omitted and the site sodded. Safdie held fast and the so-called frills were retained. In the major battles that followed he managed in most cases to get his way.

No one, including Safdie, believed the building would be ready on time. It wasn't. Drapeau adroitly suggested that the actual assembly of Habitat would entrance the visitors. "We decided to announce that Habitat 67 had been left voluntarily unfinished so that visitors could see how it was built," he said. Throughout the fair one of the apartment units was suspended high in the air from a five-storey crane. "There are no problems," the mayor remarked, "only solutions."

The day after Expo opened Safdie and his wife moved into a Habitat unit. The press, once sceptical, now raved. Visitors crawled all over the public areas—seven million people in all. Major articles in leading

297

American publications praised it. Safdie was hard put to restrain those visitors who wanted to look over his own house and photograph it. One day a group of children wandered in thinking it was an exhibit. They walked right through the house and were surprised to find Safdie and his wife in the bedroom. Whenever a head of state came to visit Pierre Dupuy, a secret agent lurked in the hallways. When U Thant was there, a bomb threat forced everybody to vacate the building; fortunately it was a false alarm.

"They were a lively six months," Safdie recalled. "Every night there would be a party on some terrace and you would hear the music as if it was coming over a distant mountain. Some of the visitors' ships docked in front of us had bands aboard and the sound was carried over the river." When their furniture arrived, Safdie and his wife held a party, covering their part of the building with coloured lights. Safdie engaged a twenty-man steel band to play on his terrace while his neighbours danced on theirs. It was a festive climax to the years spent overcoming obstacles.

The great tragedy of Habitat was the decision to scale down Moshe Safdie's original plan to one-sixth its contemplated size. Generally Expo's planners thought big, but in this case they—or more correctly, the Treasury Board—thought small. Safdie's initial scheme attacked the whole problem of urban density. But the scaled-down Habitat was no more densely populated than an ordinary apartment building. Safdie had seen Habitat as a self-sustaining village of more than five thousand people, complete with shops, services, school, clinic. None of this was possible in the scaled-down version, which meant that Habitat's tenants found themselves isolated from the city's amenities. In the original concept, much of Habitat would have been supported by the retail outlets on the ground floor while the high density would have made rents economically viable. When critics attacked Habitat for not solving the problems of density or high rents, they were really attacking the government's faintheartedness in rejecting the first bold and imaginative design.

Had this not happened, would Habitat have been finished on time?

Safdie believes it would have been—*if* it had been started early enough, say, in 1964. But even the scaled-down version wasn't completed when Expo opened; could a vast structure, six times that size, have been finished in three years?

Habitat, as Safdie first planned it, was supposed to solve the problems of urban density by supplying something more liveable than a slab-like apartment house. Oddly, its tangible impact has been not on the cities but on vacation resorts in Mexico and on the Mediterranean coast, with stepped housing and terraced housing.

One of Habitat's influences can be seen in changes in the traditional bathroom. Safdie foresaw all his units prefabricated on an assembly line, but only the bathroom, with everything moulded from a single piece of plastic, has survived, giving Canada a thriving new industry. Again, the resort areas have made the greatest use of it. Another influence has been Safdie's concept of the roof garden, although this has generally been adapted for wealthy apartment owners, not for middle-income families, as Safdie planned.

The scaling down of Safdie's concept, boosting the cost of each house, gave the impression that Habitat-style living was only for the wealthy. In vain its promoters tried to explain that Habitat was a prototype, and all prototypes, whether automobiles or housing complexes, cost money to develop. Certainly Habitat changed the thinking of some architects. As Safdie himself explains: "It got so enormously publicized that it became a kind of icon for several years so that in every school of architecture there'd be all kinds of Habitat-like projects. In that sense you had an immediate impact on the way the industry thought about housing and community design." Safdie himself embarked on a number of projects that applied both the architectural and the technical concepts of Habitat. Most were never built, partly because of resistance to the cost of such amenities as roof gardens. In a sense then, he says, "Habitat remains an ideal that you aspire to but never achieve."

By the time Expo closed, Safdie was perhaps the most talked-about architect in the world. That didn't help him in Canada. In the ten years that followed he didn't get a single commission in his adopted country. The scaled-down plan that had been forced on him had burdened him with the reputation of being an unnecessarily expensive architect.

4

"What celebrity is it, Mamma?" a little girl asked as she stood in the crush outside the Czech pavilion on a hot afternoon in mid-July.

"It's Grace Kelly, honey, and her husband, the Prince. Now you stand real still and maybe we'll see them when they come out."

Through the Expo summer, the official VIPs came at the rate of three a week—kings, reigning queens, princes, presidents, prime ministers, other heads of state, and lesser dignitaries. They turned up on the Expo grounds with their entourages, large and small, trailed by secret service men and secret policemen, newspapermen, and huge throngs of ordinary people brandishing cameras.

Some came briefly. Lyndon Johnson stayed only ninety minutes. Others found it hard to tear themselves away. Princess Grace's visit lasted five days and ended in Montreal's Royal Victoria Hospital because of a miscarriage she suffered during her Expo tour.

Everybody who was anybody, it seemed, was there. The governor of New York, Nelson Rockefeller, arrived to glad-hand his way through the crowds, denying rather lamely that he was on the campaign trail. The Queen was in attendance, her security so tight that it was thought for a time she would never be seen by the crowds. Then she expressed a desire to ride the minirail (so it was said) and protocol was tossed out the window to accommodate her, to the delight of the press and the public. In fact, that so-called spontaneous minirail ride had been planned months in advance and was carefully monitored every foot of the way.

Lady Bird Johnson, the president's wife, arrived some weeks after her husband's whirlwind tour and spent two days enjoying herself on the grounds. She impressed Philippe Beaubien's wife Nan-b more than any of the other big shots, for she stood on no ceremony and even revealed that she ate a box of Cracker Jack once a week "to remind myself where I came from." Some of the African heads of state—dictators, sheiks, princes, and presidents—were less informal. For them, the trip to Expo was a chance to splurge, to throw lavish parties, and to clean out the more expensive shops in Montreal. One woman insisted on buying fur coats for every female in her entourage. The seventy-four-year-old Haile Selassie, Emperor of Ethiopia, the 255th direct descendant of King Solomon and the Queen of Sheba, was accompanied by a retinue of forty persons—doctors, dentists, barbers, nurses, cooks, and servants—and his wretched little dog, Lulu, which he carried everywhere. Dogs were strictly forbidden on the Expo grounds, and the Lion of Judah was forced to fidget until Beaubien told the security guards, "What the hell. Let him in. We can't afford to affront an emperor." At Place des Nations, just before the customary ceremony of greeting, the dog responded by defecating directly in front of the podium. Guards were hastily summoned to clean up the mess before the ceremony began.

Haile Selassie encountered a more serious problem when he and his entourage were invited to inspect the British pavilion. After the party boarded the mobile stairs for the second floor, the accompanying hostess tripped the switch by accident and the stairs reversed direction. The commissioner of the pavilion and his assistant grabbed the king and proceeded to run him up the escalator faster than people could begin to come down. When, breathless, they reached the top, they found the rest of the entourage was piled in a heap at the bottom. As soon as the emperor had found his feet again he was invited to sign the visitors' book with a gold pen that had been carefully crafted by the British for their queen and her consort. Haile Selassie liked the pen so much he put it in his pocket. As Beaubien said, "What could we do? There goes a two-thousand-dollar pen, and you can't just say to the head of state, 'Give it back!'"

And so they came, day after day: Bobby Kennedy and his six children; John Lindsay, mayor of New York, with his three; Prince Takamatsu, brother of the Japanese emperor; Queen Juliana of the

Netherlands. Each was given a welcoming address, a state dinner, and a conducted tour. But in all that glittering assembly, one tall eminence stands out. No other state visitor caused one fraction of the fuss that General Charles de Gaulle, president of France, stirred up when, at the invitation of Jean Drapeau, he deigned to undertake a state visit to Man and His World.

The general arrived at Wolfe's Cove, Quebec City, on Sunday morning, July 23, standing tall in the bow of the French cruiser *Colbert*, flagship of France's Mediterranean fleet, that had picked him up at St. Pierre and Miquelon after his flight from France. As he disembarked, the tremendous crowd greeted him with thunderous cheers; for the new governor general, Roland Michener, there were only scattered boos. The elder Daniel Johnson, the Quebec premier who had unseated Jean Lesage the previous year, drove him away in an open car, leading him from the dockside through seas of waving fleur-de-lis flags and crowds chanting "De Gaulle! De Gaulle! *Vive la France!*" They circled the Plains of Abraham and drove down Rue St-Louis to the city hall. There some four thousand people were massed to greet him, chanting in unison until he appeared at a door draped with fleur-de-lis and tricolour flags. As he stood on the grey stone steps, his oratorical magic caught fire while the band played "La Marseillaise" and the general, his long arms raised high, cried, *"Vive la nouvelle France"*. . . *"Vive le Canada français!"* The crowd chanted back: *"Vive la France!"* In an unscheduled speech, de Gaulle came close to backing the Quebec separatist movement when he told the crowd, "We have fallen in step with our century and every day we acquire a bit more the ways and means of being ourselves."

It was de Gaulle's show from start to finish. In a testy, behind-the-scenes struggle for control, the federal government had been virtually shut out.

Johnson did his best to paper over the long tedious battle about protocol. "Political wrangles," he had told the press, "are all in the past." But at almost every turn Quebec had got its way, protocol or no protocol, and so had the general.

Since the previous year the Prime Minister had been apprehensive

302

about any visit by de Gaulle. He didn't want it, but he couldn't stop it; after all, every major head of state was visiting Canada in its centennial year, going both to Ottawa and to Expo. Pearson's worries grew when, on August 4, 1966, Johnson informed him that he intended to send a personal invitation to de Gaulle to visit the fair. (Canada had already sent its informal invitation in the spring of that year.) That muddied the diplomatic waters.

The Prime Minister had reason to be apprehensive. Relations with France had been rocky, to say the least. In November 1966, de Gaulle had delivered a major snub by refusing to meet Jean Marchand, the highly popular cabinet minister who, it was hoped, would help smooth over the difficulties between the two countries. De Gaulle's excuse was that he would see only foreign ministers, yet that same year he had seen the education and cultural affairs minister of Quebec and also the mayor of Montreal. The following spring Canada was again affronted when France refused to send a representative to the fiftieth anniversary of Canada's victory at Vimy Ridge. When the sensitive general learned that Prince Philip had been invited to attend first, he was outraged and declined to take any part in the ceremony.

De Gaulle had not yet replied to either invitation, but it was rumoured that he did indeed intend to arrive by French warship and thus, in defiance of protocol, visit Quebec before the Canadian capital. In fact, such plans had been tentatively agreed upon by officials in both Quebec and France.

Pearson was determined that if de Gaulle didn't come to Ottawa, there would be no visit. It *must* begin in Ottawa, not Quebec City, and the entire affair must be controlled by the federal government. But the French were adamant and so was Quebec. In this diplomatic contretemps we can see the beginnings of the long, painful debate on sovereignty. Ottawa gave in. If de Gaulle came by ship, as he fully intended, he would have to land at Quebec first. It was decided that he could do so, provided there would be a strong federal presence in the welcoming group. It was even hoped—a vain hope!—that perhaps if the general knew his final words in Canada would be spoken in the nation's capital, he might be less disruptive.

Ottawa had been outmanoeuvred, and the Quebec government made the most of it. The day before de Gaulle disembarked, an unnamed Quebec official told the press that the general's personal decision to begin his visit in the Quebec capital represented recognition of "the state of Quebec" because "whenever de Gaulle goes to a country, he goes to its capital." De Gaulle was certainly calling the shots. He was determined to hold a reception aboard the *Colbert* at five o'clock on the afternoon of his arrival, the same time the governor general was slated to hold a reception at the Citadel in his honour!

Meanwhile, the government of Quebec was preparing what the press called "the biggest, brashest and costliest bash in history"—a state dinner in the gilded ballroom of the Château Frontenac that evening. By this time, the plans to operate a press headquarters in the cavernous stone armouries on the Plains of Abraham were aborted. Quebec government officials simply walked out of the armouries and set up their own press offices in the Château. So much for a federal presence in Quebec.

The diplomatic wrangling continued regarding the state dinner. Who should host it? Ottawa insisted that the place of honour should go to the governor general, but in the end it went to the Quebec premier. Paul Hellyer, the cabinet minister representing Ottawa, found himself moved to a second head table to be replaced by a French-Canadian colleague. Only at the last minute was Paul Martin, secretary of state for external affairs, allowed a seat at the first head table. There were many speeches, even one from the president of a steamship company, but none from any federal representative. As Hellyer wrote, "It was a deliberate French snub of the feds." The CBC's undoubtedly French network, Hellyer noted, filmed only provincial politicians "to the point of cutting a conversational group in half when taking a picture. 'The "cold war" was intensifying.'"

In his own speech the general again came perilously close to giving aid and comfort to the separatists. He described the people of Quebec as "French with the appellation Canadian tagged on afterwards." Then, "What we are witnessing here, as in many parts of the world, is the advent of a people, which wishes, in every field, to determine its own future and take its destiny in its own hands." ("The world will know we exist," Daniel Johnson had proudly remarked to the press before de Gaulle's arrival. He could not know how true that prophecy would be.)

The following day de Gaulle rode in a Lincoln convertible leading a cavalcade of fourteen limousines down the recently named Chemin du Roi on a triumphal procession to Montreal. Quebec fleur-de-lis flags and French tricolours were attached to every pole along that historic route. Even the tarmac had been painted, mile after mile, with the fleur-de-lis. Well-organized crowds along the route cheered the general's words when he told them that Quebec was a country becoming its own master. "I can feel it," he said. "A country that takes its destiny in hand, that is indispensable today. A people, be it the French people, French Canadians, or French of Canada, must depend only on itself."

The spectacle had all the trappings of an election campaign. A pack of fifty-seven station wagons and three buses jammed with reporters, photographers, and television crews—three hundred persons in all—broadcast every word.

By the time de Gaulle arrived at the Montreal city hall seven thousand people were waiting for him in the square. An electric sense of anticipation rippled through the crowd. All that day reports of the general's tour down the highway had been pouring in, gathering in intensity. Now the moment had come, and, as René Lévesque recalled, everyone was saying, "If he goes on at this rate, something's going to happen that our grandchildren will still be talking about."

The young activists of the Rassemblement pour l'Indépendance Nationale—the RIN—had been prominent all along the route, leading the cheering. Here, they seized the best tactical positions in the crowd. "*QUÉBEC LIBRE*," their placards read. Their young leader, the charismatic Pierre Bourgault, would soon be overshadowed by Lévesque, but this was his moment. The best-known separatist in the province, he provoked among his screaming followers the kind of adulation usually reserved for pop stars. At one mass election rally, after *La Presse* likened him to a Beatle, ardent admirers had tried to tear his clothes off.

The police formed a flying wedge around de Gaulle as he made his way up the steps and entered the city hall to sign the Golden Book for distinguished visitors. After the signing the general indicated to Drapeau that he would like to step out on the little balcony to greet the chanting throng who had just booed the playing of "O Canada" so lustily that the music was drowned out. This was the last thing the mayor wanted. He made an excuse that the microphone wasn't hooked up, but a CBC technician explained that he could fix it in a jiffy.

"Then do so, my friend," de Gaulle told him. "Do so."

"My heart is filled with a vast emotion," de Gaulle began conversationally as the crowed quieted, "as I see before me the French city of Montreal. In the name of the old country, in the name of France, I salute you with all my heart.

"I will tell you a secret that you will not repeat. Here tonight and all along the route, I found myself in an atmosphere like that of the Liberation." He was, of course, referring to the liberation of France in 1945, but his listeners could not miss his meaning. It was the spark the crowd needed. The chants and cries for "liberation" of Quebec swelled. ". . . if you only knew what confidence an awakened France brings to you and what affection it is beginning to feel for the French of Canada.

"I take with me an imperishable memory of this extraordinary meeting. France knows, sees, and hears what is going on here."

And now, with the young zealots of the RIN clamouring below him, came the stunning climax.

"Vive Montréal!" de Gaulle cried. *"Vive le Québec!"*

The crowd held its breath. Then. . .

"VIVE LE QUÉBEC LIBRE!"

There—he had said it. In the heart of French Canada, the president of France had shouted the phrase on the RIN placards. Hardly anybody heard or noticed the words that followed: *"Vive le Canada français! et vive la France!"*

De Gaulle turned to Daniel Johnson apparently puzzled. "What on earth did I say to make them explode this way?" To which the premier replied, without hesitation, "*Mon général*, you have just repeated the slogan of the separatist party, which I defeated in the last election."

"Election slogans! Bah!" said the general, and turned back into the city hall.

Soon the young Quebeckers were marching in the streets, chanting:
Québec libre, oui, oui, oui!
Québec libre, de Gaulle l'a dit!

On the long terrace behind the city hall, René Lévesque and a fellow MNA, Yves Michaud, had been watching the general on television with the other guests, regretting that they were no longer journalists covering such a historic event. De Gaulle's rallying cry left them paralysed for a few moments. Behind them a deathly silence reigned. Lévesque turned to see the faces of Drapeau's guests. "It is rare," he recalled, "to have such an opportunity to see the two Montreals so clearly. In a state of shock, frozen in a fury that was as yet emitting only a few anticipatory rumblings, stood the anglophone city. As for French Montreal, except for those constrained by office or acquaintance to reserve, they did not hide broad, complicit smiles, or even, in the background, gestures more discreet but just as enthusiastic as the crowds in the street."

As Johnson had predicted, suddenly the world knew that Quebec existed. The next day in a Peruvian *barrio*, a Montreal student sent by the Canadian government to help the community reported that the Indians came to tell him about the event and remarked that from then on they knew that Quebec existed, too.

Did the ageing general blurt out his inflammatory words on the spur of the moment? One of his biographers, Claude Mauriac, thought de Gaulle had been "carried along by events." Jean Drapeau thought so, too, and told Gérard Pelletier the following day that de Gaulle's balcony appearance had been entirely spontaneous. How could he have remained indifferent to the cheers of the crowd? Perhaps. Yet de Gaulle's earlier remarks, endlessly repeated during that triumphal procession down the Chemin du Roi, suggested that he was building up to something. He was a practised politician. He had seen the signs the RIN waved before him. How could he not know that those words would cause a diplomatic incident?

Certainly they were unexpected. The French ambassador to Ottawa was so confused that he left his briefcase behind in the limousine of one of the Quebec ministers. But in Paris, French government sources, in informal briefings to newsmen, insisted that de Gaulle's remarks were no slip of the tongue.

The Prime Minister, who had watched de Gaulle on television, was first startled, then angered. He called Paul Martin back from Montreal for a cabinet meeting. Martin's advice was to keep cool and give de Gaulle a chance to explain. But the general was expected in Ottawa two days later, after touring Expo, and there was scarcely time to mend fences.

Pearson's most effective move would have been to ignore the general's outburst, but that was impossible. Hundreds of telegrams from Anglo-Canadians were landing on his desk, demanding a response to de Gaulle. A flood of telephone calls jammed the government switchboards even before the cabinet met on the morning after the speech. All were from Anglos demanding that de Gaulle be publicly censured. (In Paris, the Canadian Embassy was similarly swamped with calls from French men and women apologizing for the general.) It was clear that, if only for political reasons, Pearson must speak out.

Two cabinet meetings that day chewed over the proper response. It took Pearson two and a half hours to draft the statement issued that evening. In it he warned the general that his remarks were unacceptable. ". . . The people of Canada are free. Every province of Canada is free. Canadians do not need to be liberated." He left a way open for conciliation by emphasizing Canada's desire for a warm friendship with France and by a declaration that he hoped de Gaulle shared that purpose. "However," he pointed out, "his statements tended to encourage a small minority of our population whose aim is to destroy Canada."

That minority included the RIN, whose strategic presence along the route from Quebec and later at the city hall had helped to orchestrate the final act of the de Gaulle drama. "I never thought he would go that far," a surprised Bourgault remarked. It was, he said, an extraordinary coup for independence; and so it was. The hero of World War Two had, by laying his enormous prestige on the line, gone a long way to legitimizing and publicizing the separatist movement.

Both Réal Caouette of the Créditiste party and Jean Lesage, the Quebec Liberal opposition leader, condemned the speech. In doing so, Lesage brought about the defection of three members from his embattled caucus. These included René Lévesque, whose position within the party was growing shakier. But Lévesque was uneasy about the speech. "It did not seem to me," he wrote, "to be at all advisable to have recourse to some external authority no matter how prestigious. . . . Québec libre by all means, but who wanted that liberty to seem an imported product?"

Meanwhile, the cause of the international uproar was grandly touring Expo where he pointedly gave ten minutes to the Canadian pavilion but half an hour to the French. Lionel Chevrier, who accompanied him as federal representative, reported to Ottawa that he was speaking openly about Quebec independence and that he, Chevrier, was being taunted by French officials. The reaction of the Quebec press was mixed. *Le Soleil* of Quebec City was most angered by what it called de Gaulle's meddling. *Le Devoir* was calmer. Claude Ryan, its editor, published a front-page editorial giving the general the benefit of the doubt but urging that he clarify his message. Both *La Presse* and *Montréal Matin* saw de Gaulle's outburst as an exhortation to French Canada to fulfil itself culturally. The major international newspapers, such as the *New York Times* and the French liberal journal *Combat*, were highly critical. The *Toronto Daily Star* echoed the Anglo-Canadian attitude when it called the general "a meddlesome old man."

The cabinet had been prepared to greet de Gaulle in Ottawa for the usual diplomatic rounds. The last thing that Pearson wanted was to be seen hounding the French president out of the country. The general solved that problem by announcing he would not visit the capital. His decision was a matter of some relief to his would-be hosts, who did not fancy greeting him under such strained conditions.

Gérard Pelletier was one member of the cabinet who disagreed with the way de Gaulle was handled, though he too deplored the general's excursion into Canadian internal affairs. At this time Pelletier broke with Trudeau and Marchand, the other two "wise men." Pelletier objected to the haste with which Ottawa had reacted, to the argument put forward to condemn de Gaulle, and to "the way in which he was shown the door." How, he wondered, could his two colleagues defend the government's action? Was it cabinet solidarity? Yet cabinet documents for July 25 show that Trudeau was on Pearson's side. The people of France, he said, would think the government was weak if it didn't react. Marchand took a softer line. It was important, he said, that Pearson's statement not be interpreted as being anti-French or anti-Quebec. De Gaulle should, as far as possible, be separated from France and from Quebec. Pelletier's point was that Pearson's statement, aimed at calming anglophone indignation, paid little attention to Quebec. He feared, correctly, that "the incident, treated in this way, might become a powerful auxiliary force for the take-off of Quebec separatism."

In fact, de Gaulle had placed the Canadian government in a no-win situation. No matter what it did, no matter what it said, it would offend one section of the voting public. Here, in the centennial year, of all years, the old Canadian dilemma was re-emerging.

It remained for the mayor of Montreal, who had been caught in the middle of the controversy, to calm troubled waters and issue a mild rebuke to the cause of it all, and he did it without grating on de Gaulle's touchy feelings.

To read Drapeau's speech at the banquet for de Gaulle thirty years later is to marvel at his impeccable choice of phrase and the manner in which he managed to stroke his imperious guest while making his own point of view clear.

He began at the outset by making it explicit that his words were a response and not a rebuttal. "There had been an explosion of sentiment," he agreed, "a veritable explosion that cannot be denied." There hadn't been nostalgia, however. "One cannot be nostalgic after four centuries." Was there gratitude? Gratitude to de Gaulle, yes, but gratitude to France?

Here Drapeau was gentle but blunt: "Posing the question is to express a doubt because we have learned to survive alone for two centuries." The mayor then softened his clear suggestion that France had ignored its former colony by declaring that "no other had ever attached the importance which you have, Mr. President, and have been willing to express to the French Canadians."

The outpouring of emotion, he repeated, was neither nostalgia nor gratitude because the role that French Canada could play in North America "has never been, until you appeared, Mr. President, the object of any special interest." For a century there had been no relations with France, but now it was his hope that de Gaulle's pledge of support "will be inspired by the same spirit that inspired our ancestors," who had given so much to North America by way of culture, language, and religion. He hoped that those who helped to accentuate the renewal of French Canada would "be animated by the same spirit so that French Canadians will better serve all of Canada."

Through Expo, the mayor pointed out, thousands of Americans were discovering French Canada. Just as de Gaulle had devoted his life to ensuring that France could assume her rightful place in Europe and the world after the humiliation of the Pétain regime, so he would well understand that French Canada could also hope for the place it deserved. "We believe it is possible for us to play a role in North America analogous to the one you played in France for Europe and for humanity.

"If we serve our country better as Canadians of French origin, so we serve France better and our humanity better. . . . We do not ask for anything more than an enlargement. . . of our own destiny to better serve the land of our ancestors."

Having thus delivered to de Gaulle a genial rebuke wrapped up in a history lesson, and having made it clear that he saw a Quebec that operated within the federal structure, Drapeau then raised his glass in a toast to which de Gaulle responded graciously. "If one fact, one event could alone justify my trip," he declared, ". . . it would be the truly moving and profound speech you have just delivered." Then he was off to the airport to return home, unruffled and unrepentant.

Two prescient remarks served to illuminate the controversy as the curtain slowly dropped on the de Gaulle visit. One anonymous French official put matters neatly when he said, "There is no de Gaulle problem, but a Canadian problem." And Daniel Johnson, who believed that Ottawa had acted too hastily in the de Gaulle affair, put his thoughts in a final quip as the general's plane soared out over the Atlantic.

"Well," said the premier, "de Gaulle is now up in the air, and so are we."

SEVEN: THE WORST OF TIMES

1

The white nigger

2

Mme Chaput Rolland's odyssey

3

René's choice

4

Bye-bye, Bi-Bi

1

The white nigger On January 13, 1967, Pierre Vallières returned to his native Quebec and was taken into custody, having completed, three days before, his manuscript of *White Niggers of America*, a passionate call for violent revolution in French Canada. That explosive little book would become the Bible not only for the Front de Libération du Québec—the FLQ—but also for revolutionaries everywhere. Stokely Carmichael, the black activist in the United States, was only one of many who offered Vallières their support. "Your experiences are no different from those of true patriots everywhere and at any time who resist against tyranny," he wrote.

Vallières did not mince words. "Only a total revolution," he wrote, "will allow Québécois, in collaboration with other people of the earth, to build a totally free and totally sovereign Québec. Such a revolution will not come about without war and without violence."

The FLQ was only one of many similar phenomena. Revolutionary fronts were raging everywhere that year. "Liberation" was the operative word. The Six-Day War in the Middle East hardened the Palestinian resistance into long-term guerrilla warfare; Yasser Arafat would soon assume the leadership of the Palestine Liberation Organization. At the same time, George Habash's Popular Front for the Liberation of Palestine was in the crucible; it would be responsible for most of the hijackings that followed. In Francisco Franco's Spain, the Basque people had their own Socialist Liberation Movement, pledged to a separate Basque state.

Black America was in a ferment. Seventy-five bloody riots in black ghettoes in the summer of 1967 had caused eighty-three deaths. One thousand people had been wounded, more than sixteen thousand arrested, and damage exceeded $600 million. Stokely Carmichael had created a phrase that was sweeping around the world: Black Power (Vallières saw this as the African-American equivalent of Quebec separatism). That October, the Cuban revolutionary Che Guevara was gunned down in the Bolivian jungle to become a martyr for revolutionary protests

314

everywhere. Fidel Castro, at the first conference of the Organization of Latin American Solidarity that year, gave his support to the Black Power struggle. "We are very happy," Vallières wrote at the time, "that the Black Americans were represented. . . . We are certain that Quebec revolutionaries will not be forgotten at the next Solidarity conference."

All over the globe in 1967 the seeds of future violence were being sown by student revolutionaries. That January in Germany, Horst Mahler led a student demonstration against the Berlin police. He would be a future organizer for the Baader-Meinhof gang, the most notorious of the urban guerrilla terrorist organizations. One of its founders, Ulrike Meinhof, the so-called bandit queen, was already making her name that spring as a radical journalist opposing the visit to Germany of the Shah of Iran—a visit that would spark a bloody riot at the Berlin Opera House. In Italy that same fall, Renato Curcio, the future leader of the terrorist Red Brigades, managed to bring the University of Trento to a halt.

The entire student world, it seemed, was rising up—a loose international movement fuelled by opposition to the Vietnam War; worries over the threat of nuclear war; the racism of some ruling classes, from Georgia to Rhodesia; various incitements of Marxism in its extreme form, from Mao to Castro; and, of course, the overwhelming influence of television, which for the first time brought street demonstrations into the homes of the bourgeoisie.

The revolutionaries formed proletarian movements of students, disenchanted workers, and intellectuals. Their object was to overturn society by "any means necessary," in Malcolm X's phrase. The FLQ, though concerned almost entirely with Quebec's position in Canada, was very much a part of that worldwide trend.

White Niggers of America is an angry polemic that seems to have been written in blood. Vallières's analogy between Negro slaves and French Canadians may have seemed a little extreme to some, but it certainly struck a chord among his own people. When it was published at last in 1968 it sent shock waves around the western world— in France, the United States, English Canada, West Germany, Italy, and Mexico. Of all the revolutionary books published in Quebec,

315

Nègres blancs d'Amérique had the greatest worldwide circulation.

"To be a 'nigger' in America is to be not a man but someone's slave," Vallières's manuscript began. "For the rich white man of Yankee America, the nigger is sub-man. Even the poor whites consider the nigger their inferior. . . . Very often they do not even suspect that they too are niggers, slaves, 'white niggers.' White racism hides the reality from them by giving them the opportunity to despise an inferior. . . .

"In Quebec the French Canadians are not subject to this irrational racism. . . . They can take no credit for that, since in Quebec there is no 'black problem.' The liberation struggle launched by the American blacks nevertheless arouses growing interest among the French Canadian population, for the workers of Quebec are aware of their condition as niggers, exploited men, second-class citizens. Have they not been, ever since the establishment of New France in the seventeenth century, the servants of the imperialists, the white niggers of America? Were they not *imported*, like the American blacks, to serve as cheap labor in the New World? The only difference between them is the color of their skin and the continent they came from. After three centuries their condition remains the same. They still constitute a reservoir of cheap labor, whom the capitalists are completely free to put to work or reduce to unemployment, as it suits their financial interests, whom they are completely free to underpay, mistreat and trample underfoot, whom they are completely free, according to law, to have clubbed down by the police and locked up by the judges 'in the public interest,' when their profits seem to be in danger."

Vallières had already spent three and a half months in an American prison. The FLQ's program was to organize a general uprising of workers in Quebec to overthrow, through revolution, the imperialist bourgeoisie and establish a Marxist state. The previous year, a bomb planted in a box in the offices of a shoe factory to symbolize the start of a new wave of FLQ action had killed a sixty-four-year-old woman. Vallières and his compatriot Charles Gagnon fled to New York and distributed a statement of solidarity to delegations at the United Nations. Their demands for justice were now being carried into French-Canadian

316

homes by television. At that, with the collusion of Canadian authorities they were arrested for "illegal entry," confined in the Manhattan House of Detention for Men, New York's notorious Tombs, and charged in absentia by Canadian authorities with murder in connection with the shoe factory bombing.

There Vallières wrote his *White Niggers of America*—part autobiography, part confession, part manifesto, part polemic—immediately after a twenty-nine-day hunger strike in the Tombs. It is a testimony to his burning determination to get his views out that he managed to write in spite of the surrounding conditions. There was a constant noise of cells being opened and banged shut and of the cries of guards and prisoners shouting back and forth, all "within the framework of an absurd discipline. . . invented and applied for the purpose of brutalizing the inmates as much as possible."

He and Gagnon were held in cells designed for mentally ill prisoners, drug addicts, men accused of murder, prisoners in a depressed state, "and, lastly, 'political' madmen, like Charles and me, whom the officers regard more or less as 'deranged.'"

Periodically one of their fellow inmates would slit his veins out of despair or simply to attract attention. Vallières could understand that, for he too was affected by the "boundless solitude" that each man felt, "especially during those hours of depression when it becomes impossible to communicate with others." Their wretchedness was intensified by rules that forbade them to go outdoors "to get a breath of fresh air and an occasional look at the sun."

White Niggers is a cry from the heart, a bitter, impassioned tract in which Vallières sees no difference between the treatment of his fellow French Canadians and the black sharecroppers of the American South. Even though the metaphor was overdrawn, a growing number of Vallières's countrymen agreed with it. For them, Jean Lesage's Quiet Revolution was proceeding too slowly. They were angered by the domination of Quebeckers by English-speaking capitalists, irritated by the refusal of the rest of Canada to understand their problem, and goaded by the minority's unwillingness to learn their language or understand their culture. Shunned as dangerous by Quebec bookstores, *White Niggers* would sell briskly in the United States, "a revolutionary document," in the *New York Times*'s estimate, "that clutches one's throat like a drowning hand."

Pierre Vallières was about to turn twenty-nine when he returned to Canada at the dawn of the centennial year. His life, as one critic described it, had been "a mosaic of continuity." He had already been a student, a stockbroker's clerk, a bookseller, a journalist, an émigré intellectual, and a political polemicist. He was raised in poverty first in the East End of Montreal and then, after he was seven, in squalid, Dickensian surroundings on the South Shore. His family settled in Longueuil-Annexe, a shack town of tarpaper and Insulbrick hovels. Since there was no municipal government, they had no water, no sewage disposal, no paved roads, and—this was the only appeal—no taxes. Housewives had to buy their water at five cents a pail from the backs of trucks whose owners enjoyed monopolies purchased from local politicians. It is under conditions such as these that revolutionaries are shaped.

"Many families, including mine, had to tighten their belts to buy water for cooking, bathing, doing laundry, etc. That lasted for years, years during which Duplessis was letting the Americans loot the rich iron deposits of Northern Quebec."

At the classical *collège*, subsidized by the church, Vallières felt a hypocrite because he was pretending to study for the priesthood in order to get a subsidy. To him, the instruction was worthless, especially in history—and notably the history of Quebec—but he put up with it because of the material advantages education offered; expulsion meant a life sentence of poverty. He hated the church for which he was apparently destined. He stood first in his class, showing "great promise," but he was playing a game he didn't believe in, going to Mass every Friday only for selfish reasons. He no longer believed in God. He was merely exploiting his faith because it was a ticket to university.

"Faith doesn't give a damn about Justice!" he wrote. "Why should *we* be afraid to not give a damn about Faith and to take advantage of

318

it! Charity doesn't give a damn about low wages and unemployment! . . . It certainly isn't our fault if the Church and High Finance imprison us in an empire (their empire) in which men have to alienate themselves. . . if they don't want to die like rats."

He was not alone. Many of the young men of his generation were beginning to rebel, at least in their hearts, against the priest-ridden domination of their province. Vallières went further. "One day I couldn't take it any longer, and I began to publicly ridicule this masquerade, this monumental farce." He told one of the priests that "they were all a bunch of whores and the worst enemies of the people of Quebec."

When the school year ended, he resolved never to set foot in the *collège* again. A friend got him a job as a brokerage clerk that he held for two years. He gave half his wages to his family and spent the rest on books, voraciously reading his way through Gide, Malraux, Sartre, Camus, Proust, Mauriac, and Dostoyevsky. To him, white-collar workers were even more alienated than blue-collar workers or farmers. He tried to lead an office revolt but got nowhere. He hated the job but kept at it because it left him free time to read and to write. "I wrote like a madman, for hours on end, and sometimes for entire nights."

By 1956 he had met and come under the influence of Gaston Miron, whom he described in his book as "this great living poet who (despite his youth) is the spiritual father of the FLQ." It was Miron who developed his political consciousness, encouraged him to write articles for *Le Devoir*, and introduced him to contemporary poetry and "the literature of colonized peoples."

Vallières's account of his life in the sixties is a chronicle of impotent rage and despair. He was clearly searching for something, a principle to live by, a star to guide him, a goal worthy of his quest. In 1959 he enrolled briefly as a philosophy student at a theological college in Quebec, later working in a campus bookstore. But the book trade "made me sick" and "the rage that I experienced at the college took hold of me again." After a few months he quit and took a job as a labourer on a construction site. By September 1962, he had had enough. He set off for exile in Paris "intending never to return to Quebec again."

France was a letdown, "a dreary, disillusioned country," rent by the Algerian war and nourished by Gaullism. It was here, however, in the "Red" region of Dijon that he discovered Marxism and realized that "revolution was not a gratuitous choice but a vital necessity for all workers." Yet Paris was "a veritable hell," and the bureaucracy of the Communist Party revolted him. He searched about for a suitable revolutionary organization to join but found none. Everybody talked; nobody acted. To him, the French Left had "the stupidest leaders in the world."

He was penniless, unable to find a job, dependent on the charity of a few friends. He lost his appetite, roamed the streets of Paris like a sleepwalker, tried to throw himself into the Seine but was too weak to carry it out. In the end, to avoid suicide, he decided to return to Quebec and did so in March 1963, thanks to a loan from his mother. Here, Gérard Pelletier offered him a job on *La Presse*, and he jumped at it.

Pelletier, who, with Pierre Trudeau, had helped found the intellectual periodical *Cité libre*, urged Vallières to write for it also, as he had briefly done before his exile. That fall, he became a co-editor. His plan was to turn the journal "into a weapon and put it exclusively at the service of the Québécois workers." That did not sit well with Trudeau and Pelletier. The following March, after a spirited attack on the pair, Vallières was forced out.

By this time he had broken with his mother. To him she represented the passive French Canadian—the Uncle Tom of Quebec, to use his analogy. She "wanted to force me back into the passivity, docility, resignation, and humiliation, which were precisely what I wanted to escape from once and for all." By 1967 Vallières had lost track of her—didn't know whether she was dead or alive. He always had more sympathy for his father, who worked for the CPR's Angus Shops. "His life no longer had the slightest meaning. All his acts were nothing but habits. His life: a routine. His body: a machine, reduced to skin and bones, nerves and tendons. His mind: a lamp with run-out batteries. His strength was abandoning him. In a few years he would die of exhaustion. . . . Why would he have lived? For nothing. To serve as

320

cheap labour for the CPR." Eventually Vallières stopped speaking to his family.

He and Charles Gagnon secretly joined the FLQ in 1965 and met frequently with others "to lay the foundations of a revolutionary movement that would exclusively serve the exploited of Quebec."

The Front's collection of cells and networks had grown out of the left wing of the RIN, some of whose members wanted to develop more radical and spectacular forms of action, daubing slogans on buildings and mailboxes and undertaking small acts of sabotage. By 1965 the majority had decided on a course of clandestine action that within a year turned to violence. The first death occurred on April 20, 1966, when a night watchman was killed by a bomb behind a Canadian Army recruiting centre. The war was on, and it would not end until the crisis of October 1970.

There were more bombs (not all exploded): in a Legion headquarters, in a post office, in a mining company headquarters, in a Black Watch barracks, in an army service unit, in oil refineries, and in a mailbox in Westmount, where a sergeant major in a bomb disposal unit lost his arm. Panic set in. The police adopted draconian methods: arrest without warrant, confinement without trial, interrogation with no lawyers present, and, some charged, beatings as well. Three activists were found guilty of taking part in bomb attacks. The sentences went as high as twelve years in prison, but by the end of the centennial year all were paroled.

One cell of the FLQ network was broken up; another survived to publish *La Cognée*, the Front's official if clandestine newspaper; a third called itself l'Armée de Libération du Québec. The violence continued—more fires, more bombings, more dynamite, and, most significantly, a daytime raid on a military arsenal that yielded an enormous horde of weapons and ammunition. Again the police broke up the FLQ, sending six of its leaders to jail and carrying out a series of raids that put more behind bars.

Shortly after Vallières and Gagnon joined the FLQ it became apparent that they were not in sympathy with the Front's loose organization or with its strategy and tactics. In *La Cognée*, Vallières castigated the FLQ as "a vague collection of tiny, more or less active groups, whose members are all known to the police and to each other." The people, he said, were looking for a stronger FLQ. "When are we really going to start working seriously to organize it?"

Instead of working to unite the old and discredited networks, Vallières and Gagnon started one of their own—a new FLQ, in effect, radically different from the original but still divided into cells and networks under the control of a central committee. In 1966, Vallières made its objective clear in a secret document calling for "a violent, organized, armed struggle." The task of the Front, he wrote, was to organize that violence.

Unlike the old FLQ, the new Front was Marxist. To Vallières, the struggle was not between the federalists and the separatists but between the proletariat and the bourgeoisie. He had by this time fallen under the spells of Che Guevara and Mao Tse-tung, whose work impressed him more than that of Lenin.

The Vallières-Gagnon group was held responsible for the shoe-box bombing in May 1966 and the death of Thérèse Morin. Another bomb exploded at the strike-plagued Dominion Textile mill at Drummondville. A third exploded at the Paul Sauvé Arena in Montreal during the big Liberal windup just ten days before the provincial election. Surprisingly, the Lesage government was defeated partly because of the independence vote, most of which went to Pierre Bourgault's RIN.

On July 14, a young student activist was killed trying to plant a bomb in a textile plant in Saint-Henri. Vallières, in a confidential memo, had written that "Quebec is the only place in North America where conditions are ripe for a revolution to break out and succeed." But by this time he and Gagnon were in New York and the object of an intense police search, while the tensions within the Action Network of the Front were such as to cause it to cease its activities.

Publicly identified as the leaders of the network and with warrants issued for their arrest in connection with the shoe-box bombing, the pair organized a co-ordinating committee of all North American liberation movements. They did not hide; instead they began picketing the United Nations headquarters in New York.

When the U.S. immigration department tried to extradite them, accusing them of illegal entry, they successfully fought removal and, after their incarceration in the Tombs, were released—but only briefly. Officers of the immigration department literally kidnapped them and took them to the airport, where they were led aboard a plane, flown to Montreal, and deposited in the arms of the waiting RCMP, who put them once again under arrest. As the nation began its feverish celebration of the country's one hundredth birthday, the pair appeared in court on a dozen charges, the most serious of which was murder.

It is hard to believe that Vallières would spend almost four years in jail simply because of what he had written. It was clearly a political trial—one that might have been expected in a small South American dictatorship but not from a Canadian court. The indictment was changed twice; many charges were dropped. Though Vallières was charged with murder he was, after a six-week trial, found guilty only of manslaughter. It didn't matter; he was sentenced to life imprisonment anyway. Almost eighteen months after that the court of appeal finally held that the judge and prosecutor had "appealed to passion or fear" and not to the question of who killed Mlle Morin. It ordered a new trial.

Altogether, Vallières would spend forty-four months behind bars and Gagnon forty-one while their cases wound through the courts. In the end both men were acquitted. The court of appeal stated explicitly that Vallières had been convicted, not for any overt action, but only for "his words, writings, and opinions."

Both men were out of action in 1967, but the FLQ was very much alive. On the very first day of the birthday year, a bomb blew a mailbox to bits in Montreal's financial district. *La Cognée* denounced "100 years of exploitation of the people of Quebec" and threatened "special celebrations." The RIN distributed licence plates carrying the slogan "1867-1967, 100 Years of Injustice." On April 15, *La Cognée* closed down as a result of an intensive campaign of "selective interviews" by the police.

De Gaulle's *Vive le Québec libre* speech caused a bigger explosion than any bomb. The general himself was unrepentant. Back in France, he gave more aid and comfort to the separatist cause when, at a November press conference, he declared "Quebec would take her place as a sovereign state and master of her national existence, and she would negotiate with the rest of Canada, freely and as an equal, the terms of their co-operation."

Three months after the general's outburst, the Prime Minister called his security panel together. Although the Cold War was at its height, separatism was now seen as a greater danger than communism in Canada. In Commissioner William Kelly's words, it was at "a critical turning point in the broadening of the RCMP's security intelligence coverage of separatism." It was more than a security threat, Kelly declared, it was also a serious political threat. The movement was becoming too popular for Ottawa's liking. As Louis Fournier points out in his study of the FLQ, 1967 "marked the beginning of the vast RCMP spy operation against a 'foreign power'—France—now elevated to the rank of 'enemy power' because of its special relationship with Quebec."

In November, the FLQ made its presence felt when it launched a new official organ, *La Victoire*, to replace *La Cognée*. "Let us take all the time we need to get ready," the paper advised its activist readers. "And when we strike, the blow will be so powerful that the enemy will not soon recover." The paper saw its task as educational. It published diagrams showing how to make a Molotov cocktail, lessons on how to acquire semi-automatic weapons, and how to fight and survive in the bush together with general information on organization, recruiting, and the training of action groups. From all this it was quite clear that the FLQ was now a quasi-military organization.

That fall, student demonstrations became more violent. On November 17, twenty people were wounded and forty-six arrested when police charged into a crowd in front of the U.S. Consulate in Montreal protesting the bombing of Hanoi. The RCMP blamed "terrorist sympathizers" for creating campus unrest and, in clear violation of Lester Pearson's instructions to the contrary in November 1963, started carrying out political espionage and surveillance on university campuses, using spies and recruiting informers among students and professors.

As for the FLQ, it seemed determined that the centennial year, which had opened with a bang, should also close with one. That December a gunsmith's shop at Cap-de-la-Madeleine was looted of nine thousand dollars' worth of heavy calibre guns, revolvers, and ammunition. There was no doubt who the burglars were. They left a note reading, "Thank you. F.L.Q." And, as a panicky populace would realize three years later, that was only the beginning.

2

As her centennial project, Solange Chaput Rolland, a prominent Quebec broadcaster, journalist, and playwright, chose to visit a foreign land and keep a diary of her experiences. Her expenses were paid by a bursary from the Centennial Commission, and the foreign land was English Canada. She crossed it, from sea to sea, and on the eve of the Centennial she published her diary under the title *My Country, Canada or Quebec?* (It's intriguing to note that in French Canada the words were reversed, giving precedence to Quebec.) *Mme Chaput Rolland's odyssey*

The commission had originally offered the bursary to both Chaput Rolland and the novelist Gwethalyn Graham to continue the dialogue they had initiated in the best-selling *Dear Enemies*, a series of letters expressing their divergent views on Canada and Quebec's place in Confederation. But her co-author died, and so Chaput Rolland set off alone from Newfoundland to the borders of Alaska.

"I am now faced with the question which has haunted me since the publication of *Dear Enemies*," her first diary entry read. "Is my country Canada or Quebec?"

Mme Chaput Rolland was not a separatist, but she was certainly a Quebec nationalist. In 1955, she had founded *Points de Vue*, an anti-Duplessis, pro-labour periodical. "I am a French Canadian passionately proud of belonging to the French community of this world," she wrote. "When I sing 'O Canada,' I think of Quebec first because French was the first and only language of this country for more than two centuries. . . . I think of Quebec first because this province is the only one which allows me to live freely in French twenty-four hours a day."

Although Mme Chaput Rolland was no stranger to parts of English-speaking Canada and had many anglophone friends, her journey was very much like an exploration into an unknown country. The book is not a Gallup poll, only an account of a series of encounters between a sophisticated, responsive Quebec woman and various English-speaking Canadians, from St. John's to Victoria. One reads it with considerable dismay. How insensitive some of our English-speaking countrymen seem in this otherwise cordial centennial period! As Mme Chaput Rolland pursues her travels, one senses in her a growing despair at our intransigence and our stubborn refusal to understand what it is that Quebec wants, even though Quebec has tried to tell us, time and again. By the end of the journey, Chaput Rolland remains a federalist of sorts, but it is clear that her experience has shaken her.

Early in 1967 after her book was published, she began to receive letters, mainly from English-speaking Canadians. She had thought she could contribute to a rapprochement between French and English, but after the book's publication she found herself "living a strange experience."

"The resentment and animosity of English Canada towards Quebec has turned on me. . . . As I read the letters. . . piled up on my table. . . I wonder sometimes if I live in the same country as most of my correspondents. I also wonder if it is possible to write a book whose French version appears honest and unruffled but whose English is judged dishonest, cruel, aggressive, uninspired, arbitrary. I have the crazy sensation of sitting on a fence that divides two fields whose climates are different and whose longitudes do not correspond."

In a second diary, written in 1967, excerpted in *Maclean's*, and published in English as *Reflections: Quebec Year One*, she quoted two typical letters from Western Canadians. From Kamloops, B.C.:

"All I can say is if you don't like Canada go back to France and de Gaulle, if he will have you. Why try to force your stupid language on the rest of us? By the way, you stupid French keep talking about your culture. What is the French culture? Raising a lot of kids for the Pope and then let the rest of Canada look after them. You people are just fantastic. Any time you wish to leave Confederation, I am sure we should be only too glad to see you go. Bunch of frogs.''

From Saskatoon:

"I have read your article in *Maclean's*. I can assure you that I have never read before anything so biased, unrealistic and emotional. . . . All you want to do is shove the Quebec French down everybody's throat. . . . I would like to see Quebeckers shut up, clean up their own province, their own Augean stable.''

This astonishing attitude—that Quebeckers were trying to force their language on the rest of Canada—would dominate much of the controversy to come. But on the first leg of her voyage of discovery—the night flight to Halifax—Chaput Rolland experienced the other side of the problem. The stewardess (not yet a "flight attendant") spoke only English and, because there were no Quebec magazines available, offered her a token of Air Canada's respect for bilingualism in the form of the French periodical *Paris Match*. How much easier it would be, she thought, if her name were Sue Rowland. Then she would not feel dispossessed of everything she held dear. Twenty minutes out of Dorval she had lost her name as well as her language, her newspapers, her Quebec magazines. Now she was "Soulange-Chapoote-Rollande.''

Every traveller leaves his country behind when he travels, she mused, "but as a French Canadian I become a stranger in my own land simply by crossing a street! All French Canadians feel this estrangement when they travel in Canada, and most of them resent it. I do too." She found herself, of necessity, switching to English but could not help feeling a little humiliated, a little angry, because her plane was still flying over her home province. Yet she understood the expediency of speaking "the Queen's English.''

In Halifax, she was the guest of a young French-Canadian woman who taught French to Grade 7 children and who also appeared on television, reading, singing, and telling stories in French. Her staff of cameramen, prop men, producers, and directors had been listening to her for two years but were still unable to speak one word of French. "I am beginning to wonder whether there is a congenital infirmity in most English-Canadian brains prohibiting them from becoming bilingual," she told her diary.

I cannot read Chaput Rolland's centennial diary thirty years later without sensing the frustration that ordinary Quebeckers must have experienced when they travelled into the anglophone world. French Canadians were criticized at the time for their insularity because, it was said, they never left their own province to explore the rest of Canada. But the lack of understanding, the various misconceptions that English-speaking Canadians held about her province conspired against the kind of travelogue in which Mme Chaput Rolland found herself involved. The anglophones whom she met and often stayed with were unfailingly polite and hospitable, but when the subject of relations with Quebec came up, she faced a wall of ignorance and prejudice.

"What do you want or expect of Quebec?" she asked a group of students at Dalhousie University during a history lecture. The answer was blunt: "We want you to shut up and leave us alone."

She had arrived during French Week at Dalhousie, but the Halifax papers virtually ignored it. When Claude Ryan of *Le Devoir* tried to answer the slightly irritating question, "What does Quebec want?" in an address to some five hundred students, he got just ten lines of comment hidden on the last page of the local paper. Mme Chaput Rolland was astonished when one of the professors, who wanted to discuss the situation with her in private, asked her not to quote him by name. "It would not be good for my job if I was suspected of leaning toward Quebec." How painful, she thought, that an English-speaking Canadian taking Quebec's side should be ostracized in his own community! Was there something contemptible in being known as a friend of Quebec? she wondered.

The end of that day left her "empty of feelings, of faith, of hopes." In her belief, English Canada was not yet willing "to yield one inch of its privileges to make room for us in Canada." She was not a separatist—not yet—but she knew if she were to remain long in English Canada, she would become one in self-defence. As a journalist she was wise enough and experienced enough to see both sides of the great Canadian quandary. After all, in Quebec she tended to flare up when some French Canadians condemned *a priori* their anglophone counterparts. "But as hard as I try to remain objective and fair, here in English Canada I am bruised by the summary judgments with which many English Canadians reject us."

Though there was a great difference between Halifax and Vancouver, she was aware of a growing conviction that "this whole country becomes a monolithic block when it reflects on the situation of Quebec." In less than a week she was told three times that "some of us are quite ready to go back on the Plains of Abraham and clean up your mess." This blinkered response kept turning up everywhere she went.

One student from Jamaica told her that Halifax businessmen seemed baffled when he approached them for funds for Dalhousie's French Week. "Why a French Week?" they asked. More than one remarked that "the problem of Quebec was settled centuries ago, on the Plains of Abraham." She was irritated to discover that Charlottetown's spanking new Confederation Centre was unilingual. In the library there wasn't a book, newspaper, or magazine in French. In the art gallery, English was the only language used in notes about the artists. In her Fredericton hotel she tried to get a copy of the province's French-language newspaper. The maid, who had lived in the capital all her life, had never heard of it.

Ontario was no different. In London she discussed Quebec's poetry with Professor Ronald Bates, an expert on French-Canadian literature. She asked to address his class and then suffered a bad attack of stage fright—and no wonder. "My young audience is polite, and politely bored. I do not sense any curiosity. They quietly voice their fear of bilingualism and they all are a little shocked to realize Quebec might disturb their pleasant way of life by demanding a special status in Confederation."

She also spoke to Mason Wade's history class and was distressed to find that Wade, the author of a much-admired tome about the French Canadians, "suspects every French Canadian who believes in independence of being close to lunacy." Perhaps they were, but she also remembered André Laurendeau's comment, a few years before, that "some of us prefer lunacy to certain death."

Once again, she found herself toying with separatism. The more she defended her separatist friends, the closer she came to their views. In the eyes of the English Canadians, the separatists were villains and traitors, but to Mme Chaput Rolland they were sincere "and as honest with their hopes for Quebec as I hope I am."

The big cities were more cosmopolitan than she had realized. Toronto wasn't anti-Quebec, but some Torontonians were fed up with French Canada. Yet Montreal could not be called a separatist town, though many Montrealers were separatists. These musings were rudely interrupted when she picked up a copy of the *Telegram* and came across an article entitled "Either shut up or get out."

In Toronto she came to see me, among others. "Why does English Canada hate us so much?" she asked me.

"Because," I answered, "we are afraid of the unknown, because you know what you are and we don't, and because you have an identity and some of us are still looking for one."

A fortnight or so later, Mme Chaput Rolland set off for British Columbia. On board the CNR train, a young sailor asked if she was the lady writing a book about Canada. When she confessed, he replied, "Take care what you say about us, lady, for we English are just about to fix you."

"I'll be honest with you, madame," said another traveller. "How can you expect us to feel at home in Quebec when so few speak our language?" To which Chaput Rolland replied, but only to her diary: "Who is aware that I must forget *my* language in nine provinces?"

The inevitable irritating question followed: "Do you speak Parisian French or Quebec French?" She found it a ridiculous question coming from somebody unable to speak a decent word of French.

330

"Non, monsieur," she replied evenly, "I definitely and proudly do not speak Parisian French. I try to speak international French with, of course, a Quebec accent. Do you speak London English?"

A high CBC official, Will Hankinson, opened her eyes to one of the reasons for British Columbia's resentment. The corporation was about to broadcast in French on the FM network. "Here," Hankinson tells her, "one often hears the expression, 'If you had lived with those dirty frogs during the war, you would hate them as I do.'" The Vancouver press had a somewhat similar attitude: "Now Ottawa wants to impose French culture on our way of life."

In her book, Solange Chaput Rolland keeps a tight rein on her emotions. One sympathizes with her irritation; one senses that she must be seething inwardly at those unthinking responses that grate on her like a fingernail on a blackboard. But she is too civilized and too much of a journalist to respond with a furious and unseemly outburst. She keeps her cool for the most part, but sometimes in her diary there is a small cry from the heart in which she confesses to her frustration and fatigue.

By the time she reached Calgary, she tells us, she was suffering from "complete intellectual exhaustion." For twenty days she had spoken, written, discussed, and argued in English; now she was empty of words. "No one seems to understand why I suddenly fumble with every sentence. At the end of a long day of discussion, in English only, on the advantages of bilingualism, I have great difficulty resisting the urge to throw my glass up in the air when one of my guests remarks lightly: 'Oh, let's all be Canadians.'"

In Calgary, no one except journalists was interested in asking questions about Quebec. But everyone she interviewed told her "what we are supposed to want, and what we will not get!" She quoted a couple of examples in her diary:

"You want too much for yourself and you give nothing to others."

"You have nothing to offer us anyway" (this from a Calgary businessman).

Again she encountered the narrow provincialism that, because of its geological structure, is the great curse of Canada. We are, in effect, an archipelago of population islands. Vast barriers divide us: the angry ocean, the implacable desert of the Canadian Shield, the triple wall of plumed mountains that corrugates the interior of British Columbia. Unlike the United States, Canada is a horizontal country, four thousand miles long but no more than three hundred miles thick in terms of population, its people hived in enclaves, separated by vast distances and by geographical obstacles that also act as psychological barriers.

"The Calgarian," Chaput Rolland wrote in her diary, "does not impress me as having a fond feeling for his neighbours. 'Vancouver? A land of lotus-eaters,' he says with contempt, and his 'down east' is articulated with a false sense of superiority." French Canadians, she found, were rejected as a group though not as individuals. When she spoke as a French Canadian, "faces close, smiles disappear, cordiality freezes." People showered her with affection but could not understand why she resented their attitude towards her people, her province, her identity. "It is absolutely futile to hope that one day a French Canadian will be a full citizen in Western Canada."

"Why hang on to a Confederation which has succeeded in kindling such animosity, such jealousy, such misunderstandings between provinces?" she was forced to ask herself. "Here, it is a common practice to hear one province attack another. I do not react as a French Canadian to this national pettiness but as a human being drained of love, of affection, of mutual respect." She was advised not to judge English Canada "on 'your impressions of Vancouver or Victoria. British Columbia is a selfish province only concerned with its own needs. Alberta is more open than Ontario. . . in the Maritimes we Westerners are as much strangers as you are.'"

In Edmonton, she learned to her dismay that the major student organization in Quebec—l'Union Générale des Étudiants du Québec—had refused to take part in a project sponsored by students at the University of Alberta to celebrate Confederation. Why? Because they rejected all centennial celebrations.

She found herself torn by a strange paradox: her journey had been made possible because of a centennial grant, yet the more she saw of

Canada, the less reason she found to celebrate a hundred years of living together.

She was learning a truth about Canada that had escaped her until this odyssey—that it was not really a united country. "Before this trip, I had anticipated that our concept of national unity would differ from that of the English provinces, but still I felt a certain admiration for what I had imagined to be a Canadian solidarity. I have greatly changed my opinion since, and I have lost confidence in English Canada's open-mindedness. It is easy for the other provinces to accuse Quebec of narrow nationalism, but because each province thinks it is better than the other, there are ten Canadas, each little concerned with unity but aggressively sure that it is the only one in the right."

"In Regina," she was told, "we recognize the equality of all Canadians." Yet only a few hours before she heard that smug declaration, a group of New Canadians told her how hard it was for them to be accepted by the Anglo-Saxon *minority*. "In Quebec, you want to go too fast," she was told. It was true: "In Quebec, we are in a hurry. We have no time to lose, we are busy building, repairing, studying. . . . Granted, in Quebec we do a million things wrongly, but at least we do something! In some parts of Canada, I feel as if I were living in slow motion. Suddenly it seems urgent for. . . me to hear new words, bold ideas about Canada and its future."

In Winnipeg she was appalled when the noted western historian W.L. Morton told her he was ready to accept the cultural duality of Canada, "but if we must be forced into political duality, then I think it would be best for Quebec to secede." To that she responded with sudden and uncharacteristic bitterness, "You would rather break Canada than share its destiny with us. If an historian of your reputation and of your authority thinks along these lines, I really do not see what I am doing in your country. I might as well go home, and say quite definitely in answer to the question of my book, that my country is Quebec."

At the *Winnipeg Free Press* she discussed Walter Gordon's book *A Choice for Canada* with the publisher Richard Malone, who dismissed Gordon's nationalism. That provoked within her a shrewd suspicion—

that one of the schisms between French and English Canada rested on the fact that Quebec wanted too much independence and the rest of the country too little.

Three weeks later she found herself in Newfoundland, where people talked about Canada as if it were a foreign country. An islander, she realized, was a Newfoundlander first, a Canadian second. "Where have I heard this point of view before?"

Everywhere she heard the same refrain: "Every province in Canada is different, but Newfoundland is more different." She had come to realize, after her long exploration, "that Canada as a whole does not exist, but is regionalized into eleven different republics. I write eleven, because English Quebec is an entity of its own on this continent."

She visited with the premier, Joey Smallwood. "If the pretensions of Quebec to think itself equal with the rest of this country were not so ridiculous, I would die with laughter," he told her. Then, oblivious to her rising anger, he added, "The French Canadian is one of the most lovable human beings in Canada, but collectively he deserves a swift kick."

And so Solange Chaput Rolland's long voyage of discovery ended and she returned to her native province. Having been interviewed by the media in every province, she began to receive mail from all parts of the country. A great many letters from the West suggested she remain in French Canada and lead her province out of Confederation once and for all, since Quebeckers were all a bunch of terrorists who had never given much to the country. From Quebec, the letters accused her of being a turncoat, a "dangerous 'bourgeoise and capitalist,' selling out to English Canada," and a prime candidate for the firing squad on the morning of Quebec's first Independence Day. She did not take these very seriously, but they did illustrate "the lack of respect for the other person's point of view."

If the centennial celebrations had been launched to help the cause of national unity in Canada, Chaput Rolland's experiences suggest that the experiment was not an unqualified success. No one, it seemed, was prepared to listen to any point of view but his or her own, and that included the quarrel in Quebec over separatism.

"For example, when Jean Lesage mentions young separatists, he fumes with rage. Why? When on the other hand some separatists speak of federalists, they often laugh at them. They become vulgar, violently impolite, and their tantrums always fail to convince our population of their sincerity. When English Canadians, in turn, do their utmost to ignore the identity of the French Canadians living in their provinces, are they respectful of the rights of a minority group? As human beings, French Canadians are neither better nor worse than their English counterparts. The new Quebec takes self-criticism in its stride. I wonder if English Canada is ready for self-examination?"

3

René's choice

The great historical event of 1967, as far as Canada's future was concerned, was neither the centennial celebrations (in which Quebec did not join) nor the great exposition in Montreal (in which, of course, it took the lead). It was the departure of René Lévesque from the Lesage Liberals and the formation, under his leadership, of a separatist movement that led to the birth of the Parti Québécois. In a watershed year in which attitudes and mores were changing swiftly, this was the greatest turning point of all. René Lévesque gave the struggling and divided separatist movement unity and legitimacy.

This was no wild-eyed radical with a bomb in one hand and a manifesto in the other. "I am a nationalist," he had declared after the early FLQ bombings, "if that means being, for oneself, fiercely for or against something or against a given situation. But never against someone. Nationalism that means racism or fascism makes me vomit." As much as Jean Lesage he had been responsible for the Quiet Revolution that set Quebec on a new course, free at last of Duplessis's old-style politics and of church domination. Nor was his vision confined to the narrow horizons of his own province. He had seen the world as a war correspondent in Europe, not as a Canadian journalist but for the U.S. Office of War Information ("though I was willing to go overseas, I was not willing to go in the uniform of His Majesty") and later as a Canadian war correspondent in Korea.

He was among the first to discover the horrors of Dachau and, later, the first journalist to interview Nikita Khrushchev. The war opened up the world to him. Until that time, he had had little contact with anything outside his own province, except through books. "The war," he told an interviewer, "made me an internationalist." Radio-Canada sent him off to cover the Korean War (an assignment that turned him into a pacifist) and then to the coronation of the new queen.

More than anything else, however, he was a child of television, which was launched in Quebec in 1952. The news analysis program *Point de Mire* turned him into a star. There his ability to synthesize a complicated issue and render it understandable to a mass audience made him the most talked-about journalist in the province. It was this gift for reducing complex issues to thirty-second sound bites on TV, together with his brilliant oratory, that made him a political figure to be reckoned with.

But he was not a traditional politician. He wasn't elected to office until the eve of his fortieth year. Shortly after that he was propelled into the Lesage cabinet, where he emerged as a tribune of the people. Early in 1962, after months of careful preparation, he unleashed on his party a bombshell as potent as any detonated by the FLQ. This was his proposal to nationalize the Quebec electrical industry. He chose his moment carefully, slipping a single sentence into a routine speech he had been scheduled to give on the subject of energy. "The future in this sector," he said, "is state business."

As Lévesque recalled, "the next morning all hell broke loose. I was told Lesage was beside himself." But Lesage, who knew a winning issue when he heard one, seized on the slogan "The people of Quebec versus the electrical trust," a rallying cry that resolved itself into the even more potent *Maîtres chez nous*—"Masters in our own house."

When Lévesque broke with his party after the de Gaulle speech to join the separatist movement, or, more accurately, the *sovereigntist* movement, he was a media star who was also a political star of the first magnitude. He was honest, that was clear. He was not ambitious in the self-serving sense; he had shown no inclination to succeed Lesage as Liberal Party leader. He did not care about money, and, above all, he was sincere. He had apparently sacrificed a political career for what he believed in.

His own background had no similarity to the impoverished upbringing of the impassioned Pierre Vallières. His biographer Peter Desbarats has described his childhood on the Gaspé Peninsula as "secure, almost idyllic and typically Canadian in its main influences." The son of a country lawyer, he enrolled at Laval's law school but did not finish the course. An indifferent student, he skipped lectures, preferring to sit around playing cards or going to the movies. His job with the U.S. Office of War Information helped change his life.

The real turning point came in 1958–59 with the strike of seventy-four French-language radio and television producers against the CBC. The producers wanted to form a union; the CBC refused, claiming they were part of management. To that point, Lévesque had shown no interest in politics. Now, two things grated on him. John Diefenbaker, then prime minister, was totally unsympathetic. Worse, the English-speaking producers didn't want to be involved. As Lévesque put it later, "the whole bloody French network became virtually non-existent, and nobody cared." If Radio-Canada was supposed to be so important to a bilingual country, how was it that nobody seemed to give a damn? The non-Quebec labour unions, in Lévesque's words, "tried to stab us in the back." The Diefenbaker government thought the strike would be over in a few days and refused to intervene. To the rest of the country the strike was a big yawn. What had happened to Solidarity Forever?

The administration of Radio-Canada was a federal responsibility, but Ottawa was lying low. Lévesque was part of a delegation that went to the capital to request an audience with the minister of labour, Michael Starr. Sixty-eight days elapsed before they received a reply. If the dispute had arisen on the CBC's English-language network, Lévesque believed it would have been settled in two or three days. "I was scarred, even traumatized by that experience," Lévesque recalled. Sooner or later, he realized, he would have to enter politics. For him this was the moment of truth. "I learned then that French was really very secondary in the rest of Canada's mind, certainly in Ottawa's."

The producers' strike ended in March 1959. Jean Lesage had been named leader of the provincial Liberals a few months before. Lévesque joined him and when the party won a narrow majority in 1960 became a member of the Quebec legislature.

Immediately after the election he spent an evening with Father Georges-Henri Lévesque, whom he called "the liberating conscience of our generation." As they stood at the edge of the Montmorency Falls, the priest turned to him, and over the roar of the water, shouted, "Hurry up! What's happening is a revolution. Don't let it slip through your fingers."

Those first few weeks, Lévesque later recalled, "were absolutely staggering." The so-called Quiet Revolution was under way. The new government was dedicated to the difficult task of cleaning out the Augean stable of corruption that had been part of Quebec politics. Lévesque found himself in the cabinet, and soon he began attending informal meetings with some of the most progressive figures in French Canada—Gérard Pelletier, André Laurendeau, and Pierre Trudeau— usually at Pelletier's house. There, Lévesque gave them "a backstage view of public life" and they responded with plenty of blunt advice.

It was Lévesque's plan to serve his province for a decade and then return to journalism. But, as a result of the party's unexpected defeat in 1966, he found himself the organizer of an informal group of reformers who met regularly to discuss the party's future in the private Saint-Denis Club on Sherbrooke Street. The dominant members were Eric Kierans, Paul Gérin-Lajoie, and Lévesque himself. Kierans had been one of Lévesque's chief supporters in the Lesage cabinet. Gérin-Lajoie, Quebec's first minister of education, had been the architect of the new secular school system that replaced the old church-dominated institutions. As 1967 dawned, the membership of the Saint-Denis group had swelled to one hundred and had become, in Lévesque's words, "the think tank of the party."

338

The Liberals were now split between the Saint-Denis reformers and the Lesage old guard. It had become more obvious during the party's convention in November 1966, when its outgoing president, Dr. Irénée Lapierre, told a radio interviewer that Lévesque no longer belonged in the party and would soon be a liability. "If he doesn't leave us now," he said, "he'll go tomorrow." When Lesage tried to explain away that gaffe, he was booed and shouted down by a majority of the delegates.

The reformers scored a victory when Kierans was elected president of the Liberal Federation. A committed federalist, he had no sympathy for the separatist cause. Lévesque and other members of the original Saint-Denis Club were still pressing for more constitutional debate. But, as events developed, this was the beginning of the end for Lévesque as a Lesage Liberal. Within a year Kierans, his closest political ally, would turn against him and drive him from the party.

Kierans had been brought up in Saint-Henri, an Irish enclave of Montreal whose population was largely made up of railway workers. He obtained a full scholarship to Loyola College, where he opted for a business career rather than the priesthood. In 1953 he became head of McGill's school of economics where he jousted with the principal, Cyril James, an early example of the windmill-tilting that would mark his career. Later, as head of the Montreal and Canadian stock exchanges, he developed a reputation as a maverick—a man who thought nothing of upsetting the staid Montreal Club by bringing along as his luncheon guest the unspeakable René Lévesque.

Kierans also made a determined effort to learn French—a rarity for a businessman at the time—often rising at five in the morning to struggle with the language. After Jean Lesage's 1962 victory, he quit the exchanges and, after winning a seat in the by-election, joined the cabinet and became minister of revenue. A member of the party's progressive wing, he supported Lévesque, who liked him because "he really acted as a Quebecker on the move."

To the press, Kierans was "the English René Lévesque." The pair were dubbed "Jean Lesage's terrible twins." They stood on what the anglophone businessmen would consider the wrong side of many issues.

Kierans was for the rapid development of an expanded provincial government with a reduced role for the English-speaking élite. This made him Lévesque's natural ally, but Kieran's advocacy of decentralization was always made in the context of a united Canada.

Although one of the mainstays of the Saint-Denis group, Kierans was opposed to separatism both emotionally, as a keen federalist, and practically because he believed a separate Quebec would cause a decline of between 10 and 15 percent in the province's standard of living. He left the group in the spring of 1967. Its influence was diminishing, but Lévesque stayed on.

Lévesque had been moving closer to separatism since 1965. In his view, the province's affairs, especially in the economic field, were being left in the hands of outsiders while political decisions made in Ottawa were profoundly affecting the collective life of French Canadians.

The growing rift between Lévesque and the party came to a head in the centennial year. In April, a group of leading Liberals met at Mont-Tremblant in the Laurentians to discuss future party policy. There Lévesque spelled out his ideas about the future of the province in what one participant called "the best speech that I ever heard him give." What Lévesque was advocating was sovereignty association, though that phrase had yet to be coined.

A climax was approaching. In a confidential letter to Pierre Laporte, one of Lesage's closest advisers, a leading party organizer, Paul Desrochers, identified Lévesque as "the most controversial personality" in the party and reported that the majority of Liberals thought that "he has to fit in with the thinking of the party or get out!"

Identified as a Liberal maverick, Lévesque was demanding that Quebec's private media monopolies be disbanded and the companies made to pump their profits into programming. That was as worrisome to the party's right wing as was his continued speculation over Quebec's place in the Canadian nation. When the party executive, which included Kierans, rejected any discussion of the constitutional issue at the upcoming Liberal convention in October, the stage was set for a dramatic confrontation.

Even as the opposing camps jockeyed for position, General de Gaulle entered the scene with his July 24 *Vive le Québec libre* speech. Lesage and most of his followers insisted on repudiating the French president's remarks, forcing one member, François Aquin, to quit the caucus. Lévesque wrote to Lesage that he considered that caucus meeting "stifling and surly" and the decision to disclaim the general "a grave mistake which was and will remain indefinitely hard to swallow."

Lévesque had promised the remaining members of the Saint-Denis Club that he would outline his position when he returned from a U.S. vacation. The result was a six-thousand-word manifesto outlining his vision of a new political order for Canada. "Quebec must become sovereign as soon as possible," he declared, adding that "this sovereignty should be open to association with others. . . . This, new adaptation of the current 'common market' formula, might be called the Canadian Union—l'Union canadienne."

The party moved quickly to diminish Lévesque's authority within its ranks. The province's Young Liberals voted against sovereignty, 67 to 45. Lesage stated publicly that he would "never lead a party that preached separatism," and Kierans declared that "if the Liberal party accepts René's resolution for separatism, for a sovereign Quebec, I could not remain in the Liberal party."

At a final meeting of Lévesque's supporters before the fall convention, Yves Michaud, a new member for the Montreal riding of Dorion and a close friend of Lévesque, made an impassioned plea that "the Rocky Mountains are part of our heritage. . . Marquette and Joliet. . . we were there first. You are going to deprive us of a heritage that is ours," he told Lévesque.

"Well, if you still want your Rocky Mountains," Lévesque shot back, "keep them!"

Six years later, Michaud joined the ranks of the separatists to run in the election of 1973. Later he became founding editor of the movement's first daily newspaper, *Le Jour*.

No amount of compromising on the part of Robert Bourassa, who acted as a link between Lesage and Lévesque, could heal the breach that was widening between them. An hour-long CBC debate between Kierans and Lévesque on September 26 made their differences public.

"René and I are two predictable people," Kierans told the radio audience. "I knew he was heading to this. He knew I would fight him."

"Basically, I am a Quebecker first," Lévesque declared, "and Eric is a Canadian first."

The night before the October convention, Lévesque and his followers met in the Clarendon Hotel in Quebec City. "If we have 25 percent, then I'm staying," Lévesque reportedly told them. He still believed that there was a chance he might remain in the party. But with the powerful men against him—Laporte, Kierans, Lesage—his support was dropping. "We haven't come to discuss Lévesque's thesis," one of the delegates told the press. "We're after his head."

The convention opened on October 13, devoid of the American-style hoopla that the Tories brought to Canada. The party organizers, anxious to project an image of serious debate, had banned all demonstrations. The fifteen hundred delegates crammed into the Château Frontenac's elegantly cavernous ballroom were faced with three conflicting motions. One was Lévesque's call for a separate Quebec with a negotiated economic association with the rest of Canada. A second motion by Gérin-Lajoie was similar but did not call for independence. The party hierarchy had its own motion that unequivocally rejected "separatism in all its forms."

The convention was on Lesage's side. It hooted down and rejected Lévesque's motion calling for a secret ballot. Kierans, as party president, followed and, looking straight at Lévesque, declared, "If anyone feels that separatism is the way the party should go, then he should go and form his own party."

The federal Liberals were nervous. Walter Gordon phoned Kierans to make sure the provincial party wouldn't come out for independence. Lester Pearson, it was said, carried a pocket radio to follow the proceedings.

On Saturday afternoon, Laporte introduced a motion stating that the Gérin-Lajoie motion should be tabled and the party should reject any

342

form of separatism. When Lévesque entered the ballroom, his opponents began to shout, "*Lévesque dehors!*"—Lévesque out.

At 6:00 p.m., Lévesque was given the right to speak for his resolution for five minutes. He was on the verge of tears as he told them that "the party is in danger of dying if it returns to being a private club."

He walked down the aisle. From one row to the next he recognized a throng of familiar faces. Some made friendly, discreet little signs, but most, as Lévesque later noted, "acted as though I ceased to exist." Only Gérin-Lajoie "dared cross the psychological barrier and step forward with outstretched hands."

Lévesque felt a twinge in his heart as he recognized former colleagues from every region in the province who had shared his successes and his failures. But he was relieved to be leaving the party—he never was a party animal. "For me," he said, "any political party is basically just a necessary evil, one of the instruments that a democratic society needs when the time comes to delegate to the elected representatives the responsibility of looking after their common interests." To him, there was nothing traumatic about the Liberal rejection of him. "I wasn't breaking up with my family, just an old, outmoded party, falling into sterility." It was the loss of old comrades-in-arms that saddened him.

That evening, he met with his most dedicated supporters at the Clarendon Hotel. Their subject: What next? "A decision in principle was made that we had to have further political action, that we were starting, not finishing." With Lévesque out, most Quebec newspapers praised him for his reforming zeal and his part in the regeneration of the Liberal Party. The most prescient of the journalists, Claude Ryan of *Le Devoir*, warned: "The truth is that a major surgical operation has been performed, and no one can yet predict what the long-term effects will be." But he knew what was coming. René Lévesque would soon be called on to lead the separatist forces in the province. The confrontation at the convention was only the first of many.

Lévesque's ascendancy to the leadership of the separatist movement in Quebec meant the eventual disappearance of the RIN as a political force and the overshadowing of the fiery young leader Pierre Bourgault. Bourgault, who had once suggested (on my TV program) that the separatists could block the St. Lawrence Seaway by sinking a boat in mid-channel, was too volatile for Lévesque's tastes. The two had met several times, but Lévesque was not enthusiastic about the RIN's tactics, which had helped heat up the crowds during the de Gaulle visit. Bourgault told Peter Desbarats that "it was our bum image that he didn't like. We were always on the street demonstrating and Lévesque was completely against this."

Bourgault, Lévesque realized, would not be an asset to the kind of movement he was contemplating—Mouvement Souveraineté-Association. It was born in mid-November during a weekend meeting of 380 supporters. It was not yet a political party, but in less than a year it would be. For the next two decades Lévesque's features—the high dome, the sad eyes, the mouth with its inevitable cigarette dangling loosely from a corner—would be the most recognizable in his native province.

Thus were sown the seeds of Canada's potential dismemberment. How ironic that Lévesque's moment should come even as the nation wound up the spectacular birthday bash that was originally conceived to celebrate the triumph of its nationhood and the unity of its people.

4

Bye-bye,   At five o'clock on the afternoon of November 29, 1967, André Lau-
Bi-Bi   rendeau, the co-chairman (with Davidson Dunton) of the Royal Commission on Bilingualism and Biculturalism, handed the first volume of the report to Lester Pearson after four years of exhaustive hearings and deliberations. It had been the most expensive royal commission in history and also the longest, and there were many who felt, not without reason, that events had already conspired to render it out-of-date.

It could have been presented earlier in the year, but the Prime Minister, who had once been frustrated by the glacial pace of its deliberations, had suggested it be held back until the end of the centennial year. "Up to this point," he had told Laurendeau and Dunton (then president of Carleton University) the previous February, "I would have tended to ask you to hurry. But this time my wish is for the opposite. If your report brings to light disastrous situations, if your first book tends to confirm the view of certain Québécois who believe Confederation is a totally negative experience for French Canadians and makes them want to say 'we told you so,' then we may as well wait."

This was an odd reaction. Royal commissions are supposed to expose the cancers in the body politic, to dig out the facts no matter how unpalatable, even to rock the boat—or are they? Are they not the government's method of postponing unpalatable truths? The last thing the Prime Minister wanted, in this jubilant year, was, in the vernacular of the day, to "lay a guilt trip" on the country and, at the same time, provide an unassailable document that would give aid and comfort to those who felt the country wasn't working.

A few days later, as Laurendeau and Neil Morrison, the commission's secretary, crossed Wellington Street on their way to the House of Commons where the first volume of the report was to be tabled, Laurendeau seemed depressed and disappointed. Morrison tried to cheer him up. There would be more recognition, he pointed out, and a higher status for the French language in Ottawa and in the rest of the country as a result of the commission's findings. Laurendeau remained pessimistic. "But, Neil," he said, "it does nothing for Quebec." And, as Morrison later wrote, he was right.

At this point Laurendeau was exhausted. For four years he had led "an impossible life," crisscrossing the country, cut off from his home province, unable to pursue his chosen career as a political journalist—unable even, as a neutral commissioner, to comment publicly on matters that had preoccupied him for most of his life. The very monotony of the hearings became numbing after a time. "Each day," Laurendeau wrote, "we come into contact with a large number of individuals, we hear many things that touch and move us, often in contradictory ways, and the next day the same experience begins again in a new place. It is exactly like being subjected to machine-gun fire. . . . It's rough going for everyone, and at the same time I believe it is profoundly useful."

This nomadic life, much of it spent in what was to him a strange and even foreign country, had taken its toll by 1967. The migraines, the insomnia, the severe back pains to which he had been subject were increasing. The stultifying parochialism that he had encountered from Victoria to Charlottetown had dismayed and depressed him. "Faced with certain anglophones," he had written early in 1964, "I feel an inner urge toward separatism. They're too deaf, they don't listen to anything but force. But when I get home, the separatists make me a Canadian again: they're too naïve, too unaware of political reality—or else strangely fickle and superficial."

By the time the first report was published, events in Quebec were moving at an accelerated speed that made it seem passé. René Lévesque's new separatist movement and Daniel Johnson's aggressive stand at the Confederation for Tomorrow Conference in Toronto that fall both overshadowed the Bi-Bi Report. As for André Laurendeau, he himself was suffering "from the fatigue that comes from being a Canadian."

Why had he taken the job? Chiefly because he had been advocating just that sort of royal commission in the pages of *Le Devoir* and he felt it would have been hypocritical to refuse to take part in the very cause that had concerned him for all his adult life. As a twenty-year-old nationalist, and a spokesman for the nationalist youth movement, Jeune-Canada, he'd been rebuffed by R.B. Bennett when he tried to protest the treatment of French Canadians in the federal civil service. Thirty years later, another Tory prime minister, John Diefenbaker, rebuffed him again when Laurendeau called for a federal inquiry into Canadian bilingualism and the participation of French Canadians in the civil service. That same year, Lester Pearson made the issue party policy. "I believe," he told the House, "that we have now reached a stage where we should seriously and collectively. . . review the bicultural and bilingual situation in our country."

At Laurendeau's suggestion, the party committed itself to a federal

346

inquiry when and if it came to power, even if the provinces refused to co-operate. Laurendeau was no Liberal; Pearson's flip-flop over nuclear warheads in Canada had aroused his scorn in *Le Devoir*. Nonetheless, shortly after his victory in 1963, Pearson phoned Laurendeau at the newspaper, pointed out that he was "in a certain way the father of the commission," and asked him to serve.

Laurendeau was faced with an agonizing choice. On the one hand, there was his position as the leading journalist in Quebec. The province was clearly about to enter a turbulent and historic era that would cry out for the kind of forthright and reasoned comment for which he was known. How could he stay on the sidelines, his voice stilled, his pen no longer active? On the other hand, he had been the leading advocate for this kind of major inquiry. How could he, in conscience, refuse Pearson's offer?

His first instinct was to say no, but his colleague Claude Ryan pointed out how awkward it would be if "the father of the commission" refused to serve. Laurendeau consulted with other colleagues, and "no one could see how I could refuse." He met with Lévesque in a Chinese restaurant. On one side of a napkin Lévesque had scrawled the reasons why it was a bad idea to accept. On the other he had written one positive foreseeable result: Laurendeau could resign with a bang. "In other words, one of the rare reasons for my working on this commission would be the fuss it would make if I left it."

In the end Laurendeau accepted the co-chairmanship with Dunton. It seemed to him that this was the first step towards achieving for French Canadians both linguistic and cultural equality within Canada. "What is at stake," he wrote, "is the destiny of a people." As he told his readers in *Le Devoir*, "I have been calling for an investigation since January 1962. I believe in it. I am diving in."

It was an unusual royal commission, a two-headed organization with equal representation from French and English Canada and two of its ten members from other ethnic groups. All were bilingual, and as the historian Ramsay Cook pointed out in the *Canadian Forum*, "every single member. . . had a background in the field of what might be called mass education—university teaching, the media, trade unionism." As Cook remarked, few English Canadians were aware of Laurendeau's varied and controversial background. "Indeed, there could certainly have been some. . . who would have turned the radio off very quickly and hoisted the Union Jack if they had realized that at various times since 1935, M. Laurendeau had been a separatist, a neutralist, an editor of *Action Nationale*, a leader of La Ligue pour la défense du Canada, which opposed conscription during World War Two, a founder of the *Bloc Populaire*, and one-time *Bloc* member of the Quebec Legislature. For a brief period he was even associated with the Quebec wing of the CCF." But that was in his youth. Over the years he had developed into "a profoundly intelligent and sensitive humanist."

That last assessment was written in 1962. A little more than a year later, Laurendeau found himself presiding over a unique coast-to-coast dialogue exploring the strengths and weaknesses of the pact originally made between the two founding peoples.

Laurendeau's discovery of English Canada, recorded in a series of diary entries between 1964 and 1967, is reminiscent of Mme Chaput Rolland's centennial-inspired peregrinations. Like her, he was appalled by the parochialism he encountered from east to west. "Provincialism is strong everywhere," he wrote when the commission reached Edmonton. "They call themselves Canadians, but they look at things first and foremost as Albertans or Manitobans. The only way to make any headway with them is to remind them that they *are* Canadians, that Quebec is part of Canada, and that if separatism splits the country apart they would feel the effects."

At a meeting with some notables from Prince Edward Island he was "astounded by the extent of their provincialism—although perhaps we shouldn't have been, as we're in the island of Lilliput." In Halifax, he described the Maritimer as "a Canadian dissatisfied with Canada, who remembers the period before Confederation as a period of prosperity, and who feels a constant need for interventions, at least on the financial level—which means grants from Ottawa." It was not just a political attitude, he realized, "it's a profound part of his psychology. He considers himself mistreated almost as much as the Quebecker does, but since he feels weaker economically, and less different from a cultural point of view, his criticisms always lead to more requests for money rather than a demand for greater autonomy."

"In the West. . . there is resentment against the East: that is, against the economic domination of Bay Street and St. James Street. According to this point of view, French Canadians belong to the group of exploiters, and Montreal appears as a suburb of Toronto. Also, at least in Saskatchewan, we become more likeable when we describe ourselves as exploited too."

In 1964, when René Lévesque was still a Liberal, albeit a maverick one, Laurendeau noted that in the West, as in the Maritimes, Lévesque's statements, even more than those of the separatists, were perceived as disastrous. "And yet, after several conversations that were depressing because of the ignorance and lack of curiosity of those I spoke with, I came to understand the absolute need for a René Lévesque. Not only for internal reasons, but to trouble—even dangerously so—these communities that are so closed in on themselves."

The more Laurendeau experienced the intransigent attitudes of English-speaking Canadians, the more he came to understand the separatist point of view. "A separatist going through what we're experiencing," he wrote of the commission's public hearings, "would come out of it far more convinced of his position. A young nationalist would certainly be tempted by separatism." He himself confessed that "left to myself there's no doubt that I feel several times each week, and even several times a day, real inner urges toward separatism."

Laurendeau was no wild-eyed nationalist; he had long been a committed federalist and so paid no more than passing attention to these emotional reactions. Yet, if he—an intelligent, well-educated, and sophisticated journalist—could understand and sympathize with the separatist cause, how much more inviting would it appear to the younger generation?

In his reflective moments he had come to realize the extent to which society was changing: ". . . some of its young people refuse to listen to what one says to them—it doesn't matter to them. And so I find myself cut off from those who interest me the most, and who formerly. . . were my best listeners. Is this a new state of things or a temporary crisis? Is it going to be necessary to adopt a new language in order to be heard?"

In his travels across the country, Laurendeau made it a point to call upon all the provincial premiers. They rarely impressed him. Bennett of British Columbia, he told his diary, "drowns all problems in his smile and his general expressions of optimism." As for Manning of Alberta, "what we have to say doesn't interest him in the slightest. He recognizes the existence of a grave and dramatic crisis in Quebec, adds that it must be paid attention to, and moves on to other subjects." Indeed, Laurendeau had been told, the premier even objected to the use of French on airlines flying in and out of Alberta.

His encounter with John Robarts of Ontario and his minister of education, William Davis, was disappointing. To Laurendeau, the premier was "a man who. . . doesn't seem to ask himself many questions, except about matters he has to deal with directly. . . . I don't think he asked us a single question." Roblin of Manitoba he found excessively prudent: "[He] will do all he can for cultural equality in Canada, but. . . he will carefully measure the implications of each of his acts; and. . . unless there is a major change in the cultural climate, he won't be able to do much."

His interview with Louis-Joseph Robichaud, the Acadian premier of New Brunswick, was more agreeable, perhaps because Robichaud asked him what language he'd like to use and also because in his answers he looked directly at Laurendeau, unlike the others who directed all their remarks to Dunton.

His meeting with Woodrow Lloyd, premier of Saskatchewan, produced "a radical change of climate," perhaps because Lloyd was a better listener. He and his minister of health, Allan Blakeney, a future premier, Laurendeau found "broad minded and much more aware of belonging to Canada." The meeting in Regina, he wrote, "was the most interesting and possibly the most fruitful" of all those held on the prairies.

The apathy he found in English Canada distressed him. In Winnipeg he, too, had a visit with Richard Malone of the *Free Press*, "a fellow who is apparently satisfied with the status quo and doesn't want to challenge it; he has remarkably little curiosity. In short, for him the solution lies in unending patience." So much for the views of the vice-president of a once great newspaper that had, under John Wesley Dafoe, been the voice and the conscience of Western Canada.

Now Laurendeau found "an astonishing lack of self-criticism in all of Anglo-Canadian society, whether in the West or the Maritimes. They don't examine the postulates on which their society is based, and at the same time several of them jump on our statements about ourselves, which immediately falsifies the dialogue."

The general attitude was "Let's not rock the boat," an ostrich-like approach since the boat was already being rocked in Quebec. "When we meet with a group, whether in Edmonton, Winnipeg, Charlottetown or Halifax, everyone always starts by saying there is no problem in their region or locality; in other words, don't start stirring things up. They repeat it over and over again, until certain problems start emerging almost in spite of them. But these problems are almost always provincial matters, and it's very difficult to bring them to another level of discussion. I can't get over the provincialism that one meets up with everywhere."

At lunch with a group of businessmen in Edmonton, Laurendeau found the atmosphere very negative. "To hear these men, you'd think the Commission was creating an artificial problem, and that French is fated to disappear, or at least that it only exists in the East, that biculturalism is an old quarrel between Ontario and Quebec and that's the end of it." The idea that the commission itself was creating the crisis seemed to be widely held. "Only a few state this but many imply it." Again and again Laurendeau and his colleagues were obliged to insist that the commission was created because the problem was very real.

In Quebec, the commissioners came up against radicals and separatists who loudly dominated the meetings and vilified those commissioners who were French Canadians as sellouts. At the regional meetings they heard again and again from French-speaking Quebeckers who testified to their frustrations at being obliged for economic reasons to speak English. The anglophone members of the commission were shocked to find that many who appeared before them thought the only way to combat the problem was to create a unilingual state.

One could not come away from these hearings without the conviction that the country was in a state of real crisis and that much of English Canada was oblivious to the danger. It was this realization that prompted the commission to produce, in 1965, an interim report entitled *The Canadian Crisis*. The Prime Minister objected to the title, indeed to any title at all, because there was no precedent for putting a title on a royal commission report. Pearson was still held hostage by his fear that the leader of the opposition would accuse him of having manufactured a crisis to justify his policies. As Laurendeau noted, "He seemed a little obsessed by Mr. Diefenbaker." Nonetheless, Pearson came around to Laurendeau's point of view, and when the report was presented to him on February 11 pronounced it "a good report, though somewhat gloomy." Laurendeau got the impression that the Prime Minister found the analysis lucid, "but he's not unaware that this lucidity may cause him some problems."

"It seems to us," the commissioners reported, "to be no longer a traditional conflict between a majority and a minority. It is rather a conflict between two majorities: that which is a majority in all of Canada and that which is a majority in the entity of Quebec." The split in the country's personality, though not new, was more serious than ever before, the commissioners reported. A change of attitude was needed. English Canadians must be prepared to provide better guarantees for the security of the minority: "To some extent they must be prepared to pay by way of new conditions for the future of Canada as one country, and to realize that their partner of tomorrow will be quite different from their partner of yesterday. French Canadians must try to overcome their self-serving minority complex. Problems affecting all of Canada are their problems, too. They would need to be aware of the kind of thinking that puts 'la nation' above all other considerations and values."

John Diefenbaker predictably savaged the interim report as "a collection of generalities and platitudes." The general reaction, however, was positive. Some Western newspapers continued to insist that the commission was manufacturing a crisis. A few commentators, such as Charles Lynch of the *Ottawa Citizen*, claimed that French-Canadian commissioners had dominated the report—that it was "a French-Canadian report—a French-Canadian victory." That wounded Laurendeau, who had made a point of leaning in the opposite direction.

The report's blunt conclusion that Canada was passing through "the greatest crisis in its history" was widely criticized in English-speaking Canada as alarmist. That may be one reason why it was a best-seller (for a government document). Certainly, Laurendeau's main purpose was achieved—to wake the country up to a continuing problem. In French Canada the reaction was remarkably positive. When Laurendeau and Dunton visited Lesage in Quebec City, wondering whether he would accept the idea of the state of Quebec being "investigated" by a federal commission, they found him unexpectedly co-operative. And when Dunton asked the Quebec premier whether he found the interim report unduly pessimistic and "if the situation seemed less serious this year than last," Lesage told him, "It's much worse. In Quebec we're all walking on a volcano."

Now, near the close of the centennial year, with the final report complete, the climate in Canada—especially English-speaking Canada—had changed. First, Expo 67 had made the public aware of the vigour and élan of Quebeckers and the obvious fruits of co-operation between the two societies. Second, de Gaulle's spectacular performance had made it clear that a good many Quebeckers were unhappy with their position in Canada. Because of these changes, as a writer in the *Canadian Forum* pointed out, it was now possible for Torontonians to applaud an opera in which a heroic and tragic Louis Riel is the victim of Orange Ontarians who would "hang him up the river with a yah, yah, yah."

The Bi-Bi Report was essentially a plan for action. It declared English and French the official languages, of Canada. It proposed a sweeping new charter for French and English language rights as a tool to tackle the country's unity crisis. It called for a concept based on "equal partnership" and for the enshrining of these rights in the constitution. It urged English-speaking Canadians to face up to the French fact and language and repeated the warnings of the 1965 interim report. It urged two provinces, New Brunswick and Ontario, to declare themselves bilingual and suggested that any province where the minority exceeded 10 percent declare itself bilingual. Both languages should be used in all provincial legislatures, and bilingual districts should be established throughout Canada. In the federal capital, the report called for sweeping bilingualism.

These recommendations, many of which seem mild enough today, were not universally accepted, especially in British Columbia, whose premier remained inflexible on the subject of language instruction in the schools. Even Robert Strachan, the province's NDP leader, broke with his party to decry the report as "seven million dollars' worth of trouble for Canada."

In addition to language, the commissioners were concerned about two other problems. One was multiculturalism and the way it was perceived, especially in the West. The other was the overwhelming influence of the United States.

In Regina, with its large Ukrainian population, the commissioners said, "[We] began to formulate for ourselves an understanding of the situation we've been observing; that is, a multiculturalism that is an undeniable fact and must be taken into account, but which manifests itself differently according to locality. Over and above it is the great problem of French-English relations in Canada. How can we get across the point that an 'ethnic group,' even one that is relatively large provincially, but only represents 3% of the total Canadian population, is not at all the same thing as an organized society like Quebec, with a large population, its own institutions, and a long and specific history?" Now it seemed that every large group of newcomers wanted its language enshrined with that of the two founding nations. Laurendeau was disturbed that the ethnic groups "seem to believe that to grant something to the French is to take something away from them. . . for if they accept to a great extent the necessity of losing their languages, why shouldn't everyone in Canada have to do so." He found this especially true of the Ukrainian Canadians, perhaps because, being accustomed to a constant struggle in the old country, they tended to perpetuate it in the new land.

As the commission moved from one region to another, Laurendeau had taken note of the second problem: each region was influenced by the corresponding American region. "No matter where you go, across three thousand miles. . . you're always dangerously close to the United States. So Canada resembles a large ship that's leaking like a sieve." As Ralph Hedlin, a writer and management consultant in Winnipeg, told him, "The facts are too overwhelming to be denied, even struggled against—except by something stronger than a fact: an idea!"

There was, as Laurendeau said, "a fatigue that comes from being Canadian—an almost impossible undertaking and a heavy responsibility, given the proximity of the United States."

Certainly he himself felt the fatigue. After more than four years on the commission, "the years ahead," he wrote in his diary, "look like thankless ones." When he presented the first volume to the Prime Minister that day in November, it should have been an occasion for rejoicing, but as Neil Morrison noted, Laurendeau was depressed and disappointed. During the presentation meeting he became aware that the Prime Minister was directing all his remarks to Dunton. "I think he feels ill at ease with me," Laurendeau wrote. "I am not of his race."

The previous February, when his wife was ill, he had written that "all the work, the emotion, not to speak of the heavy household chores, have worn me out." A year later a close family friend found him haggard, exhausted, and suffering from terrible headaches. She urged that he find a replacement for himself on the commission before it was too late, but all he could think of was finishing the job. "You may be right," he told her. "I'd better hurry. I don't know if I'll have time to finish the last report. I feel responsible for it." But others would finish it in his stead. On May 15, 1968, after a press conference, he suffered a brain aneurysm. Fifteen days later, at the age of fifty-eight, he was dead. There were many who believed the Bi-Bi Commission had done him in.

AFTERWORD: GOODBYE
TO A GOLDEN YEAR

On December 14, with the centennial celebrations wrapped up, Lester Pearson called it quits. His decision came as no surprise. Since the previous spring, insiders (and some outsiders, too) had known that the Prime Minister was determined to see the year out but intent on leaving office once the captains and the kings had departed. He was weary of politics; indeed, it might be said that he had always been. He left on a high note, with the international hosannas still ringing in his ears, but there's no doubt that he left with an enormous sigh of relief.

And so the long-running Pearson–Diefenbaker vaudeville act came to an end, as did so many entrenched institutions in that watershed year. That is how I see them in retrospect—a pair of hoofers, complete with straw hats, striped blazers, and malacca canes, tripping across the national stage in Question Period, cartoon figures created by Duncan Macpherson, locked in an absurd, symbiotic relationship. With their passing, the face of Canadian politics was transformed.

In the wings, still in the shadows, a different kind of performer was awaiting his turn in the bright light of the baby spot. When the moment came it would be blinding—but not quite yet. First: the *entr'acte*—a gaggle of Liberal has-beens tottering across the stage, each pathetically eager for stardom, each totally convinced that he had been given the royal jelly that would enable him to seize the imagination of the audience. A new word, "charisma," a legacy of the Kennedy years, was being bandied about. *Charisma?* In Paul Martin, Sr.? In Mitchell Sharp? In Robert Winters? You could almost hear the stage manager's call to send in the clowns.

As the year ended, and the televised audience on Parliament Hill once again sang "O Canada," few commentators invoked the name of Pierre Elliott Trudeau as a possible successor to Lester Pearson. He had made his mark that December with one memorable aphorism that caught the public's imagination: "There is no place for the state in the bedrooms of the nation." It was uttered specifically in support of his bill to ease legal restrictions on homosexuals, but it had broader connotations. This had been the year in which the state—meaning the establishment—had tried, with limited success, to come down hard on the new morality. The

358

burgeoning youth culture resented it. The Pill would make them free: what business did the state have telling them how they should behave in private? What business did the state have interfering in such personal matters as sex, birth control, divorce? In one brilliant sentence, uttered at the close of a remarkable year, Trudeau had put into words what a good many Canadians were coming to believe.

A fresh wind was blowing across the land. Its genesis was Expo and the often wacky centennial projects that, to use the phrase of the day, had turned people on. Early in the New Year that odd phenomenon, Trudeaumania, would sweep the country, especially among the under-thirty contingent. It was as if Canadians didn't want the year to end, hoping the hoopla would go on forever. Now we had our own Kennedy, our own Beatle. He seemed to suit the iconoclasm of the period, a politician publicly rebuked by that most obsolete of public figures, John Diefenbaker, for wearing sandals and ascot scarf in the Commons, a sure signal to those multitudes who saw unconventional dress as a form of protest.

I remember him at the Liberal convention in the spring of 1968 when Trudeaumania reached its peak and hordes of attractive young women carried his message through the convention hall. The press was drawn to him like hornets to a cookout. You could tell at once how the wind was blowing by the media mob encircling him as he sat in his place. Not far away were the members of the old guard, wistful and alone. From the outset it was no contest.

Could he have won the leadership race and the election that followed if there had been no centennial celebration, no Expo 67? Possibly. But it was the events of that year that paved the way for a new kind of politician and helped make his victory a sure thing.

There was nothing meek about Trudeau, as later events would prove. He seemed to epitomize the new Canadian attitude that, with Expo under our belts, we didn't have to take a back seat in the world community. Canada stood tall that year, just as Trudeau would later stand tall and unmoved on that Saint-Jean-Baptiste Day in 1968 when others ducked in the face of threats and taunts.

There was nothing meek about the new generation, either—the Trudeau Generation, as some would call it. He was older, but he was one of them. The resurrected photographs showing him as a bearded backpacker roaming through Mao's China made that clear. In the centennial year a variety of social groups began to demand their place in society—not just the bearded and beaded hippies but also the women, the aboriginals, the homosexuals, and, yes, the French Canadians. Even as Walter Gordon was calling for a loosening of ties with the United States, so René Lévesque was calling for a breaking of ties between Quebec and Canada. Everybody, it seemed, wanted to be master in his own house.

The single most significant slogan in that turning-point year was surely Charles de Gaulle's provocative cry, *"Vive le Québec libre!"* It wasn't just that it helped legitimize the growing separatist movement. It was the aftermath of the speech—the bitterness and the fury of English-speaking Canada and the Anglo-Canadian media—that dismayed and angered those Quebeckers who were certainly Quebec nationalists but in no sense separatists. If fervent federalists such as Gérard Pelletier and Solange Chaput Rolland were disturbed by the uproar in the rest of Canada, what did it say to those French Canadians who were leaning towards but still uncommitted to the separatist cause? Pelletier had broken with his fellow wise men, Trudeau and Marchand, over the bluntness of the government's response, "on the *haste* with which Ottawa reacted, on the *arguments* put forward to condemn the visitor, and the way in which he was shown the door."

"I had the impression that the communiqué was primarily aimed at calming Anglophone opinion and paid little attention to Quebec," he wrote. "I feared that the incident, treated in this way, might become a powerful auxiliary force for the take-off of Quebec separatism."

Pelletier had put his finger on the problem. In rushing to spurn de Gaulle, Ottawa had once again ignored the feelings of French Canadians. Even those Quebeckers who felt affronted by de Gaulle's meddling were basking in the international attention his visit had brought to their province. As Chaput Rolland wrote a few days after the event, de Gaulle "ended our three centuries of anonymity." The spontaneous enthusiasm that greeted his speech did not shock her, but "the hysteria, the bad taste, and the visceral Francophobia of the large part of Canada and the Canadian press" did. The violence of the anglophone commentators had touched her people on the raw. ". . . [T]o horrified Quebeckers who watched hatred of the French fact surge through the country, that historic procession down the Chemin du Roi will not easily be forgotten."

The feeling of isolation from the rest of North America, the long, weary, and, until this moment, unappreciated struggle for recognition come through loud and clear in the words that Chaput Rolland scribbled in her diary at the peak of the controversy: "A great Frenchman with no role in our affairs, but knowing our will to survive, has resolutely taken our side, and with a word that could be called arrogant or undiplomatic, has disregarded world opinion and the niceties of protocol to give us his resounding accolade in the face of the whole continent." It was in this climate that René Lévesque made his break with the past and set his province on a new and radical course.

Quebec separatism represented the reverse side of the coin of nationalism fostered in English-speaking Canada by Walter Gordon amid the heady atmosphere of Expo. Gordon had grown disillusioned with politics long before the year ended, but his influence cannot be overestimated. Quietly, without much fanfare, he put his voice and his money into various nationalist institutions and causes—the best known being the Committee for an Independent Canada—that he hoped would help unite the country against the incursions of a foreign culture.

He was not always successful. In 1971, at the height of the nationalist fervour, he tried to persuade the CBC to devise programs common to both languages, including a bilingual news broadcast. Through Bernard Hodgetts of the Canada Studies Foundation (backed with Gordon's money), he asked me to chair two meetings with the CBC hierarchy in Toronto and Montreal, but I was met in both cities, and later in Ottawa, with a wall of indifference. Why, I asked, could the corporation not use the same bilingual reporters on both networks for some of its international reports? Why send two men or women to cover a news story when one, who spoke both languages, could do the job? It would not only save money but would also give the audience a sense of being part of a bilingual society.

The answer, from Eugene Hallman, weatherman now turned showman, was that the viewers didn't like to hear newscasters who spoke with accents. I found that response patronizing and, worse, racist. Hallman wasn't really talking about an antipathy towards accents on the CBC. After all, one of the corporation's top newscasters, Joseph Schlesinger, had an Austrian accent and nobody had complained. Hallman meant French-Canadian accents and no other. I left that meeting with the same sense of despair that Laurendeau and Chaput Rolland had felt during their travels in English Canada.

Few Canadians gave much thought to these problems in the heady climate of the Centennial. The Bi-Bi Commission's preliminary report had issued a warning that few took seriously. Separatism was an irritant to many Canadians, but not a danger; hippies were seen as a greater threat. In the exhilaration of the birthday party, who wanted to look on the dark side? After ten years of depression, six years of war, and two decades of readjustment and growth, the country was experiencing a return of confidence and pride, thanks to the big fair, and an abiding sense of country, thanks to the centennial celebrations.

Two of the great dividends were the new respect given to Canadian literature and the new interest in the Canadian past and the Canadian psyche. The birthday year and those that followed witnessed an outpouring of popular and scholarly works dealing with all the aspects of the Canadian experience. In fact, a literary renaissance was in the making. Every community, it seemed, was producing a local history. Major publishers vied with each other to tell the Canadian story with books that were lavishly illustrated and expensively produced, such as the National Film Board's *Canada—A Year of the Land* and Roloff Beny's *To Everything There Is a Season*. The country's leading publisher, McClelland and Stewart, whose owner, not surprisingly, had helped found the Committee for an Independent Canada, doubled its output of books in the centennial year. Jack McClelland's Canadian Centenary Series covered the entire scope of Canadian history and ran eventually to nineteen volumes. His Canadian Centennial Library and its three successors, all large-format, illustrated books, ran to some fifty volumes and sold millions of copies. When the centennial year opened there were seventeen book publishers in Canada. Within two years there were thirty-nine.

The centennial grants to publishers and authors—ninety-five in all—were part of what Peter Aykroyd called "a civilizing year." One hundred million dollars' worth of arts centres, community halls, sports arenas, and theatres helped Canada come of age culturally. More than ninety small towns enjoyed one hundred million dollars' worth of ballet, opera, symphonic music, and drama that would not ordinarily have come their way.

But there was more to the Centennial than that. The individual and community centennial projects, a few of which are mentioned in this book, were by far the most important and lasting of all the centennial activities. Our hundredth birthday celebration in Kleinburg, when we resurrected the historic Binder Twine Delivery Night as a centennial street fair, lived on and draws forty thousand people to the village every fall. The profit from this thirty-year-old venture (which was originally intended as a one-shot celebration) underwrites a number of local organizations—Scouts, Guides, seniors—purchases new computers for the school, sends children on various excursions, originated Binder Twine Park, with its tennis courts and ball diamond, and recently created the Kleinburg New Forest on a forty-acre cornfield.

The real bonus, however, is to be found in the community spirit that the centennial project engendered. In Kleinburg, a town of some 2,500, everybody knows everybody else because all are involved with the annual festivities. They are the glue (some would say the twine) that binds the community together. Newcomers in Kleinburg are not strangers for long; the Binder Twine Committee always needs new blood. But without that centennial push, this would not have happened. In a sense, Kleinburg is Canada in microcosm. The country learns to know and to appreciate itself through scores of similar village projects begun in 1967.

It was a golden year, and so it seems in retrospect—a year in which we let off steam like schoolboys whooping and hollering at term's end. We all thought big that year. The symbolic birthday cake on Parliament Hill stood thirty feet high: ice cream and cake for thirty thousand kids and hang the expense! Over and over again we showed the world what Canadians could do: Nancy Greene grabbing the World Cup for skiing; Elaine Tanner, the aquatic Mighty Mouse, taking four medals at the Pan-American Games; Marshall McLuhan on every magazine cover.

By a number of measurements we are a great deal better off today than we were thirty years ago. We are healthier and we are wealthier than we were in 1967. The real net worth of the average Canadian is almost double what it was back then. Babies born today can expect to live longer—six years more than the centennial crop of babies. The death rate for infants has dropped from twenty-two per thousand to six. Far fewer mothers die in childbirth. And, as far as minority groups are concerned, we live in a much more tolerant society and one that is far less repressed.

Why, then, do we look back to 1967 as a golden year compared to 1997? If we are better off today, why all the hand wringing? There are several reasons, but the big one, certainly, is the very real fear that the country we celebrated so joyously thirty years ago is in the process of falling apart. In that sense, 1967 was the last good year before all Canadians began to be concerned about the future of our country.

To many of us, 1967 represents the days of our youth. We are all thirty years older today, and the pain and struggle that were part of those times are seen through a haze of nostalgia. In 1967, when 55 percent of the population was under thirty, young men and women were warned by their peers not to trust anybody over that age. Three decades later those twenty-five-year-olds have passed middle age. Some, like Dan McLeod, driving to work from his Shaughnessy home in his spanking Infiniti, have joined the establishment. Others have shed their long hair but followed vocations that in a sense parallel their youthful interests. Howard Szafer wears a beard, plays four instruments professionally (clarinet, mandolin, saxophone, and double bass), runs a scissors sharpening business (Howard's Hand Honing), and has become an acknowledged international expert on mushrooms. Russell Alldread, the part-time transvestite, still appears in drag performances but without being hassled by the police. George Hislop, who was caught in the act in Philosophers' Walk, has become a spokesman for the gay community. David DePoe is now a high school teacher. June Callwood, thanks to her experience with the Digger community in Yorkville, founded three charitable hospices—Casey House, Jessie's, and Nellie's. Michael Snow continues to paint and make experimental films. Michael Valpy writes a column for the *Globe and Mail* that reflects his earlier humanitarian outlook. Moshe Safdie, back after a long exile, has produced some of Canada's most striking buildings, including the Vancouver Public Library and the National Art Gallery. Philippe de Gaspé Beaubien went into private business and not politics, as some of his colleagues hoped he would. Pierre Vallières renounced violence and joined a religious order. Blake Brown is a captain in the Delta, B.C., fire department. Daryl Duke, *Sunday*'s producer, founded a new television station in Vancouver, sold it, became a prominent motion-picture director, and has been a major critic of the CBC. Peter Aykroyd, together with his son, Dan, the actor and comedian, is looking forward to another Anniversary Compulsion (his phrase) in the year 2000, which he calls the Milleniard, a name he has patented.

Most of these men and women belonged to the so-called Younger Generation in 1967. For some, retirement is already a fact; for others it is just around the corner. As for the members of the Older Generation, many of whom looked askance in 1967 at long hair, hippie dress, "loose" morals, and outrageous ideas, most are either dead or in their dotage.

In 1967, a better world seemed to beckon—a world no longer uptight, where marriage ceased to be slavery, where birth control was everybody's right, where the social services were expanding and universal medicare was just around the corner—a more tolerant world that treated women and minorities with respect, in which everybody could do his own thing without attracting the police.

In 1967 we looked forward with anticipation. In 1997 we look backward with regret to the "good old days" when nobody talked about the deficit or "downsizing." Though we are better off, we have less ready cash, partly because of the need to pay for the new social services and for an accumulation of expensive modern gadgets, from microwave ovens and laptop computers to CD-ROMs and gas barbecues, that didn't exist in those carefree days when Bobby Gimby came to town.

The Centennial encouraged us all to go high, wide, and handsome when it came to spending money. The government set the example. "Are you sure you're asking for enough?" was the response Peter Aykroyd had got when he presented his budget. Expo cost us more than $268 million (net), and nobody whimpered; it was, after all, no more than a drop in the public bucket. In the immediate centennial period— the three years including 1966 and 1968—government spending jumped by $2.5 billion—an increase of 75 percent over the previous three years. At the same time public debt rose by 20 percent and continued to rise.

We were all high in 1967, like somebody who has just won the lottery. Expo taught us to go first class, and we revelled in the pride that inspired. In those days we felt secure as Canadians, confident enough to push for a better, freer life. We did not count the cost until the bills began to come in. The years that followed had some of the effect of a hangover after a binge.

Jean Drapeau's Montreal suffered most from the exuberance of the Expo year, or perhaps simply from Drapeau's personal exuberance. Basking in the praise lavished on his city, the mayor sought further glory a decade later in capturing the Olympic Games. "The Olympics can no more have a deficit than a man can have a baby," he said at the time—and lived to regret it. In the Olympic stadium he got the tower he hungered for. The runaway cost all but beggared a city already reeling from the anglophone exodus propelled by the growing separatist movement.

In spite of this, breathes there a Canadian today who would turn back history and say we should have scrapped our hundredth birthday party? That we should not have danced in the streets, followed our own pied piper down the byways of the nation, or built our own dreamland on those magic islands in the St. Lawrence? I think not. Without that great adventure, what kind of people would we be now? How would we see ourselves? The stereotype of the dull, unimaginative, cautious Canadian was never a true picture, but we half believed it in the days before the centennial year. We tended to see ourselves (as, indeed, others saw us) as stick-in-the-muds, while the Americans looked like gamblers and risk takers. No more. Nineteen-sixty-seven was a watershed year in more ways than one, a revolutionary year in which old concepts were turned upside down. But the greatest revolution was the revelation that we had created a world-class, forward-looking nation.

Some of the changes described in this book would have taken place without any celebration; the emerging generation would have seen to that. But, as Judy LaMarsh said, the great triumph of the Centennial was not to be measured in the number of cultural monuments we erected across the land. Rather it flourished because of an awakening of spirit that seduced all of us. For an entire year we shared an invisible bond as we pondered our past and present and resolved to build a brighter future. "Since 1967," LaMarsh wrote, "no one has asked what it is to be a Canadian. Perhaps we can't yet articulate it, but we know: we grew up to be one hundred together, and we all shared that experience. We learned to have our own style. . . . We cast off the bonds of our conformity, and slipped out of our cloak of grey anonymity forever. The year 1967 changed us all profoundly, and we will never look back."

Author's Note

A work of this complexity requires the strong presence of a backup team to rescue the author from his own imbecilities. I have been fortunate over the years to have had the services of a small but effective editorial group without whose advice and hard work a book like this would not have been possible. They are old-timers now, and I have learned to lean on them. This is the fourteenth book to which my research assistant, Barbara Sears, has contributed her remarkable talents. She not only searched out the official documents, films, books, newspaper stories, and magazine articles that provide the underpinnings for the narrative but she also set up the interviews that I conducted with more than forty participants—to whom I owe an equal debt (their names are listed in the bibliography). Janice Tyrwhitt, who has been my editor on almost as many books, again forced me to revise, rewrite, cut, change, and/or expand entire sections of the manuscript. Janet Craig, who has copy-edited my work for the best part of three decades, saved me, as she always does, from many follies. She was backstopped by my wife (another Janet), whose phenomenal eye spotted misprints and inaccuracies that had somehow slipped through the editorial net. I want to thank my longtime agent and producer, Elsa Franklin, for her sensible comments on an earlier draft of the manuscript, and also John Pearce of Doubleday, who, having arrived in Canada after the centennial year, brought a fresh eye and some useful comments to the narrative. Once again, the manuscript, in all its progressive variations, was typed at incredible speed by my secretary, Emily Bradshaw. If there are errors (and there usually are), blame me.

Select Bibliography

Interviews
Russell Alldread; Doris Anderson; Bill Armstrong; Peter Aykroyd; George
Baird; Philippe de Gaspé Beaubien; Mme Nan-bowles de Gaspé Beaubien;
Jules Brabant; Blake Brown; June Callwood; Dalton Camp; Keith Davey;
David DePoe; Daryl Duke; Barbara Hall; George Hislop; Allan King;
Andrew Kniewasser; John Laxton; Jim Liles; Dan McLeod; Steven Marks;
Knowlton Nash; Abraham Rotstein; Moshe Safdie; Michael Snow;
Don Starkell; Howard Szafer; John Turner; Michael Valpy; Mel Watkins;
Patrick Watson; Jack Webster; Mary Winstone; Basil Zarov.

Canadian Lesbian and Gay Archives
1967 file
Everett Klippert file
ASK, 1967

Hockey Hall of Fame
Vertical files on players and coaches, Toronto Maple Leafs and Montreal
     Canadiens

National Archives of Canada
RG69 Records of the Centennial Commission of Canada
RG71 Records of the Canadian Corporation for the 1967 World Exhibition—
     Expo 67
MG26 Pearson Papers

Ontario Jewish Archives
Joint Community Relations Committee Collective Box 33, File 171

Privy Council Office
Files on visit of General Charles de Gaulle, 1967. FOI request.
Cabinet documents relating to Expo released under FOI, 1963–64, Cabinet
     minutes re Expo, 1967.

Unpublished Sources
Kinsman, Gary. "Official Discourse as Sexual Regulation: The Social
     Organization of the Sexual Policing of Gay Men." Ph.D. thesis,
     University of Toronto, 1989.
Morris, Cerise. "No More Than Simple Justice: The Royal Commission on
     the Status of Women and Social Change in Canada." Ph.D. thesis,
     McGill University, 1982.

"Sixth Annual and Final Report of the Centennial Commission for the Fiscal Year 1967–8."

PUBLISHED SOURCES

GOVERNMENT DOCUMENTS
Canada. Hansard. *Minutes of Proceedings of the Special Joint Committee on the National and Royal Anthems.*
Ontario Department of Labour. *Annual Report, 1966/67; 1967/68.*
Ontario Human Rights Commission. *Case Studies and Community Action Programs under the Ontario Human Rights Code and the Age Discrimination Act.* Toronto, 1968.
———. *Human Rights.* Toronto: 1965.
Report of the Royal Commission on the Status of Women. Ottawa: Information Canada, 1970.
Royal Commission on Bilingualism and Biculturalism:
    Preliminary report, 1965.
    Final report, 1967.

NEWSPAPERS
Calgary Herald
Financial Post
Georgia Straight
Globe and Mail
Halifax *Chronicle-Herald*
Montreal *Gazette*
Montreal Star
Regina *Leader Post*
Toronto Daily Star
Vancouver Sun
Winnipeg Free Press

MAGAZINES
artsCanada
Atlantic Advocate
Canadian
Chatelaine
Maclean's
Star Weekly
Time (Canada)
Weekend

BOOKS

Anderson, Doris. *Rebel Daughter.* Toronto: Key Porter, 1996.

Aykroyd, Peter. *The Anniversary Compulsion: Canada's Centennial Celebration.* Toronto: Dundurn Press, 1992.

Batten, Jack. *The Leafs: An Anecdotal History.* Toronto: Key Porter, 1994.

Becker, Jillian. *Hitler's Children: The Story of the Baader-Meinhof Terrorist Gang.* Philadelphia: J.B. Lippincott, 1977.

Berton, Pierre. *The Smug Minority.* Toronto: McClelland and Stewart, 1968.

Bird, Florence. *Anne Francis: An Autobiography.* Toronto: Clarke, Irwin, 1974.

Bothwell, Robert. *Pearson: His Life and World.* Toronto: McGraw-Hill Ryerson, 1978.

Braddon, Russell. *Roy Thomson of Fleet Street.* London: Collins, 1965.

Camp, Dalton. *Gentlemen, Players and Politicians.* Toronto: McClelland and Stewart, 1970.

Chaput Rolland, Solange. *My Country, Canada or Quebec?* Toronto: Macmillan, 1966.

———. *Reflections: Quebec Year One.* Montreal: Chateau Books, 1968.

Clarkson, Stephen, and McCall, Christina. *Trudeau and Our Times.* 2 vols. Toronto: McClelland and Stewart, 1990–94.

Cole, Stephen. *The Last Hurrah: A Celebration of Hockey's Greatest Season '66–'67.* Toronto: Viking, 1995.

Daly, Margaret. *The Revolution Game: The Short, Unhappy Life of the Company of Young Canadians.* Toronto: New Press, 1970.

Davies, Robertson; Mitchell, W.O.; Murphy, Arthur L.; Nicol, Eric; and Theriault, Yves. *Centennial Play.* Ottawa: Centennial Commission, 1967.

Desbarats, Peter. *René: A Canadian in Search of a Country.* Toronto: McClelland and Stewart, 1976.

Diamond, Dan, ed. *The Official NHL Stanley Cup Centennial Book.* Toronto: McClelland and Stewart, 1993.

———. *Years of Glory 1942–67.* Toronto: McClelland and Stewart, 1994.

Dompierre, Louise. *Walking Woman Works: Michael Snow 1961–67.* Kingston: Agnes Etherington Art Centre/Queen's University Press, 1983.

Expo 67, Official Guide. Toronto: Maclean-Hunter, 1967.

Fetherling, Douglas. *Travels by Night: A Memoir of the Sixties.* Toronto: Lester Publishing, 1994.

Fleming, Donald. *So Very Near: The Political Memoirs of the Honourable Donald M. Fleming.* Toronto: McClelland and Stewart, 1985.

Fraser, Ronald. *1968: A Student Generation in Revolt.* London: Chatto & Windus, 1988.

Frayne, Trent. *The Mad Men of Hockey.* Toronto: McClelland and Stewart, 1974.

Friedrich, Otto. *Glenn Gould: A Life and Variations.* Toronto: Lester & Orpen Dennys, 1989.

371

Fulford, Robert. *Best Seat in the House: Memoirs of a Lucky Man.* Toronto: Collins, 1988.

———. *Remember Expo: A Pictorial Record.* Toronto: McClelland and Stewart, 1968.

———. *This Was Expo.* Toronto: McClelland and Stewart, 1968.

Goldenberg, Susan. *The Thomson Empire.* Toronto: Methuen, 1984.

Goodman, Eddie. *Life of the Party: The Memoirs of Eddie Goodman.* Toronto: Key Porter Books, 1988.

Gordon, Walter. *A Choice for Canada: Independence or Colonial Status.* Toronto: McClelland and Stewart, 1966.

———. *A Political Memoir.* Toronto: McClelland and Stewart, 1977.

Grigg, John. *The History of The Times: The Thomson Years 1966–81.* London: Times Books, 1993.

Gwyn, Richard. *Smallwood, The Unlikely Revolutionary.* Toronto: McClelland and Stewart, 1968.

———. *The Northern Magus.* Toronto: McClelland and Stewart, 1980.

Haig-Brown, Alan. *Hell, No, We Won't Go: Vietnam Draft Resisters in Canada.* Vancouver: Raincoast Books, 1996.

Hamilton, Denis. *Editor-in-Chief: The Fleet Street Memoirs of Sir Denis Hamilton.* London: Hamish Hamilton, 1989.

Hamilton, Ian. *The Children's Crusade: The Story of the Company of Young Canadians.* Toronto: Peter Martin, 1970.

Hellyer, Paul. *Damn the Torpedoes: My Fight to Unify Canada's Armed Forces.* Toronto: McClelland and Stewart, 1990.

Henderson, Maxwell. *Plain Talk! Memoirs of an Auditor-General.* Toronto: McClelland and Stewart, 1984.

Hogg, Helen S., ed. *Man and His World.* Toronto: University of Toronto Press, 1968.

Horton, Donald. *André Laurendeau: French Canadian Nationalist 1912–1968.* Toronto: Oxford University Press, 1992.

Horwood, Harold. *Joey.* Don Mills: Stoddart, 1989.

Houston, William. *Inside Maple Leaf Gardens: The Rise and Fall of the Toronto Maple Leafs.* Toronto: McGraw-Hill Ryerson, 1989.

Howard, Philip. *We Thundered Out.* London: Times Books, 1985.

Hunter, Douglas. *Open Ice: The Tim Horton Story.* Toronto: Penguin, 1994.

Imlach, Punch, with Young, Scott. *Hockey Is a Battle.* Toronto: Macmillan, 1969.

Irvin, Dick. *The Habs: An Oral History of the Montreal Canadiens 1940–1980.* Toronto: McClelland and Stewart, 1991.

Jenish, D'Arcy. *The Stanley Cup: A Hundred Years of Hockey at Its Best.* Toronto: McClelland and Stewart, 1992.

Kazdin, Andrew. *Glenn Gould at Work: Creative Lying*. New York: E.P. Dutton, 1989.

Kierans, Eric. *Challenge of Confidence: Kierans on Canada*. Toronto: McClelland and Stewart, 1967.

Killmer, Richard L.; Lecky, Robert S.; and Wiley, Debrah S. *They Can't Go Home Again: The Story of America's Political Refugees*. Philadelphia: Pilgrim Press, 1971.

Kinsman, Gary. *The Regulation of Desire: Sexuality in Canada*. Montreal: Black Rose Books, 1987.

Kostelanetz, Richard. *Master Minds*. New York: Macmillan, 1969.

LaMarsh, Judy. *Memoirs of a Bird in a Gilded Cage*. Toronto: McClelland and Stewart, 1968.

Laurendeau, André. *André Laurendeau: Witness for Quebec. Essays Selected and Translated by Philip Stratford*. Toronto: Macmillan of Canada, 1973.

Lévesque, René. *Memoirs*. Translated by Philip Stratford. Toronto: McClelland and Stewart, 1986.

———. *My Québec*. Toronto: Methuen, 1979.

McDonald, Iverach. *The History of the Times: Struggles in War and Peace 1939–1966*. London: Times Books, 1984.

McDougall, John N. *The Politics and Economics of Eric Kierans: A Man for All Canadas*. Montreal: McGill-Queen's University Press, 1993.

McFarlane, Brian. *100 Years of Hockey*. Toronto: Deneau, 1989.

McKenna, Brian, and Purcell, Susan. *Drapeau*. Toronto: Clarke, Irwin, 1980.

McLeod, Donald W. *Lesbian and Gay Liberation in Canada: A Selected Annotated Chronology 1964–1975*. Toronto: ECW Press/Homewood Books, 1996.

McLuhan, Marshall. *The Gutenberg Galaxy: The Making of Typographic Man*. Toronto: University of Toronto Press, 1992 (first published 1962).

———. *Understanding Media: The Extensions of Man*. Cambridge: MIT Press, 1994 (first published 1964).

———. and Fiore, Quentin. *The Medium Is the Massage*. New York: Bantam, 1967.

Man and His World: International Fine Arts Exhibition Expo 67, Montreal, Canada 28 April–27 October. Montreal: National Gallery of Canada, 1967.

Marchand, Philip. *Marshall McLuhan: The Medium and the Messenger, A Biography*. Toronto: Random House of Canada, 1989.

Martin, Paul. *A Very Public Life*. Ottawa: Deneau, 1983.

Meade, Robert C. *Red Brigades: The Story of Italian Terrorism*. London: Macmillan, 1990.

Miller, Mary Jane. *Turn Up the Contrast: CBC Television Drama since 1952*. Vancouver: UBC Press, 1987.

Mitchell, David Joseph. *W.A.C. Bennett and the Rise of British Columbia*. Vancouver: Douglas and McIntyre, 1983.

Molinaro, Matie; McLuhan, Corinne; and Toye, William, eds. *The Letters of Marshall McLuhan.* Toronto: Oxford University Press, 1987.

Munro, John A., and Inglis, Alex, eds. *Mike: The Memoirs of the Right Honourable Lester B. Pearson. Volume 3, 1957–1968.* Toronto: University of Toronto Press, 1975.

Nash, Knowlton. *History on the Run: The Trenchcoat Memoirs of a Foreign Correspondent.* Toronto: McClelland and Stewart, 1984.

———. *The Microphone Wars: A History of Triumph and Betrayal at the CBC.* Toronto: McClelland and Stewart, 1994.

Nevitt, Barrington, with McLuhan, Maurice. *Who Was Marshall McLuhan?: Exploring a Mosaic of Impressions.* Toronto: Stoddart, 1994.

Newman, Peter C. *The Distemper of Our Times: Canadian Politics in Transition 1963–68.* Toronto: McClelland and Stewart, 1968.

Payzant, Geoffrey. *Glenn Gould: Music & Mind.* Toronto: Key Porter Books, 1984.

Peers, Frank. *The Public Eye: Television and the Politics of Canadian Broadcasting 1952–1968.* Toronto: University of Toronto Press, 1979.

Pelletier, Gérard. *Years of Choice, 1960–1968.* Translated by Alan Brown. Toronto: Methuen, 1987.

Powe, Bruce W. *A Climate Charged.* Oakville, Ont.: Mosaic Press, 1984.

Radwanski, George. *Trudeau.* Toronto: Macmillan of Canada, 1978.

Regush, Nicholas M. *Pierre Vallières: The Revolutionary Process in Quebec.* New York: Dial Press, 1973.

Reid, Alison, ed. *Allan King: An Interview with Bruce Martin.* Ottawa: Canadian Film Institute, 1970.

Roberts, John L., and Guertin, Ghyslaine, eds. *Glenn Gould, Selected Letters.* Toronto: Oxford University Press, 1992.

Rosenthal, Raymond B. *McLuhan: Pro and Con.* New York: Funk and Wagnalls, 1968.

Roy, Gabrielle. *Terre des Hommes, Man and His World.* Montréal: La Compagnie Canadienne de l'exposition universelle de 1967, 1967.

Safdie, Moshe. *Beyond Habitat by 20 Years.* Montreal: Tundra Books, 1987.

Satin, Mark. *Manual for Draft-Age Immigrants to Canada.* 2nd ed. Toronto: House of Anansi Press, 1968.

———. *New Options for America.* Fresno: Press at California State University Fresno, 1991.

Sharp, Mitchell. *Which Reminds Me: A Memoir.* Toronto: University of Toronto Press, 1994.

Smallwood, Joseph Roberts. *I Chose Canada: The Memoirs of the Honourable Joseph R. "Joey" Smallwood.* Toronto: Macmillan of Canada, 1973.

Smart, Patricia, ed. *The Diary of André Laurendeau.* Toronto: James Lorimer, 1991.

Smith, Denis. *Gentle Patriot: A Political Biography of Walter Gordon.* Edmonton: Hurtig Publishers, 1973.

———. *Rogue Tory: The Life and Legend of John G. Diefenbaker.* Toronto: Macfarlane, Walter and Ross, 1995.

Stevens, Geoffrey. *Stanfield.* Toronto: McClelland and Stewart, 1973.

Swift, Jamie. *Odd Man Out: The Life and Times of Eric Kierans.* Vancouver: Douglas and McIntyre, 1988.

Thomson of Fleet, Roy Herbert Thomson, Baron. *After I Was Sixty: A Chapter of Autobiography.* Toronto: Nelson, 1975.

Trudeau, Pierre Elliott. *Memoirs.* Toronto: McClelland and Stewart, 1993.

Uscem, Michael. *Conscription, Protest and Social Conflict: The Life and Death of a Draft Resistance Movement.* New York: John Wiley & Sons, 1973.

Vallières, Pierre. *White Niggers of America.* Toronto: McClelland and Stewart, 1971.

Visual Art 1951–1993 [the Michael Snow Project]. Toronto: Alfred A. Knopf, 1993.

Williams, Roger Neville. *The New Exiles: American War Resisters in Canada.* New York: Liveright Publishers, 1971.

Wolfe, Tom. *The Pump House Gang.* New York: Farrar, Straus, Giroux, 1968.

Woods, Oliver, and Bishop, James. *The Story of the Times.* London: Michael Joseph, 1984.

Worsley, Lorne, with Moriarty, Tim. *They Call Me Gump.* New York: Dodd, Mead, 1975.

ARTICLES

Alter, Susan, and Holmes, Nancy. "Human Rights and the Courts in Canada." Ottawa: Library of Parliament background paper, 1994.

Bliss, Michael. "False Prophet," *Saturday Night,* May 1988.

Brien, Alan. "Child's Guide to McLuhanology," *New Statesman,* 10 Feb. 1967.

Charney, Ann. "The Transformation of a White Nigger," *Maclean's,* May 1973.

Clausen, Oliver. "Boys Without a Country," *New York Times Magazine,* 21 May 1967.

Cooper, Barry. "Vallières Confession," *Journal of Canadian Studies,* Vol. 6, no. 2, May 1971.

Desbarats, Peter. "Quebec's Imprisoned Revolutionary," *Saturday Night,* February 1970.

Dunton, A. Davidson. "The Muddy Waters of Bilingualism," *Language and Society,* Autumn 1979.

Erland, Anastasia. "Mark Satin, Draft Dodger," *Saturday Night,* September 1967.

Gault, John. "Company of Not-So-Young Canadians," *Toronto Life,* November 1991.

"Graphics Convey Message in the Medium is the Massage," *Publisher's Weekly,* 3 April 1967.

Hamill, Pete. "Who's Afraid of Marshall McLuhan?", *Cosmopolitan,*
     December 1967.
Katz, Sidney. "The Harsh Facts of Life in the Not So Gay World," *Maclean's,*
     7 March 1964.
————. "The Homosexual Next Door," *Maclean's,* 22 Feb. 1964.
Kermode, Frank. "Marshall McLuhan Interviewed," *The Month,* April 1969.
Knight, Arthur. "Marshalling McLuhanism," *Saturday Review,* 12 Aug. 1967.
Kostelanetz, Richard. "Glenn Gould As a Radio Composer," *Massachusetts
     Review,* Vol. 29, Fall 1988.
————. "Understanding McLuhan (in part)," *New York Times Magazine,*
     29 Jan. 1967.
Krutch, Joseph. "If You Don't Mind My Saying So," *American Scholar,*
     Autumn 1967.
Lapham, Lewis. "Prime Time McLuhan," *Saturday Night,* September 1994.
————. "Terms of Endearment," *Harper's,* September 1994.
McLuhan, Marshall. "Love," *Saturday Night,* February 1967.
————. "McLuhan's Toronto," *Toronto Life,* September 1967.
————. "What TV Is Really Doing to Your Children," *Family Circle,*
     March 1967.
————, with Leonard, George. "The Future of Education," *Look,* 21 Feb. 1967.
————, with Leonard, George. "The Future of Sex," *Look,* 25 July 1967.
Marsden, Lorna, and Busby, Joan E. "Feminist Influence Through the Senate:
     The Case of Divorce, 1967," *Atlantis,* Vol. 14, no. 2, 1967.
"The Message of Marshall McLuhan," *Newsweek,* 6 March 1967.
Muggeridge, Malcolm. "The Medium Is McLuhan," *New Statesman,*
     1 Sept. 1967.
Rockett, Eve. "So Judy LaMarsh, What Are You Up To Now?" *Chatelaine,*
     October 1973.
Roddy, Joseph. "Apollonian," *New Yorker,* 14 May 1960.
Schickel, Richard. "Canada's Intellectual Comet," *Harper's,* November 1965.
Woodcock, George. "Inquest on McLuhan," *The Nation,* 1 Nov. 1971.

DOCUMENTARY FILMS

America, Love It or Leave It. Alioli Associates, Ltd., 1990.
The Children's Crusade. National Film Board, 1984.
Flowers on a One Way Street. National Film Board, 1967.
Jim Loves Jack: The James Egan Story. David Adkin Productions.
Never a Backward Step. National Film Board, 1966.
Summer of 67. National Film Board, 1994.
Warrendale. Allan King Associates, 1967.

RADIO DOCUMENTARY

"The Idea of North." CBC, 1967.

376

Index

378

379

380

385

386

University College, 181; Victoria College, 220
University of Victoria, 174
University Women's Club, 130

Vachon, Rogatien, 79, 81
Vallières, Pierre, 314-23, 337, 365
Valpy, Michael, 175-76, 183, 185, 365
Vancouver, B.C., 37, 44, 186-87, 190-95, 202
Vancouver Council of Women, 137
Vancouver *Province*, 192
Vancouver Sun, 14, 187, 189, 194, 196, 246, 264, 275; *quoted*, 64, 107, 152
Van Ginkel, Sandy, 290, 291
Vanier, Georges, 24
Vanier, Madame Pauline, 28, 33
Vickers and Benson, 30
Victoria, B.C., 23, 34-36, 173
Vietnam War, 17, 66-67, 161, 176, 182, 187, 197-203 *passim*, 216-17, 315
Vimy Ridge, 256, 303
Voice of Women, 127-28
Von Thadden, Adolf, 89
Voyageur pageant, 23, 49-56

Wade, Mason, 330
Wain, John, 211
Walker, Bud, 91
Walker-Sawka, Mary, 98
Walking Woman Works, 281-83
Warhol, Andy, 282
Warrendale, 85-86
Warrendale (film), 86-87
Washington Post, *quoted*, 274
Watkins, Mel, 67-69
Watkins Report, 67, 69
Watson, Patrick, 85, 86, 89, 90, 92, 93
Wavelength (film), 283
Webb and Knapp, 293
Webster, Jack, *quoted*, 187
Welles, George Orson, 219
Well-Tempered Clavier, 235-36
Wetzel, Hans, 166, 168
Wharram, Kenny, 77
White Niggers of America (*Nègres blancs d'Amérique*), 314, 315-16, 317-18
White Spot restaurants, 192

Whitton, Charlotte, 137
Wichita Falls, Texas, 197
Wieland, Joyce, 282
Williams, Roger Neville, 203
Williams, Tommy, 69
Wilson, Halford, 188
Wilson, Harold, 250
Wilson, J. Tuzo, 257
Windsor, N.S., 176, 179
Winnipeg, 15, 33, 51, 180, 333, 351
Winnipeg Free Press, 14, 136, 333; *quoted*, 153
Winnipegosis, Lake, 52-53
Winstone, Jenny, 35-36
Winstone, Mary Isobel, 35-36
Winters, Robert, 64, 296, 297, 358
Wolfe, Tom, 215-16
Wolfenden Report (U.K.), 148
Women's issues, 112-19, 120-38; royal commission for, 126, 128, 131-38
World War, First, 216
World War, Second, 216, 336
Worsley, Gump, 71, 80, 82
Wright, Jean, 125

York Centre (riding), 244-45
Yorkville (Toronto), 163-67, 169-72, 181, 183
Yorkville Ave., 169, 171, 184
Yorkville Cultural Activities Committee, 168
Yukon, 23-24, 276
YWCA, 130

Credits

FIRST ALBUM

1: *above*, University of Manitoba, *below*, *Globe and Mail*; 2/3: *Globe and Mail*; 4: Canapress; 5: National Archives PA–185471; 6: National Archives, Malak–LZ6756; 7: *above* and *below*, Canapress; 8: *Vancouver Sun*.

SECOND ALBUM

1: Canapress; 2: Frank Prazak/Hockey Hall of Fame; 3: *above*, Graphic Artists/Hockey Hall of Fame, *below*, *left* and *right*, Canapress; 4: *above* and *below*, Canapress; 5: *above*, Daryl Duke, *below*, *Toronto Star*; 6: Barbara Hall; 7: *above*, courtesy *Chatelaine* magazine © Maclean Hunter Publishing Ltd., *below*, *Vancouver Sun*; 8: *above* and *below*, *Globe and Mail*.

THIRD ALBUM

1: *above*, Canapress, *below*, *Vancouver Sun*; 2/3: *Toronto Star*; 4: *above* and *below*, Canapress; 5: *above*, Philippe de Gaspé Beaubien, *below*, Moshe Safdie; 6: *above* and *below*, Canapress; 7: *above* and *below*, Canapress; 8: *Toronto Star*.

CARTOONS

Pages 9, 57, 157, 313, 357: Duncan Macpherson, courtesy Toronto Star Syndicate.
Page 109: Courtesy Len Norris/*Vancouver Sun*.
Page 205: Drawing by W. Miller © 1966, The New Yorker Magazine Inc.
Page 255: Courtesy *Globe and Mail*.